Flying Saucers 101

Everything You Ever Wanted to Know
About UFOs and Alien Beings

By

Harold E. Burt

Alien2U Publishing

San Diego, California

USA

Flying Saucers 101

2012 Edition

Alien2U Publishing • San Diego, California
USA

The Invasion From Mars: A Study in the Psychology of Panic
© 1940 Princeton University Press
1966 Preface © Hadley Cantril

ISBN-10: 0615642977
ISBN-13: 978-0-615-64297-0

Dedication

This book is dedicated to my wonderful parents, Harold and Lillian Burt. One of the greatest gifts they gave me was encouragement to meet and respect people from all backgrounds, races, countries, and walks of life. From them I learned to cherish the differences. They openly welcomed all the friends I brought home. Little did they know where that would lead.

I also dedicate this book to the rest of my family and all my friends.

Acknowledgments

My Wife
I want to acknowledge and share the creation of this book with my lovely and beautiful wife, Gina. Without her support this journey would not have been possible.

My Agent
Bill Birnes. Bill, thanks for all your support and expertise. I could not have done it without you.

My Editor
If you have never written a book, then you cannot appreciate what a good editor really means. So thank you, thank you, thank you, Nancy Birnes. Nancy also did the layout and design of this book.

My Publisher and the Staff at UFO Magazine
Thank you for having the vision and the patience to see this project through.

Artists
James Neff, Christine "Kesara" Dennett and Bill McDonald. If you need your experience or sighting recreated, contact them. James, Christine and Bill are simply the best in this field. Enough said. Thanks, team.

Cover Artists
Richard Montoya. Thanks Richard, the cover is awesome.

Content Editors
Marika Morgan, Ron Press. Thanks for lending me your eyes and ears.

The UFO Research Community
These are people whose work, dedication, and courage in bringing you the truth has made them true heroes of this planet. Their work is equal to the efforts of the great men and women who established this country of ours. They are the Paul Revere's and Betsy Rosses of our time. Their contributions are that significant. At the risk of excluding someone, I

would like to list some of those people whose dedication and courage has been compelling and inspirational to me:

MUFON Orange County Board of Directors
Belisario Alanis, Phil Bettencourt, Lyne Friedland, Steve Gill, Eric Hartman, Jan C. Harzan, Tom Kardos, George Meadows, Lena Miller, Ron Regehr, Dena South, Debbie Stock, Dr. Bob Wood.

At Large
Sherry Adamniak (in memoriam), Shawn Atlanti, Darryl Anka, Jean Noel Bassior, Hugo and Julio Battallanos, Art Bell, Bill Birnes, Nancy Birnes, Alan Boal, Peter Brookesmith, Jackie Brust, Mark J. Carlotto, Kim Carlsberg, John S. Carpenter, Bill Cooper, Gordon Cooper, Col. Philip J. Corso (in memoriam), Robert O. Dean, Cecelia Dean, Christine 'Kesara' Dennett, Preston Dennett, Carlos Diaz, Jim Dilettoso, Jimmy Doughtie, Don Ecker, Vicki Ecker, Edith Fiore, Stanton Friedman, Ron Garner, Timothy Goode, Steven Greer M.D., Bill Hamilton, Pam Hamilton, Sharon Higgins, Richard C. Hoagland, Linda Moulton Howe, J. Allen Hynek, Philip Imbrogno, David M. Jacobs, Bond Johnson, Philip Krapf, Bob Lazar, Roger Leir, Melinda Leslie, John E. Mack M.D.(in memoriam), Jesse Marcel, Jesse Marcel Jr., Jim Marrs, Jaime Maussan, Bill McDonald, Jim Miller, Reg Miller, Story Musgrave, Brian O'Leary, Ron Press, Christina Reece, Jenny Randles, Carl Sagan (in memoriam), Steven Schiff (in memoriam), Ed Sherwood, Derrel Sims, Brenda Smith, Yvonne Smith, Col. Wendelle Stevens (Ret.)(in memoriam), Michael Talbot (in memoriam), Whitley Streiber, Jaques Vallee, Don Waldrip.

Contents

INTRODUCTION

Throughout our history much of our behavior has been based on assumptions, beliefs, and traditions within society. Over time these assumptions are continually being changed and corrected.

Some previous assumptions:

- *The world is flat*
- *The sun revolves around the earth.*
- *We are the only intelligent beings living in the universe.*

All "facts" except the last assumption have been challenged, changed, and corrected. Progress was achieved by a few people boldly speaking out in the face of ridicule, followed by a ground swell of others. These others did not change their opinions, they simply came to know the truth.

This book is a foundation for you to come to know the truth. You will become a part of the ground swell that will change the greatest incorrect assumption in human history!

Consider yourself lucky. You must truly be special to have the opportunity to live during this, the most dramatic time of transition and revelation in the history of mankind! Hold onto your seats.

Harold Burt

How I Came to Write This Book

From my earliest days in grade school, something seemed out of place. Some things didn't fit. My first realization of this came when I was in about the fourth or fifth grade. The teachers at school kept telling us that if we worked hard, any one of us could become president of the United States.

Well, that flat-out wasn't true. If you were black or had a last name like Wong, Valdez or Obayashi, you couldn't be president. I don't care how smart you were or what your grades were; if you were a girl, you couldn't be president, period! It didn't matter what the rules said, it was a lie.

I knew it, the teachers knew it, everybody in the school knew it. Then how come they kept saying it? I wasn't angry or even upset about the whole deal. I just thought it was weird. It caused me to have a strange feeling I can't quite describe. Nobody would talk about it and everybody continued to stick to the lie.

Recent Update

The above paragraph was written for the printed version of this book, *Flying Saucers 101*. I had initially written that paragraph several years ago. With the election of Barack Obama as President and strong runs by Hillary Clinton and Sarah Palin I had planned to delete it. However, I was encouraged by many people to leave it in as a reminder of the recent past and as an example of how rapidly and dramatically things can change.

We're the Only Ones? How Can That Be?

About the same time in school, I remember thinking that the assumption there were no other people in outer space was just as weird as the president thing. To me it was the same as saying that if you found a strange little insect you would assume that it was the only one of its kind. And, where insects and other science was concerned, it has always been assumed that it was not the only one. Once again, it just didn't seem to make sense. Hey, but who was I? I was just a kid playing Little League who wanted to make the majors.

Not Even Science Fiction

Throughout the rest of my scholastic career I was a decent student, but not exceptional. Most of the time, college included, I thought school was pretty boring and irrelevant. I wasn't even particularly interested in space launches, although I did have a poster showing John Glenn's flight on my bedroom wall after he first went up. His trip was very cool and very exciting. I read a little science fiction; you know: Asimov, Heinlein, those guys. But I never even saw a complete episode of the original Star Trek until decades after it first came on. (However, I became an avid fan of *Star Trek, The Next Generation, Star Trek Voyager and Deep Space Nine.)*

Go to the Moon? No Way!

When President Kennedy said we were going to the moon, I thought that was cool. For him to boldly step out there and speak that way was unlike anything we had ever heard from a president before. But quite frankly, I never thought I would see it in my lifetime.

1969

In 1969 I was a hippy in full bell bottoms, listening to Jimi Hendrix. When NASA landed Neil and Buzz on the moon, I thought, "Man, if I die right now, it's cool, because I actually lived long enough to see man land on the moon." I had just turned twenty.

Fast Forward

Sometime around 1986 a friend gave me an audio cassette and told me I would enjoy it. I assumed it had music on it. I took it to the beach and put it in my Walkman. I was completely surprised when it turned out to be someone talking about flying saucers. To this day, I have no idea why this friend gave me the tape and we have since lost touch with one another. For some reason, the sound of the audience in the background intrigued me. I could hear them audibly gasp when he showed them some videotape. Over the next several weeks I became kind of obsessed with finding out where I could hear this guy or someone like him speak. Why? I don't know.

With a few inquiries at some local New Age bookstores, I learned there was going to be a UFO conference in a few weeks in San Diego, not far from where I lived.

UFO Conference

So I went, and I continued to go to other UFO conferences over the next several years. I heard some pretty strange stuff, but I had the overwhelming feeling that *all* these people couldn't be lying, could they? I also continued to investigate and research flying saucers on my own. As time went on, I began to encounter more and more ex-military people, many of high rank, as well as commercial airline pilots who all told the same story. All their experiences lined up. I couldn't find any holes. Soon, it became abundantly clear - by God, these things were real!

It Won't Stay Secret Forever

At first I thought, 'Well, it will never become public in my lifetime.' Then I remembered how wrong I had been about man going to the moon. I also now realize how rapidly things can change – like the president thing. As the evidence began to mount and the numbers of people who knew the truth began to swell, I knew it *would* become public in my lifetime!

Uncontrolled Excitement

Wow! I was actually going to see the entire planet realize we are not alone! It seemed beyond the wildest experience I could expect to have during my entire lifetime. It reminded me of a particular episode of the Star Trek Voyager series. I was going to participate in the greatest transition in human history. I knew it would affect every aspect of our existence. And I was lucky enough to get an advance heads-up on the whole thing.

The excitement of this inevitable event took over and consumed my life. I could hardly think of anything else. Suddenly, I became interested in things I had no interest in before; computers, physics, history, archaeology, math, geometry, astronomy, sociology, human potential, how the mind works, how the brain works (they are not the same thing).

My aptitude for these subjects didn't increase, but my interest alone gave me new understandings about the universe that I never had before. I could hardly believe it, but I found myself reading introductory books on quantum physics for fun! If I had been this interested in studying when I was in high school, I could have stormed Harvard or Stanford and forced a degree out of them.

That Funny Feeling Was Back

That strange, indescribable feeling I had when I was in fifth grade was back and this time it was huge! You know, that weird feeling, the big lie nobody wanted to talk about. However, unlike the "president" thing, not everybody knew about this big lie. Some people were going to freak when they found out the truth. After all, the public has for the most part not been prepared for this.

For My Friends, Family and for Young People

I wrote this book for my friends and family. I wanted them all to stay calm and enjoy the spectacular experience they are going to have. We are all going to witness unbelievable events. I also wrote this book for all people under the age of twenty, whether in age or spirit: For those of you who have the elasticity to enjoy the party and not succumb to fear of the new and unknown. Remember, we are all one, and that includes the aliens. You have been invited to the greatest party in the universe, but you can't go unless you bring everybody!

How To Use This Book

If you really want to learn about flying saucers, then read this book. You'll know more than 99 percent of the people on the entire planet about flying saucers and alien beings. You will also know more about the true abilities of human beings than the world's best scientists.

How the Book is Organized

Flying Saucers 101 has ten major parts. Each part is divided into several chapters. Each chapter is complete by itself - some are longer than others, because some topics are larger or more important than others. At least I think so. Almost every chapter will direct you to where you can get additional information about the topic. The book is thoroughly cross-referenced and offers easy guides to related items of information. Some of the things in this book are repeated. When you see this, I didn't goof; It's simply something that is so important, it is related to more than one topic.

This topic of aliens, flying saucers and UFOs is huge. It is going to affect every aspect of humanity. To cover everything in its entirety would take a hundred volumes, this is volume one.

The Basic Things You Need To Know

- *Flying Saucers exist and they are real.*
- *The leaders of every nation on the planet know they are real.*

You picked up this book because you either know this or strongly suspect it's true. We're going to reward you for your curiosity. You're going to learn the ins and outs of flying saucers and how to explain them to others in a way that makes sense. You're also going to get some facts to back up your statements. All humanity will soon be confronted with the fact that flying saucers are real. There will be a real scramble with people seeking answers and information. Last, but not least, you are going to have a real good time!

Gallup Poll

You have lots of company. A Gallup poll taken in 1996 showed 71 percent of the American public believes the U.S. Government knows more about UFOs than they are telling us. A 2002 Roper poll showed that 74% of the American public claim they are at least somewhat psychologically prepared for the discovery of extraterrestrial life, and nearly half are very prepared.

You are going to have a lot of company and support as you begin to pursue this fascinating adventure. As you will learn, leaders world-wide are waging a losing battle to keep this information secret and hidden from the public. This issue is much larger than you ever imagined. You may be surprised when you discover how much other countries know about flying saucers. The dam `of` secrecy has a huge crack in it and there is going to be a major flood soon. Consider this book to be your emergency kit.

Fun or Fear: The Choice is Yours

For your friends and family, you can make the flying saucer reality fun, exciting, and informative. Help them prepare for this information now. If your family is anything like mine, they may panic if they are not prepared. Then the information would be sudden, shocking, and fearful. So dig in and get the facts.

Ignorance Is No Longer an Option

As usual, the public is the last to know. Not only do world political leaders already know about flying saucers, but, so do leaders in every field, including science, education, industry, the media - even sports. Public ignorance of the existence of flying saucers is no longer an option!

The Benefits of Knowing About Flying Saucers

- *The world is going to be a better place.*
- *You have fantastic hidden abilities.*
- *It's the first step to finding the truth.*

Sheer fun and excitement! This is a major benefit. You are going to discover you have been invited to the greatest party in the entire universe! You're on the "A" list and there's no waiting in line. As I said before, you must bring everybody.

Making the World a Better Place

You are going to help make the world a better place. Simply by sharing this information and helping people integrate it into their daily lives, you are going to radically alter the planet and all its population. As you discover we are not alone in the universe, you will learn to value and appreciate the differences between human beings. We will no longer see the differences between us as a threat, but instead as one of our most cherished virtues. This will be a necessary change before we can be included with the rest of the societies in our universe.

You Have Fantastic Abilities

As a human being, you have fantastic abilities you have not yet realized. You will discover that these abilities are of great interest to our alien visitors. They have also been the subject of much research by our government's covert scientific community. You have heard we use only 5 percent of our brain's capacity. Now you're going to find out what the other 95 percent can do.

The Expansion of Humanity

Because of this interaction with flying saucers and other beings, we will be forced to expand our concepts of science, reality, and even our own humanity. You will be a guide for this growth. You are also going to grow and change. It has already begun.

There is more opportunity for growth now than there has ever been before in your lifetime. You will be helping people understand they are part of a much larger community. Are you ready? It's going to be a wild ride!

Without It, We Can't Achieve Worldwide Goals

Without knowing the truth about the existence of flying saucers and alien beings, humanity will never be able to accomplish its most sought-after goals, such as ending world hunger, preserving the environment, eliminating disease, creating pollution-free energy, or traveling to the stars.

To not know the truth of flying saucers is like not knowing the earth is round, not knowing microorganisms exist, not knowing the laws of physics, or not knowing how children are conceived.

To know of the existence of alien beings is as important and basic as all the concepts listed above. This knowledge incorporates who and what we really are, our true history, and our real future. It explains how the universe actually works. It will dramatically affect how we view the universe, or understand how the human body works, or how we comprehend the untold wonders that physics and mathematics hold.

EVERYDAY MISCONCEPTIONS

"You could see a lot, just by observing."

Yogi Berra

[Famous philosopher and Hall of Fame baseball catcher for the New York Yankees. Yogi played in 14 World Series, more than any other player in baseball history.]

Heads Up!

There are many things around us, which don't make any sense - things we accept as true, when in fact, they are not. Our lives and culture are permeated with such things. The truth of them, however is right in front of us. And, with a little observation and common sense, you can see the plain and honest truth right before your eyes. You will be shocked that you never saw it or realized it before.

Let's look at a few innocent examples that are firmly ingrained in our culture. These examples are innocent and harmless, but they can change your powers of observation so you can more clearly see the UFO/Alien phenomenon.

Smokey is Blowing Smoke

Smokey the Bear says: "Only YOU can prevent forest fires." Sorry Smokey, we *cannot* prevent forest fires. Not only that, but we have nothing to do with most of them. The real fact is that 99 percent of forest fires are started by lightning!

(Smokey has recently changed his message say "Wildfires".)

Speaking of lightning, we often think lightning never strikes in the same place twice. Wrong. The Empire State building alone gets hit by lightning twenty-five to thirty times each year. In fact, you only see lightning *after* it strikes. The visible lightning we see is the return of the electrical charge after it strikes something on earth.

Holy Cow

Cows give milk. Yes, they do. However, most people think they give milk all the time, automatically. The truth is, cows only give milk after they have been pregnant! If a cow has never been pregnant - no milk. But for some reason, we think cows give milk simply because that is what cows do.

Duck Soup

What do ducks eat? Quick! Answer this question in three seconds. (Turn to the next page for the answer.)

Please give these examples some thought. They are meant to be fun and whimsical, but also deadly serious in alerting you to tune up your powers of perception and observation. When you apply your alerted powers of observation to the flying-saucer phenomenon, you can see that extraterrestrial spacecraft and alien beings really do exist and the facts are sitting right in front of your face.

A FRAMEWORK FOR INVESTIGATION

"To know the true nature and thoughts of a man, judge him not by his words, but by his behavior."

Dr. Lawrence Jones

Behavior is the Key to Our Investigation

The topic of flying saucers is so exciting, so dynamic and challenging, it's easy to get lost in the smoke. Try to stay focused on the behavior of the people I have written about. Look not only at their words, but consider what would prompt them to behave (speak their words) in this manner. What could be their motive? Money? Notoriety? Or simply the desire to share the truth?

Answer To The Duck Question

If you said "Bread" you are dead wrong. For some reason 99 percent of the American population gives this silly answer to the duck question. In fact, ducks eat fish. However, they are omnivores and will eat most anything. But "Bread" is not the right answer. To say ducks eat bread is like saying the human diet consists of candy bars.

Putting Things in Context

One of the big problems people have with the idea of space-traveling aliens is that we have nothing else in our day-to-day experience to help us integrate this information. Where in your brain do you file it? You haven't set up a file folder for that topic. So what do we do with the information? The information is disjointed, and we have no context in which to frame the information.

Historical Context

The dramatic information that alien beings are real is not unlike other humanity-changing revelations that have happened in times past. Imagine you are living in the year 1492. You work on the shipping docks in Spain. Over the past few years you keep hearing from sailors that they firmly believed the world was round. It didn't seem possible because you had been taught from childhood by people you trusted that the world was flat.

However, now suppose that you are an adult and you simply can not ignore the hundreds of sailors who have sailed the oceans and who have said there were many clear indications that the world was round. And, this is in spite of what government officials and the general population believe. You could not ignore your own simple observation that everything you see in the heavens appears to be round. It might well take several years and more information before you are finally able to accept and understand the fact that the earth is truly round.

You are in exactly that same position now. The seeds of the truth are
before you. Combined with your own observation and a little more
information, you will soon know the truth: aliens exist and are real. It
may actually take you a couple of years, but you will eventually confirm it
to your own satisfaction.

Copernicus

Copernicus was the Old World astronomer who discovered the earth was
not the center of the universe. He found out the earth revolved around
the sun and not vice versa. This was considered such volatile information
that it was hidden from the public for nearly two hundred years! Scientists, Government and church officials felt the public could not handle
such a revelation. The same thing is happening right now with the
existence of alien beings and flying saucers.

Magellan, The Ancient Explorer

> *"The church says that the earth is flat, but I have seen the shadow of
> the moon and I have more faith in the shadow than I have in the
> church."*
>
> **Ferdinand Magellan**

During one of Magellan's travels, he was the first foreign visitor to a
remote island. The natives had never seen anything like Magellan and his
crew before. Magellan had anchored his boat offshore and rowed in
using one of the ship's small row boats. When the natives asked him how
he got to their island, Magellan pointed to his large ship. The natives had
never seen a large boat. Such a concept was not in their consciousness.
The natives thought the large ships were living creatures, and the small
row boats were the children of the large ships. That same kind of consciousness "vacancy" is happening today when it comes to flying saucers.

Here's another example, this one from C. G. Jung, one of the world's
most influential psychiatrists, writing in *Modern Man in Search of a Soul:*

> "I once showed some native hunters, who were as keen-sighted as
> hawks, magazine pictures in which any of our children would have
> instantly recognized human figures. But my hunters turned the

pictures round and round until one of them, tracing the outlines with his finger, finally exclaimed: "These are white men." It was hailed by all as a great discovery.

Receiving Information

The context in which a person receives information is extremely important. Consider this example. If you are in a swimming pool with your swim suit on and someone throws a bucket of water over you, it's no big deal. It's fun, you laugh, and respond in kind. But if you are sitting at your desk in your business suit and someone pours a bucket of water on you, you'll have a completely different response. Identical bucket of water, different context.

It's the same with information. I want to help put it in context, so the recipient can perceive it as fun and exciting. As I proceed, this will be one of our primary goals.

Don't Tell Me, I Don't Want to Know

The truth is not always helpful to the person receiving it. Although it may seem strange, a brief discussion of stomach ulcers will illustrate what I mean.

A Pain In The Gut

In the United States stomach ulcers are a major problem. They are not only painful and inconvenient, but they are also dangerous. Ulcers can eat through blood vessels and cause fatal internal bleeding. Ulcers are also expensive. Americans have spent over $25 billion over the last five years on antacids to curtail the production of stomach acid. Several billion more dollars have been spent by patients on office visits to the doctor for ulcer treatment.

What a complete waste! The truth is stomach acid has nothing to do with causing ulcers! Neither does stress, by the way. Ulcers are caused by a bacteria, period. The bacteria is known as H. Pylori. It can be eliminated in as little as two weeks with treatment by an antibiotic. No bacteria, no ulcer. The medical community is completely aware of this.

People who have ulcers and learn from their doctors that they can eliminate the ulcer-causing bacteria often choose not to. For them it's inconvenient. The antibiotic does not provide the immediate pain relief antacids do. People would rather get the instant relief than eliminate the cause, even though the ulcerous condition will cause years of future pain and possibly even death.

I Want an Expert

People generally want information from someone they consider an expert. Often the so-called "experts" are the last people to recognize new information. In our previous example about ulcers, the discovery of the H. Pylori bacteria was made by an everyday practicing physician. He made the simple observation that nearly every ulcer patient he had ever seen had the H. Pylori bacteria in their stomachs while non-ulcer patients didn't. Simple enough; at least it seemed to be worth investigating. The medical community and experts fought this doctor and vilified him for ten years before they recognized and admitted the simple truth that lay before their eyes the entire time. [1]

In 2005, this physician, Dr. Barry Marshall and his colleague Dr. Robin Warren were awarded the Nobel Prize for Medicine for making the discovery that H. Pylori was the cause of ulcers.

Where's a Bum When You Need Him?

Imagine you have exactly a thousand dollars in your bank account. It is the only money you have, and you need it to pay your rent. You withdraw the money from the bank and walk outside. A pickpocket walks by and steals your wallet. You quickly realize what has happened and you watch the pickpocket go around the corner. You chase him. When you round the corner, you find yourself in a dead-end alley with three closed doors. There is also a bum lying on the ground. The bum raises a shaking finger, points to the second door and says, "He's in there."

What would you do? Would you start with the second door? What's more important, the information or the source?

The Point

With flying saucers, it's the information that is most important. Your traditional sources of information - radio, TV, and newspapers - are simply uninformed. With flying saucers, you're on your own, for now. There are no experts. You are more likely to get useful information from your friends and neighbors than anywhere else, as you will see.

Two Basic Things You Need to Know

- *It is not easy for people to receive information not connected to anything they are familiar with.*

- *The truth is not always useful to people.*

Chapter 1: The Basics

FLYING SAUCERS VS. UFOs

- *What "UFO" really means.*
- *Flying saucers are vehicles.*
- *The first flying saucers.*
- *Sizes and shapes of flying saucers*

No More UFOs

A suggestion: try to stop using the term UFO. I know this is a tall order. UFO is part of our national vocabulary and is ingrained in our culture. Even in this book I use the term because it's easy to say and write quickly. But, whenever possible, try to use the term *flying saucer* instead. Following are some reasons why:

UFO originally meant *unconventional flying object*, not *unidentified* flying object. The military has known since the 1940s that these were intelligently piloted craft. To confirm this, simply review the Air Force intelligence documents from 1958, which are listed in Chapter 3.

The term *flying saucer* has been used in hundreds of government and military intelligence documents precisely because they are known to be flying, piloted craft. A change in mind-set is needed. It is not just a matter of semantics; it is similar to the difference between referring to someone as a victim or a survivor.

If you saw what appeared to be a boat several miles out in the ocean, you would not say, "Hey, I see a UFO - an unidentified floating object." You would make the assumption it is an example of an intelligently piloted craft that we commonly call a boat. Whether you were actually right or wrong is beside the point. It may actually have been a whale or a buoy. However, you empowered yourself to make an intelligent assessment and committed to it.

When you say this you are saying you have some idea of what you saw and people will generally take your assessment at face value.

However, when you say you saw a UFO, you are confirming in your own words that what you saw is unidentified; you have no idea what you saw, or if you saw anything at all, so why should anybody listen?

Craft, Not Clouds

Flying saucers are not like clouds just drifting by. They are more like cars on a freeway; they contain "people" in them and they are on their way to or from a specific destination. Please spend some time thinking about this, since it is an important concept. When you fully embrace this idea you will begin to see the flying-saucer phenomenon in a new light, and some more of the pieces will begin to fall into place.

Origin of the Term

The first reported modern-day sighting of flying saucers occurred on June 24, 1947. A private pilot, Kenneth Arnold, spotted nine disk-shaped objects flying in formation over the Cascade Mountains in the state of Washington. Based on this sighting the term flying saucers was born. The following July 29, 1947, Arnold saw approximately twenty-five more disks that flew within four hundred yards of his plane. An official CIA account of Kenneth Arnold's sightings can be viewed at www.FlyingSaucers101.com and www.ufomag.com

Keep in mind the year these sightings occurred: 1947. In 1947 flying craft of any kind, even airplanes, were rarely seen by citizens. In 1947 it is estimated that less than 1 percent of the American population had ever seen a helicopter. And, for all intents and purposes, there was no television.

Sizes and Shapes of Flying Saucers

Besides the classic "saucer" shape of these alien craft, there are many other forms that have been seen by civilians and noted in military documents. There are as many configurations of craft as there are shapes of cars and trucks on our planet. Here are some of the ones seen most often.

Saucer or Disk-Shaped Craft

These come in different configurations and sizes. Some have small domes or cupolas on top, and some do not. The dome configuration can be rounded or square. These are known to be primarily scout ships and short-range research vehicles.

Cigar-Shaped Craft

These vehicles are generally larger than the saucers. They are known to be small mother ships containing eight to ten saucer-shaped craft. They are long and cylindrical with a taper at both ends; thus the name.

Triangle-Shaped Craft

These ships are huge; many stretch over several miles along a single edge. These are the craft that were sighted over Belgium in the wave of sightings taking place there in 1989-1990. It is estimated that over 70 percent of the entire population of Belgium saw these craft firsthand, and as a result, Belgium is the only country that officially recognizes the existence of flying saucers.

Boomerang

These craft are also gigantic. They differ somewhat from the triangle-shaped craft in that one arm of the boomerang ship is longer than the other. These are the sort of craft that have been seen and videotaped by thousands of citizens in Phoenix, Arizona in March and April, 1997.

Giant Cylinders

Very large craft, a thousand feet or more in length (picture a 70 story building on its side). These craft are not tapered. Many photographs of these have been taken. In photos they look just like a giant, hovering telephone pole on its side and don't look like a craft at all.

The Roswell Craft

One of the most famous flying saucers of all time, the Roswell craft was not really shaped like a flying saucer. Researcher and forensic artist Bill McDonald has reconstructed the Roswell craft from several eyewitness testimonies. Bill received confirmation from contacts he has within the U.S. intelligence community. It was McDonald's re-creation of the craft that the Testor Model Company used for their commercially sold scale model. The Roswell vehicle looks very much like the V-shaped Stealth aircraft the U.S. military built years later.

McDonald's intelligence agency sources have stated that Jack Northrup and Kelly Johnson, who were the founders of Northrop and Lockheed's "Skunk Works," had direct access to the data and configuration measurements of the Roswell spacecraft.1 It was said that this information was adapted and applied to the development of the X-33 and X-38 aerospace shuttle planes, NASA's space shuttles, the VentureStar, U.S. Stealth aircraft and the TR-3 Black Manta.

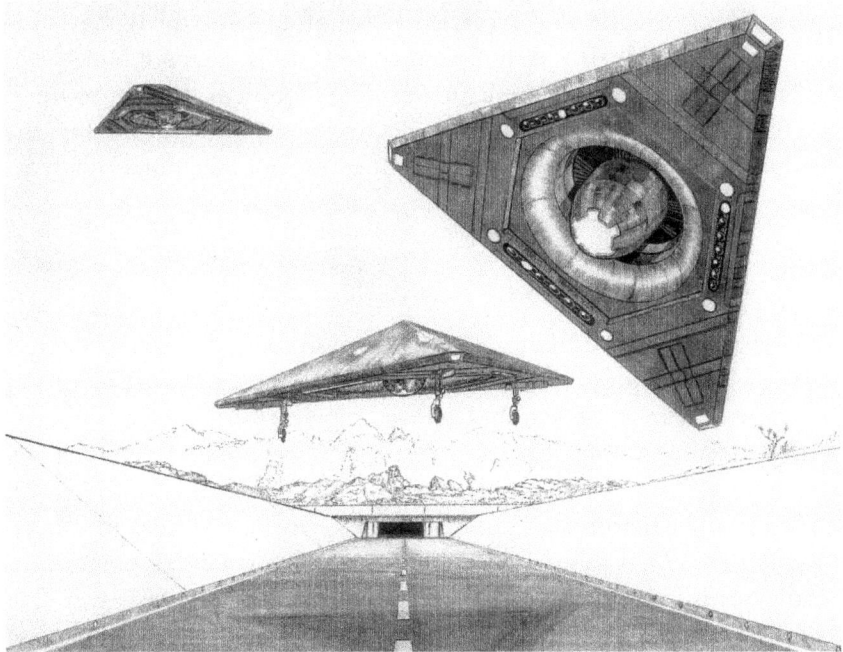

Triangle-shaped craft. Former aerospace and intelligence officials have said that these craft are man-made UFOs based on technology recovered from crashed flying saucers. (©1997 William L. McDonald)

Other Characteristics of Flying Saucers

There are a few characteristics of flying saucers that are not generally known to the public at large. Although these characteristics are never depicted in the movies, you should know about them.

THE WOBBLE

Flying saucers often wobble when they fly. It is very pronounced at lower speeds, giving the saucer a surreal look. It is often this characteristic which first draws the viewer's attention.

This wobble immediately distinguishes the flight of a flying saucer from that of an airplane. It was the wobble that attracted pilot Kenneth Arnold's attention to the first saucers, which he spotted in 1947.

When a saucer is caught on videotape, people often think the tape is fake because of the wobble. It is reminiscent of a model rocket wobbling on a string like in the old Buck Rogers movies. The wobble is thought to be caused by fluctuations of waves in the electromagnetic fields that the saucers use to overcome gravity. To imagine how it looks, think of a high-speed boat bouncing off the water as it moves forward.

MORPHING DISKS

Another characteristic of these alien craft is morphing; that is, the shape of the saucer changes right before your eyes. Often a saucer will elongate and become a cigar-shaped craft. This transmutation effect has also been caught on videotape.

Jaime Maussan, a reporter and investigator for a show similar to our *60 Minutes* in Mexico, has thousands of videotapes, all from different individuals, showing this morphing capability. Maussan has collected over five thousand videotapes of flying saucers from the citizens of Mexico, including many videos taken of the same craft shot at the same time from many different parts of Mexico City. In Mexico, Jaime Maussan is as well known and as well respected as Dan Rather or Peter Jennings. Jaime Maussan has videotapes that show over fifty flying saucers at one time. They often hold themselves stationary while forming strange designs, like some kind of array of symbols in the sky. This isn't as dramatic as landing on the White House lawn, but it's pretty close.

In March 1998 Jaime told me, "Nobody in Mexico laughs at UFOs. Nobody. They are frequently around the volcano, which now has the strongest electromagnetic field in the world. " There have been times when all the traffic in Mexico City was stopped, with millions of people standing outside their cars pointing to the skies. Yet, not one American newspaper has ever carried the story."2

HYPERSPACE JUMPS
Videotapes have also captured what have come to be known as "hyper-space jumps." This is when a flying saucer will jump a distance of fifteen to twenty miles in less than one-tenth of a second. Basically the craft is disappearing and reappearing in another location almost instantly. To the viewer, from a distance it looks like a "jump."

Different Names for Flying Saucers
Flying saucers are a world-wide phenomenon. They are called different things in different countries. In Mexico they are known as *flying plates*. In China they are known as flying woks. In many European countries they are known as *flying shields*. This term originated in ancient times and continues in use today in Europe. For background on the origin of this term, see Chapter Two: "UFOs In History."

Sizes of the Craft
Just as with the shapes, there is a wide variety of sizes. Most of the flying saucers we see are scout ships and are about 30 feet across. Their size is often deceiving because although there are larger disks, which are also seen, they are sometimes seen at a great distance and they appear smaller than they actually are.

Some Are Huge
As I mentioned earlier, some of these ships appearing in our atmosphere are huge! People regularly report seeing craft several miles across. A woman in Phoenix was driving with her two sons when a boomerang craft flew over them and hovered over the isolated stretch of highway where they were traveling. Out of fear, she accelerated to over 85 miles per hour. One of her teenage sons decided to time how long it would take them to get from beneath the craft. He started timing well after they

had driven under the craft, and it took them just over two minutes at 85 miles an hour to get from under the wingspan of the ship. That makes the wingspan approximately three miles across!

Satellite Photos

Some of these large craft have been caught on film by our orbiting weather satellites. Judging by the grid on the camera lens and knowing the distance of the satellite's orbit, calculations show these craft to be hundreds of miles across! I have included some of the satellite photos in Chapter Seven: "Watch The Skies."

Estimating Sizes

I don't know about you, but I have difficulty gauging sizes and distances. For instance, if someone says an object is 300 feet away, I don't have a clue how far that is. On the state driving test, the words "stay a hundred feet behind the next vehicle" mean nothing to me. But, I do like football, so I can gauge a hundred yards pretty accurately. I also get a clear picture if someone tells me a building is ten stories tall. For some reason, it's easy for me to relate to.

Now I use the reference of a building to help me understand how big something is. For example, it is often reported that flying saucers are about 50 feet across. Translated, this means it was as long as a four-story building on its side. That's pretty big. Bigger than the words *fifty feet* seem to indicate to me.

Six Hundred Feet Across

We found several military sources who have seen craft 600 feet across. That's a 45-story building on its side. That's large!

Folding Space

Just a little teaser to whet your imagination. Aliens beings have the ability to "fold" space. I cover this in more detail later, but here's what this means in relation to space-craft size: Often, the inside of the saucer is much larger than it appears to be from the outside. People who have worked on recovered craft often recall doing a double-take when they first stick their heads inside of a flying saucer. They can't believe it can be that big inside and they pull their head out to look at the outside of the craft. They are in total disbelief. What appears to be a 30-foot craft on the outside is three times that size on the inside.

OFFICIAL PROOF

Is there any evidence, Any Proof? Papers, Photos? Something Solid?

Virtually every U.S. president since the 1940s has contributed a statement or action addressing the existence of flying saucers or extraterrestrial beings. I've included them here. Not only U.S. presidents, but hundreds of military officers, elected officials, heads of government agencies, and world leaders have clearly established the fact, through their words and actions, that flying saucers exist. There are so many people in this category that I have chosen to include only the most notable.

Intelligence Agency Documents

This is what most people want to see, some acknowledgment by our elected or appointed officials. Keep in mind, meanwhile, that for the most part the so-called "smoking gun" documents have remained highly classified and hidden from public view. However, you really don't need them to put two and two together. Thousands of formerly classified documents have been released to the public through the Freedom of Information Act (FOIA).

Some of these documents are over 40 years old and still have key phrases blacked out. You have to wonder what kind of national security issues from 40 years ago could still be a concern today. These defense and intelligence agency documents show a clear interest, belief, and concern about UFOs, and they cover a time span of 50 years.

Photographs From Around the World

Most people have never seen really good, clear UFO photos. That's because many of them have been confiscated from well-meaning citizens by officials from the government. However, there are literally thousands and thousands of clear photographs taken by ordinary citizens around the world. Some of the best, well-documented photos have been preserved by the UFO Archives under the guidance of former Lt. Col. Wendelle Stevens. He was kind enough to let me share some of these dramatic images with you.

Chapter 2: UFOs in History

"All truth passes through three stages. First, it is ridiculed. Second, it is violently opposed. Third, it is accepted as being self-evident"

Schopenhauer, German philosopher
1788 – 1860

Once you know flying saucers are real, you'll also discover they didn't just show up yesterday. They have been here during our entire existence. When the Roman Empire was in full bloom, they were there. When Columbus crossed the Atlantic, they were there. When Christ was born, they were there!

Let's take a little journey back in time and look at some ancient events through newly enlightened eyes. I'm only going to describe a few events, but it will be enough to give you an idea of what we're about to discuss. Noted UFO researcher John Carpenter has traveled around the world investigating ancient examples of visitations to earth by extraterrestrial beings. Here is some of what he has uncovered.

Language

Keep this in mind: Language was completely different in past centuries. There were only a limited number of words that could be used to describe things which might be, frankly, indescribable. Try to describe an airplane using only the language available two thousand years ago and you'll see what I mean.

A Large Silver Disc

St. Athanasius of Alexandria, a bishop, wrote a biography of St. Antony in A.D. 373. In it is a section titled "A Disc in the Desert." Here's what it says:

> Yet once more the Enemy (Satan), seeing (Antony's) zeal and wishing to check it, threw in his way the form of a large silver disc of silver. Antony, understanding the deceit of the Evil one, stood and looked at the disc and confuted the demon in it, saying, "Whence a disc in the desert, this is not a trodden road, and there is no track of any faring this way. And, it could not have fallen unnoticed, being of huge size.

> Great is the number in the air around us, and they are not far from us. But, there is much difference in them. It would be long to speak of their nature and differences, and such discourse is for others greater than us.

> Weaving phantoms, taking forms of women, of beasts and reptiles, and gigantic bodies, they pretend to prophesy and to foretell things to come, and to show themselves taller than the roof and as vast phantoms to those whom they could not beguile with thoughts. 8

Burning Globes

In Rome during the reign of Theodsius, A.D. 393, it was recorded that a huge luminous sphere accompanied by many smaller ones appeared over the fields outside of town. It was also recorded that the citizens basically panicked. 1

Roman writer Julius Obsequens told of people who had seen "burning globes" and "round shields" flying over Rome at night and during the day. 2

Dragons in the Sky

It was reported that large "flame-breathing dragons" were flying over China in approximately A.D. 747. The records also speak of "men in airships" 1,200 years before airplanes were invented! 3

Aerial Sailors

The Archbishop of Lyons recorded that three men and a woman were seen disembarking from an "aerial ship." A gathering crowd panicked and began to stone the visitors. The archbishop also said that "aerial sailors" were arriving on ships in the clouds and bedeviled members of his church. 4

The following is a report from the Saxons, around A.D. 900.

> Those watching outside in that place, of whom many still live to this very day, say they beheld the likeness of two large shields, reddish in colour, in motion above the church, and when the pagans who were outside saw this sign, they were at once thrown into confusion and, terrified with great fear, they began to flee from the castle. 5

On August 3, 989, three glowing objects appeared over Japan. The objects all joined together to form one large brilliant ball in the sky. 6

Fiery Worms

Citizens in Switzerland in 1104 noted what appeared to be "fiery worms" in the sky. A professor at the University of Basil recorded, "They flew in the air and took away the light of the sun as if they had been clouds." 10

A Flying Pan?

Ancient Japanese records describe an "earthenware vessel" that flew out of a mountain in the Kii Province on October 27, 1180. This occurred about midnight and the "vessel" left behind a luminous trail. 9

Swimming in the Air

People attending church in 1211 at Gravesend in Kent, England, ran outside to watch a ship in the sky that had people on it! Some of the people on the ship "jumped off and swam in the air."

1271

During a scheduled execution in Tasunokuchi, Kamakura, Japan, a UFO appeared and scared off the populace. According to reports, "There appeared in the sky an object like a full moon, shiny and bright." The intended victim who was to be beheaded, a well-known priest named Nichiren, was spared.

1290

William of Newburgh's *Chronicle* in Yorkshire, England contains this description: "The abbot and monks were at a meal, when a flat, round, shining, silvery object flew over the abbey and caused the utmost terror."

1361

A flying craft came out of the inland sea on the western side of Japan. Observers described it as "shaped like a drum about twenty feet in diameter." 11

1431

The entire population of the village of Angkor Wat mysteriously vanished. Large airships were seen in the area.

1453

Strange lights were seen circling over Constantinople the night before the Turks conquered it. Some of the lights flew straight up at high speed and then split into many smaller lights. 12

March 17, 1458

Five "stars" appeared over Japan. They circled the moon, changed colors three times, then disappeared. The citizens of Kyoto, Japan, were so distressed by this event that they ran and hid, expecting the arrival of horrible disasters.

November 1, 1461

The French Duke of Bourgogne wrote in his memoirs that "an object appeared in the sky over France on the night of November 1, 1461. It was as long and wide as a half moon; it hung stationary for about a quarter of an hour, clearly visible, then suddenly...spiraled, twisted and turned like a spring and rose into the heavens." 13

1468

A large object making a "sound like a wheel" flies out of Mt. Kasuga. None of the citizens had seen anything like it before. 14

1479

A large "comet" is reported flying over Arabia. The comet is reported as having numerous windows on it. 15

1492

From the personal log of Christopher Columbus, during his famous voyage, comes this entry:

> *Saturday, 15 September, 1492*
> And on this night, at the beginning of it, they saw fall from the sky a marvelous branch of fire into the sea at a distance of four to five leagues from them." 39

August 7, 1566

In Basel, Switzerland, a large number of black spheres were flying all over the sky. They appeared to be fighting one another. This battle was witnessed by hundreds, if not thousands, of people. In describing this activity, a newspaper article written by Samuel Coccius said, "Many became fiery and red, ending by being consumed and vanishing." 16

April 4, 1561

Over two hundred large cylinders, globes, and "spinning disks" flew over the skies of Nuremberg, Germany. People also reported seeing red, black, and orange globes, as well as "smoking spheres" coming out of the cylinders in the sky. 17

October 24, 1593

In Manila, Philippines, a soldier completely vanishes. The next day he reappeared in Mexico City! The man was able to completely describe the previous day's news from the Philippines. (Remember, there were no airplanes, no radio, no television, no telephones).

1606

Large numbers of "spinning fireballs" are reported over Kyoto, Japan. A "whirling, red wheel" hovered over the Nijo Castle. The Samurai guards were put on alert. [18]

August, 1666

A ball of light was seen by the citizens of Robozero, Russia, in the middle of a cloudless day. The ball was brighter than the sun. [19]

July 9, 1686

A large ball flies across the sky in Leipzig, Germany and two smaller, glowing balls come out of it. [20]

December 9, 1731

In Sheffield, England, Thomas Short described the following: "A dark red cloud, below which was a luminous body which emitted intense beams of light. The light beams moved slowly for awhile, then stopped. Suddenly, it became so hot that I could take off my shirt even though I was out of doors." Note: this event occurred in the middle of December.

A similar object appeared on the same day over Romania. Old manuscripts described it like this: "There appeared in the West, a great sign in the sky, blood-red and very large. It stayed in place for two hours, separated into two parts which then rejoined, and the object disappeared towards the west. [22]

January 2, 1749

Three globes "like the moon" appeared over Japan. People were so frightened that riots broke out. To try and calm things down, the government ordered anybody rioting "because of the globes" to be executed. Later "three moons" appeared. Days after that, "two suns" appeared. [23]

1766

In Sweden three objects "like the moon" appeared in the sky and stayed for four days, then vanished never to be seen again. [24]

In another incident that same year, a luminous globe appeared at night and projected beams of light out of it. 21 These seemingly minor incidents are quite remarkable because there was nothing in the skies in 1766 that could project a beam of light, except sunbeams coming through clouds.

THE BIBLE

The Bible has many references to other-worldly beings and flying saucers. If you are a student of the Bible, you can go back and reread the entire text with a new understanding. You will be astounded.

Here is one remarkable passage from the books of Infancy and Protevangelion, taken from *The Lost Books of the Bible*. It actually describes the same experience many abductees have in our times, particularly the aspect of everything being stopped and all surrounding people being "switched off." (See Chapter 5, "Abductions.") Following is an event which happened to Joseph, just before the birth of Christ. Here is Joseph's description:

> I looked into the air, and I saw the clouds astonished, and the fowls of the air stopping in the midst of their flight. And I looked down towards the earth, and saw a table spread, and working people sitting around it, but their hands were upon the table, and they did not move to eat. They who had meat in their mouths did not eat. They who lifted their hands up to their heads did not draw them back. And they who lifted them up to their mouths did not put anything in, but all their faces were fixed upwards. And I beheld the sheep dispersed, and yet the sheep stood still. And the shepherd lifted up his hand to smit them, and his hand continued up. And I looked unto a river, and saw the kids with their mouths close to the water, and touching it, but they did not drink. 26

> Then a bright cloud overshadowed the cave, and the mid-wife said, "This day my soul is magnified, for mine eyes have seen surprising things, and salvation is brought forth to Israel." But on a sudden the cloud became a bright light in the cave, so that their eyes could not bear it. And, behold, it was all filled with lights, greater than the light of lamps and candles, and greater than the light of the sun itself." 27

ANCIENT ART

There are plenty of examples of ancient art that clearly depict the fact that UFOs and extraterrestrial beings were around in those days. ET's and flying saucers appear in cave paintings, tapestries, woodcuts and paintings.

A sixteenth century fresco from a church shows an ancient astronaut rocketing across the sky. This was hundreds of years before the concept of aircraft came about.

Roman Fresco

In March, 1998, archaeologists unearthed a fresco in the ruins surrounding Rome. The fresco was a detailed painting of ancient Rome, yet the view was from the air! Scholars are dumbfounded; they can't figure out how it was done.

Flemish Painting

A painting made in 1710 by the Flemish painter Gelder, depicts the baptism of Christ. In the background there is a clear image of a flying disk with beams of light coming from it and shining down on the infant.

The painting has not been retouched or altered in any way. It is on display at the Fitzwilliam Museum in Cambridge, England.

A note about old paintings: If you were a artist living in the 13th through 18th centuries, you had to follow certain unwritten rules. If you wanted to depict something strange or different in a painting, you had to put that strange item in the background of the painting. In the foreground, you had to paint a religious scene or depict religious figures. Otherwise, you would be denounced as a devil worshiper and literally burned at the stake or beheaded. That's why all the UFOs in these ancient works of art are rendered small and in the background. 28

Ancient Woodcut

A woodcut done by Hans Glaser depicts a battle among flying disks and flying cylinders that occurred over Nuremberg, Germany, on April 4, 1561. 31

Australian Rock Art

Throughout the continent of Australia there are ancient drawings on the rocks which show beings with enlarged bald heads, large slanted eyes, and slits for mouths. They also depict orange globes floating in the skies. 29

African Cave Painting

An African cave painting depicts a being wearing headgear with antennae and flying through the air. The being is holding an animal in its arms. The painting is in Tassili-N-Ajer, Africa. The being has large, black slanted eyes and thin lips. 30

Russian Plate

A Russian archaeologist discovered an ancient plate in the mountains of Nepal. It is known as the Valenov Plate. The plate has been dated at about a thousand years old. The material the plate is made from is a combination of metal and ceramic, a process that even today is not possible. The plate very clearly shows a flying saucer and alien being. 32

Medieval Tapestry

A tapestry from medieval times is in the Collegiale Notre Dame, Beaune,
France. In the foreground is a depiction of the Virgin Mary; however, in
the background is a clear rendition of a flying saucer! 33

Fifteenth Century Painting

A painting done in the fifteenth century by Ghirlandaio shows the Virgin
Mary in the foreground. In the background there is a man looking up at a
disk. The disk has large sparks coming from it and the man is shielding
his eyes from the disk. A dog at the man's side is barking up at the UFO.
The painting is entitled *Madonna and St. Giovannino*, and can be found in
the Loeser Collection, Palazzo Vecchio, in Florence, Italy. 34

*A sixteenth century painting of the
Virgin Mary shows a UFO in the
background. A man is pointing up
at it and his dog is barking at the
object.*

THE ANCIENTS

The items that follow are not
necessarily UFO-related. I have
simply included them because they
are interesting and are further
evidence that the true history of
our planet has not been fully
uncovered or truthfully told.

The Pyramids of Egypt

It is now generally acknowledged by the world's top archaeologists that
the pyramids and the Sphinx in Egypt are at least ten thousand years

older than previously thought. Basically, what this means is that the Egyptian pharaohs did not build them!

The world's leading expert in archaeological wind erosion, who was based at Harvard University, decided to pay a visit to the Sphinx. After all, he was the world's best authority on wind erosion and he had never visited the most famous wind-eroded artifact. When he got there he found, to his shock, that the Sphinx exhibited virtually no signs of wind erosion. Instead, it was completely water-eroded.

When he returned to Harvard he approached a colleague who was a water-erosion expert. He pulled out a picture of the Sphinx, which he had partially covered, except for certain sections showing the eroded stone. Thus, his colleague would not know what the object was before he offered his opinion. He asked the water erosion expert if he could determine what had eroded the stone. The man laughed and said, "You know as well as I that this building has been water-eroded." When he pulled away the cover to reveal that the object was indeed the Sphinx, his colleague said, "Oh, no, oh no. I'm not going to touch this with a ten-foot pole." He immediately knew the water erosion was clear evidence the Sphinx was not made by the Egyptians.

Humans and Dinosaurs Together

Here is another one nobody wants to touch. In a riverbed in Paluxy, Texas, archaeologists have found both dinosaur tracks and human footprints together. Both made at the same time. And, not just one track, but dozens. All the tracks are the same age, about 140 million years old, and they were made together. From the spacing of the footprints it is clear the ancient person was clearly tracking the dinosaur. 35 Several scientists have said it is not possible; however, those that say this have never gone to visit the prints themselves.

In 1983 a report appeared in the *Moscow News*. The article reported that human footprints that were 150 million years old were found in Jurassic rock next to a dinosaur footprint that had three toes. 40.

Other fossils were found in 1968 in Utah. There were human footprints found there as well, and these footprints are 440 million years old! Not only that, but the feet had shoes on them! One of the footprints has an ancient marine animal called a *trilobite* squashed under it. The shoe print with the trilobite in it is in perfect condition. 36

Giant Footprint

In 1912 in South Africa a giant human-like footprint was found in solid granite. The footprint is of a left foot and is approximately 4 feet long and 18 centimeters deep. It is distinct enough to clearly show where mud had squished up between the toes. The footprint is estimated to be about a million years old. 37

Another footprint, almost identical to the one in South Africa, except it is an imprint of a right foot, has been found in Sri Lanka. Nobody knows who or what made it. Scientists who have seen it and dated it simply agree it is not a hoax. 38

Thousands of Other Artifacts

Geologists, archaeologists and paleontologists around the world have found literally thousands of artifacts clearly made by intelligent beings that date back 200-500 million years ago!

WAR OF THE WORLDS

On Sunday night, October 30, 1938 a young man named Orson Welles presented a radio broadcast with a group of players on the "Mercury Theatre on the Air." It is probably the single greatest radio broadcast in American history. Welles and his group created a radio play adapted from H. G. Wells' (no relation, different spelling) novel, *War of The Worlds*. Thousands of listeners believed the story was an actual news bulletin and they panicked, many leaving their homes and literally heading for the hills. Lillian Gardiner of Wilmington, Delaware recalls the event vividly:

> Mr. Hodges from across the street came over and told daddy, "Mr. Gardiner, turn on the radio, something terrible is happening over in New Jersey." My mother and I were really scared, as were the other neighbors.

Orson Welles was only 25 years old at the time. He later went on to write, produce, and star in the film *Citizen Kane*, which by the way, many call the greatest film ever made. Hell of a career for one guy, huh? The "War of the Worlds" broadcast has become so famous that even sixty years later it is still used as the benchmark for mass public reaction. This event comes up so often in discussions about flying saucers and abductions that I feel compelled to discuss it and clarify it.

This case is important for two reasons: first, to eliminate the idea of mass hysteria which often comes up when discussing flying saucers. In particular, the response to the Orson Welles' broadcast is commonly and mistakenly referred to as mass hysteria. And second, to eliminate the weak-kneed excuse bureaucrats and military honchos use: that to tell the public the truth about flying saucers would result in complete and total panic on the part of the public.

People always use the Orson Welles broadcast as an example of this. They are wrong; the public will not panic. The real panic is happening among world leaders who fear that the public will not only find out the truth, but also learn that they have been lied to for decades about the existence of flying saucers.

Are alien abductions really just a case of mass hysteria or psychosis, like the Orson Welles broadcast? The direct answer is simply no!

"Mass" anything means that something is being directly transferred from one person to the next. If anyone can explain how the abduction descriptions can be passed from one person to another through cultural, geographical, and language barriers, that person will win a Nobel Prize.

Mass hysteria is excessive, uncontrollable emotion such as fear or panic being passed from one person to the next. Probably the best example would be a concert by a popular singing group like the early Beatles, or Elvis. With abductions, the various abductees are not in close proximity with someone on the other side of the planet. In addition, people who have been abducted at the same time are generally unaware that the other person was abducted until it is recalled under hypnosis.

Psychosis is a mental disorder marked by derangement of personality, loss of contact with reality, and a deterioration of normal social functioning. If anything, abductees represent the complete opposite of this profile. Outside of their abduction experiences, they are completely normal. Noted psychiatrist John Mack states that none of the abductees he has seen exhibit any symptoms of psychosis or any other mental disorder.

Clearly a Case of Panic

Any scientist, sociologist, or psychologist who studies the "War of the Worlds" broadcast will tell you it was a clear case of panic. Panic occurs "When some highly cherished value is threatened and no certain elimination of that threat is in sight." [1].

Those who panicked knew exactly where the information was coming from, it was in the voice of a most trusted source, their radio news announcer. It was specific information (although false) telling them that they were in extreme danger and were being threatened. There was nothing imagined here. They were being told by a trusted "friend" that they were in mortal danger.

To give you a flavor of the program, here are a few lines from the broadcast:

> *Look, the darn thing's unscrewing!*
> *Keep back, there! Keep back I tell you.*
> *Maybe there's men in it trying to escape!*
> *It's red hot, they'll burn to a cinder!*
> *Keep back there! Keep those idiots back!*

(SUDDENLY THE CLANKING SOUND OF A HUGE PIECE OF METAL FALLING)

VOICES
> *She's off! The top's loose!*
> *Look out there! Stand Back!*
> *Ladies and gentlemen, this is the most terrifying thing I have ever witnessed.... Wait a minute! Someone's crawling out of the hollow top.*

Someone or ... something. I can see peering out of that black hole two luminous disks ... are they eyes? It might be a face. It might be ...

CROWD SCREAMS

Good heavens, something's wriggling out of the shadow like a grey snake. Now it's another one and another. They look like tentacles to me. There, I can see the thing's body. It's as large as a bear and it glistens like wet leather. But that face. It ... it's indescribable. I can hardly force myself to keep looking at it. The eyes are black and gleam like a serpent. The mouth is V-shaped with saliva dripping from its rimless lips that seem to quiver and pulsate. The monster or whatever it is can hardly move. It seems weighed down by ...

Sounds a little hokey now, but it was scary stuff back in 1938 when almost none of the population had ever even seen an airplane. To repeat, the Orson Welles broadcast is a case of panic to a perceived real threat, originating from real, albeit false, information coming from a known reliable source. Whew!

Some Facts About the Broadcast

Despite its notoriety the majority of the public never heard the original broadcast. And they still haven't. Welles' station was competing in the same time slot against the most popular radio show in the world at that time, "The Charlie McCarthy Program" with Edgar Bergen (Murphy Brown's dad). Charlie McCarthy was a wooden dummy and this show alone had ten times more listeners than Welles' station. [2]

The people most frightened were those living closest to where the Martians were supposed to be taking over. Subsequent interviews showed that those living in New York, New Jersey, and Pennsylvania were most frightened because the broadcast used real street names and neighborhoods people were familiar with. Those less familiar with the area of attack basically didn't care too much. [3]

In 1938 more people had radios than plumbing. At the time, radio was the most trusted way for the population to get news. Radio was the vehicle for important news announcements. There was no TV. Only a few weeks before, it was radio that carried the news of Europe preparing to enter a war, World War II. Of 32 million families, 27.5 million had radios. 4

Less than 5 percent of the population heard the broadcast and reacted in fear. Nationwide, 32 million people were listening to the radio that night, and only 6 million people heard the original broadcast. Approximately one million listeners, 16 percent of the audience, became disturbed or frightened. Although a million people is quite a lot, it's not anywhere near what the legend has grown to. 5

There was enough concern to take a survey of the population. High school principals were polled shortly after the event to see what effect the broadcast had on students. Only 5 percent admitted to being afraid, but the actual number was probably much higher.

The public loved it. Although the FCC made Welles apologize, 91 percent of the public applauded the broadcast. Newspaper surveys showed an even higher approval rate. For the most part the public thought it was exciting. They had a good time. (After they found out the truth.) 6

SCANDINAVIAN GHOST ROCKETS

Scandinavia, of all places, was once a hotbed of UFO activity. For a period of 5 years prior to World War II, from 1932 to 1937, there were hundreds of reports from the citizenry of unknown aircraft flying over Finland, Norway, and Sweden. Remember, in those days an airplane was an extremely rare sighting. There were so many aircraft reported that more were seen at one time in the air than were known to be in all of Scandinavia. Thus, officials knew they weren't local.

Huge craft were reported, some of which had eight engines. There were just not any airplanes like that in 1932. Strange multicolored lights were also frequently seen accompanying these craft. The ships were seen hovering over military installations, much as flying saucers do today. Then as mysteriously as they had first appeared, they disappeared and were no longer seen after 1937.

1946

In 1946 strange vehicles appeared in the skies over Scandinavia again. Many were seen diving into lakes. After checking with Allied armed forces, the Scandinavian countries confirmed they were not from any of the Allied countries. Nor did their behavior match the flight patterns of German V-2 rockets.

Many observers reported sightings of this craft traveling at high rates of speed and making hairpin turns at high speeds. Nobody had technology capable of that in 1946, and we still don't, even now. These craft were sighted from June through August of 1946, and then they disappeared, just like before. Since no one knew where they came from they became known as "Ghost Rockets."

THE WORLD AT WAR

 Nobody could have foreseen the unbelievable costs. The losses both financially and in the sheer numbers of people killed were huge, unprecedented, and unanticipated. Everybody suffered, even the so-called "winners."

World War I: No One Could Have Imagined

Huge portions of Europe had been completely demolished by what was known then as the "World War." Business and banking institutions had literally been blown away. A total of 1.4 million people in France had died. Germany lost 1.8 million people. Tiny England lost 900,000 citizens. Italy lost 650,000 people. In Russia, the toll was so high they just lost count. As a comparison, the United States lost 53,000 men and women in Vietnam. 1. As of November 2011, there were 6,331 men and women killed in Iraq and Afghanistan, combined.

Hundreds of thousands of men, women, and children were simply missing, and presumed dead. No one knows or ever will know exactly what happened to them. Many others died later from starvation, disease, exposure, and infection. Psychologically, no surviving person or family was ever the same again.

The War Never Ended

At 10:55 a.m. on November 11, 1918, Britain's Prime Minister David Lloyd George came out of his residence at 10 Downing Street and shouted at startled pedestrians: "At 11:00 o'clock this morning, the war will be over!"

But, not really. Here are just a few of the many incidents that happened during the next 21 years.

1918 - 1939

October 27, 1921
    Mussolini becomes Premiere of Italy.

December 25, 1926
    Hirohito becomes Emperor of Japan, succeeding his father.

September 18, 1931
    Japan invades Manchuria.

January 30, 1933
    Hitler becomes Chancellor of Germany.

October 3, 1935
    Italy invades Ethiopia.

July 17, 1936
    Civil War breaks out in Spain.

July 7, 1937
    War breaks out between China and Japan.

March 12, 1938
    Germany invades Austria.

October 1, 1938
    Germany invades Czechoslovakia.

September 1, 1939
Germany invades Poland.

September 3, 1939
Britain and France declare war on Germany.

November 30, 1939
The Soviet Union invades Finland.

This pattern continues until 1941 when the United States enters what will be known as World War II. By this time the following countries had already been swept up in the conflict: Egypt, the Philippines, Guam, Yugoslavia, the African nations, Greece, Scotland, Libya, Bulgaria, and the Wake Islands. 4

WORLD WAR II

As you can see, nearly the entire planet was already at war before the United States even entered it. Every country on the globe was involved. World War II affected every human being living on the face of the earth. Again, like World War I, the devastation was tremendous. New research has shown that Russia alone had over 25 million deaths. Here are some of the losses:

Russia	25 million people dead
China	15 million people dead
Poland	6 million people dead
Yugoslavia	2 million people dead
Germany	4 million people dead
Japan	2 million people dead
Great Britain	400,000 people dead
United States	300,000 people dead

Again, as a comparison, the United States lost 53,000 men and women in Vietnam. A total of 6,598 American men and women have been killed in Iraq and Afghanistan combined.

The total number of people killed on the planet during the two world wars was over 60 million human beings!

World War II formally ended on September 2, 1945.

Oh, No. Not Again

During the two years immediately following the end of World War II, the Communist party took over Yugoslavia, Poland, and Romania. It almost looked like the war cycle was starting over again, for the third time! 3

Eisenhower

Let's take General Eisenhower, who was later to become president of the United States. Here is a man who fought in World War I. For the next twenty years he and his colleagues watched as another cloud of war grew and encircled the planet again, almost from the first day after World War I. For all intents and purposes, for the next twenty years Eisenhower and the rest of the military were never *not* at war!

The same pattern seemed to be following World War II. Because of past experience and what they were seeing happening between 1945 and 1947, men in the military believed they were still at war, in anticipation of the next conflict that they would be involved in.

General Dwight D. Eisenhower, c. 1950
(U.S. National Archives and Records)

Put Yourself in Their Shoes

Try and imagine the devastation, trauma, and horror of two all-encompassing world wars that together killed over 65 million people in less than 20 years!

Imagine the mind-set and vigilance that men and women in the military had to adopt to insure not just their own survival, but all humanity. World War II had ushered in the age of the atomic bomb. Our very existence as a species was at risk.

To Make Sure It Doesn't Happen

Despite the all-encompassing nature of both world wars, one major tragedy was avoided: The United States was never occupied by the forces of another nation. Not a single building in the United States was lost to a bomb. No matter what, our military had stood their ground. They were going to make sure that nobody ever entered our boundaries or penetrated the skies above our cities. Only by stepping into their shoes for a brief moment can you begin to understand the military's reaction to the wave of flying saucer sightings that began in 1947.

LOS ANGELES AIR RAID

On February 25, 1942, less than three months after the bombing of Pearl Harbor, defense forces in Los Angeles, California went on full alert. American radar had picked up a formation of aircraft coming in over the ocean from the west. Remember, radar was still such a new invention that most of the general public didn't know it existed.

Air Raid Alert

When the craft crossed the coast, a barrage of anti-aircraft fire was released. Some 1,430 rounds of anti-aircraft ammunition were fired. This was witnessed by thousands of people who were diving for cover as air raid sirens wailed. Several homes and public buildings were destroyed from falling debris and six people died from heart attacks and auto accidents caused by the event.

The *Los Angeles Evening Herald Examiner* reporter Peter Jenkins said: "I could clearly see the "V" formation of about twenty-five silvery planes overhead moving slowly across the sky toward Long Beach." 1

Too Fast to be Planes

The objects were so quick they were able to dodge and dart between exploding shells. The event was witnessed by Paul Collins, a Douglas Aircraft employee. Collins said that he and others with him estimated that on the conservative side the craft sometimes moved at up to five miles per second. That equals 18,000 miles per hour! What's even more amazing is that Collins' estimate is dead-on the same speed that the Russians have learned to time flying saucers by using radar and sophisticated instruments - but a full 40 years later!

Too Slow to be Planes

There was also a large "mothership" that cruised by. A reporter from the *Long Beach Independent* estimated that the larger craft never exceeded 60 miles per hour. This is significant. A plane cannot fly that slowly! At sixty miles per hour, there is not enough airlift to keep it aloft. In the full glare of wartime searchlights, this larger craft took many direct hits and suffered no effect. 2

"Somebody, Get the President"

On our website, www.flyingsaucers101.com, there is a copy of the memo that Chief of Staff General George C. Marshall sent to then-President Franklin Delano Roosevelt the day after the Los Angeles air raid. Marshall's memo states that the objects traveled at 200 miles per hour, but thousands of eyewitnesses put the speed at almost ten times that.

Key Points

This event was witnessed by thousands of people. The event was described in full detail on the front page of every newspaper in southern California, complete with photographs showing the disks under fire from anti-aircraft batteries. The event is well-chronicled in military and presidential documents.

FOO FIGHTERS

Foo fighters! This is what World War II fighter pilots called the brightly colored balls of light that zipped in between their flying formations during battle. During the final years of World War II it was common to have these little "foo" fighters follow Allied aircraft for long periods of time. The foo fighters often appeared in groups of ten or more. Years later, German pilots reported similar occurrences. At the time, both sides feared the other had a secret weapon or tracking device.

Foo

The name originated with the French word *feu* which means fire. A popular comic strip of the time, "Smokey Stover," often used the line "Where there's foo, there's fire."

Present at Every War

UFOs have been consistently present at every major war from World War II on. If you were an alien sociologist, there is no better venue to observe man engaging in his most consistent and troubling behavior: killing members of his own species.

The Korean War

During the Korean War there were many encounters with alien space-craft. The significant thing about these encounters is that almost all the military maneuvers were joint efforts combining infantry and air combat units, and so many of the sightings and encounters were witnessed by both ground and air personnel. [1]

Wartime UFOs

Specific encounters between military pilots and alien spacecraft occurred in North Korea on March 10, 1951; on January 29, 1952; on February 24, 1952 over Antung; and on May 31, 1952 near Chorwon. During one of the sightings, military ground forces directed rifle fire at one of the alien spacecraft. [2]

The spacecraft responded by emitting a pulsating ray. This was witnessed by both military pilots and ground forces. The men on the ground who were hit by the ray became so weakened they could not walk. Over the next several days they literally had to be carried off of the front lines.

The Vietnam War

There are many dramatic stories and anecdotes involving aliens and spacecraft encountering U.S. military forces in Vietnam. The problem of confirming and validating each story is virtually impossible to resolve. The Vietnam war itself is an enigma. The American public still can't get the whole story even about their own men, the POWs, and MIAs.

Therefore, there is little hope (at present) of getting a confirmed version of Vietnam alien encounters. 3

1947: THE YEAR OF THE WAVE

1947 is known as the year of the first "wave" of modern flying saucer sightings. A study of U.S. newspapers that year documents over 832 sightings in the United States just in the 30 days between June 15, 1947 and July 15, 1947. For the entire year there were over 1,500 reports. Include on our website is a CIA report tracking saucer sightings in 1947. This report was secret and withheld from the public for decades. 1

The Kenneth Arnold Case

This is the first key flying saucer case of modern times. As you can see from the previous sections, reports of flying objects are certainly not unique to our century. However, this is the case that caught the attention of the media and re-informed the contemporary world that flying saucers existed.

The Facts

Kenneth Arnold was a private pilot and a businessman. He was also a member of the Idaho Search and Rescue Mercy Flyers and a Federal Deputy Marshall. On June 24, 1947 Arnold joined in a search mission to find a Marine Curtis C-46 transport plane that was believed to have crashed in the Cascade Mountains.

While flying at about 9,000 feet at 2:00 p.m., Arnold saw nine silver disks moving in formation directly across his flight path. He estimated them to be about 25 miles away. Since they were unusual, to say the least, Arnold decided to time them to estimate their speed. He checked his watch as they passed Mt. Rainier and again when they passed Mt. Adams. It took them 1 minute and 42 seconds. After landing and checking the distance between the two peaks, Arnold realized the disks had been traveling over 1,700 miles per hour! This was twice the speed of sound, and the world airspeed record in 1947 was only about 650 miles per hour!

"They Flew Like a Saucer"

Not only Arnold, but people flying in a nearby Douglas DC-4 also saw the flying disks. In addition, disks were seen by hundreds of people on the ground. The disks made no sound. They were completely silent. In an interview with *The East Oregonian* newspaper, Arnold said: "They flew like a saucer would if you skipped it across the water."

When the Associated Press picked up the story, they called the disks "saucer-like objects." From this, the term *Flying Saucer* was officially made an integral part of the human language. Be sure to check out the CIA's official report on the Kenneth Arnold sighting at our website, www.flyingsaucers101.com

Headline from 1947 reporting sightings and landings of flying saucers.
(Courtesy Seattle Post Intelligencer)

OTHER SIGHTINGS

June 14, 1947
Richard Rankin saw a triangular formation of ten disks over Bakersfield, California while flying from Chicago to Los Angeles. He estimated their speed at 600 m.p.h.

June 21, 1947
Residents in Spokane, Washington saw eight disks flying at an estimated speed of 600 miles per hour at 11:00 A.M.

June 21, 1947
A salesman driving through Yukon, Oklahoma saw six disks flying in formation at an "incredible rate of speed."

June 24, 1947
Three disks were seen above Richmond, Washington. They were wobbling as they zipped across the sky. This is the same day Kenneth Arnold saw his disks. He also noted that the disks were "wobbling."

June 27, 1947
A woman sees disks "wobbling from side to side," fly past the Cascade Mountains at phenomenal speed while in formation. She was quoted as saying, "They looked like silver plates."

June 28, 1947
Two pilots from Maxwell Air Base in Alabama, see a bright light traveling at high speed make a 90-degree turn and disappear. Six other witnesses, including two intelligence officers, see the same thing.

June 28, 1947 A farmer in Wisconsin by the name of Beuscher sees several silent disks zoom over his farm. At the same time, reports of flying disks overhead come in from across the state of Illinois.

June 29, 1947
The driver of the De Moines-Mason City bus in Iowa sees five disks streak across the sky. Shortly after that sighting, he counts thirteen more coming from the opposite direction.

Scientists at White Sands Proving Grounds in New Mexico spot "silvery disks" flying across restricted airspace at speeds greater than sound. In 1947 White Sands was the only nuclear air base in the world. The appearance of these saucers over this facility generated a flurry of military activity and concern. See the copies of top-secret memos concerning this at www.flyingsaucers101.com.

June 30, 1947
Near Williams field in Arizona, a U.S. Navy pilot sees two disks appear to land about 20 miles south of the Grand Canyon. The pilot described them as having "inconceivable speed."

Newspaper headline and article describing high-speed disks flying over U.S. military bases in 1947.

STORIES ALL OVER

Flying Disk Reported Seen At Air Station

By Associated Press

A recruiting officer at the Naval Air Station at Grand Prairie said Friday he saw what appeared to be a flying disk streak under a B 34 bomber for a second and then disappear.

Chief Petty Officer Charles Lewis 36, said he looked up to watch the B 34 go over Thursday and I saw a very bright object racing at it at an incredible speed.

It got under the bomber as seemed to hang there for a couple of seconds or so. Lewis said it then broke away at a 45 deg

June 30, 1947

Portland, Oregon police officers see "five shiny chromium hub caps" disappear and reappear while flying by. The hub caps "wobbled from side to side" as they flew. The disks were seen by officer K. McDowell along with two other officers and a pilot.

Note: Wobbling from side to side was a commonly observed characteristic of flying saucers in the late 1940s and early 1950s. Since then the aliens apparently have re-engineered their craft to reduce this. They now fly straight, with less wobble, and they are frequently tilted sideways.

July 4, 1947

Let the fireworks begin! Campers at Twin Falls, Smoke River Canyon in Idaho see more than thirty disks traveling at a high rate of speed.

United Airlines crew, pilot E. J. Smith, copilot Ralph Stevens and stewardess Martie Morrow see nine disks while flying over Idaho. The disks put on a fantastic display. They perform acrobatics, merge together, then split apart again. They also disappear and reappear.

On July 4, 1947, that day alone, there were 88 major disk sightings reported by over 400 people across twenty-four states. It is estimated at least 10 million people saw flying saucers on this day.

July 4, 1947

The crash at Roswell happens. Shortly before midnight in an explosive thunderstorm, the now-famous flying saucer crash at Roswell, New Mexico occurred. It is also known as "The Crash at Corona" because Corona, New Mexico is about 40 miles closer to the crash site than

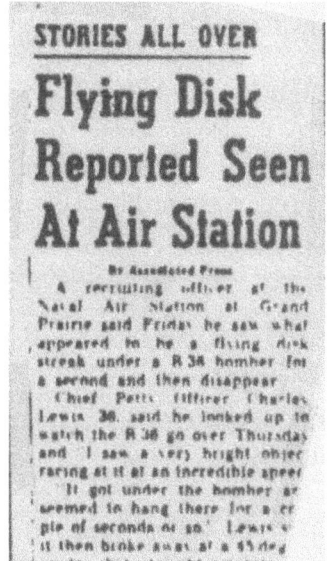

Roswell. However, the crash debris was taken to Roswell Air Base, hence the name "Roswell."

October 9, 1947
Las Vegas, Nevada. Air Force pilots flying over Las Vegas spot a disk traveling at a thousand miles per hour. It does a 180-degree turn at that speed. Any earthly airplane trying that maneuver would have self-destructed.

SIGHTINGS IN EUROPE

April 20, 1947
Citizens in Col de Serres, France report seeing disks flying over the valley.

May 21, 1947
Slow-moving, large cigar-shaped objects are seen in Sweden.

Another newspaper headline during the 1947 UFO "Wave."

June 10, 1947
Fast-moving flying objects are seen in Finland.

July 7, 1947
In Sussex, England people see disks fly over the coast and out to sea. Citizens in Naples, Italy report a slow-moving, shiny disk overhead. Astronomers at Del Satto Observatory in Chile spot disks. Estimated speed: 3,000 miles per hour! Japan and Holland also report seeing high-speed disks on this day.

July 18, 1947
Norway: Two objects are seen diving into Lake Mjosa.

July 19, 1947
Several witnesses see an object dive into Lake Kolmjorv, Sweden.

Even Aircraft Recognition Expert Is Stumped Over Flying Disks

W. J. Schanz, war veteran who served as an instructor in aircraft recognition, was stumped when called upon for his expert opinion on what may have been Flying Disks over Roswell Tuesday afternoon. Harvey Sparkman, fellow employee at the Jennings Fixture Co., 1008 W. Tilden, called Schanz out after spying several mysterious airborne objects.

Six people were in the group which saw the articles, of whom Mr. Sparkman was first. His seeing of them came about in a very unique manner.

The fellows in the shop had been

Two additional objects had seemingly followed the first into view.

The appearance of the articles had everybody baffled, including Mr. Schanz. During his time as an instructor in the air forces, he had seen every type of plane in existence, and he said, "the objects did not have any characteristics of any plane I have ever seen." His description of the flying somethings-or-others was, "they did not seem to be exactly round, and rather than spinning through space they appeared to somersault, with no definite pattern of movement." Their speed could not be estimated.

Article (1947) discussing the fact that military experts have no idea what the flying saucers are, or where they are from.

July 23, 1947
Workers near Pitanga, Brazil witness the landing of a craft. Three 6-foot tall beings get out wearing transparent suits emerge from the craft.

August 11, 1947
In Sweden over 400 people see fast-moving disks fly overhead.

August 14, 1947
Italy: A citizen, R. L. Johannis, comes across two small beings with large heads and large eyes.

September 1, 1947
Greece: British army units see "mystery projectiles." (Don't you just love the British? They don't see disks or saucers, they see "projectiles.")

KEY EVENTS IN 1947

- *There was a huge number of flying-saucer sightings.*
- *The sightings were worldwide.*
- *They were witnessed by millions of people.*
- *Almost all the sightings were in broad daylight.*
- *The Roswell crash did not happen out of the blue, it was just one of thousands of fly-overs.*

ROSWELL – Alien Crash

Alien contact had begun! In one of the most astounding events in human history, alien bodies were recovered from a downed spacecraft in Roswell, New Mexico in July, 1947.

This was the beginning of modern confirmation that we are not alone in the universe. The story involves the recovery of bodies, secrecy, and death threats. Dozens of witnesses have sworn and testified to what they saw.

The occurrence at Roswell has been the most talked-about UFO event in American history. Most Americans have a fleeting acquaintance with the words *Roswell, New Mexico*. Here is a synopsis of what happened and when. It is designed to give you a factual account to use as a foundation for your own investigations and discovery of information about flying saucers and alien beings. Remember, the Bible, the Torah, the Koran, the law of relativity and virtually everything we know to be true is "hearsay" and based on secondhand descriptions.

Here is the text of First Lieutenant Walter Haut's press release dated July 8, 1947:

The many rumors regarding the flying disc became a reality yesterday when the Intelligence office of the 509th Bomb Group of the Eighth Air Force, Roswell Army Air Field, was fortunate enough to gain possession of a disc through the cooperation of one of the local ranchers and the sheriff's office of Chaves County.

The flying object landed on a ranch near Roswell sometime last week. Not having phone facilities, the rancher stored the disc until such time as he was able to contact the sheriff's office, who in turn notified Maj. Jesse A. Marcel of the 509th Bomb Group Intelligence Office.

Action was immediately taken and the disc was picked up at the rancher's home. It was inspected at Roswell Army Air Field and subsequently loaned by Major Marcel to higher headquarters.

STANTON T. FRIEDMAN

Nuclear physicist Stanton Friedman has been investigating and documenting the existence of flying saucers and extraterrestrial beings for over 30 years. He has written several books on the subject and has spoken to over a thousand colleges and universities. Friedman was the person who initially uncovered the incident at Roswell, New Mexico. As a trained scientist, he has brought a deliberate and thorough approach to researching this large and very complex subject. If Friedman is discussing an issue, you can believe it has been well-researched. For an absolutely intriguing story, get a copy of his *MJ-12 Report*, or his CD-Rom: "UFOs, The Real Story. How the Roswell story came to light."

Hidden for Thirty Years

Although the incident at Roswell Army Air Base happened in 1947, it was completely unknown to anyone except the participants, an inner circle of very high-level military personnel, and the president of the United States. That is, until 1978. Friedman was being interviewed at a radio station in Baton Rouge Louisiana. Friedman had been involved in investigating the world-wide sightings of UFOs for several years. He had been in town to give a lecture at Louisiana State University on February 20.

Would You Like a Saucer With Your Coffee?

While having a coffee break, the director of the radio station said to Friedman in a casual manner, "The person you really ought to talk to is Jesse Marcel. He handled pieces of one of those things." Friedman contacted Marcel, who at that time was living in Louisiana, and the rest is history. Roswell was out of the bag.

More Witnesses

Over the next several years Friedman would uncover dozens of firsthand witnesses to a truly remarkable event: the crash and recovery of a craft not made on earth. Friedman's research is impeccable and unbiased. Check the Bibliography for a list of his books. Start there. The best, most accurate reporting on Roswell, you simply can't go wrong with Stanton. His work is a must for serious research.

Physicist Stanton Friedman, the man who first uncovered the story about the crash at Roswell, New Mexico.
(Photo courtesy Debbie Stock)

An unprecedented Fifty-year Leap

In the 50 years since the extra-terrestrial spacecraft crashes in New Mexico, there has been a quantum leap in technology, unprecedented in all human history. Despite the fact that man has not changed one iota physiologically, the technological advancements that have occurred in the last 50 years would normally have taken at least 200 years to make. There's a reason. We had help. That help came from technology found in downed alien spacecraft.

> The government is not some monolithic piece of granite that never moves or reacts. To those of us inside the military/government machine, the government is dynamic, highly reactive and even proactive when it comes to devising ways to protect its most closely held secrets.

For years after Roswell we weren't just one step ahead of people wanting to know what really happened, we were a hundred steps ahead, a thousand, even more. In fact, we never hid the truth from anybody, we just camouflaged it. It was always there, people just didn't know what to look for or recognize it for what it was when they found it. And, they found it over and over again.15

Colonel Philip J. Corso (Ret.)

Many technological items were filtered out to private industry through the use of government contracts. Some of the things that were borrowed or developed from recovered alien craft were:

Night Vision Goggles
When soldiers looked into the craft at Roswell in the middle of the night, they could see through the portholes. They were astonished to be able to see their comrades outside the ship walking around as if it were broad daylight, the only difference was that there was a greenish quality to the light, just like today's night-vision glasses.

Lasers
It was not immediately known what this device was when they found it. They couldn't figure it out; later they turned it on by accident.

Atomically Aligned Fibers
Military scientists discovered that the suits the aliens were wearing were composed of materials that were atomically aligned. All the molecules are lined up in one direction. The only thing found on earth made this way is a spider's web. A single strand of this material, weighing only 15 ounces, could be stretched for 50 miles without breaking. This was the beginning of super-tenacity fibers such as Kevlar, the material used to make bullet-proof vests.

Chips, Weapons And Optics
In addition, prototypical examples of integrated chips, directed energy beam weapons, and fiber optics were first found at the Roswell crash site. No one had ever seen anything like them and it was years before it was finally figured out what they were.

Reverse-engineered Craft

The U.S. military has built several craft based upon what they learned from the crashed flying saucers they have recovered. This is known as *reverse engineering*; that is, taking something apart and rebuilding a new one based upon what you learned during the dismantling.

There have been approximately twenty-nine saucers recovered or built and test-flown out of Area 51 in Nevada and the site known as S-4, which is adjacent to Area 51. Although we have successfully flown the craft we have not been able to get these craft to leave earth's atmosphere. So far the tests have been limited to low-altitude levels. These are the craft viewers have seen from the hills surrounding Area 51.

ROSWELL: THE BEST EVIDENCE

The incident at Roswell is truly an astonishing story of excitement, discovery, and intrigue! However, it has been 50 years since this event occurred. There are many different versions and a lot of confusion about what actually happened. It is a tough job sifting through all this info, conflicting reports, and supporting testimony.

After looking at all the available information and evidence, here is the most accurate version of this event. As often as possible I've used direct quotes to substantiate any conclusions. See the Bibliography for additional research you may want to conduct on your own.

The Saucer Crash Was Real!

Once you look at the facts it's clear that something extraordinary did occur at Roswell in July, 1947. Recent Air Force statements - that it was merely a weather balloon, or it was just some test dummies that were recovered - are embarrassing. Anyone who spends just ten minutes looking into this event can see that.

It will take you no more than a few minutes to finish reading this chapter. Draw your own conclusions. You can determine if the weather balloon story makes any sense.

What Happened

On the night of July 4, 1947 an object crashed in the desert of New Mexico sometime around midnight. Many writers mistakenly state that the crash occurred July 2. However, documents, affidavits, and eyewitness testimony clearly date the crash as occurring on July 4. It was on July 1 and 2 that military radar and eyewitnesses first spotted fast-moving objects in the sky. The crash may have happened just after midnight on the fourth, which would actually have been the fifth of July.

A particularly violent thunderstorm occurred on the evening of July 4. It is speculated that a bolt of lightning may have struck the crashed object. Around 11:30 P.M. several people in the area heard an unusual exploding sound, unlike normal thunder, followed by an object which roared overhead and appeared to crash nearby.

Where Did It Happen? Roswell? Corona? Or Socorro?

The crash did not actually occur at Roswell. Roswell is a small town in New Mexico quietly nestled around an Army Air Base located there. A crash site was discovered on a ranch almost midway between the towns of Corona and Roswell. Both towns are about 75 miles away from the initial crash site. The town of Socorro is a little farther west of Corona. Another site was discovered about 35 miles outside of Roswell. The crash is commonly called "Roswell" because the debris and bodies were taken to the Roswell Army Air Base. However, this crash has also been called three different names: the crash at Corona, the crash at Roswell, and the crash at Socorro.

More Than One Crash Site

In addition to the different names for the Roswell crash, there were also two separate crash sites. It appears the vehicle may have split in two pieces and crash landed over several miles apart.

The Plains of San Augustin

This is a yet another crash site in addition to the three that are called *Roswell*. This is a separate crash location not linked to the other Roswell sites. All indications are that this crash occurred several days before Roswell, most likely around July 2 or 3, 1947.

The plains of San Augustin are in the Roswell area, and the recovery of bodies and craft parts was also done by military personnel from Roswell Army Air Base. The evidence for this case is based on secondhand testimony. However, there is an air of credibility about it for this simple reason: The man who claimed to have witnessed the recovery made his statements decades before the existence of the Roswell crashes came to light. In fact, he died 10 years before Roswell became known by anybody who was not involved in the Roswell affair.

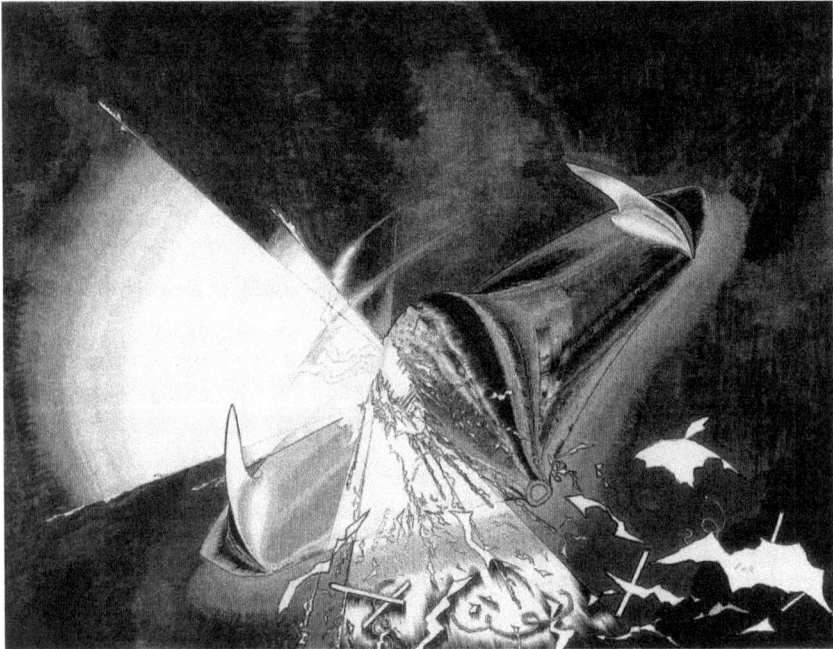

Lightning struck the craft around midnight on July 4, 1947, tearing a gash in its side before the craft hit the ground and gouged a large trench in the earth. (©1997 William L. McDonald)

Barney Barnett

Grady "Barney" Barnett stumbled upon the "Plains of San Augustin" crash site. Barnett was a soil engineer who worked in the area for the U.S. Conservation Service. When he arrived, some private citizens were already on the scene, supposedly another group of archaeologists. He saw them looking at several dead bodies and a large metallic object stuck in the ground. Barnett died in 1969, but the following account is what his family and friends say he told them. The craft was still mostly intact. The beings were small with odd-shaped heads and no hair. The eyes were small but had a different spacing between them as compared to humans. The bodies were dressed in form-fitting, silver jumpsuits.

Shortly after he got there the military showed up and cordoned off the area. They told him he was never to discuss this matter with anyone. The existence of this crash site would also account for all the bodies reported. If you add up all the bodies seen by eyewitnesses, the number exceeds the number of bodies seen at any one site.

Barnett told his story to close friends Vern and Jean Maltais. He also told his story to William Leed, a retired colonel in the military who was investigating the Roswell crash.

Alien Crash Retrievals

Be patient and stay with me here. Some researchers also say there have been as many as eighteen crash retrievals in the American southwest. Evidence for these other crash retrievals or C/Rs, as they' re called, is weak and sketchy. Most of the evidence consists of secondhand statements.

Eighteen More Crashes?

Other possible crash retrievals were first brought up by Frank Scully. Scully had supposedly gotten the information from a lecture given by Silas Newton. Newton had given his lecture about crashed flying saucers in early March 1950 at Denver University. Newton had gotten his information from a Texas oilman named Leo GeBauer. GeBauer heard the information from a geologist who did some work for him and had done some work for the U.S. military. So the information is fourth-hand with no documents and no confirming eyewitnesses.

Twenty-eight years later in 1978, another guy by the name of Len Stringfield came forward and made the same claims about the existence of many more crash retrievals, and not just Roswell. He also had no verification in the form of documents or witnesses. This makes everything more than a little suspect except there are a few very interesting details. But first, here is a list of some other alleged saucer crash retrievals, including those Scully and Stringfield think occurred.

1947
- Crash near Socorro, New Mexico on June 1.
- Crash in New Mexico. Robert Morningsky says his grandfather and others found a downed saucer and a live alien while on a tribal vision quest.

1948
- Crash in Mexico.

1952
- Crash in California, out in the desert. Unconfirmed story about a film the military has in its possession showing a crashed saucer.

1953
- Recovered saucer in Kingman, Arizona. Confirmed by firsthand eyewitness Bill Uhouse.
- Crash in Montana, supposedly with military and civilian witnesses.

1957
- Crash in the American Southwest.

1962
- Crash in New Mexico, with two alien bodies recovered.

1973
- Crash in the Paradise Valley area of Arizona.

Follow-up to the Undocumented Crash Retrievals
Although neither Frank Scully nor Len Stringfield had any concrete evidence of additional crash retrievals, here are some interesting points.

Frank Scully describes recovered saucer material in his book *Behind The Flying Saucers* as being like lightweight, indestructible aluminum, and also that pieces of recovered disks had "hieroglyphics" on them. This was written more than 25 years before any Roswell information came to light.

An FBI memo dated March 31, 1950 (released by the Freedom of Information Act) discusses a Texas oilman who is talking about crashed UFOs and recovered alien beings.

Another FBI memo dated March 22, 1950 and addressed directly to FBI Director J. Edgar Hoover states that an Air Force investigator said three flying saucers had been recovered in New Mexico. The memo also says the government believed "radar interfered with the controlling mechanism of saucers."

Researcher Ted Loman, in trying to confirm the alleged saucer crashes, discovered something very interesting. While researching back issues of local newspapers in the areas where the crashes supposedly had occurred he found that all the back issues were there except the days of the crashes and the two days following them. All those back issues of the newspapers were missing. This included several different newspapers located in different towns, the towns closest to each crash site. In all the 50 years of newspaper records, those are the only ones missing. 18

How Many Fingers? Four? Five? Or Six?

Keep in mind that there are many different kinds of beings visiting our planet. Different reports from crashes describe beings with different numbers of fingers. Some of the beings are more human-looking, with smaller eyes than the classic little gray aliens depicted in the movies.

There is no way at this time to sort this out completely, but you should be aware that different alien beings have been reported with four fingers, five fingers, and six fingers. Whether this includes a thumb I don't know, but different eyewitnesses report different numbers of fingers on alien beings.

Artist's rendition of the cockpit of the Roswell craft and its pilots shortly before being struck by lightning.   (©1997 William L. McDonald)

What They Found: The Main Crash Site

Very early on the morning of July 5 some civilians came upon a crash site. They found three alien bodies lying outside of the craft and they thought they could see at least one more through a large hole ripped in the side of the craft. All the occupants were dead, although rumors persist that at least one being was still alive. These civilians were at the crash site before the military arrived and secured the area. This site was the closer of the two sites to the town of Roswell, located only about thirty-five miles outside of town.

The craft they found was not actually disk-shaped. It was shaped more like a strange airplane without wings, and it had a large crescent-shaped section near the front. News reports later referred to it as a "disk" but that could be because flying disks had been seen in the area for several days just prior to the crash or because part of an actual disk-shaped craft was blown off leaving the remaining crescent. This site is the one I will refer to as the *main crash site*. This is where the main body of the craft was found, along with the alien bodies.

The Debris Field

The second crash site is what I will refer to as the *debris field*. This is the site most people think of when someone says *Roswell*. The debris found at this site was unlike anything ever seen before. There were very thin pieces of metal very much like tin foil. Some of these pieces could be crumpled easily. However, after a few seconds and if left alone, the piece would completely un-crumple like liquid and flatten out perfectly smooth, all by itself. Other pieces of the foil-like material could not be cut, dented with a sledgehammer, or burned with a blowtorch. Several pieces looked like small I-beams and had strange symbols on them resembling hieroglyphics. There were no bodies found at this site.

The Bodies

The occupants were small, approximately 3 to 4-feet tall, with four fingers and no thumbs on their hands. They had finely featured faces and did not resemble the big-eyed gray aliens depicted in stories and commercials on TV. Official autopsy reports are classified, and for all practical purposes, non-existent. However, several written statements are available describing the bodies and autopsies in detail, written by physicians a few years later in the early 1950s.

This raises a question for those who believe this event involved a weather balloon. Why are documents still classified regarding the activities at Roswell Army Air Base during the first week in July, 1947? National security for a weather balloon, after 50 years?

Why So Many Crashes?

Assuming there may have been more than one crash, why were there so many? Well, no one knows for sure because the military isn't talking. However, here are some things to think about. First, there were a lot of saucers flying around in the American southwest during the summer of 1947. Roswell was the only nuclear air base in the world at the time; White Sands Proving grounds were where all the top-secret missile testing was taking place. These locations, along with Los Alamos and

Alamogordo Labs where the atomic bomb was developed, were all within a 150-mile radius of one another. It's pretty clear our alien visitors were having a good look at humanity's "progress."

Second, it appears the U.S. Military had some capability (whether intentional or unintentional) for throwing off the guidance systems of the saucers through the use of radar or other newly developed electronic devices. A case has been made for the idea that the U.S. military intentionally sought to down and recover some of these craft.

The Kingman, Arizona Landing

Credence for that concept comes from an event that happened several years later in 1953 at Kingman, Arizona. At Kingman the aliens simply landed a craft and left it there intact, for the military, ostensibly to give the military what it so actively sought and thus lessen the efforts to shoot a saucer down.

Eyewitness Bill Uhouse has gone on record to state that a "disk" was left at Kingman with the hatch open. The first soldiers to enter it became disoriented and nauseous. The disk was transported to what is now known as area 51. It made loud humming noises the whole time. The military didn't know what to do. They weren't sure if it was going to explode or what, so they left it sitting out in the open, on the tarmac, for 9 months! Uhouse joins several other people who have come forward and said they worked alongside "gray" aliens at U.S. military bases for years.

Eyewitnesses

There are over 150 firsthand eyewitnesses to the crash sites, alien bodies, and debris. They are doctors, nurses, military personnel, and civilians. All were sworn to secrecy. Most have since come forward and given sworn statements verifying the Roswell event. (See the entire list at the end of this chapter.) Virtually none of these people have made any money from their statements and none appear to have asked for any. For more detail about the witnesses, see the timeline that follows.

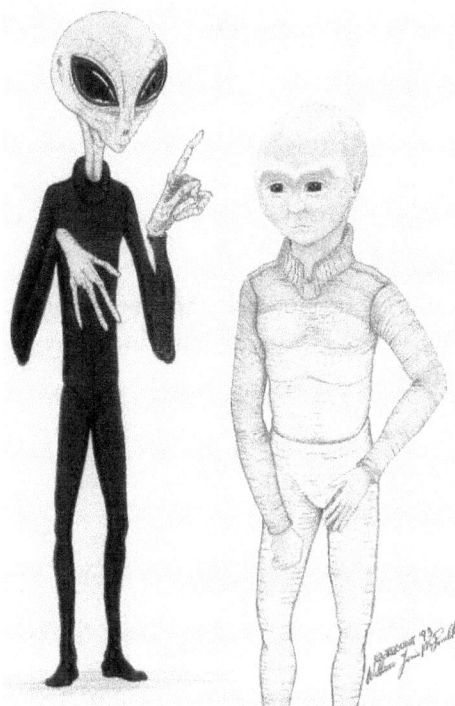

A "gray" alien being is shown on the left; The kind of being that crashed at Roswell is on the right. (©1997 William L. McDonald)

The Threats

Over the next several months following the crash, military personnel and civilians, including women and children, were threatened with death by the U.S. military if they spoke of what they saw at Roswell. Many, many civilians have sworn affidavits stating that U.S. military officers threatened them overtly, boldly, and face to face.

This is compelling. These threats come a scant 2 years after the U.S. defeated Hitler in World War II. Even when fighting against Hitler, private citizens and children were not threatened with death if they spoke to a fellow countryman, but here in Roswell, they were! All for a weather balloon? Think again!

While people are certainly capable of making up weird stories, what reason would a mother have for falsely stating that her children were threatened with murder by soldiers from her own country? There were many women who have made such statements about the incident at Roswell.

Even the most hardened police officers will tell you that suspects will say anything and witnesses may be unclear on what they saw, but people who are not involved in criminal activity never make up threats. It just doesn't happen. Actual statements about these threats appear later in this chapter.

News Reports

Reports of the crashed craft were published in over a thousand U.S. newspapers and over four hundred foreign papers over the next three days following the crash. The military's public information officer based at Roswell Army Air Base sent out the original press release.

"I Didn't Mean It, I Take It Back"

On July 8 the military retracted their initial press release and stated that the found object was a weather balloon. Here is a handy timeline to help you keep track of all the elements of this amazing story.

ROSWELL TIME LINE

Tuesday, July 1, 1947
Military installations at White Sands, Alamogordo, and Roswell, New Mexico track high-speed objects on radar, all flying at speeds well above what current jet fighters were capable of doing. With the radar blips penetrating highly secure air space at will, all three facilities go on full alert. [19]

Wednesday, July 2, 1947
Civilians spot disk-shaped craft flying over Roswell. Numerous reports come in from the public. The number of radar blips increase. Now there is almost a constant presence of the unidentified objects showing on radar.

Friday, July 4, 1947
Late at night during a tremendous thunderstorm, a fast-moving object disappears from military radar screens and local citizens hear a loud, unusual explosion and watch an object traveling overhead crash into the desert. Radar operator Steve Arnold watches a blip on the radar screen pulsate, enlarge, and then explode, disappearing from the screen. [20]

Colonel William Blanchard thinks an enemy aircraft has penetrated the defense systems and has crashed nearby. He immediately sends out a team to investigate the crash. Blanchard desperately wants to know what kind of aircraft could make hairpin turns at 3,000 miles per hour, which he just had witnessed on the radar screens.

Saturday, July 5, 1947
About 4:00 a.m. the military team reaches the still-smoldering wreckage. They call local sheriff George Wilcox and tell him to send out the fire department.

The Main Crash Site

Among the military team members is Steve Arnold and what he sees amazes him. The craft was still almost completely intact and partially buried in the sand as the result of a terrific impact. By comparison, Arnold feels an airplane would have been completely demolished. The craft appeared to be crescent-shaped, or like a rounded delta shape. Arnold sees several small, dark-gray bodies sprawled on the sand near the craft. He also sees another one near an opening in the craft. Arnold initially thinks it must be some kind of secret Russian craft.

One being is still alive. It tries to run away. Some of the soldiers yell at it to stop running, while at the same time locking rounds into the chambers of their guns. They end up firing on and killing the alien. Immediately after the alien is shot, an officer turns to Arnold and tells him to prevent a group of civilians who have shown up from getting any closer to the craft and bodies.

Fireman Steve Dwyer arrives with the Roswell fire department. He too sees the strange, crashed craft and alien bodies. As one is being carried right by him on a stretcher, Dwyer gets close enough to look down into the alien being's eyes. Dwyer gets some kind of mental information from the being telling him it knows it is dying.

A number of private citizens report that the downed craft crashed into the side of a ravine, about 5:30 or 6:00 A.M. Saturday morning. These people include:

Dr. W. Curry Holden

An archaeologist from Texas Tech University, he is on a field trip with a group of students. At first Holden thinks it's a plane and sends one of his student to go call the local sheriff. Holden and the others see three small bodies, two outside the craft and one still inside they can see through a hole in the body of the craft. When the military arrived, the entire group was escorted to the Roswell Army Air Base, where they were detained and told not to talk about the incident.

Later that same day Holden ran into another scientist in Roswell, Dr. C. Bertrand Schultz, a paleontologist who had been working in the area. Holden told Schultz what he had seen. Schultz was impressed enough that he recorded his meeting with Holden in his personal diary. Holden later confirmed in an interview that he had in fact been at the site of the crash. Holden is a credible witness. He had been the Chairman of the Department of History and Anthropology at Texas Tech. Holden died in 1993 at the age of 94.

The main crash site at Roswell. More than two dozen civilians saw military activity at this site. (©1997 William L. McDonald)

James Ragsdale

Along with his friend Trudy Truelove, Ragsdale said he saw the craft roar overhead about 11:30 P.M. the night before when they were out camping. They got in their jeep and drove into the desert to find out what crashed. They found the craft stuck in the side of a small hill. It looked very unusual and they thought it was an experimental military craft. They didn't see any movement in their flashlight beam, so they decided to leave and come back in the morning.

When they went back the next day they could see the craft more clearly. It looked like an airplane with little crescent-shaped wings. The front end was collapsed, but the rear part was intact. They also saw several bodies "about four or five feet long - they looked like midgets." They both picked up pieces of debris. As Ragsdale said, "You could take that stuff and wad it up and it would straighten itself out."

Shortly thereafter the military showed up in force with six or seven trucks and a staff car. Ragsdale and Truelove were afraid they would get in trouble, so they threw down the pieces they had picked up and hid. They stayed hidden while they watched the military completely clear away and pick up every piece of debris and the bodies. Ragsdale said they even raked the ground afterward. Ragsdale's story has been confirmed by other family members.

Sergeant Thomas Gonzales
Gonzales was one of the men assigned to guard the site. In an interview years later he recalled seeing small bodies with eyes not much larger than human eyes and a slightly enlarged head.

Major Edwin Easley
The man in charge of the MPs who were guarding the site during clean-up, Easley said he told his men to surround the ship with their backs to it. He told them not to let anyone come near it unless they had proper clearance. 21

Steve MacKenzie
He has signed a sworn affidavit stating his experience in the Roswell affair. He had been stationed at Roswell Army Air Base. On July 2, 1947 he was told to report to White Sands where he monitored the fast-moving disks flying over the area. On July 5, while back at Roswell, he was told to go out to the crash site, immediately, along with a special team from Washington.

When they got there MacKenzie said they just stood there staring at the crashed object because they realized it was one of the things they had been tracking on radar and had watched it disappear from the screen. MacKenzie said, "We were all smoking cigarettes and talking about how in the hell we were going to handle this thing. We were all concerned and a little scared." MacKenzie also confirmed that the Army completely cleaned the site, even using vacuum cleaners to complete the job.

MacKenzie personally said he saw four small bodies, one still inside the craft sprawled across a seat. He later learned there was a fifth body at the crash site.

When the military arrives they discover five alien bodies at this, the main-impact site. Melvin E. Brown, a soldier on guard, is told to get inside a truck with the recovered bodies. Although he is told not to, he lifts a tarp covering the bodies and sees them. He later stated that they were small with large heads and odd-colored skin.

"A.K."

Years later in an interview with physicist Stanton Friedman, an Army Air Force photographer who Friedman identifies as A.K. said that in July of 1947 he was stationed at Anacostia Naval Air Station in Washington D.C. He also made the following statement:

> One morning (in July 1947) they came in and they said, "Pack up your bags and we'll have the cameras there, ready for you." (They were then flown to Roswell Army Air Base.)

> We got in a staff car and we headed out about an hour and a half, we was headin' north. We got out there and there was a helluva lot of people out there, in a closed tent. All kinds of brass runnin' around. And, they was tellin' us what to do; shoot this, shoot that!

> There was four bodies I could see when the flash went off. I remember they was thin and looked like they had too big a head.9

Someone calls Sheriff George Wilcox in Roswell and tells him about the crash. Wilcox sends out several members of the local fire department to the main crash site. At this point, this is the only crash site that has been reported.

The local mortician in Roswell, Glenn Dennis, receives three phone calls from the Air Base asking him about the availability of small, child-sized coffins. He is also asked about various chemicals and their effects on body tissue. He is then asked about how to prepare a body that has been laying out in the desert.

Interview With Glenn Dennis

During an interview I did with Glenn Dennis in 1998, he told me some additional details:

Dennis said that at the time of the Roswell incident, he was a young man, only 22 or 23 years old. When he received the phone call from the Army Airbase, his boss had gone to lunch and Dennis was holding down the office. He was surprised when the military asked for child-sized caskets because children were never allowed on the base. Also, they were asking for more than one casket, which made it even more unusual. He wanted to get the right information so his boss wouldn't yell at him when he returned. So, he asked the officer on the phone if there had been a school bus accident near the base. The officer on the phone yelled at Dennis, telling him to shut up and do as he was told.

Dennis also operated the local ambulance service. Later that day he transports an injured soldier to Roswell Army Air Base. While standing around the loading dock in the back of the hospital, he sees a lot of unusual activity. Two military officers, obviously upset at seeing him there, approach him and threaten him. They tell Dennis, "If you open your mouth, we'll be picking your bones out of the sand."

The alien bodies arrive at the hospital and are pronounced dead by Dr. Jesse Johnson.

THE DEBRIS FIELD

This is the second site, the one that most people think of when they talk about Roswell, but as you will see, most people's impressions are a blurred combination of both sites. Once again there were no bodies found at this site. It is still Saturday, July 5, 1947. This debris-field site is much farther away, over 75 miles of unpaved road away from Roswell. By car it takes four and a half hours to get to it.

Saturday, July 5, 1947

Early in the morning William (Mac) Brazel rides out on horseback across the Foster Ranch to check on the livestock following the previous night's thunderstorm. He is accompanied by 7-year-old William D. Proctor. Young Proctor goes along because he likes to ride horses. On a minor point, some reports refer to Brazel as the foreman of the ranch; some call him the owner.

When they arrive at the site, they discover a large amount of strange debris strewn across the range. There is so much of it that the sheep will not walk through it. They end up having to herd the sheep almost a mile around it to get them to water.

The debris consists of pieces of lightweight material that resemble tinfoil and pieces of very light I-beams with unknown symbols engraved in their sides. The debris is so unusual that Brazel gathers up a bunch of it and takes it home.

Stanton Friedman interviewed many witnesses who actually handled the material. Here is how they described it to Friedman:

William Brazel: Something on the order of tinfoil, except (it) wouldn't tear, you could wrinkle it and it lay it back down and it immediately resumed its original shape. It was pliable but wouldn't break, weighed nothing, but you couldn't scratch it with your fingernail. **(Mac Brazel's son)**

Loretta Proctor: (Mac) had this piece of material he had picked up. He wanted to show it to us and wanted us to go down and see the rest of the debris or whatever. We cut on it with a knife and would hold a match on it and it wouldn't burn. **(William D. Proctor's mother)** 2

Mrs. Besie Brazel Schreiber: Some of these pieces had something like numbers and lettering on them, but there were no words we were able to make out. The figures were written out like you would write numbers in columns, but they didn't look like the numbers we use, at all. **(Mac Brazel's daughter)** 3

Walt Whitmore Jr.: Very much like tinfoil in appearance, but could not be torn or cut at all extremely light in weight. Some small beams that appeared to be either wood or wood-like had a sort of writing on it which looked like numbers which had either been added or multiplied (in columns). **(Son of the owner of Roswell Radio station KGFL)** 4

Sunday July 6, 1947
Rancher Mac Brazel takes a box load (load number one - remember this fact) of the debris to county sheriff George Wilcox. This involves a trip of over 75 miles on unpaved roads, taking more than 4 hours. The only reason Brazel made the long trip was to deliver this strange material to Wilcox.

After seeing the debris Wilcox decides it is strange enough that he should call the air base. He calls and speaks to Major Jesse Marcel, the Roswell Army Air Base intelligence officer.

Shortly thereafter Marcel was ordered by Base Commander William Blanchard to go out to the ranch with Brazel and take a look around. This was a major endeavor It's a four-hour trip. All for a weather balloon?

Major Marcel was accompanied by Sheridan Cavitt, who was an officer with the Counter Intelligence Corps. The men each drove separate cars. It was nightfall when they arrived at Brazel's ranch. They spent that night at the ranch in a small cottage.

Back at the Base
While Marcel and Cavitt are heading out to Brazel's ranch the following events occur:

Colonel William Blanchard, who is the Roswell Army Air Base commanding officer and Commander of the 509th Bomber Squadron, is given an order by Major General Clements McMullen, Commander of the Strategic Air Command. McMullen tells Blanchard to retrieve some of the debris in Sheriff Wilcox's possession and send it immediately to Colonel Thomas DuBose at the Fort Worth Army Air Field. The pieces of debris are sealed in a special courier pouch and flown to Fort Worth, Texas.

Roswell Army Airbase in 1947.
(U.S. National Archives and Records)

At Fort Worth Army Air Field the plane carrying the pouch is met personally by Colonel Alan D. Clark, the Base Commander. Clark takes the pouch and walks it over to a waiting B-26 airplane. The pouch is then attached to Col. Clark's wrist. Clark, with the pouch, then gets on the plane and is flown to Washington D.C., where it is received, again personally, by Major General McMullen. All this for a weather balloon?

Monday, July 7, 1947
Brazel takes Marcel and Cavitt to the site of the debris field early in the morning. Marcel held the rank of major at this time. World War II had just ended two years before. These were career military men, who saw weather balloons everyday. Simply look at their behavior in this debris field. This was no weather balloon!

Debris is spread over a large area, estimated to be at least a square mile. Both men fill their cars with debris. One of the cars was a Jeep Carry-All, a kind of old-fashioned station wagon that Jeep used to make.

Note: Marcel and Cavitt's two loads, when combined with the load Brazel took to Sheriff Wilcox, have already totaled three car-loads of debris. The biggest weather balloon ever used by the military at that time would easily fit into one box the size of a 19-inch television. So, it's very unlikely that the debris was from a weather balloon.

In an interview that Jesse Marcel gave as a retired Colonel in 1979, he stated what he saw when he and Cavitt first arrived at the debris field:

> When we arrived at the crash site it was amazing to see the vast amount of area it covered, scattered over an area of about three-quarters of a mile long, I would say, and fairly wide, several hundred feet wide. So we proceeded to pick up all the fragments we could find and load up our Jeep Carry-All. It was quite obvious to me, (my) familiarity with air activities, that it was not a weather balloon, nor was it an airplane or a missile. It was something I had never seen before, and I was pretty familiar with all air activities. We loaded up the Carry-All, but I wasn't satisfied. I told Cavitt, "You drive this vehicle back to the base and I'll go back out there and pick up as much as I can put in the car," which I did. But, we only picked up a small portion of the material that was there.

Marcel and Cavitt head back to the base. Major Marcel is impressed enough by the recovered material that he makes a special side trip to his house on the way back. He arrives at 2:00 A.M. (early Tuesday morning). It's late at night but he wakes his wife and 11-year-old son Jesse Jr. to show them the material.

Here is part of Major Marcel's firsthand description of the material he showed his family:

> A lot of it had a lot of little members with symbols that we had to call them hieroglyphics because I could not interpret them, they could not be read, they were just symbols. Those symbols were pink and purple, uh, lavender. I even tried to burn that. It would not burn.

But something that is more astonishing is that the piece of metal that we brought back was so thin, just like tinfoil in a pack of cigarette paper. So I tried to bend the stuff, it wouldn't bend. We even tried making a dent in it with a sixteen-pound sledgehammer. And, there was still no dent in it.

Eleven-year-old Jesse Marcel Jr. grows up to become a surgeon, a pilot, and a colonel in the military. He also becomes an experienced airplane crash investigator as well as Surgeon General for the State of Montana. Jesse Marcel Jr. remembers clearly the strange properties of the material his father showed him. He has never seen anything like it since.

THE RADIO STATION

Monday, July 7, 1947

It's still Monday, July 7, when the manager of a local radio station, KSWS, learns of the main crash site. The teletype operator for the station was Lydia Sleppy. She gets a call from station manager John McBoyle saying he had been to the crash site. In a 1990 interview, she tells what happened to her on July 7, 1947:

We were Mutual Broadcasting and ABC and if we had anything newsworthy, we would put it on the (teletype) machine and I was the one who did the typing. This call came in from John McBoyle. He told me he had something hot for the network. I got into it enough to know that it was a pretty big story, when the bell came on. (Then) typing came across: "This is the FBI, you will cease transmitting."

Tuesday, July 8, 1947

Marcel and Cavitt bring their two car-loads of debris on to Roswell Army Air Base about 6:00 A.M. They stop at Colonel William Blanchard's quarters and give him a description of the debris field. Blanchard orders the debris field cordoned off with armed guards posted around it. Shortly thereafter a large contingent of soldiers is sent to the debris field. An air search is also begun.

Sheriff Wilcox sends two deputies out to the debris field. The deputies find soldiers surrounding the area and they are turned away. However, they do see a large circular imprint where something hit that was so hot it turned the sand around it into molten glass, like volcanic glass.

The first newspaper report based on Lt. Walter Haut's press release
(Courtesy Roswell Daily Record)

Around 9:00 A.M. a staff meeting is held. Colonel Blanchard orders First Lieutenant Walter Haut, the Roswell Army Air Base Public Information Officer, to issue a press release saying the Army had recovered the remains of a crashed flying disk.

At 11:00 A.M. Haut delivers his press release to two local radio stations and two local newspapers. Frank Joyce, the manager of local radio station KGFL, recalls his discussion with Lt. Walter Haut when Haut delivered the press release:

> Walter Haut came into the station sometime after I got this call. He handed me a news release printed on onionskin stationary and left immediately. I called him back at the base and said, "I suggest that you not release this type of story that says you have a flying saucer or flying disc." He said, "No, it's OK, I have the OK from the C.O. (Commanding Officer, Col. Blanchard). I sent the release on the Western Union wire to the United Press Bureau."

Shortly before noon the press release hits all the wire services and the phones start ringing off the hook at Roswell Army Air Base. Sometime early in the afternoon, photographs were taken of some of the material recovered from the debris field.

Photographs of the Roswell Debris

Initial photographs taken of some of the Roswell debris have caused a bit of confusion about the whole incident. Various conflicting statements about these photos have bounced around like ping-pong balls.

Some of the principal people involved in taking these photos are still alive. I had an opportunity to meet with and speak to one of the photographers, J. Bond Johnson, about the photos. His statements, along with some investigation and observation, leads us to this summary of the Roswell photographs:

Scene 1, Take 2

On the afternoon of Tuesday July 8, 1947, Bond Johnson, then a young reporter for the Fort-Worth *Star Telegram*, was told to go out to General Ramey's office with his camera and take some pictures. When he got to the general's office he saw the floor covered with debris of some kind. Johnson used a Speed-Graphic camera and took a total of eight photographs on the two-sided film plates.

Not Very Exotic Stuff

Johnson recalls that the debris was pretty plain looking and not very exotic. This leads many critics to claim that it could not possibly have come from a high tech, space-traveling vehicle. However, the Mars Rover and Lunar Lander are pretty ordinary looking also. If one of them crashed they would also look like a pile of ordinary junk.

Brigadier General Roger Ramey (left) and Colonel Thomas J. Dubose (right) examine debris from the Roswell crash on July 8, 1947. Note the telegram in Ramey's hand and also notice that he is wearing a full dress uniform during July in New Mexico with no air conditioning. The original photo was taken by J. Bond Johnson. (Photo Courtesy Fort Worth Star-Telegram Photograph Collection, Special Collections Division, The University of Texas at Arlington Libraries.)

No Weather Balloon

Bond Johnson later became Colonel Bond Johnson and served four tours of duty at the U.S. Pentagon. Johnson states clearly that the debris he photographed was not a weather balloon. He also remembers that the debris filled the room with a strong, burned smell. Everyone who entered Ramey's office remembers the strong odor from the debris. Bond says the photos he took were of the real debris. If there was a switch for subsequent photos it occurred after he left.

Roswell Photo Update

After 50 years Johnson got a bug under his saddle to go back and look at the original photographic plates. He had not seen the plates since that fateful day of July 8, 1947. Not only that, Johnson was the last civilian to ever see the Roswell crashed flying-saucer debris.

So Johnson left his home in Southern California and went down to the University of Texas at Arlington where the original plates had been stored. With special permission, Johnson was able to examine the original plates and have photographic copies made from them. Inexplicably, one of the original plates was missing and no one knew where it was.

The Truth Is in the Telegram

When Johnson returned to California, he invited MUFON investigators Ron Regehr and Debbie Stock to examine the photos he had brought back. They made an amazing discovery that had been completely over-looked for 50 years. One of the photos clearly shows General Roger Ramey kneeling next to the debris with a piece of paper in his hand. Enlarging the photo allowed the three investigators to actually read parts of the telegram!

Johnson, Regehr, and Stock hired six separate teams of experts to blow up and examine the telegram in Ramey's hand. All six teams pretty much concluded the same thing.

"Victims, Second Crash Site..."

Besides being able to read the Western Union mark on the telegram, the telegram mentions the "victims" of a second crash site. It also contains the words: "crash story," and "weather balloons." Here are exactly the words that the researchers were able to see on the telegram:

...4 HRS THE VICTIMS OF THE...
YOU FORWARDED TO THE...AT
FORTWORTH, TEX.
...THE "CRASH" "STORY"...FOR 0984
ACKNOWLEDGES...EMERGENCY
POWERS ARE NEEDED SITE TWO
SW MAGDALENA, N MEX.
...SAFE TALK...FOR MEANING OF
STORY AND MISSION...WEATHER
BALLOONS SENT ON THE...AND
LAND...ROVER CREWS.

Order a Copy For Yourself

No need to take my word for it. You can order a copy of the photo yourself, just as I have. A 16- by 20-inch print from the original photographic plate taken by J. Bond Johnson is available for $25 from:

The University of Texas at Arlington
Special Collections Division
PO Box 19497
Arlington, Texas 76019-0497
Phone: (817) 272-3393
Fax: (817) 272-3360

Dubose Speaks

In an interview appearing in the November 24, 1991 edition of *Florida Today*, Thomas DuBose, now a retired general, stated that the material Ramey had photographed and displayed to the press later was a weather balloon and that he (DuBose) had already transferred the real debris to a lead-lined pouch which was sent to Washington D.C. Other sources quote Dubose as saying there was no switch. The material was not changed, only the story.

J. Bond Johnson, photographer of the Roswell crash debris, shows the author remarkable details later discovered in the original photos. Johnson was the last civilian to see the crash debris.   (Photo courtesy J. Bond Johnson and Debbie Stock)

Key Points

It bears repeating that both Johnson and DuBose agree on the following points:

1. No one knew what the real debris was, but they knew it was from something we didn't make.

2. They knew it was not a weather balloon. Both men were experts at identifying weather balloons and radar arrays; Bond had been a colonel and Dubose a general.

3. Major Jesse Marcel was in General Ramey's office when the first photos were taken and he appears in several of them.

4. In the initial photographs General Ramey appears in full dress uniform, with hat. This was in July in the middle of the desert with no air conditioning! The reason for this was because Ramey knew this was debris from a real flying saucer and the picture of him with it would be seen throughout the world.

5. In a recent interview Walter Haut told author Bill Birnes that
    there was absolutely no question about the fact that the debris
    was from a flying saucer and not a weather balloon.

BACK TO THE TIMELINE

The following incidents occurred between 3:00 and 5:00 P.M. on Tuesday July 8, 1947.

Brigadier General Roger Ramey announces that "the flying disc has been sent to Wright-Patterson Air Base in Ohio."

General Clements McMullen calls Colonel DuBose from Washington. He tells Dubose to tell Ramey to send some of the debris to Washington immediately and to make up a story "to get the press off our backs," and also to stop talking about a crashed saucer. Dubose recalls McMullen saying, "Do you understand me, Colonel?" Dubose replied, "Yes, Sir!"

Major Jesse Marcel learns that he will transport the debris on a specially prepared B-29 airplane heading for Fort Worth Army Air Field. Marcel describes the load of debris as "half a B-29 full." (Note: There was no weather balloon ever made that can fill half of a B-29 bomber.) Meanwhile, back at the debris field, army personnel are continuing to fill wheelbarrows with debris and load it on to trucks. Around 5:00 P.M. the Pentagon calls Roswell Army Air Base and orders a halt to all press releases.

More Photos

About 5:30 P.M., two hours after Jesse Marcel left General Ramey's office, Ramey summoned a young weather officer, Irving Newton, to his office. Newton later recalled not wanting to leave his post because no one else was there, but he was told to do so anyway and on the double! If there was a switch, this is where it occurred. Sometime before Newton arrived a weather balloon was put on Ramey's floor and a new set of photos were taken. Ramey told young Newton to identify the object as a weather balloon for the reporters who were now present.

Irving Newton (above) was later brought in and told by General Ramey to identify the debris as a "weather balloon" for the press corp. (Photo courtesy Fort Worth Star-Telegram Photograph Collection, Special Collections Division, The University at Arlington Libraries.)

In the first photos taken of Dubose and Marcel with the real debris you can clearly see Marcel's military cap and tie lying on the radiator in the background. The photo of Newton was taken hours later, after the story had been changed. You can now see Newton with a weather balloon and Marcel's cap and tie are missing from the radiator. Marcel and Dubose had long since left with the real debris. Notice how Ramey appears in a full dress jacket, in July, in New Mexico with no air conditioning. Obviously, something extraordinary was occurring.

One More Press Conference

At 8:00 P.M. Roger Ramey calls a press conference. He tells the press that he, (a brigadier general in charge of an air base and air command unit who had personally handled the debris for hours) made a mistake and misidentified what turned out to be a common weather balloon.

At 10:00 P.M. ABC News declares the Roswell wreckage was a weather balloon and as far as the public was concerned, it stopped right there.

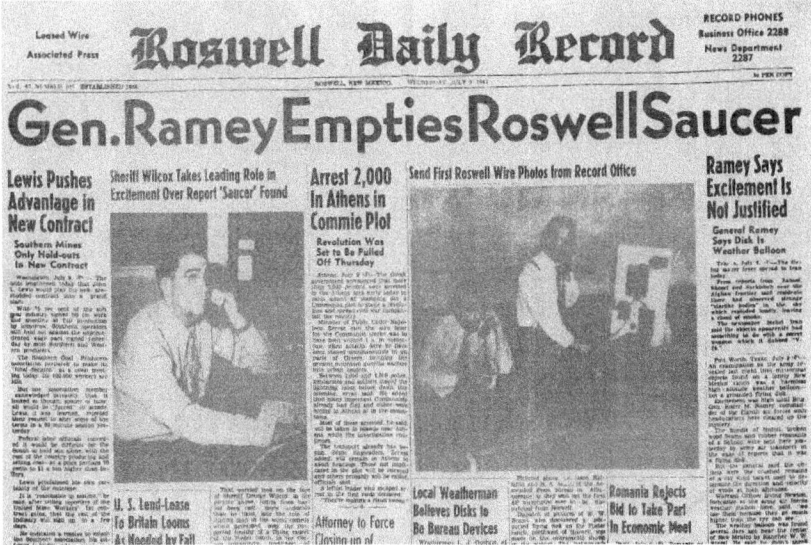

This is the famous headline in which General Ramey retracts his prior claim to have found a crashed flying saucer. (Photo courtesy Roswell Daily Record)

Wednesday, July 9, 1947

Alien bodies and a crashed disc are flown to Wright-Patterson Air Base. Photographer J. Bond Johnson notes that weather balloons have hundreds of feet of string attached to them. He points out that not a single inch of string was found in the debris, nor is any visible in the photographs.

All parties who were at Roswell agree that the debris was spread over one square mile. A square mile is the equivalent of walking four miles. Both Colonel Bond Johnson and General Thomas Dubose agree that a weather balloon or radar array would fit in a container the size of a 19-inch television. In addition, Marcel alone loaded two car-loads of debris. Other soldiers on duty loaded more truck-loads.

Also keep in mind the number of high-level personnel involved. They were all colonels and generals who were stationed at the most sophisticated air base operation in the world. They had just finished fighting World War II, and they were experts in radar arrays and weather balloons. How could all these high-level people be involved in such a great amount of activity over an entire week for something they saw every day, namely weather balloons?

Why would a group of civilians all get together and decide to lie in concert for no monetary gain about what they saw at Roswell?

Fact: Mac Brazel, the rancher who originally found the debris field, was taken into custody and held by the military for a week. You think they held the guy for a week for finding a weather balloon? Brazel had found weather balloons on his ranch many times before and nobody came out to look at them, and nobody ever asked him to return them.

Mac Brazel's son Bill lived 75 miles away in Albuquerque, New Mexico. When his dad was taken into custody he had to return to his father's ranch to take care of it and the livestock.

Here's how Bill Brazel recalls the whole affair:

> My dad found this thing and he told me a little bit about it, not much, because the Air Force asked him to take an oath that he wouldn't tell anybody in detail about it. Then, lo and behold, here comes the military. They said we understand you found some bits and pieces." I said "Yeah." And he said, "Your father turned the rest over to us, and you know he is under an oath not to tell." And he said, "We would rather you didn't talk very much about it." 23

Twining Takes a Trip

Several days later on July 17, 1947 General Nathan Twining cancels a preplanned trip. Instead, he makes an emergency trip in the middle of July, with no air conditioning, to, you guessed it! New Mexico! Check out the memo in the documents section of: www.flyingsaucers101.com

The Threats

Even law enforcement officers were told that their families would be in jeopardy if they talked about the Roswell incident. Military officers made it clear they were willing to murder children. For a weather balloon?

If you open your mouth we'll be picking your bones out of the sand.
Glenn Dennis
(threat made by two military officers.)

Don't tell anybody! When the incident (Roswell) happened, the military police came to the jailhouse and told George (Sheriff Wilcox) and I that if we ever told anything about the incident, not only would we be killed, but our entire family would be killed.
Inez Wilcox
(to her granddaughter Barbara Dugger)

The military came to our house and they basically threatened us if we said anything about it. They were going to take Mother away and they were going to take Daddy away.

The other guy was standing beside him with his rifle at half-mast, holding it pointed up right in front of their bodies.
Frankie Rowe

My sister Frankie told me about her experiences sometime in the early 1960s. Frankie told me about sitting around the table in 1947 and being threatened. My sister also mentioned seeing the material that "ran like water."[24]
Helen Cahill
(signed affidavit, November 22, 1993)

A few days later, several military personnel visited the house. I was questioned about the piece of metal I had seen. I was told that if I ever talked about it, I could be taken out into the desert never to return, or that my mother and father would be taken to Orchard Park, a former POW camp.
Frankie Rowe
(signed affidavit, November 22, 1993)

Frankie Rowe was still a child when she was threatened.

Newspaper account telling how military detained and harassed rancher
Mac Brazel. (Photo courtesy Roswell Daily Record)

We'll know if you talk; we'll know who you talk to and all you will simply disappear.
So forget everything you saw, and hightail it out of here before someone else sees you and wants to make sure you stay silent.

Local plumber Roy Danzer
(recounting threat from military officers)

Danzer had just seen a still-alive but dying alien on a stretcher at the base hospital.

They said if I didn't forget what my father had told me, that me and the rest of my family would simply disappear in the desert.

Sally Dwyer
(Dan Dwyer's daughter)

FIRSTHAND EYEWITNESSES TO ROSWELL

Below is a list of firsthand eyewitnesses to the Roswell incident. They were all interviewed personally by Kevin Randle and Donald Schmitt.

They have all confirmed their involvement and that the event did happen. 11

Shirley Brazel
William Brazel
Joe Briley
Charles A. Cashon
Mary Cavitt
Sheridan Cavitt
Arthur W. Cruikshank
Glenn Dennis
Bill DeVaugn
S. M. Dobson
Thomas DuBose
Edwin Easley
Arthur Exon
Tom Gonzales
Walter Haut
W. Curry Holden
Frank Joyce
Frank Kaufmann
Thaddeus Love
Jesse Marcel Jr.
Viaud Marcel
Felix Martucci
John McBoyle
Paul McEvoy
Charles McGee
Phyllis McGuire
Joseph Mondragon
Irving Newton
Bud Payne
Robert Porter
Loreta Proctor
Lewis Rickett
George Roberts
Frankie Rowe
Patrick Sanders
Robert Shirkey
Edgar Skelly
Robert Slusher
Robert E. Smith

Allye Tadalani
Tommy Thompson
Elizabeth Tulk
Jay Tulk
Tommy Tyree
Walt Whitmore Jr.
William Woody
Vernon D. Zorn

The following group of people have both first and secondhand knowledge of the events at Roswell. Their testimony would be allowed as evidence in any court of law. 12

Pete Anaya
Ruben Anaya
Beverly Bean
Anne Blanchard
Ada Brown
Joe Cavitt
Robert Dennis
Barbara Dugger
Robert Friend
Sappho Henderson
Sarah Holcomb
J. Bond Johnson
Mrs. Jesse B. Johnson
John Kromschroeder
Elizabeth Kyle
Shirley Linde
W. E. Lounsbury
L. W. Maltais
Art McQuiddy
Leonard Porter
Marian Strickland
Jay West
Loretta Young

The following people are all secondhand witnesses who were given information about Roswell directly by participants in the incident. 22

Gerald Anderson
Peggy Anderson

E. J. Argenbright
Harold Baca
Jo Boehms
Greg Boldra
William Boris
George Bush
Richard Chapman
Charlie Clark
Denise Clark
J. F. Danley
Jan Days
John Foard
Iris Foster
Mary Ann Gardner
Mary Catherine Groode
L. M. Hall
Peter Harrison
Bill Henderson
Ned Henderson
Imholtz Hillman
Alma Hobbs
Alice Knight
Max Little
Steve Lytle
Allene Mann
Johnny Mann
John McBoyle Jr.
Hugh Olney
Norris Proctor
Latone Ramey
Charlie Reynolds
Myra Richards
Jack Rodden
Edward M. Sager
Dan Saunders
Elaine Sparks
Peggy Sparks
Leo B. Spear
F. E. Spurlin
Leonard Stringfield
Juanita Sultemeier
John G. Tiffany

Tom Tracey
Merle Tucker
June Tyree
Juanita Valenzuela
Elaine Vegh
Helen Wachter
George Walsh
Patty Welsh
Nettie Willmuth
Terry Wilmot

What They Told the Canadians

WILBERT SMITH'S MEMO
In 1950 a radio engineer for the Canadian Department of Telecommunications spent some time working with the United States, primarily on projects involving geomagnetism. The engineer, Wilbert Smith, sent the following words in a memo to his boss, the controller of telecommunications of the Canadian Department of Transport. Here is what it said:

> I made discreet inquiries through the Canadian embassy staff in Washington who were able to obtain for me the following information:
>
> a. The matter is the most highly classified subject in the United States government, rating even higher than the H-Bomb.
> b. **Flying saucers exist.** (Emphasis added)
> c. Their modus operandi is unknown, but concentrated effort is being made by a small group headed by Doctor Vannevar Bush. (This is the MJ-12 group.)
> d. The entire matter is considered by the United States authorities to be of tremendous significance.

Wilbert B. Smith
Canadian Department of Transport
November 21, 1950

Wilbert Smith Interview Notes

Years later Wilbert Smith's son came across the following notes written in his father's handwriting. They are notes of an interview Smith conducted with Dr. Robert Sarbacher. Dr. Sarbacher was a well-connected scientist in the United States who had been the dean of the graduate school at Georgia Tech and had been a consultant to the U.S. Research and Development Board. He was listed in several directories as one of the United States' leading scientists. Here are some excerpts from Smith's interview notes with Dr. Sarbacher. 26

Smith: I am doing some work on the collapse of the earth's magnetic field as a source of energy, and I think our work may have a bearing on flying saucers.
Sarbacher: What do you want to know?

Smith: I have read (Frank) Scully's book on the saucers (Behind the Flying Saucers) and would like to know how much of it is true.
Sarbacher: The facts reported in the book are substantially correct. (Note: remember, Frank Scully is the guy who claims there have been at least eighteen downed saucers in the American southwest. He made these claims in his book.)

Smith: Then, the saucers do exist?
Sarbacher: Yes, they exist.

Smith: Do they operate as Scully suggests, on magnetic principles?
Sarbacher: We have not been able to duplicate their performance.

Smith: Do they come from another planet?
Sarbacher: All we know is, we didn't make them, and it's pretty certain they didn't originate on earth.

Smith: I understand the whole subject of saucers is classified.
Sarbacher: Yes, it is classified two points higher even than the H-Bomb. In fact, it is the most highly classified subject in the U.S. Government at the present time.

Smith: May I ask the reason for the classification?
Sarbacher: You may ask, but I can't tell you.

Wilbert Smith
(handwritten notes) September 12, 1950

Friedman's Confirmation

Stanton Friedman picked up the phone and called Dr. Sarbacher in December, 1983. Sarbacher confirmed to Friedman that the information he had given about flying saucers was, indeed, accurate!

Dr. Sarbacher

During additional investigation conducted by William Steinman,
Sarbacher made the following points to Steinman, in writing:

> Although I had been invited to participate in several discussions as-
> sociated with reported (flying saucer) recoveries, I could not person-
> ally attend the meetings.

> About the only thing I remember at this time is that certain materials
> reported to have come from flying saucer crashes were extremely
> light and very tough.

> I got the impression these "aliens" were constructed like certain in-
> sects we have observed on earth, wherein because of the low mass,
> the inertial forces involved in operation of these instruments would
> be quite low.

> I still do not know why the high order of classification has been giv-
> en and why the denial of the existence of these devices. 28

Dr. Sarbacher died in 1986.

Other Possibilities

No discussion of the Roswell incident would be complete without
discussing other possibilities about what might have occurred at Roswell
Army Air Base the first week of July, 1947.

Crash Test Dummy?

In July 1997, on the fiftieth anniversary of the Roswell crash, the Air
Force announced one final explanation for the sightings of alien bodies
by private citizens. First, it's interesting to note that the Air Force was the
branch of the military chosen to announce this. In July 1947 the United
States Air Force didn't exist! It had not yet been formed as a separate
branch of the military. Roswell was an *Army* air base. In fact, some
historians claim that one of the reasons the existence of flying saucers
was kept secret in 1947 was because the military was right in the middle
of getting congress to approve the Air Force as a separate branch and
didn't want flying saucers to hold it up.

The Air Force claimed the alien bodies civilians saw were really crash-test dummies dropped by parachute. Such tests did occur starting in 1953, according to the Air Force's own records. The Roswell crash occurred in 1947. We have a decade problem. The first of these full-sized dummies was dropped six years after the Roswell crash.

Choose

Without belaboring the point, suffice it to say there are dummies involved. The dummies are either the Air Force officials or you. This time you get to choose.

Project Mogul

In 1994 the Air Force announced they had gone back and looked at their records regarding Roswell. They concluded that the debris Mac Brazel found was a weather balloon, part of a project called Project Mogul.

Project Mogul was a series of unmanned balloon flights. Those participating were told the purpose of the project was to maintain the balloons at a constant altitude in order to monitor weather conditions. Decades later it was learned that the true purpose had been to monitor any attempts the Soviet Union might make to detonate a nuclear device.

These balloons consisted of an array, or many balloon-like objects tethered together. Some of them were quite long, stretching out over 500 feet. Past records show a number of these were being launched during the time the Roswell affair happened. Virtually all the balloons launched at that time were reported as recovered or located. One flight, Flight 9, remains unaccounted for. There are no records saying it was unaccounted for, there are simply no records. They have been "lost".

There are people who think it was this Mogul Project balloon Mac Brazel found. I don't think that was the case, and the following are some reasons for my opinion.

First of all, the amount of debris found far exceeds the amount of debris that would be left by a Mogul balloon array, even a 500-foot-long array.

Second, look at the behavior of the military. Even though Project Mogul was classified, the kind of threats received by civilians went far beyond the restrictions imposed upon civilians for any other classified project in United States history. Even the development of the atomic bomb did not result in civilians and children receiving death threats.

The testimony of dozens of high-ranking military officers who saw weather balloons and Project Mogul balloons every day, and who stated quite clearly that the debris they handled was not a weather balloon, and was not like any other material they had ever seen on earth.

Tests of German V-2 Rockets

It is true that some captured German V-2 rockets were being launched and tested at nearby White Sands Proving Grounds. This facility is about a hundred miles from Roswell. In fact, one of the V-2s was launched and then crashed across the border in Mexico on May 29, 1947. However, the episode was announced and carried in all the newspapers. Official press releases were handed out. No secret was made of the event.

On July 3, 1947, a V-2 launching was scheduled. However, an accident occurred on the launching pad and seriously injured several people. So the July 3 launch was cancelled. Newspaper accounts of the event and statements of the White Sands base commander Colonel Turner confirmed the launch cancellation. Not one person in the military has put forth a hypothesis that it was a V-2 rocket found on Mac Brazel's ranch in July.

Japanese Balloon Bombs

During World War II the Japanese launched nearly ten thousand balloons, each carrying 50- to 75-pound bombs. The last one was launched in April, 1945; 2 years before Roswell. These balloons traveled at an average speed of 35 miles per hour. At least one of them made it to U.S. shores. It was found by a family in Oregon who was out camping. The bomb exploded and killed six people. These were the only people killed on American shores due to a war-time attack. (Pearl Harbor and the Hawaiian Islands, were not a state in 1947.) After that the military made sure everyone knew of the existence of these bombs. Once again, the handling of the Japanese balloon-bomb case was in complete contrast to the military's behavior in handling the Roswell incident.

One more note. In order for Roswell to be the result of a Japanese balloon bomb, the balloon would have had to stay aloft for two years and then miraculously land within a few miles of the world's only nuclear air base.

Alien Bodies Recovered

Here is a list of flying saucer crashes and alien bodies allegedly in the possession of the United States government.

July 2, 1947	San Augustin, New Mexico	5 bodies
July 4, 1947	Roswell, New Mexico	4 bodies
Feb. 13, 1948	Aztec, New Mexico	12 bodies
July 7, 1948	Mexico (just south of Laredo, Texas)	1 body
1952	Spitzenbergen, Norway	2 bodies
Sept. 10, 1950	Albuquerque, New Mexico	3 bodies
Aug. 14, 1952	Ely, Nevada	16 bodies
April 18, 1953	Arizona	1 body
May 20, 1953	Kingman, Arizona	0 bodies
June 19, 1953	Laredo, Texas	4 bodies
July 10, 1953	Johannesburg, South Africa	5 bodies
Oct. 13, 1953	Dutton, Montana	4 bodies
May 5, 1955	Brighton, England	4 bodies
July 18, 1955	Carlsbad, New Mexico	4 bodies
June 12, 1962	New Mexico, Holloman Air Force Base	2 bodies
Nov. 10, 1964	Fort Riley, Kansas	9 bodies
Oct. 27, 1966	Arizona	1 body
1966-1968	Ohio/Kentucky/Indiana (5 Crashes)	3 bodies
July 18, 1972	Morocco	3 bodies
July 10, 1973	Arizona	5 bodies
May 12, 1976	Australia	4 bodies
April 5, 1977	Ohio	11 bodies
June 22, 1977	Arizona	5 bodies
Aug. 17, 1977	Mexico	2 bodies
May 1978	Bolivia	0 bodies
Nov. 1988	Afghanistan	7 bodies
1989	South Africa	2 ETs alive
July 1989	Siberia	9 ETs alive

THE INFAMOUS TUSKEGEE STUDY

For 40 years the U.S. government knowingly withheld treatment from critically ill people. Black men who were diagnosed with syphilis were given placebos instead of penicillin to "find out what would happen to them." The fact is the government already knew what would happen to them. The Government had based their study on a previous study done on a thousand men in Oslo, Norway. The Norway study ran from 1896 to 1910. The Tuskegee study started in 1932, almost 25 years after the Norwegian study. The affects of syphilis had been known for a quarter of a century. So they already knew the results before they even started!

Officially known as "The Tuskegee Study of Syphilis in the Untreated Negro Male," the study withheld treatment from 400 men from the years 1932 to 1972. Only 120 men were still alive when the study ended. [1]

The key point: Although the public didn't know about this, the government did know the entire time. After all, its funding was renewed year after year for 40 years. Sounds similar to something else being withheld, doesn't it?

THE ALIEN AUTOPSY FILM

In 1995 a man approached a television show producer in Great Britain and said he had actual film footage of an alien autopsy that was photographed in the late 1940s. The man's name is Ray Santilli, and the film he was describing is referred to as the "Santilli film." Santilli said there were fifteen reels of 16mm film, each about ten minutes in length. Santilli said that he got the film from a former military cameraman by the name of Jack Barnett.

Fox Airs the Film

The film was eventually aired in the United States on a Fox Network special. It was so popular that Fox had to run it several times to satisfy the public's demand.

But, Is It Real?

My opinion is, No! People have been looking into virtually every aspect of this film, and in many areas it just doesn't hold up. Here are some key points:

The supposed cameraman cannot be found. There are no military records of anyone by the name of Jack Barnett in that position during that time period. Also, Santilli has changed his story several times and said the guy's name was really Barrett. Still, no match with any military records.

Although Kodak, after analyzing the film, said the raw film could have been manufactured during this time period (1947), it's not conclusive and it could have been manufactured much later. Research into items appearing in the background of the film such as the wall clock, surgical instruments, and the telephone have also proved inconclusive.

The actual filming technique is very poor. Instead of the camera being set up in a stationary position as would be expected, it is constantly moving, a technique in documenting that did not really come about until the development of video tape decades later.

Lastly, the alien itself has a remarkable resemblance to the dummy alien on display in a Roswell museum, in fact, they are almost identical. Not only that, but the alien body seems to lack an internal structure. There is virtually no evidence of stretched skin, tendons, bones, or muscle tissue.

Disinformation

The Santilli film appears to be a classic case of disinformation. The whole Santilli episode could serve as a textbook example; I've never seen a better one. Disinformation is the practice of telling the absolute truth, but telling it in a way that can't be believed. You make it look so bogus that people dismiss the idea completely. The technique was used and refined during World War II. The Allies actually "leaked" to the Germans where the main American forces would be landing in France. But they made it so easy for Hitler to get the information and laid out the plan so simply that Hitler didn't believe the information. As a result the Allies landed right where they said they would and found the German troops out of position and undermanned.

Such an autopsy as is depicted in the Santilli film almost certainly did take place. Several physicians have come forward to say it happened. But it's not on the Santilli film. The Santilli film is illustrating a real event that took place in a way that can't be believed, in hopes that the public will dismiss the whole idea as ridiculous.

FLYING SAUCERS OVER WASHINGTON, D.C.

"Why don't they just land on the White House lawn?" This is one of the most frequently asked questions when the subject of flying saucers comes up. Well, they damn near did. Check this out. In the first year and a half of the 1950s flying saucers were being seen on an average of about once a day nationwide. Suddenly in June 1952 the rate doubled. Then in mid-July the rate quadrupled. It quadrupled again a few weeks later. The rate was now twenty-eight sightings per day, most of them by highly trained military fighter pilots. The sightings were also being confirmed by military radar.

The White House

On July 19 and 20, 1952, eight flying saucers flew directly over the White House, the Capitol building, and the Pentagon. They flew over restricted airspace, and they were tracked visually from the ground. The people in the control towers at Bolling Air Force Base, Washington National Airport, and Andrews Air Force Base all saw them as well. The radar at all three bases picked up the saucers as solid objects. Commercial airline pilots saw them and so did virtually every citizen in Washington DC. 1

Newspaper Headlines

The saucers cruised in real slow, then accelerated to astounding velocities over the Capitol. The nearby military bases all sent up jet fighters to intercept the speeding disks. As soon as they showed up the saucers literally disappeared. They simply faded away. Ten minutes after the jets would leave the saucers would reappear. This scenario was repeated over and over again. These sightings were given more front-page headline coverage in the Washington D.C. newspapers than the Democratic National Convention, which was going on at the same time.

Fifty Flying Saucers

Then to make matters worse, the saucers left, only to reappear one week later on July 26 and 27. Later investigations would show that over fifty saucers flew over Washington D.C. on a single day, May 23, 1952.

The Biggest Press Conference Since World War II

The military was embarrassed by this whole thing. Not only that, they were still concerned that we could be vulnerable to a Soviet attack by misidentifying incoming missiles or bombers as flying saucers. A press conference was called by Major General John Samford. It was the longest, largest press conference since World War II had ended 7 years earlier. I mean, there was a lot of explaining to do since everybody and his neighbor saw the saucers. [2]

The End Result

The military ended up stating that the flying disks were merely optical illusions caused by a weather condition known as a "temperature inversion." This, despite confirmation of the disks by five radar arrays all at different locations. Note that radar can only detect metallic objects. It is impossible for radar to "see" an optical illusion. Seventeen years later the military released a report saying that a temperature inversion of this magnitude is literally impossible in earth's atmosphere.

(See copy of CIA memo dated August 14, 1952, which discusses both the Washington, D.C. sightings and the press conference at www.flyingsaucers101.com and www.ufomag.com).

Military Pilots Contacted

In 1997 researcher Derrel Sims located and interviewed two of the military pilots who were sent up to intercept the flying saucers over the White House. Both men requested anonymity; however, they told Sims what happened and showed him copies of the original flight logs. [3]

The pilots told Sims that immediately following the encounter they were both called into a debriefing room along with other pilots. Once there, they were threatened. They were told they'd better not tell anybody about what they saw.

Another Pilot Speaks Up

In the fall of 1954, Lt. Guy Kirkwood and three other pilots with the 191st Fighter-Interceptor Squadron based at Salt lake City, Utah, conducted over 27 sorties in an attempt to photograph and document the UFO phenomenon. The project was assigned by the pentagon, under the direction of a Col. Perterson. The above photo is one of over 33,000 frames of 3mm film exposed by the four F-86 Sabrejet pilots.

Loyal Americans

The pilots were angry. By following orders and responding to what may have been a danger to national security and possibly putting their own lives in jeopardy, they were now the ones who were threatened! These were loyal men who had pledged their lives to protect the country, and they were being treated this way.

Resigned Commissions

The two pilots were so upset and disgusted that both resigned their commissions and quit the military! I hear stories like this over and over again. If you ask enough people you'll hear the same thing too! You'll hear it from loyal, hard-working, patriotic, honest men and women who were in the U.S. Armed Forces. Even in the face of Hitler, they didn't get this kind of treatment from their own government concerning national security.

It's time for a change! Make it happen. Let your elected officials know that it's no longer OK to threaten citizens who know about the existence of flying saucers.

TEN YEAR REVIEW

Over ten years, from 1942 to 1952

The entire world went to war against itself and killed off over 65 million people.

Though we were allies in World War II, The United States and the Soviet Union both suffered heavy losses, especially the Soviet Union. Both sides completely distrusted one another. The Cold War was begun before World War II even ended.

Front-page article from the Los Angeles Times, 1949. (Courtesy Los Angeles Times)

Many men and women on the planet had lived most of their adult lives affected by war and consequently lived in a condition of "full alert "just to insure their survival.

The Nazi issue was still unresolved. There were still many on the loose. There was a world-wide concern that those who got away still had potent weapons technology.

And finally, all of a sudden, there were solid, metallic, disk-shaped craft flying across our skies at speeds ten times greater than our fastest planes; flying completely at will over our only nuclear air base. Unaccountable craft were sited over Europe, South America, the nation's capitol, the White House, and even the Pentagon.

The Real Concerns

Little green men? Who cared? At this point the U.S. military was unconcerned whether little green men from Mars existed or not - they didn't care. Nor did they wonder if the saucers were from here or another galaxy. That was irrelevant. The only question was: "Are they dangerous?" Here are the big three concerns of the military and the reasons they responded the way they did:

1. Were we in danger of attack?

Was there a risk of nuclear bombardment similar to what we had unleashed on Hiroshima and Nagasaki? The power of these atomic bombs was so staggering that it surpassed even the scientific community's calculations. In fact, some of the reels of film footage of atomic bomb tests were withheld from the public until 1997 because the images were was so devastating.

2. What would happen if we ignored an enemy aircraft because we mistakenly thought it was a flying saucer?

What if that enemy bomber had a nuclear bomb and dropped it on us? This is the concern that resulted in a policy to try to convince the public that flying saucers were not real so the public would stop reporting so many sightings and not confuse our air defense systems.

World War II poster depicting how important it was to keep secrets during the war.

3. Was there another country or group (escaped Nazis, maybe?) with this astounding technology?

Had the Russians captured this from the Germans? Were Nazis still loose and in possession of this technology? I know this whole thing about renegade Nazis sounds a little melodramatic, but in the years immediately following the war it was a real and valid concern. It was a well-known fact that the Germans did in fact have superior technology; the V-2 rocket is just one small example. In World War II, the United States had no rockets - absolutely none.

Admiral Byrd

Admiral Byrd's now-famous trip to the South Pole in 1947 was not a scientific expedition as we were told in school. It was a full military excursion. This is well established by military films of the expedition and government documents. The ships accompanying Byrd were ice breakers and battleships. They were loaded to the gills with tanks and armaments. They were in fact, looking for a group of escaped Nazi's that military intelligence believed had set up a colony in the South Pole region. The description as a 'scientific expedition' was a cover story so as not to alert the group what the U.S. military was really after. Remember, "Loose lips, sink ships." 1

German Scientists

The U.S. government allowed a large group of German scientists to continue their work here. You might have only heard about Werner Von Braun, but there were many others.

Intelligence reports years later indicated that the Germans had recovered their own crashed flying saucer several years before the Roswell incident. Joseph Stalin of Russia was aware of this. When he heard about the crash at Roswell through his own intelligence sources he was very upset. The Germans had one, now the Americans had one, and he was the only player without a spectacular new toy.

Official Military Memo

Here's a statement from a top-secret memo written on October 28, 1947 by General Schulgen of the Air Intelligence Requirements Division:

> *While there remains a possibility of Russian manufacture, based on the perspective thinking and actual accomplishments of the Germans, it is the considered opinion of some elements that the object may in fact represent an interplanetary craft of some kind. 3*
>
> *General Schulgen*
> *Air Intelligence Requirements Division*
> *October 28, 1947*

GOVERNMENT

AT WORK

- *U.S. presidents speak about flying saucers and alien beings.*
- *Military brass talk about crashed disks.*
- *World leaders talk about extraterrestrials.*
- *Intelligence agency honchos tell what they know.*

Who Says Flying Saucers are Real? EVERYBODY!

The question really should be: "Who says they're *not* real?" It's impossible to find any government official who will flat-out say UFOs or flying saucers are not real. Check out the following quotes.

U.S. PRESIDENTS

President John F. Kennedy

> *"I'd like to tell the public about the alien situation, but my hands are tied."*

These words were spoken to Bill Holden, steward on Air Force One, flying over Germany, in the summer of 1963, when Holden asked Kennedy what he thought about UFOs.

President Bill Clinton

If I put you over at (The Dept. of) Justice, I want you to find out
two things;
     1. Who killed JFK.
     2. The truth about UFOs.

These words were spoken to Webb Hubbell (Associate Attorney General), shortly after Clinton had been elected to his first term.

President Ronald Reagan

Addressing the United Nations General Assembly, Forty-second Session, September 21, 1987:

"I occasionally think how quickly our differences worldwide
would vanish if we were facing an alien threat from outside this
world. And, yet I ask you, is not an alien force already among us?"

When Reagan said "alien force," he wasn't talking about the Democrats. I have not only confirmed this quote, I also have it on videotape, and in full color. The fact of alien visitors is well known and openly discussed inside the United Nations.

Speaking of Soviet leader Mikhail Gorbachev at the Geneva Summit Conference in 1985, Reagan said:

How much easier his task and mine might be in these meetings we
hold if suddenly there was a threat to this world from another species from another planet outside in the universe. We'd forget all
the little local differences that we have between our countries, and
we would find out once and for all that we really are all human beings here on this earth together."

President Jimmy Carter

Former President Jimmy Carter had a dramatic UFO experience when he was running for president. On his way to a two-day religious conference Carter saw a UFO. He and his entourage were so disturbed by the experience that they spent the next two days discussing UFOs and extraterrestrials instead of the planned conference agenda.

> "It was the darndest thing I've ever seen," said Carter. "It was big, it was very bright, it changed colors and it was about the size of the moon. We watched it for ten minutes, but none of us could figure out what it was. One thing's for sure, I'll never make fun of people who say they've seen unidentified flying objects in the sky."

Although he touted himself as a humble "peanut farmer," Carter was a sophisticated observer. He was a graduate in nuclear physics and served as an officer on U.S. Navy nuclear submarines. Carter later declared: "If I become president, I'll make every piece of information this country has about UFO sightings available to the public and scientists."

In 1977, after Carter had been elected president and tried to open the UFO files, he was told by the heads of the intelligence agencies that he, as president, did not have a high enough security clearance to even *see* the files! The intelligence community had immediately gone to work to prevent Carter from investigating further.

The chief of the Air Force community relations division, Colonel Charles Senn wrote the following in a letter to Lieutenant Duward Crow of NASA: "I sincerely hope that you are successful in preventing reopening of UFO investigations."

President Gerald Ford

> "In the firm belief that the American public deserves a better explanation than that thus given by the Air Force, I strongly recommend that there be a committee investigation of the UFO phenomenon. I think we owe it to the people to establish credibility regarding UFOs and to produce the greatest possible enlightenment on this subject."

Written while serving in Congress (in a letter sent to Mendel Rivers, chairman of the Armed Services Committee) March 28, 1966.

President Harry Truman

President Harry Truman formed the highly secret group (code named MJ-12) which stood for Majestic-12. The sole purpose of this group was to investigate UFOs and report their findings to the president. Majestic-12 was established by a special executive order of President Truman on September 24, 1947, three months after the crash at Roswell, New Mexico.

A briefing document describing the group for incoming president Dwight Eisenhower was leaked and is now available to almost anyone. The government denies the existence of such a group or document. The authenticity of the document cannot be proven, but the reality and the purpose of MJ-12 has been confirmed with many high-level sources over the years.

> *"I can assure you that flying saucers, given that they exist, are not constructed by any power on earth."*
>
> *President Harry Truman*
> White House Press Conference, April 4, 1950

FBI

FBI Director J. Edgar Hoover
I would do it but before agreeing to it we must insist upon full access to discs recovered. For instance in the (2nd) case the Army grabbed it and would not let us have it for cursory examination.
J. Edgar Hoover – FBI Director
handwritten note to Clyde Tolson, July 15, 1947

CIA

Victor Marchetti
We have indeed been contacted, perhaps even visited by extraterrestrial beings and the U.S. government, in collusion with the other national powers of the earth, is determined to keep this information

*from the general public. The purpose of the international conspira-
cy is to maintain a workable stability among the nations of the
world and for them, in turn, to retain institutional control over
their respective populations. Thus, for these governments to admit
there are beings from outer space ... with mentalities and technological capabilities obviously far superior to ours, could, once fully
perceived by the average person, erode the foundations of the
earth's traditional power structure.*

Victor Marchetti
former Special Assistant Executive Director of the CIA, 1979

Roscoe Hillenkoetter

*It is time for the truth to be brought out in open congressional
hearings. Behind the scenes, high-ranking Air Force officers are
soberly concerned about UFOs. But through official secrecy and
ridicule, many citizens are led to believe the unknown flying objects
are nonsense. To hide the facts, the Air Force has silenced its personnel through the issuance of a regulation.*

Vice Admiral Roscoe Hillenkoetter
former Director of the CIA (1947-1950)
member of MJ-12, 1960

MILITARY BRASS

General George C.Marshall

*The United States has recovered UFOs and their occupants. The
UFOs were from a different planet and they were friendly. They
have been hovering over defense facilities and airports. The U.S.
authorities were convinced they had nothing to fear from them. The
U.S. wanted people to concentrate on the real menace, com-
munism, and not be distracted by the visitors from space. There has
actually been contact with the men in the UFOs and there have
been landings.*

General George C. Marshall
U.S. Army Chief of Staff in World War II
Secretary of State, 1947
(as told to Dr. Rolf Alexander), 1951

Philip J. Corso

... enclosed in a thick glass container ... submerged in a thick light blue liquid.... It was a four-foot, human-shaped figure with arms, bizarre four-fingered hands, I didn't see a thumb, thin legs and feet, and an oversized incandescent light-bulb-shaped head that looked like it was floating over a balloon gondola for a chin.

What I found was an intriguing Army intelligence document describing the creature as an inhabitant of a craft that had crashed-landed in Roswell, New Mexico.

Colonel Philip J. Corso, (Ret.)
Chief of Foreign Technology Desk
U.S. Army Research and Development
member, of National Security Council

Lt. Col. Wendelle Stevens (Ret.)

I'm convinced beyond doubt that we have recovered aircraft, alien vehicles, that we have made contact with aliens, that we are communicating with them in some way or form, and that we have vehicles and bodies in preservation.

Lt. Col. Wendelle Stevens (Ret.)
Air Force Foreign Technology Division
Wright-Patterson Air Force Base

By this order, the Secretary of Air Force Office of Information must delete all evidence of UFO reality and intelligent control, which would, of course, contradict the Air Force stand that UFOs do not exist. The same rule applies to A.F. press releases and UFO information given to congress and the public.

1962 Air Force order
Disclosed by Major William T. Coleman
former Air Force headquarters spokesman
former Project Blue Book officer

NASA

I am convinced, based upon my research and the individuals with whom I have had contact within the U.S. intelligence community that the U.S. government does indeed have craft that meets the description of many UFO reports.

Robert Oeschler
NASA Mission Specialist, 1974-1977

ELECTED OFFICIALS

Congressional investigations have been held and are still being held on the problems of unidentified flying objects. Since most of the material is classified, the hearings are never printed.

William H. Ayres
Representative, Ohio.

Barry Goldwater
The subject of UFOs is one that has interested me for some long time. About ten or twelve years ago I made an effort to find out what was in the building at Wright-Patterson Air Force Base where the information is stored that has been collected by the Air Force, and I was understandably denied this request. It is still classified above Top Secret. I have, however, heard that there is a plan under way to release some, if not all, of this material in the near future. I'm just as anxious to see this material as you are, and I hope we will not have to wait much longer.

Barry Goldwater
Senator, (in a letter to Shlomo Arnon)
March 28, 1975

I have every confidence that the American public would be able to take such information without hysteria. The fear of the unknown is always greater than the fear of the known.

Walter H. Moeller
Representative, Ohio

If this information could be presented in such a way as to appeal to reason, and not to emotion, I think it would be a good thing.

Ralph J. Scott
Representative, North Carolina

I have discussed this with the affected agencies of the government, and they are of the opinion that it is unwise to publicize the matter at this time.

Richard B. Russell
Senator

DECLASSIFIED INTELLIGENCE AGENCY DOCUMENTS

- *Freedom of Information Act.*
- *Summaries of declassified intelligence agency documents.*
- *CIA and FBI summaries.*

Intelligence agency documents span a time period of over 50 years. They are fascinating to study. Just think how much time, money, and energy went into the efforts these memos talk about, and think about the meaning of all this effort for something that supposedly does not exist: flying saucers. The following pages are summaries of some of the most complete letters and memos. There are several thousand such declassified documents about flying saucers and UFOs that have been released through the Freedom of Information Act.

Patterns Emerge

Following the memos through the years you can see several patterns emerge:

- *Concern over "What are these things?"*
- *Confusion over which military branch is in charge of UFOs.*
- *Do UFOs pose a national security risk? Later memos indicate the belief that they do not threaten the national security.*
- *What do we tell the public? And, who tells them?*

- *UFO events are worldwide, occurring in every country on earth.*

Freedom of Information Act

The Freedom of Information Act was passed by congress in 1974. It is designed to give citizens access to the information and documents they own and pay for with their hard-earned money. The act is often referred to simply as FOIA. Although the idea of information availability is honorable, it is not easy to implement; the government is so large and fragmented that documents are stored in many different archives at different locations under different systems.

You cannot just call up one place and say, "Please, send me all your UFO information." It is a painstaking process. It can take years to try to get a single document, only to be told the document is not available or does not exist. You have to have a pretty good idea of what you are looking for and where it originated. Having said that, check out the document summaries on the following pages. Also included are some reference guides to tell you how and where to get more copies of declassified top secret documents.

Year: 1949

DECLASSIFIED DOCUMENT SUMMARIES

491

Memo from Special Devices Center, U.S. Navy.
Copy sent to the Director of the Central Intelligence Agency (CIA).

> The memo basically says there are continuous sightings of unidentified flying objects over White Sands Proving Grounds, which was at the time the only nuclear air base in the world. The objects appear to be under intelligent control and the observer was the Navy's foremost expert on weather balloons. Yet, he doesn't know what these objects are.

492

National Security Council Intelligence Directive to the CIA.

> Telling the CIA they are responsible for all research and intelligence gathering on unidentified flying objects. Also, that they (the CIA) are to coordinate their efforts with military researchers.

Time Check

- *The Soviet Union explodes its first atomic bomb.*
- *General Mills and Pillsbury begin marketing prepared cake mixes.*
- *Murphy's Law is proclaimed for the first time: "If anything can go wrong, it will," when Captain Edward Murphy sees an accelerometer mounted backwards on a rocket sled.*

493

OSI memo on flying saucers.

> Memo contains a graph showing a tremendous increase in UFO sightings during the months of May through August of 1947.

Year: 1952

DECLASSIFIED DOCUMENT SUMMARIES

521

National Security Council memo. Subject: flying saucers.
Directs CIA to research and solve problem of unidentified flying objects.

522

Central Intelligence Agency (CIA) memo written by CIA Director.
Subject: flying saucers.

523

1952 CIA memo. Topic: flying saucers. Discusses the following:

> "The phenomenal increase in flying saucer reports."

- Includes official CIA version of the first flying saucer sighting by Kenneth Arnold in 1947.

- Discusses hiding from the public the fact that the CIA is interested in flying saucers.
- Conclusion that flying saucers do not represent a military threat.

Time Check

- *A polio epidemic hits the U.S., afflicting 47,663 people. Jonas Salk invents polio vaccine.*
- *Jacques Cousteau invents SCUBA gear, becomes first man to use it to explore underwater wreck.*
- *Mr. Potato Head becomes the first children's toy to be advertised on television.*
- *George Jorgenson becomes Christine Jorgenson after the world's first sex change operation.*

524
Memo to Director of CIA from CIA assistant director of scientific intelligence. Subject: unidentified flying objects

> The memo states: Sightings of unexplained objects at great altitudes and traveling at high speeds in the vicinity of major U.S. defense installations are of such a nature that they are not attributable to natural phenomena or known types of aerial vehicles.

Also, the memo establishes UFOs as "a priority project throughout the intelligence and defense research and development community."

525
Memo to the heads of all military and government intelligence agencies. Subject: flying saucer problem.

> In essence, this memo says that flying saucers are a problem that should be attacked by a program of research and development.

Notice that the level of people sending and receiving these memos is the very top! No midlevel personnel involved.

Years: 1953-1958

DECLASSIFIED DOCUMENT SUMMARIES

581
CIA Advisory Panel on unidentified flying objects. 1953.

The top minds from the major areas of science are gathered solely to discuss flying saucers. They concluded that UFOs were not a military threat; however misidentifying an enemy aircraft as a UFOs was a threat.

Time Check

- *Color television broadcasts begin. 1953.*
- *Elvis records his first record. 1954.*
- *Tractors outnumber horses in the U.S. for the first time. 1955.*
- *James Brown records "Please, Please, Please." 1956.*
- *First transatlantic phone cable put in. (Prior to this all calls to Europe were made on a short-wave radio telephone.) 1956.*
- *Sputnik, the first satellite, is put in space by Russia. 1957.*
- *The first stereo records are sold. 1958.*
- *The first aluminum cans are made by Kaiser Aluminum. 1958.*

582
CIA memo. Subject: Non-conventional air vehicles. 1954.

When addressing the public, the military and the CIA call them "unidentified flying objects;" however, in-house they were known to be and referred to as "non-conventional air vehicles" as this memo shows. The term UFO originally stood for "unconventional" flying object, not "unidentified."

583
CIA memo 1955.

The CIA is responsible for all non-conventional types of air vehicles, but the project is to be considered inactive (as far as the public goes).

584
CIA memo from the assistant director. Subject: flying saucers 1956.

"Are we keeping in touch with the Air Force center on these things?"

585
CIA report from Hungary with diagram. 1956.

Flying saucers sighted flying in formation from Budapest to Moscow. Estimated speed: 12,000 kilometers per hour. Top military planes can travel only about 600 miles per hour.

586
CIA memo 1958.

The CIA has an interest in keeping track of flying saucers, but public relations and community explanations are the responsibility of the Air Force.

Years: 1963 - 1969

DECLASSIFIED DOCUMENT SUMMARIES

691
U.S. Air Force memo about Lonnie Zamora UFO sighting. 1964.

This is a famous UFO case in which a local, well-respected sheriff walked up to a UFO that was sitting on the ground with several small beings walking around it. When the beings saw Zamora, they got in the craft and took off. This occurred in the desert in New Mexico. This Air Force memo states: "Information obtained during the investigation revealed that the sighting was legitimate and there was no indication that a hoax was being perpetrated."

Time Check

- *Louie Louie is Recorded by The Kingsmen. 1963.*
- *Cassius Clay defeats Sonny Liston to become heavyweight boxing champ. 1964.*
- *The Beatles begin their first American tour. 1964.*

- *Astroturf is used for the first time in the Houston Astrodome. 1965.*
- *Jimi Hendrix releases his first single "Hey Joe." 1966.*
- *Apollo 11 lands on the moon. 1969.*
- *Woodstock music festival in upstate New York. 1969.*
- *Elvis is back in the studio for the first time since 1955. 1969.*

Years 1963-1969

692

NICAP memo. Subject: National Investigation Committee on aerial phenomena. 1965.

> States that their purpose is to obtain firsthand eyewitness accounts of UFO sightings and send copies of these accounts to various air force bases. The key statement: "We were told that there have been instances where the Air Force has attempted to intimidate witnesses and get them to sign false statements relative to UFO sightings."

693

Department of Defense memo. Subject: announcing the termination of "Project Blue Book." 1969.

> Project Blue Book was the "official" Air Force investigation into UFOs. When asked about UFOs government officials always point to this announcement made in 1969. It says the Air Force has investigated UFOs and is no longer interested. Since the Air Force would seem to be the most logical military branch to carry out this investigation, the implication is that UFOs do not exist and that no government agency is investigating them. Wrong! Forget the Air Force! Continue to read through some of the following documents and you will see that virtually every other military branch and all the intelligence agencies keep track of flying saucers.

Years: 1975 - 1987

DECLASSIFIED DOCUMENT SUMMARIES

871
National Security Council memo. 1975.

> States that we still need to study UFOs so they do not "confuse
> our early warning systems in case of an attack (by Russia)."

872
CIA memo. 1976.

> Discusses the effects of magnetic and electromagnetic fields on
> the astronauts. Key line: "This in turn is related to the possible
> propulsion systems of UFOs."

Time Check

- *The Vietnam War ends. 1975.*
- *VHS VCRs are introduced. 1976.*
- *Apple introduces the first disk drive for personal computers. 1978.*
- *Dan Ackroyd and John Belushi are the "Blues Brothers." 1980.*
- *Compact Disc (CD) players are marketed by Sony. 1982.*
- *Michael Jackson and Quincy Jones combine to make "Thriller." 1982.*
- *The space shuttle Challenger explodes. 1986.*
- *Home computers are still rare. The chief executive of a major computer manufacturing company states there is no need for a home computer. 1987.*

Year: 1990

In 1990 there is a dramatic shift in the focus of the intelligence documents now available to the public. The focus becomes the constant UFO sightings occurring in Russia and the rest of Europe, especially Belgium. Here are several CIA and Department of Defense documents that give first-hand accounts of confirmed experiences by Russian military captains.

DECLASSIFIED DOCUMENT SUMMARIES

901
Department of Defense memo and distribution list. Subject: Belgium and the UFO issue.

> Remember the memo from 1969 which said the Air Force was no longer interested or involved in UFO investigations? Well, look who IS interested. Start out by reviewing this first document. It is the distribution list for a UFO memo. The subject is UFO sightings in Belgium, a hotbed of UFO activity. Virtually every branch of the military, all the intelligence agencies, the White House, NATO, and various embassies all got a five-page memo about something which supposedly does not exist.

Time Check

- *Voyager I sends back to earth the first photograph of our solar system taken from space.*
- *Milli Vanilli gets busted for faking it and has to give back their Grammy.*
- *The space probe Magellan, launched one year before, reaches Venus.*

902
Department of Defense memo. Subject: Soviet Colonel General Maltsev's comments.

> *Rabochaya Tribuna*, a leading Soviet newspaper, states: "Colonel General Maltsev's documents are a substantial confirmation that UFOs piloted by intelligent beings of some sort have been visiting the USSR." Colonel General Igor Maltsev is the chief of the main staff of the Soviet Air Defense Forces. In other words, he is the Top Dog, the guy who runs the entire Air Defense system for Russia.

903

Department of Defense memo. Subject: Japanese expedition to Siberia.

> A Russian scientific and industrial journal, Sotsialisticheskkaya Industriyia, describes a Japanese expedition to the site of the Tunguska Meteorite in Siberia. In theory, a great meteorite exploded there in 1908, destroying trees over an area of hundreds of square miles. No meteorite has ever been found. The Japanese research team concluded that the explosion had clearly been caused by the crash of a nuclear-powered spacecraft. The Japanese scientists erected a monument at the site, the first memorial in the USSR to commemorate a UFO. This sounds exciting, but it could have been a meteorite. We now know that meteorites frequently explode just above the earth's surface with the force of an atomic bomb.

Author and science journalist Linda Moulton Howe was told by a military intelligence officer that "Aliens told us (U.S. military) that the explosion at Tunguska was the result of a nuclear-powered engine being accidentally jettisoned from an alien spacecraft."

MAJESTIC – 12 (MJ-12)

The MJ-12 documents are an eight-page memo dated November 18, 1952, outlining the establishment of a secret group by outgoing President Harry Truman. The memo was prepared for President-elect Dwight Eisenhower.

The document simply describes the fact that the U.S. government recovered a crashed alien spacecraft and bodies in 1947 outside of Roswell, New Mexico. It also states that another crash occurred in Texas near the Mexican border in 1950. At that time Truman established a group known as Majestic-12, sometimes referred to as MJ-12. The purpose of the group was to determine how to handle the implications of the Roswell incident and the existence of extraterrestrial beings. The original members of the group were the very top people in government and science. Since they have all died and the names may not be familiar to you, a list of who they were and what positions they held is included.

They are the most dramatic UFO documents ever leaked to the public!

Where Did the Documents Come From?

The MJ-12 documents were received on a roll of undeveloped 35mm film by UFO researcher Jaime Shandera in 1984. Shandera had earlier worked with a group of military intelligence personnel who referred to themselves as the "Insiders," who had expressed a desire to have the true facts about flying saucers released to the public. 2

The documents are the first to uncover the true facts of the dramatic UFO/alien body crash recovery that occurred at Roswell. The story of the investigation of the MJ-12 documents alone could fill a book, and did (see below).

The Controversy

The MJ-12 documents have undergone intense scrutiny both by people who claim they are genuine and by those who claim they are fake. Complicating matters is the fact that the actual paper documents have never been available for examination. Instead, there are only photos of the documents which Shandera received on a roll of film.

Clearing the Smoke

After clearing the smoke, here is what remains: The preponderance of evidence leans heavily towards those who think the documents are genuine. The research on the "real" side is more thorough.

The side arguing that the documents are fake have made several light-weight claims, most of which were easily refuted by research. In fact, the "fake" side, led by known UFO debunker Philip Klass, had to pay off a $1,000 bet when Klass' claims that certain parts of the document were fake were disproved. The check was written out to Stanton Friedman. Friedman has kept copies of the cancelled check, and made them available for all to see. 1

Here is the key point: Even if the documents had been faked the research into confirming their authenticity led to finding 160 eyewitnesses who saw or handled wreckage or bodies from the crashed flying saucer! Many of these eyewitnesses have signed sworn affidavits. Others have given what amounts to dying declarations, both allowable as evidence in any court of law in the United States. In addition, all their stories fit together like the workings of a fine watch. Their time frames all line up, as do their descriptions. The evidence that the crash at Roswell really did occur is now so overwhelming that the MJ-12 documents are just a confirmation of the event.

The Double Reverse

In another effort to authenticate the MJ-12 papers, one researcher used a unique but effective approach. Lee Graham, an aerospace worker, realized that anything stamped "Top Secret" (like the MJ-12 papers) fell under government security regulations; specifically, Department of Defense regulation 5200.1-R, which requires government employees or government-contracted workers to report any leak or breach of security with Top Secret documents. The forging or faking of Top Secret documents is also a violation of this statute.

The FBI Checks Them Out

Graham reported the MJ-12 documents as being either stolen or forged. The FBI spent over one year investigating whether these documents were forged or not. The FBI concluded two things:

First, if the MJ-12 papers were forged, it was an incredible forgery, unlike any they had ever seen in the past. The details of the people and events from 50 years ago were absolutely accurate and coincided with their internal documents.

And second, if the documents were real, they could not get any part of the U.S. government to acknowledge that they had lost them.

To see a complete set of the MJ-12 documents, go to these websites: www.flyingsaucers101.com or www.ufomag.com.

THE ORIGINAL MEMBERS OF MAJESTIC – 12

Dr. Lloyd V. Berkener

Explorer and scientist, he headed a group that later became the Weapons Systems Evaluation Group. He was also a member of a CIA panel that determined that UFOs did not constitute a threat to U.S. national security. Berkener was the executive director at Carnegie Institute, and was a member of the Joint Research and Development Board in 1946.

Dr. Detlev Bronk

Physiologist, aviation expert, and prominent member of the National Academy of Science, he served as president of both Johns Hopkins and Rockefeller Universities. He was chairman of the Nuclear Research Committee and the medical advisor for the Atomic Energy Commission. Bronk also served on the Scientific Advisory Committee of Brookhaven National Laboratory where he worked with Dr. Edward Condon (who completed a major UFO study for the Air Force).

Dr. Vannevar Bush

A leader in research and development at MIT and Carnegie Institute, he was at one time the head of each of the following: Office of Scientific Research and Development, the Joint Research and Development Board, and the National Advisory Committee on Aeronautics. The Office of Scientific Research and Development was responsible for the development of the atomic bomb. Bush also put together the National Defense Research Council in 1941.

James Forrestal

Forrestal was under secretary of the Navy, then secretary of the Navy. He became the first secretary of Defense in 1947, during the time of the Roswell crash. In 1949 he committed a very mysterious suicide. There was talk that he didn't want to hide the truth about flying saucers from the public. His suicide was considered to be just as weird in his day as the Vince Foster suicide is today.

Gordon Gray

Secretary of the Army, he later held several high security positions under

Presidents Truman and Eisenhower. He was also a consultant on UFOs and reported directly to CIA Director Walter B. Smith.

Admiral Roscoe Hillenkoetter
He was the first director of the Central Intelligence Agency (CIA). Later he became a member of NICAP, the National Investigations Committee on Aerial Phenomena. He publicly stated that "UFOs are real… through official secrecy and ridicule, many citizens are led to believe the unknown flying objects are nonsense."

Dr. Jerome Hunsaker
Head of the National Advisory Committee on Aeronautics; chairman of the Departments of Mechanical and Aeronautical Engineering at MIT.

Dr. Donald Menzel
Director of the Harvard College Observatory and an expert in cryptoanalysis, the science of breaking codes and deciphering unknown languages and symbols. Menzel was involved in very high-level intelligence operations during and after World War II.

General Robert M. Montegue
Head of the Armed Forces Special Weapons Center, he was also an Army general at Fort Bliss and as such had control over the White Sands Nuclear Research facility and the Sandia Atomic Energy Commission facility at Albuquerque, New Mexico during the time of the saucer crash at Roswell.

Admiral Sidney Souers
Souers was the first director of Central Intelligence, the precursor to the Central Intelligence Agency. He was also a member of the National Security Council and a special consultant for military intelligence operations.

General Nathan Twining
Chairman of the Joint Chiefs of Staff, Chief of Staff of the U.S. Air Force, Twining was also the commander of the Air Materiel Command based at Wright-Patterson Air base, where the debris and bodies from the Roswell crash were taken. Twining was known to have cancelled a scheduled trip on July 8, 1947, just days after the crash at Roswell and the

same day Roswell Army Air Base sent out a press release stating that a flying saucer had been recovered. In a now-famous memo, Twining stated that UFOs were very real.

General Hoyt Vandenburg

Chief of Staff of the U.S. Air Force and former director of Central Intelligence, he was allegedly in charge of security for the MJ-12 group.

THE PROJECTS

- *Project Sign.*
- *Project Saucer.*
- *Project Grudge.*
- *Project Blue Book.*
- *Undocumented projects.*
- *The Condon Report.*

Well, what does any civic minded government bureaucrat always do when there's a problem? Order up some studies or "Projects."

PROJECT SIGN

The members of Project Sign were the first group assigned to study flying saucers in the U.S. military. The project was begun as a result of a top-secret letter written by Lt. General Nathan Twining. Twining was the former Chief of Staff of the U.S. Army and at the time of his letter he was the Chief of the Air Material Command, Air Technical Intelligence Center at Wright-Patterson Air Force Base. Basically, Twining was the top dog in the military, particularly when it dealt with aircraft. He was the Colin Powell of his day. He was also in charge at Wright-Patterson Air Base, which is where the military took the crashed saucer and debris from the Roswell incident. In his letter dated September 23, 1947, Twining states:

> *The considered opinion of the Command concerning the so-called "flying discs" that:*

a. The phenomenon reported is something real and not visionary or fictitious.
b. There are objects probably approximating the shape of a disc, of such appreciable size as to appear as large as man-made aircraft.

Lt. General Nathan Twining
Top Secret letter, September 23, 1947

Project Sign was begun in February 1948. It lasted one year.

PROJECT SAUCER / PROJECT GRUDGE
On February 11, 1949, Project Sign was officially changed to Project Grudge. Inside the military, Project Sign had been known as "Project Saucer." The existence of the group was leaked to the press and the group's name was changed to "Grudge." (Secret Intelligence Documents on the following pages refer to the "Saucer Project.")

Project Grudge was terminated by the Air Force on December 27, 1949. The Air Force stated that they had completed their investigation of the UFO phenomenon. The concluding report is officially entitled:

Unidentified Flying Objects, Project Grudge.
Technical Report No. 102-AC-49/15-100.

Everybody just called it "The Grudge" report. At this point the military had determined that the saucers themselves were not dangerous.

PROJECT BLUE BOOK
Project Blue Book is the most famous of the flying saucer projects. Anyone who has looked into this subject has heard of Project Blue Book. In fact, the project was done for the public. At this point the military knew flying saucers were not dangerous; if they were, they could have and would have attacked us by now. And, there was no question of their superior technology. They were just zipping around watching man do his dance on this planet. The military was not afraid of flying saucers, but they were afraid of flying-saucer reports!

This is what Project Blue Book was for:

1. To assure the public that the military knew what was going on and to calm them by patiently taking reports.

2. To explain away as many reports as possible by claiming them to be naturally occurring phenomenon like swamp gas and balloons.

3. To use shame and ridicule to embarrass people into not reporting flying saucer sightings.

A Potent Technique

My own research has shown that over 35 percent of the population has seen a flying saucer and has never told their friends or family! It appears that if you want to keep a secret, the use of shame, embarrassment, and ridicule is the best way.

Some People Would Rather Die

Physicians will tell you that most people who have their first heart attack do not seek treatment at the first signs because they are embarrassed that they may be making a big deal out of nothing. Instead, they elect to do nothing. They basically decide to die rather than risk embarrassment. Thousands of people die needlessly every year because they are too embarrassed to have their rectums and colons examined. Colon cancer kills more people than breast cancer and prostate cancer combined. Have your parents ever really talked to you about sex? In graphic detail? Probably not! They are too embarrassed.

Clear Evidence

So here we are drowning in clear evidence that we are not alone in the universe. We are being visited by other intelligent beings (and I don't mean microbes), and your parents are too embarrassed to look at the facts and talk about it.

Project Blue Book is Not a Book!

Project Blue Book is a bunch of files containing over 13,000 reports of UFO and flying saucer incidents. It is not, and never was, a book. The files themselves are not even all located in the same place. These 13,000 files are the ones that were somehow designated as Blue Book files. There were over fifty thousand cases that came in during the existence of Project Blue Book that were never even catalogued. They're still sitting in a warehouse somewhere.

It Was Never Made Public

Although it was supposed to be a public project the files were never made available to the public until some years after the project ended. Project Blue Book ran from 1952 until 1969. On December 17, 1969 the Air Force ended Project Blue Book, saying they had accounted for all the sightings - and by the way, the Air Force was no longer interested in UFOs. The implication was, of course, that no one in the government was interested in UFOs.

Interested Agencies

Maybe the Air Force wasn't interested, but everyone else in the government was! If the subject is flying saucers, every branch of the military, all the intelligence agencies, many U.S. Embassies, NATO, and the White House, all got a copy!

Report Number 14

Report Number 14 is the most important part of Project Blue Book. Almost nobody knows about it and those who do don't want to talk about it. It is the most important part of Project Blue Book because Report Number 14 completely refutes the conclusions the Air Force made about flying saucers in the very same Project Blue Book. It's a classic case of "Figures lie and liars figure."

"To use shame and ridicule to embarrass people into not reporting flying saucer sightings".

Here is the data from Project Blue Book:

Type of UFO	Number	Percentage
Astronomical	3,412	26.0
Aircraft	2,237	17.0
Balloons	1,223	9.3
Radar Phen.	152	1.2
Psychological	63	0.5
Hoax	116	0.9
Meteorological	44	0.3
Birds	85	0.6
Insufficient Information	2,409	18.3
Other	2,807	21.4

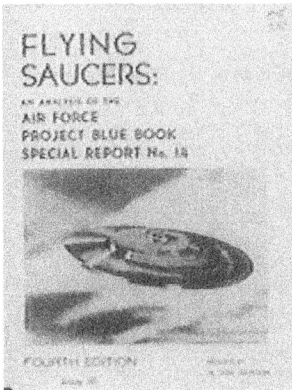

FLYING SAUCERS:
AN ANALYSIS OF THE
AIR FORCE
PROJECT BLUE BOOK
SPECIAL REPORT No. 14

FOURTH EDITION

The cover from Project Blue Book's Report # 14.

Here are the conclusions reached in Report Number 14. The report says: All evidence and analysis indicate that the reports of unidentified flying objects are the result of:

a. Misinterpretation of various conventional objects.
b. A mild form of mass hysteria.
c. Hoaxes.

Yet, look at the numbers above. Their own data show two of the categories: "Hoaxes" and "Psychological" *combined* equal only 1.2 percent!

Combining two other categories: "Insufficient Information" and "Other" totals almost 40 percent! Thus by their own data they acknowledge that almost half of all sightings are unaccounted for and are not conventional objects!

One more thing you should know: this thing about "mass hysteria." For there to be mass hysteria, the people all have to be in close proximity with each other at the time the triggering event is going on - like a rock concert, for instance. When it comes to flying-saucer sightings, the people reporting them are spread all over the globe. They are not next to each other and their sightings occur at different times. "Mass hysteria" is not a likely possibility.

In Conclusion

The next time someone brings up Project Blue Book, whip out the numbers and Report Number 14 and be done with it. It is not just the United States - all governments worldwide are withholding information about flying saucers from the public.

UNDOCUMENTED PROJECTS

These basically amount to well-founded rumors, but since it is abundantly clear that the U.S. government has been lying to us for over 50 years, rumors are fair balls. However, whenever something is a rumor or undocumented, I will tell you up front. Including rumors is not an intention to mislead you. There is simply a good chance that many rumors are in fact closer to the truth than the "truth" we have gotten from the government and the military.

Information about these projects has been leaked by so-called government sources; however, there is no way to prove if these projects are real or not. Here they are for your review:

Project Gleem
Started by President Eisenhower to study UFOs. Later became Project Aquarius.

Project Aquarius
Funded by the CIA, supposedly to gather information about alien life forms through sightings and human encounters with aliens.

Project Sigma
Created for the purpose of establishing communications with aliens. Supposedly a face-to-face meeting with aliens occurred in 1959 as a result of this project.

Project Bando
Designed to gather medical information about alien races.

Project Pounce
Created for evaluating alien space technology.

Project Snowbird
Established to test flights of recovered alien spacecraft. Supposedly, it is still going on.

The Condon Report

The Condon Report was the result of a study commissioned by the Air Force to study UFOs. It was headed by E. U. Condon and conducted with a team of thirty-six people at the University of Colorado during 1967 and 1968. The report reached the conclusion that further study of UFOs was not worthwhile. The results were released in 1969, and the Air Force used them as a basis to discontinue Project Blue Book.

Many people were critical of the findings of the report. Many sightings were classified as naturally occurring phenomena, but when looked at more closely simply could not be accounted for. For example, hard-radar readings showing craft traveling in excess of 1,500 miles per hour were called "radar bounce-back" despite statements to the contrary by experienced radar operators.

AREA 51

Dreamland is the code name for Area 51. Area 51 is a "secret" military base located about 90 miles north of Las Vegas, Nevada. It is also known as Groom Lake, named for the dry lake bed the military base is sitting on. The size of the base is 6 miles wide by 10 miles long. Recently the Federal government has seized an additional 85,000 acres surrounding the base to keep observers at a distance.

Contained somewhere on the grounds is a large air base that the U.S. government will not discuss. It is considered so sensitive that only those who take an oath of secrecy for life are allowed in. Civilian contractors and others who work at the base are flown in every morning aboard unmarked planes with blacked-out windows. It is said that structures are built deep into the desert floor, with buildings going down thirty to forty stories below the surface.

Use of Deadly Force

The perimeter of the base is covered with ground sensors and listening devices to detect even the smallest intrusion. It is also heavily patrolled by armed guards from the Wackenhut Corporation, a very serious private security firm. These guys aren't your normal rent-a-cops that local concert promoters use. In short, they will kill you. End of story.

The board of directors of the Wackenhut Corporation reads like a Who's Who of the intelligence community. Here are some of the guys who are said to be or have been on the board:

Admiral Bobby Ray Inman
Former Deputy CIA Director and a bunch of other high military positions. If you know anything about the military, you know who this guy is.

Frank Carlucci
Former Deputy Director of the CIA.

General Joseph Carroll
Former DIA (Defense Intelligence Agency) Director.

Clarence Kelly
Former FBI Director.

James J. Rowley
Former Secret Service Director.

William Casey
Former CIA Director.

So, What's the Big Deal?

Area 51 was first opened in 1955 as a testing facility for the U-2 spy plane being developed by Lockheed Aircraft. Area 51 has since become a popular symbol for the U.S. government UFO/Alien cover-up. Area 51 is supposedly where recovered alien spacecraft are being tested and reversed-engineered to learn how they work. 1

S-4

S-4 is a parcel of land that is a part of Area 51. The most secret research actually takes place there. Or so we've been told.

Secret

Secret? Hardly. This military base is so well known that every school kid in America recognizes its name. It has been a part of most UFO researcher's vocabulary for decades. Every military power in the world is aware of Area 51. As part of an international treaty called the "Open Skies Treaty," the United States Government is required to fly other countries over the base upon demand. The U.S. government has reciprocal privileges for their bases. Not only that, but Area 51 is not just a U.S. base, it is an international base being run by a consortium of many countries.

Air Surveillance Photos

Partly as a result of this arrangement there are literally thousands of air surveillance and satellite photographs available of this "secret" base. Russian surveillance photographs taken from their satellites of Area 51 are available to anyone over the Internet any day, anytime, for free! I have even included one for you in this chapter. This base may be many things, but one thing it's not is secret!

The Mainstream Media Catches Up

In April 1994 *Popular Science* magazine featured a satellite photo of the Groom Lake base on the cover. The issue contained an article on the base and its history. This ignited mainstream media interest in learning more about Area 51. Even TV personality and broadcaster Larry King has gone to Area 51 and done a whole show from a set just outside the perimeter. If Larry King knows, how secret could it be?

Aurora Superplane

When I say Aurora, I'm not talking about your dad's Oldsmobile. The
Aurora is a new kind of supersonic plane that allegedly flies out of Area
51. Its estimated cost: $15 billion! It runs on controlled explosions of
cryogenic (real cold) methane or ammonia. Estimated speed: eight times
the speed of sound, or around 6,000 miles per hour. It leaves a vapor trail
from the engine's explosions that resemble donuts strung on a rope.
The aerodynamics of the Aurora are reported to be very different from
conventional aircraft. Thus, the Aurora is a very dangerous craft to fly
and has had an exceedingly high casualty rate.

SR71 Blackbird, originally developed and flown out of Area 51.
(U.S. National Archives and Records)

Lawsuit May Lift the Veil of Secrecy

As reported in the *Wall Street Journal*, the *New York Times*, and on CBS's
60 Minutes, Area 51 is being sued. A number of workers at the base have
exhibited strange symptoms, such as watching their skin turn flaming red
and then fall off. Several have died recently and their relatives are suing
the U.S. government. Other employees have come forward and stated
that the base has engaged heavily in illegal toxic waste dumping and
burning, resulting in the employee deaths.

The lawsuit and the allegations are serious. The government is afraid the
veil of secrecy about the very existence of this base could be lifted and is
arguing that any disclosure about Area 51 could pose a "serious risk" to
national security.

President Clinton's Response

Bill Clinton signed an executive order exempting Area 51 (Groom Lake) from releasing its environmental reports to the public. See the full text of Clinton's executive order at www.flyingsaucers101.com.

Bob Lazar

Physicist Bob Lazar has claimed he has worked on alien spacecraft at Area 51. Lazar says that nine alien saucers are housed there to learn how they work. (This is known as "reverse engineering." Lazar's saga is long and controversial.

After coming forward and making his statements, Lazar's records of employment and evidence of his attending school all disappeared. He was later indicted and plea-bargained on a charge of pandering and solicitation.

However, Lazar was working as a bookkeeper at the time. One of his clients was running a prostitution ring on the side. It was well established that Lazar was bookkeeping only for the client's legitimate business and was not involved in his client's shady side business. It was evident from the beginning that the real target was Lazar. Many of the things Lazar initially said sounded outlandish, but have since been confirmed by other sources.

Jarod 2

Another Area 51 worker who goes by the name of Jarod 2 confirms Lazar's story. Supposedly, Jarod (pronounced Jay-rod) was the name given an alien who was housed at the base. The alias, Jarod 2, is a reference to this alien being.

Jarod 2 is a 70-year old retired engineer. He says he worked for thirty years designing reproductions of alien flying saucers. He also says he has seen gray alien beings during his work on the project.

Jarod 2 says his former employers have given him permission to speak semi-publicly about his experiences in order to help prepare the American public about the truth of alien existence. Jarod 2 states that the project is even more advanced than Lazar was aware of.

THE MEN IN BLACK

"Who Are Those Guys?"

Paul Newman
From the movie, *'Butch Cassidy and the Sundance Kid'*

Thanks to the hit movie starring Will Smith and Tommie Lee Jones everybody has heard of the *Men in Black*. The movie proposed that their job is to protect the earth from the "scum of the universe." Well, that's just movie talk. The truth is a lot harder to get a handle on. Nobody knows if these guys are government agents, aliens in disguise, or just a group of intelligence operatives trying to keep a secret.

Here's what I do know: They're real. They generally show up when ordinary citizens have an extraordinary sighting or encounter with a flying saucer or its occupants. They seem bent on intimidating those individuals into not talking about what they have seen. They even attempt to do this with law-enforcement officers and military personnel. There have been hundreds if not thousands of incidents reported about these men in black.

What "Black" Means
The word black when used in this context means covert, undercover, not seen. When a person enters the intelligence community and becomes involved in operations and projects, all their government files basically disappear. They are no longer accessible through the normal channels. When this happens it is said the person has "gone black."

Some people think the MIBs are Aliens
Complicating matters is the fact that many times it appears that the men in black are humanoid-type aliens masquerading as humans. Many people in the military are aware that this may be the case (in some instances).

Dr. Herbert Hopkins

Dr. Hopkins was actively investigating a UFO abduction case in 1976 when one evening during the summer a stranger called him on the phone and asked if he could come by and talk to him about the case. This was despite the fact that the case had not been publicized at all. Hopkins agreed, hung up the phone, and immediately walked to his door to turn on the porch light so the caller could see the steps when he arrived. Hopkins was surprised to see a man walking up the stairs of the porch as he was turning on the light. He was shocked when the man introduced himself as the person who had just called him. (There were no cellular phones in 1976.) [1]

The Black Suit Routine

The man was dressed in black suit, black tie, black hat, and gray gloves. In the summertime! The man's skin was a pale sickly color and he appeared to be wearing bright red lipstick, a fact which turned out to be true as Hopkins later watched some of the lipstick rub onto the man's gray glove.

Vanished Into Thin Air

The man asked Hopkins to take out the two coins that were in Hopkins' pocket. Stunned, Hopkins did it. He told Hopkins to watch the coins in his hand. The two coins simply vanished into thin air! Then the man told him, "Neither you nor anyone else on this planet will ever see those coins again."

The man then said his "energy was running low" and left. Shortly after stepping off Hopkins' porch, the man himself disappeared.

When the Scare Started

The first widely acknowledged case of Men In Black intimidating UFO witnesses occurred in 1953. A fellow by the name of Albert K. Bender was the editor of a magazine called *Space Review*. He was also the founder of an organization called the International Flying Saucer Bureau. [2]

During the summer of 1953 Bender apparently discovered some vital information pointing to the cover-up of the existence of flying saucers by the U.S. government. He had written several articles scheduled to appear in the next issue of his magazine. The next thing he knew, three guys show up at his door all dressed in black: black suits, black hats, and sunglasses. They told him they had read his article, even though it had not yet been published. They told him his information was accurate, but that he better not publish the article. In fact, they told him that he'd better not publish anything more about flying saucers. They said, "We advise those engaged in saucer work to please be very cautious." They basically scared him so badly that Bender officially retired from UFO investigations.

Other MIB Reports
- *A teenager is threatened by MIBs and has photos of flying saucers seized from him.*
- *MIBs make a coin disappear from a UFO witness and tell him, "Your heart will do the same if you talk."*
- *A former Air Force officer who learned about information on extra-terrestrials from NASA was harassed, tranquilized, and interrogated.*

Even the Military Doesn't Know Who MIB's Are
In 1967 the United States Air Force expressed concern about finding out more about these guys in black who were going around scaring people and saying they were from the U.S. armed services. Here's a statement by Colonel George P. Freeman, the spokesperson for Project Blue Book at the Pentagon:

> Mysterious men dressed in Air Force uniforms or all in black and bearing impressive credentials from government agencies have been silencing UFO witnesses. We have checked a number of these cases, and these men are not connected to the Air Force in any way. We haven't been able to find out anything about these men. By posing as Air Force officers and government agents, they are committing a Federal offense. We would sure like to catch one, unfortunately the trail is always too cold by the time we hear about these cases, but we are still trying.

The Joint Chiefs of Staff are in the Dark, Too!
Assistant Vice Chief of Staff of the United States Air Force Lt. General

Hewitt T. Wheless sent a memo on March 1, 1967 to various agencies in the Department of Defense. Here's what it said:

> Information, not verifiable, has reached Hq.USAF that persons claiming to represent the Air Force or other Defense establishments have contacted citizens who have sighted unidentified flying objects. In one reported case, an individual in civilian clothes, who represented himself as a member of NORAD, demanded and received photos belonging to a private citizen. In another, a person in an Air Force uniform approached local police and other citizens who had sighted a UFO, assembled them in a school room and told them that they did not see what they thought they saw and that they should not talk to anyone about the sighting. All military and civilian personnel and particularly information officers and UFO investigating officers who hear of such reports should immediately notify their local OSI offices.

THREE REAL CASES

Here are three encounters with the Men in Black that were told to me personally. In each case the person told me about this event without my initiating the conversation on this topic. Each person asked that I not use his or her real name if I told anyone else. In honoring those requests I'm using a pseudonym for the individual. Understandably, there seems to be a need to tell someone about what happened. With the secrecy and intimidation still surrounding any event that has to do with flying saucers or alien beings, people who have these encounters generally don't trust telling someone who doesn't have a clue that these guys even exist.

Larry

Larry approached me following a meeting on UFOs. He was about 25 years old, casually but nicely dressed. He walked up to me and said, "You know, I had something very strange happen to me and my buddy. I don't like to talk about it because it kind of scares me." So I asked him what happened. He was clearly nervous and even stuttered a little. Here's what he told me:

Late one night in a state of semi-sleep, he felt a presence in his bedroom. The "presence" communicated with him and let him know it was from another world. Larry asked why all the secrecy and if they were real why they didn't just show up in the daytime. They told him that the next time he was with his best friend (whom they called by name) he would indeed see them and he would know it was them.

Larry said the entire conversation did not exactly take place using words. It was more like he understood what they were thinking and feeling without actual words. I know it sounds weird, but this is very common in human/alien interactions. For the most part, none of the aliens use verbal language, it is all telepathic, and sometimes it's in the human's own language. Many times it is a combination of feeling, "a knowingness", and understanding on a level we have not yet discovered how to describe.

When Larry woke in the morning he wasn't sure if he had been dreaming or not, but the experience was so vivid and unlike any dream he had ever had before that he thought about it daily for months afterwards.

Larry's best friend was now in the military and he didn't see him for months. His friend returned home just in time for the Fourth of July, and they decided to go down to a local park where some of his family members were holding a big picnic. The two of them were just kind of standing around, when a black van pulled up about 50 yards away. The two front doors opened and two men dressed all in black suits with black hats and dark sunglasses got out. Larry was startled because he began to remember his "dream." The two men opened the sliding door on the side of the van and two more guys got out. They too were head-to-toe in black, with shades.

Larry said:

> First of all, it was hot. It was the middle of the afternoon and well over 80 degrees, and these guys were in black, with hats! Next, the two guys who got out of the side looked different. They didn't look human. I can't describe it, but their arms looked too long or something. Then they sat down at a picnic table and they all turned around and looked right at me and my buddy. After that he got real quiet. Then they just got back in the van and drove off. My buddy won't talk about it. He pretends like nothing happened, but I know he saw them and he knows I know.

Christine

Christine was a career military person. She is a pilot and flew in the Armed Forces of the United States. She is even a member of the now infamous "Tailhook Association." For those who don't know, Tailhook is an association for Navy Fighter pilots. The name *tailhook* comes from the hook on the back of fighter jets that is used to catch the planes when they land on an aircraft carrier. Here is what Christine told me:

> One night a large UFO showed up and hovered over the base for about forty minutes. Everybody saw it. We were all pilots and we knew it wasn't ours. We could also tell because the brass didn't know what it was either. When it left, it took off at phenomenal speed. The next day a bunch of black sedans showed up on the base. Each one had four guys all dressed in black with hats. They got out and went to every building on the base and "encouraged" us not to talk about what we saw. I'm not easily intimidated. I know how to use a firearm and I've flown in combat conditions, but these guys meant business.

Colonel Rogers

Colonel Rogers had retired from the military and lived alone. Rogers had mentioned to some people he had seen UFOs and his work in the military had assured them that they were real. Several days later a man dressed in black showed up at his door. When Rogers opened it the man began to warn him about not talking about UFOs. Rogers told the man, "OK, just a minute." He excused himself went into his bedroom and came back to the front door with a loaded .45 pistol. He cocked it, pointed it at the man's head and said, "I don't know if you are CIA, NSA, or an alien, but somebody will have a lot of explaining to do if I blow your head off. Now get out of here."

The next day another man showed up wearing regular business attire (no black suit with shades). He hailed the colonel from the front yard with his arms raised, said he was unarmed, and asked if he could talk to him briefly. The colonel allowed the guy to approach. The guy said, "Look Colonel, we're sorry, no more guys will show up at your house. Some of this UFO information is still classified and we would appreciate it if you just didn't talk too much about it. OK? Thanks." And, then the guy left.

Black Helicopters

These are similar to the Men in Black. Abductees, contactees, and people who have UFO encounters often report being followed by black helicopters. Once again, no one is sure if these are government aircraft or alien craft disguised as helicopters. There are cases which point to both.

One contactee, author Kim Carlsberg, has recorded being followed by black helicopters on the days following a nighttime abduction experience.

It's Probably the Army

Unconfirmed sources say these black helicopters belong to the U.S. Army, 160th SOAR Division. The helicopters are black, or in some cases a very dark green, because they are "stealth aircraft" technology and cannot be detected by radar, just like the stealth bombers and fighters. Apparently these craft are also made available to other government agencies, including but not limited to the CIA, FEMA, and NSA.

FEMA Again

I mention this again. FEMA stands for the Federal Emergency Management Agency. This is the organization you hear about on your local news whenever there has been a hurricane, tornado, earthquake, flood, or any other major catastrophe. FEMA manages the funds that are doled out by the government to states and individuals to help them recover from these events.

In looking into covert or "black" operations, FEMA comes up again and again. It appears that FEMA is used as a cover to direct funds into these covert operations. Can I prove it? No. However, FEMA turns up again and again from all kinds of different sources whenever government secrecy and funding is the topic. No other "civilian" agency does. Not the FDA, FAA, or USDA! Not only that, but after any major disaster people seem to have a hard time getting relief from this agency, as if there were not enough money there. Let's get a budget review done of FEMA funds and check it out!

A Dad at FEMA

Shortly after the first printed version of this book came out, a very good friend of mine named Kevin told me the following:

Kevin said that his dad worked at FEMA. He said his dad often had to make quick unplanned business trips. His dad never talked about his work, unlike his friends dads. One evening when he and his dad were watching TV, Kevin asked his dad, "Dad, what exactly do you do?" At that moment the television was showing a news report picturing President Richard Nixon and then Secretary of State, Henry Kissinger. His dad pointed at the TV screen and said: "You see those two fella's there? I was in a meeting room with them yesterday." At that point, his dad shut up and never said another word.

The Disclosure Project

It is extremely important that you know about the Disclosure Project. I put it at this point in the book, because I did not want to confuse you. This project is not a government sponsored project (like those I have discussed earlier).

The Disclosure Project is a nonprofit research project working to fully disclose the facts about UFOs, extraterrestrial intelligence, and classified advanced energy and propulsion systems. (They) have over 500 government, military and intelligence community witnesses testifying to their direct, personal, firsthand experience with UFOs, ETs, ET technology and the cover-up that keeps this information secret. 1.

The Disclosure Project was founded by Dr. Steven Greer M.D. and has uncovered eyewitnesses from defense contractors, NASA, the U.S. military, Central Intelligence Agency and other covert intelligence organizations that confirm the existence of extraterrestrial beings. Their testimonies are huge, all-encompassing and beyond refute.

The media and the rest of the world are very aware of the Disclosure Project and the information it has gathered. On Wednesday, May 9th, 2001, over twenty military, intelligence, government, corporate and scientific witnesses came forward at the National Press Club in Washington, DC to establish the reality of UFOs, extraterrestrial vehicles, extraterrestrial life forms, and resulting advanced energy and propulsion technologies. 2.

Many U.S. Senators and Congressmen sent aides to attend this event. (Guess they didn't have the courage to show up themselves.) Most of them had already been briefed privately anyway.

Every major US network was also in attendance, as well as major networks from countries around the world. There were dozens of out of state, local stations represented also.

It is mandatory that you go to their website and stay connected to The Disclosure Project: **www.Disclosureproject.org.**

NASA

As Americans, we have loved and been proud of the National Aeronautics and Space Administration (NASA). Who didn't feel a rush while
watching a shuttle lift-off? Who didn't have dreams of adventure when
ordinary men and women were allowed to go into space on the shuttle?

It wasn't just rocket fuel that got them off the launching pad. It was our
hearts, our faith, and our paychecks. Think of all the men and women
who worked so hard and those who died to put our dreams in space, and
never a complaint from a single taxpayer about footing the bill.

NASA Is Lying to Us!

NASA really stands for Never A Straight Answer. There is no easy way
to put this: NASA has been hiding from the public clear and dramatic
evidence of intelligent life in our universe.

From all indications the cover-up has been going on for decades. While
researching this book, I came to certain conclusions. I didn't want to
indict a whole agency and all the decent, honest men and women who
work there. However, it is time to pull back the curtain on the wizard.
NASA is lying to us.

NASA personnel appear to be confused by the things they are seeing.
They think they must have all the answers before releasing important
data to the scientific community and the public.

They are also threatening and holding hostage the scientists and engineers who work there. Something clearly stinks, and too many insiders
and former employees are coming forward to tell the truth. They can no
longer live with this violation of the American heart, spirit, and paycheck.
And neither can we.

We say to NASA: If you want to lie to us and withhold your findings, fine. Go get your funding privately. We're not going pay for it anymore. We can get someone to lie to us for free!

> These laws prohibit NASA from withholding information
> from the public for any reason:
>
> US Federal Law Section: 5 U.S.C. 552 (a) (4) (B) - (G)
> *and*
> Federal Register Notice: 14 CFR Part 1206 Subpart 8 (Failure to
> Release Records to the Public)

A specific example: There have been too many instances over the years of NASA withholding data and intimidating employees under the guise of national security concerns. So let's just concentrate on one; one you can confirm for yourself.

A NASA Cover up Right Before Your Very Eyes: The Mars Pathfinder Rover

NASA is withholding photos from the public and has gone back and altered the original images that came from the Mars Pathfinder Rover, the little car the scientists that wobbled along and took pictures of the Martian landscape and the rock they named "Yogi."

The Rover has the capability of transmitting high-resolution images. That means very clear, sharp, and detailed pictures. NASA acknowledges that they have received such images. However, the images that have been released to the public are the low-resolution images. They refuse to release any high-resolution images to the public or the scientific community. Try and get some of the high-resolution pictures. Call NASA chief administrator, Charles F. Bolden at (202) 358-0001.

What are they hiding? Withholding the high-resolution images is against the law. The images belong to you. You paid for them. All the images coming from the Mars Rover are numbered. Here are three to begin with. They appear on www.flyingsaucers101.com.

80881
Taken on Sol 2/July 5. Here is the original version. Good luck at finding this. NASA no longer posts this image on their website or makes it available to anyone.

80904
The same image as 80881, but it has been altered. Notice the right/front portion of the picture and you will see crude cuts and fractals. Fractals are those blurred squares in the picture that hide the detail.

80807
Has had the color balance altered to eliminate the details in the photo.

If you have an image editing program like Adobe Photoshop, or 'print screen' on your personal computer, you can blow up different portions of the images. If you do, you will clearly see where crude alterations have been made. In any images that were not altered what you will see on the blow-up will astound you.

A Noted Geologist Speaks Up

Ronald Nicks has a degree in geology and he is a registered geologist in Oregon and California, a registered engineering geologist in Oregon, and is certified by the American Institute of Professional Geologists. Nicks has also held numerous high-level management positions in geology for the U.S. Department of Energy. He has over 35 years of southwestern (Mars-like), desert geological experience. He also has a strong familiarity with archaeological sites and excavation.

Nicks made a close up examination of some of the original unaltered images. (Some of the images were sent in the first 7 minutes of the Mars Rover's transmission. These images were apparently not expected by NASA to be transmitted, because the computer program sent them through sooner than expected.) What follows is what he discovered.

What the Martian "Rocks" Really Are

Here it is in a nutshell: the rocks may not be "rocks." They appear to be artifacts! Artifacts are things that have been made by intelligent beings, such as arrowheads or a piece of pottery. What Nicks says is this: If you are out roaming around the desert, you may find a single rock in any one given shape. That is, you may find a rock shaped like a triangle. You may find another shaped like a circle and another shaped like a rectangle. But you won't find a rock with all three distinct shapes in it. You will find this only in artifacts made by intelligent beings. If you blow up many of the Mars Rover images, you will clearly see several different geometric shapes in the same item! You will see many right angles, evenly spaced, and you will see tubes and wheels. You will see items resembling gear cogs, all evenly spaced. This does not happen naturally.

They Don't Want You to See This

For some reason NASA does not want you to see this. Why? We're not sure. Investigations by John David Oates shows that part of the Mars Rover mission may have been deployment of a weapon.

Demand Your Rights as a Citizen

Call Charles F. Bolden. Call your congressman. Ask for your copy of the high-resolution, unaltered Mars Rover images. After all, they belong to you. You don't have to wait. You can go right now to the Web. Download a bunch of the "rock" images. Start blowing them up on your computer. You can see for yourself.

MODERN AIRCRAFT TECHNOLOGY

Fly From Los Angeles to New York in One Hour!

The U.S. military has an airplane that can fly from Los Angeles to New York in one hour. During this flight it can survey a 30-mile-wide strip of every state it passes over. It can fly at an altitude of 85,000 feet.

Here's the point: This plane was retired in 1965 due to obsolescence!

The plane is the Lockheed A-12 Blackbird. You can find one of them on display at the San Diego Aeronautical and Space Museum in Balboa Park. There is also one on display at Lockheed Aircraft in Palmdale, California. The display is open to the public and is known as "Blackbird Park."

Military sources tell us their technology is at least 150 years ahead of where the public thinks it is. Think about that. One hundred and fifty years ago was 1848. The American Civil War had not yet started and the automobile was still 50 years away from being invented. One hundred fifty years into the future easily represents being able to travel to the other planets in our solar system. So that means we have craft right now that are capable of doing it!

In my interviews with a military officer who holds a security clearance well above Top Secret I was told that he had been flown in an unknown aircraft from the West Coast of the United States to central Europe and back in less than two hours! That's 7,000 miles per hour!

To the Moon and Back

According to my sources, the military has aircraft that can fly from the tarmac to the moon and back as easily as flying across the country.

Advanced Propulsion Systems

Work is being conducted on many different advanced systems of propulsion, including:

* *Nuclear fission systems*
* *Nuclear fusion systems*
* *Electromagnetic systems*
* *Anti-gravity systems*
* *Cryogenic fuel systems*

The Head of Lockheed Aircraft

Ben Rich was the former head of Lockheed Aircraft. Shortly before he died he stated, "We already have the technology to move among the stars. What a shame it is that such breakthroughs are being hidden from humanity." 3

Senate Testimony

On April 9, 1997 scientist David Adair testified under oath to the U.S. Congress about recovered extraterrestrial spacecraft and reverse engineering. Just so you know, committing perjury or lies while under oath to the U.S. Congress is punishable by 20 years in a Federal penitentiary. Congress confirmed his story, including names and dates. Everything he said checked out as being true. Here are some of the things Adair told Congress:

He was taken to Area 51 on June 20 in 1971 and shown an engine from a recovered alien spacecraft. The engine had an organic sentience, which means the engine could literally feel and sense emotions and instructions from the pilot of the craft! There were organic-looking tubes surrounding the engine and cascading in the exact configuration of a brain stem and nerve fibers. 1

Though it sounds improbable, our intelligence sources say the U.S. military has working sentient capability built into advanced, highly classified jet fighters, right now. 6 Supposedly, this engine is fully capable of driving a spacecraft at light speed. And remember, the military had it in 1971! 7

THE RUSSIAN EXPERIENCE

The Soviet Union, as we once knew it, has toppled. Vast amounts of information are now flowing out of Russia about experiences with flying saucers and beings from other worlds.

Officially Documented Proof

The Soviet Military Review is a journal which is published monthly in seven languages: Russian, English, Dary, Arabic, Spanish, Portuguese, and French. Many detailed articles on UFOs have appeared in this journal over the years. In an issue dated June, 1989, then-Soviet Chief of Air Defenses Igor Maltsev stated:

> For both skeptics and non-skeptics, this information can serve as officially documented proof of UFO validity. We hope that this open acknowledgment of the phenomenon will put an end to ambiguous speculations and will make the fact of its existence beyond doubt.

> Now we have grounds to tell that UFOs are not optical or hallucinated phenomena which were allegedly caused by global psychosis.

The objects have been spotted by technological means. Pictures are available for specialists. 2

From Russia

After the changes that occurred in Russia all kinds of things went on sale. The KGB files were sold in their entirety to Yale University, and two U.S. film companies bought the rights to the KGB UFO files. Soviet scientists and cosmonauts also came forward with what they knew. In 1990 Colonel Marina Popovich held a press conference in San Francisco at the Russian Consulate. During the conference she showed amazing photographs of cigar-shaped alien craft in space that were each, fifteen miles long. The photos were taken by a Russian space, probe which mysteriously stopped working, then disappeared completely, shortly after taking the photographs.

(For more information on missing space probes see the chapter, "Star Wars and Satellites.")

Popovich knows her stuff. Besides being a colonel in the Soviet Armed Forces, she is also the wife of famed cosmonaut Pavel Popovich. Pavel Popovich was head of a Soviet Committee on UFOs. 1

Colonel Marina Lavrentevna Popovich

Col. Popovich has flown every kind of aircraft there is in the Soviet Union, from large transport planes to MIG-21s. She holds ninety flight records. She's even been called the Chuck Yeager of the Soviet Union. Popovich has a Ph.D. in technical sciences and her focus now is to get the truth about the existence of flying saucers out to the public. Here are some of the things she has to say about flying saucers and alien beings:

- *Soviet satellites have taken photographs of flying saucers. 6*
- *Soviet scientists have concluded that flying saucers have been around for as long as our planet. 7*
- *Popovich has seen photographs of alien/human hybrid children.*

More From Russia

In Moscow there is a UFO Center for research called the All-Union UFO Center. Among many other books and papers, it houses the work of Dr. Felix Zigel, who documented over fifty thousand UFO sightings in the Soviet Union.

There have been more than seventy UFO incidents that occurred at the Bhunice Atomic Energy Plant in the Slovak Republic. A log was kept of each individual incident. 3

The soviets have stated that their Mir space station has been under observation by UFOs almost continuously. 4

In 1993 declassified Soviet documents stated the following:

> The ministry of Security of the Russian Federation, along with the (American) CIA, and other covert services, have enough evidence to conclude that there is a detachment of observers from other worlds traveling in near-earth orbit.

Scientist, oceanographer, and former Soviet submarine captain Dr. Vladimir Azhazha has stated:

> UFOs trans-morph, going from saucer shape to cigar shape to a spiral in minutes. They can materialize and dematerialize at will. The craft and occupants are varied and may be from dozens of different sources and civilizations. 5

The Soviets have confirmed that they have pictures of the moon's surface that show large objects clearly made by intelligent beings. Among them:

> Eight huge obelisks or monuments, shaped much like our Washington monument in Washington D.C.

> Dozens of smaller, but evenly spaced monuments forming patterns congruent with those of the pyramids of Egypt.

Long "Runway" formations.

These objects have been documented and confirmed on both Soviet Luna 9 photographs and America's Orbiter 3 and Apollo mission photographs.

THE ASTRONAUTS

"Oh, my God! You wouldn't believe it! These babies are huge, sir! Enormous! I'm telling you there are other spacecraft out there. Lined up on the far side of the crater edge! They're on the moon watching us!"

Apollo 11

"What's there? Mission Control calling Apollo 11."

Former NASA employee Otto Binder states that the above exchange was picked up by HAM radio operators with their own VHF receiving facilities that did not go through NASA's broadcasting channels. Apollo 11 was the mission manned by Neil Armstrong and Edwin "Buzz" Aldrin; both men were the first to land on the moon July 21, 1969.

They Never Said Anything

Many people have asked about what the astronauts might have seen when they were in space. Did they see UFOs? The astronauts are a unique group. They have had experiences and have been places the rest of humanity can only dream about. Over the years many astronauts have been badly misquoted and have had statements attributed to them that they never made. It has made many of them media-shy and reluctant to discuss the topic at all.

Down Here, But Not Up There

Basically, most of the astronauts deny ever seeing UFOs while on space missions; however, they almost all admit to seeing them while doing duty as test pilots in jet planes. A list of their exact statements is at the end of this chapter. Stories continue to swirl around NASA and the astronauts. One fact is clear: Astronauts are military personnel. They have to follow military regulations in order to keep their pensions. Many of NASA's programs are paid for by the Department of Defense, even though NASA is a civilian agency.

The Stories Are True

Russian and American scientists confirm that stories about the astronauts seeing UFOs and other strange things are true.

Former Chief of NASA Communications Systems Maurice Chatelain and Russian scientists say there are large geometric structures on the moon, as well as ruins. Russia's Luna 9 and the United States Orbiter 2 have photographed these structures. The U.S. photos were taken by Orbiter 2 in 1966 on November 20. The photos were of an area of the moon known as The Sea of Tranquility. NASA has classified hundreds of lunar photographs and has never released them, despite the fact that this action is illegal.

This photo of Buzz Aldrin on the moon was taken by Neil Armstrong. This is the photo that former NASA scientist and researcher Richard Hoagland says on close examination shows ruins in the background, reflected in the face mask of Buzz Aldrin's helmet.
(U.S. National Archives and Records)

Egypt Checks In

There's more. These objects on the moon are not natural rock formations like the tower-shaped rocks in Utah and Arizona. These are
artifacts; the remains of structures built by an intelligent civilization,
similar to the cliff dwellings in Mesa Verde, Colorado.

Russian scientists led by Alexander Abramov discovered that there are
large objects arranged in the same grid pattern, including distances
between the objects, as the pyramids in Egypt. Richard Hoagland, U.S.
researcher and former NASA consultant, has discovered the same thing.

Buzz Aldrin in front of U.S. flag on the moon.
(U.S. National Archives and Records)

Abramov has applied the Egyptian pyramid pattern called an *abaka*, a
grid of forty-nine squares, to the structures on the moon. They match
exactly. In addition, William Blair of the Boeing Institute of Biotechnolo-
gy has discovered "obelisks" on the moon that form six isosceles triangles.

Review the Orbiter 2 Photos

It is against the law for NASA to classify data. So ask for it. Citizens should demand to see the entire series of Orbiter 2 photos. They are all numbered and in sequence. We will know if some are missing.

Next, these are public officials. A dollar says their salaries are higher than yours. Demand that they take a polygraph test and a drug screen to keep their jobs, just like the rest of us, and during the screening process, we should ask them about the missing data.

The Eagle Has Landed

When Apollo 11 landed on the moon, they put down in the Sea of Tranquility. Researcher Richard Hoagland claims that his computer analysis of the reflections off the space helmets of the astronauts claims to show ruins in the background.

Dr. Vladimir Azhazha also states that Neil Armstrong radioed mission control that UFOs were watching them during their romp on the moon.

THE ASTRONAUT'S STATEMENTS

Neil Armstrong and Edwin "Buzz" Aldrin
Both Neil Armstrong and Buzz Aldrin saw spacecraft shortly after landing on the moon. Here is what Russian scientists claim after having had a few conversations with Armstrong:

Neil Armstrong relayed the message to Mission Control that two large objects were watching them after having landed, near the moon module. But this message was never heard by the public, because NASA censored it.

Dr. Vladimir Azhazha
Dr. Aleksandr Kasantsev states that Aldrin took color movie film of the UFOs from inside the module and continued filming them after Armstrong went outside. Soviets say Armstrong said the story is true. He also told them the CIA was behind the cover-up.

Major Gordon Cooper

Major Gordon Cooper was one of the original Mercury astronauts and the last American to fly in space alone. On May 15, 1963 he blasted into space in a Mercury capsule for a 22-orbit journey around the planet.

In 1978 Major Cooper appeared before the UN General Assembly and asked for "open discussions" on the unidentified spacecraft matter. Cooper says the secrecy started out back in World War II or shortly thereafter.

> I think they thought the public would be frightened by knowing somebody had some vehicles that had so much better performance than anything we had, that maybe it would create panic if the public learned about them."

> They probably tried hushing it up until they found out more about them. Then as time went on, it just got more embarrassing trying to cover it up.

Cooper also wrote the following:

> As far as I'm concerned there have been far too many unexplained examples of unidentified flying objects to rule out the possibility that some other life form exists out beyond our own world.

> With the potential for there to be billions of planets out there, it seems pretty arrogant to think God would not have put life on some of them.

Major Cooper also viewed film taken by a crew of U.S. Air Force photographers using three different cameras to film landings during test flights. He describes what he saw on film:

> It was a typical double-inverted lenticular saucer. It had three (landing) gear on it and it put down on the lake bed. They were filming it as it sat there and they filmed it as it lifted up. It appeared to be big enough to have a crew of full-sized people on it.

Ed White and James McDivitt

Astronauts Ed White (the first American to walk in space) and James

McDivitt were passing over the Hawaiian Islands in the Gemini space-craft in June, 1965. They saw a strange-looking metallic object with long arms coming from it. The pictures have never been released. Astronaut Gordon Cooper later confirmed that McDivitt did, indeed, film something in space.

Donald Slayton

Donald Slayton, a Mercury astronaut, revealed in an interview that he had seen UFOs in 1951.

The astronauts didn't tell you everything they saw when they walked on the moon. Others may have been there before them.   (U.S. National Archives and Records)

Major Robert White

During a 58-mile-high flight of an X-15 aircraft on July 17, 1962, according to a *Time* magazine article, Major White exclaimed over the radio:

> I have no idea what it could be. It was grayish in color and about 30 to 40 feet away. There are things out there! There absolutely is!

James Lovell and Frank Borman
Astronauts James Lovell and Frank Borman were in a Gemini spacecraft
when they saw a UFO during their second orbit of a 14-day flight in
space in December, 1965. Borman reported that he saw an unidentified
spacecraft some distance from their capsule. Gemini control told him he
was seeing the final stage of their own Titan booster rocket. Borman
confirmed that he could see the booster rocket, but that he could also see
something else, something completely different. Here is the radio transcript:
> Gemini 7: "Bogey at 10 o'clock high"
> Control: "This is Houston. Say again 7."
> Gemini 7: "Said we have a bogey at 10 o'clock high."
> Control: "Gemini 7, is that the booster or is it an actual sighting?"
> Gemini 7: "We have several, actual sighting."
> Control: "Estimated size or distance?"
> Gemini 7: "We also have the booster in sight!"

Joseph Walker
NASA pilot Joseph Walker said that one of his tasks was to detect UFOs
during his X-15 test flights.

Eugene Cernan
Eugene Cernan was the Commander of Apollo 17. In a *Los Angeles Times*
article in 1973, he said this about UFOs:

> I've been asked (about UFOs) and I've said publicly I thought they
> were somebody else, some other civilization.

Maurice Chatelain
In 1979 Maurice Chatelain, former Chief of NASA Communications
Systems, confirmed that Neil Armstrong had reported seeing two
spacecraft on the rim of a crater when he was walking on the moon.
Chatelain was a respected scientist and engineer. He had received 11
patents and was formerly the head of Engineering Radar and Communications Systems for Ryan Electronics.

Says Chatelain:

> The encounter was common knowledge in NASA, but nobody
> talked about it until now. I think that Wally Schirra, aboard Mercury

8, was the first of the astronauts to use the code name "Santa Claus" to indicate the presence of flying saucers next to space capsules.

When James Lovell was on Apollo 8 he stated over his radio: "Please be informed that there is a Santa Claus," as he came around from the backside of the moon.

Mission Control celebrating man landing on the moon for the first first time in 1969. (Courtesy NASA)

Donald B. Ratsch

Donald B. Ratsch is an investigator and researcher. His specialty is collecting film footage from NASA space flights that show UFOs being present during the space flights. In November 1997 a personal friend of his arranged for him to meet with a man who said he had worked for NASA during the Apollo space missions. The man has requested anonymity, but here is what he told Ratsch.

During the Apollo missions he was one of the people who sat in front of the consoles monitoring information. The man was not exactly sure of which mission, but he figures it was most likely Apollo 12. He knew it did not happen during Apollo 11, because he was clear of the events surrounding the first landing on the moon, which was Apollo 11. He also knows it was not Apollo 13 because he distinctly remembers the problems surrounding the Apollo 13 flight.

He recalls that one evening during one of the flights, things got rather slow and there were not a lot of people around. So the man tuned into the transmissions being broadcast from the spacecraft on the air-to-ground/ground-to-air communications system. Things were rather mundane until about 8:30 P.M. when he heard the following exchange:

APOLLO: We have company.
HOUSTON: Say again?
APOLLO: I say we have company. (Short period of silence)
HOUSTON: (Emphatically) You were told not to make transmissions such as that! Put it on the flight recorder and we'll discuss it when you get back! (Long period of silence) 4

Dr. Edward Condon
There are three visual sightings made by the astronauts while in orbit which in the judgement of the writer (Condon) have not been adequately explained. These are:

1. Gemini 4, Astronaut McDivitt. Observation of a cylindrical object with a protuberance.
2. Gemini 4, Astronaut McDivitt. Observation of a moving bright light at a level higher than the Gemini spacecraft.
3. Gemini 7, Astronaut Borman saw what he referred to as a "bogey" flying in formation with the spacecraft.

The training and perspicacity of the astronauts put their reports of sightings in the highest category of credibility… Especially puzzling is the first one on the list, the daytime sighting of an object showing details such as arms (antennas?) protruding from an object having no noticeable angular extension.

Dr. Edward Condon, Project Director
Final Report of the Scientific Study of Unidentified Flying Objects
conducted for the U.S. Air Force.

The First Words on the Moon
The first words spoken on the moon were not Neil Armstrong's famous line: "That's one small step for man, one giant leap for mankind." The

actual first words were: "Contact light. Okay, engine stop," and they were spoken by Buzz Aldrin. The next words were spoken by Armstrong and they were: "Houston, Tranquility Base here. The Eagle has landed."

Neil's First Step

Back to Neil's step. With the whole world watching, he blew his lines. He was supposed to say: "That's one small step for a man. But, he left out the "a", resulting in a sentence which is redundant. Neil says he did say "a", but that it got lost in the transmission.

"Let's Get This Mother Out of Here"

"Let's get this mother out of here," were the actual last words spoken by an American astronaut, Eugene Cernan, on the moon. However, the "official" last words were:

> "We leave the moon as we came, and, God willing, as we shall return, with peace and hope for all mankind. Godspeed from the crew of Apollo 17."

THE MOON

- *What the astronauts really saw on the moon.*
- *Things you don't know about the moon.*

Bright Lights

Strange lights and moving shadows have been seen on the moon by astronomers so often that NASA has even published a catalog of them. From the year 1540 to 1967, NASA lists over 570 strange moon events in a report called "Chronological Catalogue of Reported Lunar Events." The report is also known as NASA Technical Report # R-277.

Lights on the moon were being seen so regularly that NASA started a study, called Operation Moonblink, to investigate them. NASA commissioned observatories from around the world to just watch and photograph the moon. Within months there were more than twenty-eight documented lunar events. Several of these events were confirmed by astronomers outside the program. Photographs of these events have never been released to the public. Why?

All Around the World

It turns out that the 570 "lunar lights" events cataloged by NASA are just a few of literally thousands of such observations that are regularly being made around the world by amateur astronomers. In fact, NASA took these 570 events from over 2,600 such events they had observed. In countries such as Japan and Great Britain, where astronomy is a national passion, these lunar activities have been well documented on film as well as still photographs. Huge objects, 4 to 5 miles in diameter have been seen moving across vast lunar craters at speeds up to 6,000 miles per hour! In addition, beams and long-distance rays of light have also been seen, as well as clouds, fog, and mists. All these anomalies on the moon have been cataloged for decades by credible scientists. 2

Moongate: Suppressed Findings of the U.S. Space Program, published in 1982, detailed a NASA film taken by astronauts on the moon that the author was able to get his hands on. It shows Apollo 11 astronauts planting the American Flag on the moon. Immediately after, a gust of wind blows the flag and it billows out. The astronauts run towards the camera and cover the lens with their hands. From then on, all flags sent up with the astronauts had wires in them to hold them out. 8

How Was the Moon Created?

Basically, nobody knows how the moon was created; however, there are two main schools of thought. One is the "Big Whack" theory. It says that something, maybe an asteroid, hit the earth millions of years ago, leaving a cloud of debris. The particles were eventually drawn together and formed the moon.

The other theory is that the moon broke off from the earth when it was a molten mass spinning rapidly, so rapidly that it formed a dumbbell shape and one end broke off. This theory was originally proposed in 1880 by Sir George Darwin, the son of famed evolutionist Charles Darwin.

The important thing is this: all modern theories of how the moon was formed are based on the premise that at one time the earth and the moon were one.

Eighth Grade Science

Here's what your eight grade science teacher didn't tell you. (It's not her fault; she didn't know either!) When the astronauts landed on the moon and brought back moon rocks in 1969, scientists scrutinized them carefully. They were shocked by what they discovered. Here's what they should have told you but didn't:

- *The moon rocks are over a billion years older than our earth!*
- *The moon dust is a billion years older than the rocks!*
- *Both the rocks and moon dust the astronauts brought back are older than our sun and our entire solar system!* 1
- *Chemical analysis showed that the composition of the moon rocks and moon dust was completely different, not even closely related to one another as would be expected.*

What this means is that it appears as if the moon was created somewhere else and someplace else! Also, it means that the moon rocks somehow got placed on the surface from somewhere else a billion years after the dust had formed.

That's just the start. The moon's orbit is nearly a perfect circle. Not only that, but the moon rotates just enough that one side, the same side, is always facing the earth.

The only objects I know of that do this are the satellites we launch. The moon behaves exactly like a satellite! The odds against the moon falling naturally into this kind of circular, limited spin orbit are astronomical! No pun intended.

Moon Measurements

Ultrasensitive seismic equipment has been placed on the moon by the astronauts. When Apollo 12 and Apollo 13 left the moon, they jettisoned the ascent stages of their spacecraft. The pieces of the craft fell back and hit the moon. Despite the relatively small size of these objects, when they struck, the entire moon reverberated for over 8 minutes! The moon registered as being more hollow than full! Scientists at NASA said, "It reacted like a gong!" They are at a loss to explain this, and so they avoid discussing it with the public.

Russian Findings

According to Soviet Col. Marina Popovich, Russian scientists have concluded that Phobos, one of the moons of Mars, is also an artificial structure, and hollow, as well! 9

The Shard

The Shard is an object that was photographed by Orbiter 3, a United States spacecraft that was launched before the Apollo space missions took place. It is a monument and it is a mile and a half high! World-renowned geologists agree with Dr. Bruce Cornet, who says: "No known natural process can explain such a structure."

The Shard is a huge and very distinctive feature. No astronomer or scientist denies its existence. Isn't it odd that you never heard of it before? According to Dr. Farouk El Baz, there are many undiscovered caverns suspected to exist beneath the surface of the moon. Several experiments have been flown to the moon to see if there were actually such caverns. 3. The public has never been given the results of these experiments.

The Tower

The Tower is another major structure on moon that has been photo-graphed from different altitudes and five different angles. The Tower is five miles high! Standing close to The Shard, The Tower is comprised of cubes, some as large as a mile wide. These two monuments were built by someone, they did not occur naturally. NASA has clear photographs of these two monuments. These photos belong to you; you paid for them, but NASA has never shown them to the public.

Contact NASA and tell them you want a copy of all Orbiter 3 photo series, un-retouched. Fax NASA Chief Administrator Charles F. Bolden at: (202) 358-4338.

The Bridge

On July 29, 1953 *New York Herald Tribune* science editor John J. O'Neill saw a 12-mile long bridge on the moon. He reported his find to the Association of Lunar and Planetary Observers. At the time, they laughed at him. Then a month later an astronomer from England, Dr. H. P. Wilkens, came forward and said that he too had seen The Bridge. Wilkens told the British Broadcasting Company:

> It looks artificial. It's almost incredible that such a thing could have formed in the first instance, or if it was formed, could have lasted during the ages in which the moon has been in existence.

The Bridge was confirmed again by a member of the British Astronomical Association, Patrick Moore. Moore said The Bridge had appeared overnight. 4

The Man in the Moon

Researcher and writer George Leonard spent years poring over NASA lunar photographs. Leonard has said:

> The moon is occupied by an intelligent race or races which probably moved in from outside the solar system. The moon is firmly in possession of these occupants.

Leonard goes on to say:

> Evidence of their presence is everywhere, on the surface, on the near side and the hidden side, in the craters, on the maria, and in the highlands. They are changing its face. Suspicion or recognition of that triggered the U.S. and Soviet moon programs.

"Somebody Else Is on the Moon"

The above headline is also the title of Leonard's 1977 book. In it, he publishes photographs of The Bridge and photos showing tracks in the moon dust and large domes in the center of artificially lit craters. There are domes and ruins on the moon. Leonard states that a NASA scientist told him he was right, but that the discoveries had not been made public yet. 5

Astronaut Underground

Rumors swirl around what the astronauts have or have not seen. Underground sources claiming to have intelligence connections say the astronauts saw plenty, and that they were sent to the moon specifically to confirm indications of intelligent life. Naturally, the astronauts, as a group, deny seeing anything. However, the evidence is so overwhelming against their denials that it's obvious we have not been told the truth.

Researcher and author Timothy Goode states that a personal friend of his who was with British military intelligence was with a scientist who was having a discussion with a very prominent astronaut. The astronaut told the scientist that NASA had been warned to stay off the moon by other beings. That's why after 30 years since the last landing we have never been back. 6

Russian Findings

Russia's Luna 9 has also photographed artificially made moon structures. The Russians have discovered several other objects, among them huge obelisks. Russian scientist and engineer Alexander Abramov has calculated that these obelisks are arranged in exactly the same position as the tops of the great pyramids of Egypt. The location of each of these monuments is based on a grid of 49 squares called an *abaka*.

Pyramids on the Moon

The structures the Russians identified as obelisks have also been reported in the U.S. They are especially visible in The Sea of Tranquility area, right where the Apollo astronauts landed. U.S. observers have sometimes referred to them as narrow pyramids. On November 22, 1966 the *Washington Post* featured them on the front page. The headline read: "Six Mysterious Statuesque Shadows Photographed on the moon by Orbiter."

The Hubble Space Telescope

On April 16, 1999, NASA finally released for the first time Hubble Space Telescope images taken of the moon. Astronomers, researchers and scientists worldwide were stunned. Ever since the Hubble had been put in space, NASA had been telling the scientific community that the Hubble Space Telescope did not have the capability to take clear images of the moon.

When asked, NASA consistently said that the telescope's instruments were too sensitive to record the moon surface because it was too bright. This, in spite of the fact that the telescopes instruments were calibrated by focusing on the clouds surrounding the earth, which are several times brighter than the moon's surface. NASA claimed that even the dark side and shadow edges of the moon's surface were too bright. When confronted with this obvious contradiction, NASA refused to comment.

Upon the release of the moon photos, mainstream astronomy publication, *Sky and Telescope Magazine* noted the discrepancy and stated:

> The Space telescope Science Institute (STSI Division of NASA) released pictures of a celestial object that most people thought the Hubble Telescope was not allowed to view: our own moon.

The recently released images from the Hubble were poor and once again, NASA refused to release any high resolution images or any infra-red images that the Hubble also records. The Hubble has taken stunning high resolution images of objects that are millions of miles away, such as the planets Saturn and Jupiter, yet NASA claims that the Hubble can't do the same for the moon which is only 250,000 miles away. [1]

Enough is Enough

There is so much evidence of other beings on the moon that I could go on forever. The bottom line is this: There were and currently are other beings on "our" moon. Here are some things you can do:

1. Ask NASA for your copies of the Orbiter 2 and Orbiter 3 lunar photos.

2. Ask NASA for your copy of film footage taken of the dark side of the moon during the moon missions. They have it; why haven't you seen it? Why have they never released it to the public?

3. Get a telescope. Look at the moon for ten minutes a night for the next couple of months. You may be surprised at what you see.

Lunar Probe Attempts

In their first attempts to land a probe on the moon, both the U.S. and the Russians failed miserably.

The United States

Ranger 3: Missed the moon completely.
Ranger 4: Crashed into the moon.
Ranger 5: Missed the moon by 450 miles.
Ranger 6: Electrical system failed.

The Soviet Union

Luna 5: Crashed into the moon going full speed.
Luna 6: Missed the moon.
Luna 7: Crashed on the moon.
Luna 8: Crashed on the moon.
Luna 9: Landed successfully.

Not Enough Gravity?

After Luna 9's successful landing things got much better for both space programs. Luna 9 was able to take gravitational readings from the moon's surface. The problem appears to have been miscalculations of the moon's gravitational forces. The first lunar missions were based on the moon being a solid, homogenous object. After Luna 9 scientists were able to determine that the moon was more like a hollow ball, with several large centers of gravity just below the moon's surface, almost as if there were huge structures built underground. These large concentrations of gravity are known as *mascons*.

As NASA scientist Robin Brett once said: "It seems easier to explain the non-existence of the moon, than its existence." [7]

THE FACE ON MARS

Mars has a face! No doubt you've seen pictures of it on the covers of tabloids at your local supermarket. Yet there is much more to the story than the mere resemblance of some blurry photos to a human face.

The Story

Photographs taken by NASA's 1976 Viking space probe show what appears to be a humanoid face in the Cydonia region of the planet Mars. In addition there appear to be other manufactured items, or artifacts. These other artifacts appear to be large pyramids and other structures. They were discovered by NASA scientists who closely examined thousands of photographs using modern computer technology not available in 1976 when the photos were taken. 3

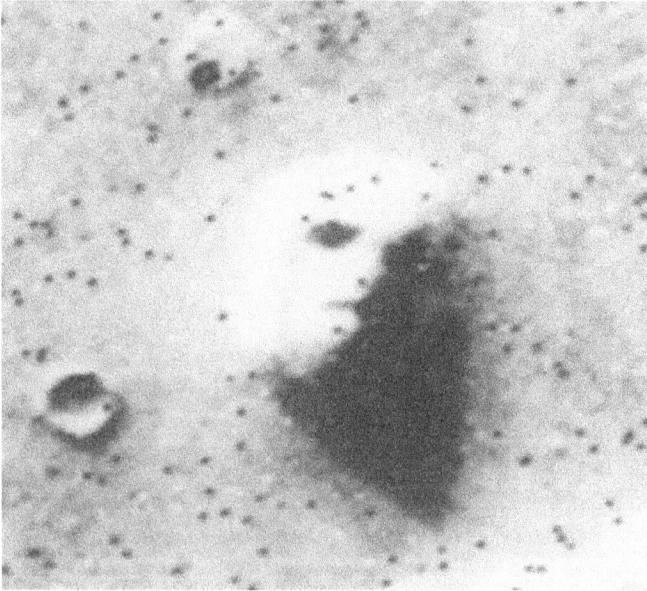

This is the famous Face on Mars, photographed by the Viking space probe in 1976. The face appears to be manufactured and not naturally occurring.
(Courtesy NASA)

What They Found

The "face" and other structures have mathematical and geometrical correlations that match those of the Sphinx and pyramids found in Egypt. 2

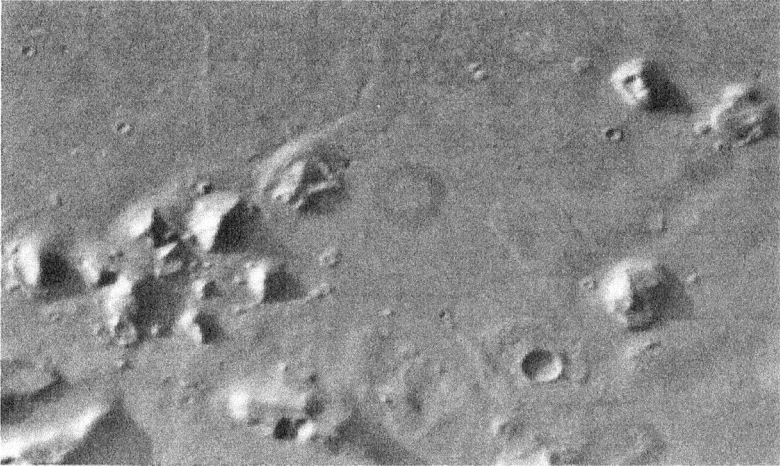

Here is the Cydonia region of Mars. Along with the Face, there are huge pyramids which appear in the center and upper-left portion of the photo. From space, these structures are identical to our planet's Egyptian pyramids. (Courtesy NASA)

Richard Hoagland

The key scientist investigating this phenomenon is a fellow by the name of Richard Hoagland. Although some conventional scientists deride his conclusions, his work has been extraordinary. He has been supported by many scientists and engineers at NASA and the Jet Propulsion Laboratory (JPL) in Pasadena, CA. In fact, I was present during one of his presentations when some scientists from JPL walked up and handed him high-resolution photos of Mars, showing clearly that intelligent life forms had built structures there. One of them said to Hoagland, "We were wondering when you were going to see this." Referring to the fact that Hoagland had already identified many other "built" structures on Mars and the moon. Hoagland has spent over 10 years investigating Martian and Lunar photos using computer-enhancement technology. 1

The United Nations

Hoagland has been invited on several occasions to present his findings to the United Nations. His U.N. presentations are now available on videotape. Hoagland is a legitimate and brilliant scientist who worked for NASA for many years. He was one of the originators of the "Calling Card" plaque that was put on the Pioneer 10 space probe. The plaque describes humans, our science, and culture to any beings who may come in contact with the probe.

Richard Hoagland has been the science advisor to Walter Cronkite at CBS and Kevin Sanders at CNN. He was also the editor of *Star & Sky Magazine*. He is a past winner of the prestigious Angstrom Award, and has appeared on *Nightline*, Art Bell's radio show and *Coast to Coast* with George Noory. He is the author of several books, including *The Monuments of Mars*. He knows what he's talking about!

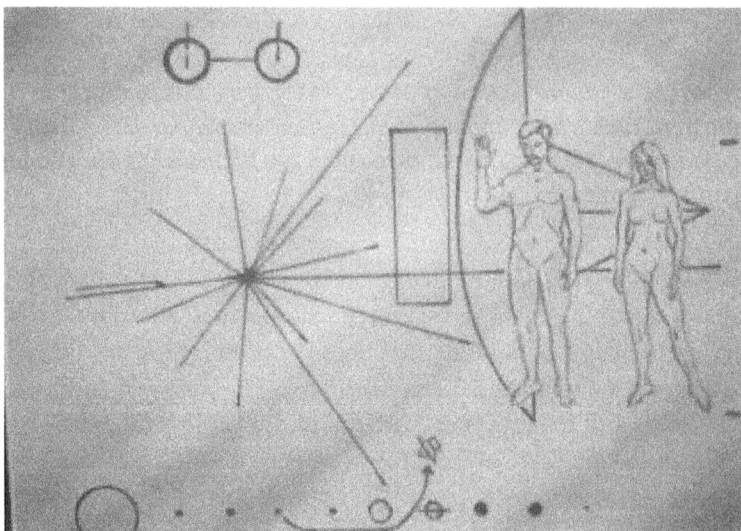

This is the plaque placed on the Voyager spacecraft by NASA which describes humans and the location of Earth in the event that alien beings encounter the craft. (Courtesy NASA)

Another Scientist Speaks Up

At the 191st national meeting of the American Astronomical Society (AAS), Dr. Tom Van Flandern presented his conclusions that the face on Mars is not an optical illusion nor is it a naturally occurring feature. Dr. Van Flandern holds a doctorate in astronomy from Yale University. He was also chief of celestial mechanics at the U.S. Naval Observatory, a highly respected astronomical facility. Van Flandern said there was less than a 1 percent chance the face was not made by intelligent hands. 4

Van Flandern based his conclusions on new analysis of the existing data. He concluded his discussion by telling the five hundred astronomers who were listening to his presentation: "I suggest that in view of these test results, we prepare ourselves for a cultural shock certainly unrivaled in recent times."

NASA Speaks

In response to an avalanche of questions from the public and amateur astronomers NASA recently issued a lengthy and technical statement. The statement began by saying that NASA would look further into the "face" on Mars issue. They also stated they were not responding to public pressure.

The Controversy

Another probe, the Mars Observer, was scheduled to reach Mars in 1992. It had the capability to clearly photograph objects on Mars as small as a coffee table. In an unprecedented move, as the Observer began to orbit Mars NASA turned off the transmitter. They then claimed that they could not turn it back on.

More Lost Probes

In case you were asleep, late in 1995 and again in mid 1996, NASA "lost" two more space probes. No explosion, no explanation, just lost! The stories of these lost probes were carried in the back pages of most American newspapers.

Several NASA insiders have come forward to say that the agency "pulled the plug" on these probes to keep the public from finding out about extraterrestrial beings.

Lost Power on the Mars Rover

Early in March 1998, NASA announced that the Mars Rover lost complete power and was unable to send back any more pictures. Is this possible? Of course. Mars is a long way off and malfunctions do happen. Is it likely? No! Given NASA's history of deceit and lies to the American public, you can assume they are lying once again.

Venus, Too!

NASA has also discovered a complex consisting of a Sphinx and pyramids identical to the ones in Egypt on the planet Venus in 1985. They didn't tell you about that find either. NASA is bound by law to release all their findings, so here's what they did. They broadcast the report over a small station almost nobody could get, and of course, since nobody else was broadcasting this information, those who heard it didn't believe it.

It's the old disinformation technique of telling people the absolute truth, but doing it in such a way that no one will believe it. Just so you know, NASA has mapped over 90 percent of the total surface of Venus. 5

STAR WARS AND SATELLITES

- *What Star Wars really does.*
- *What the Soviet Union really fears.*
- *Lost satellites.*

Our Satellites Are Picking up Flying Saucers

There are over two thousand satellites circling the planet. They're up there for various reasons: spying, communications, weather forecasting, military purposes, and scientific exploration. Some are orbiting and others are geo-stationary, which means they stay in the same position over the planet because they orbit at exactly the same speed as the earth's rotation, effectively staying in the same place at an altitude of 22,800 miles above the earth. Polar-orbiting satellites circle the earth from south to north or vice-versa, at lower altitudes of 500 to 1,000 miles. Our satellites are picking up flying saucers in photographs, infrared images, and with electromagnetic sensors on a consistent, regular basis.

Weather Satellites

The weather satellites take thousands of photographs daily to track world-wide weather patterns. On many photos clear images of flying saucers and other large spacecraft have appeared, especially some of the triangle-shaped craft. The most well-known of the weather satellites are the NOAA series.

The photographs in this chapter were taken by the NOAA 12 satellite. The objects in the photos are many miles below the satellite, which means they are huge! Many of the craft have a wing-span of several miles! These are the classic triangle craft that have been seen over Belgium in 1989 and video-taped over Phoenix in March and April, 1997. Since the satellite cameras have grid lines across the lenses, you can tell if something was really there or not. If something was there due to a transmission flaw, you would know because the grid lines would not appear. In all cases, the grid lines are intact.

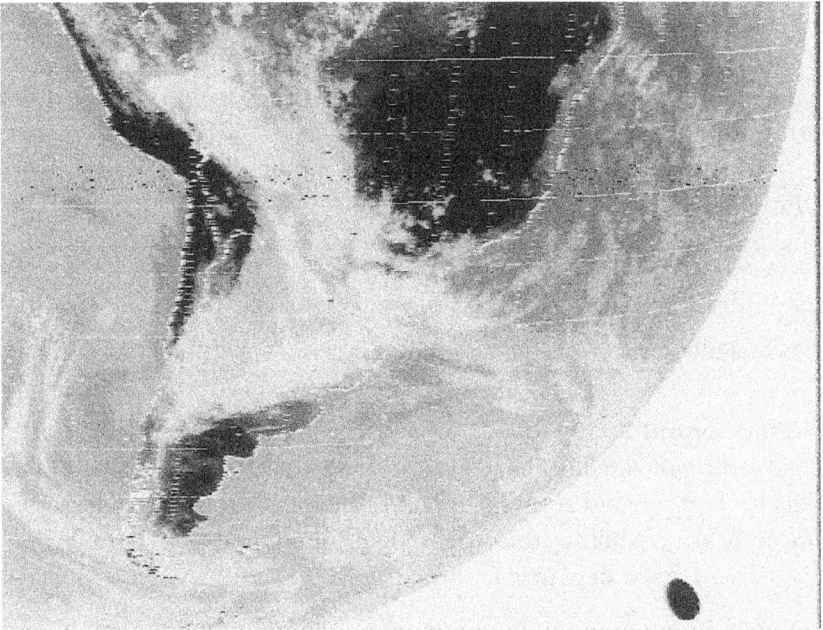

Photo of a flying saucer taken by a weather satellite at an altitude of 28,800 miles. Also recorded were infrared signatures from the craft.
(Photo courtesy Phil Imbrogno.)

Infrared photos taken by satellite indicate that flying saucers give off a tremendous amount of energy called plasma energy, and it is often accompanied by strong magnetic fields. Other wave-lengths of energy are given off and affect light-sensitive film, thus causing many flying saucer photographs to be blurry. They are also strong emitters of infrared energy.

U.S. Surveillance Satellites

NOAA Series
Meteorological polar satellites.

GOES Series
Geo-stationary weather satellite.

Corona
Highest resolution of all reconnaissance satellites.

Defense Support Program
For detection of missile launches. Uses infrared, radiation, visible (DSP) electromagnetic, and other special sensors.

Keyhole Series
Digital imaging and radar reconnaissance satellite.

Ferret
Electromagnetic reconnaissance satellite.

Strange Signals
U.S. government satellites have also been receiving strange signals. The signals have originated from just behind the moon and are being bounced off our satellites to some undetermined point on earth. Some of the signals are even in Morse Code.

Star Wars
The Star Wars satellite defense system is also tracking flying saucers. Though the primary purpose of satellite defense systems is to track incoming missiles, there are many who believe that tracking flying saucers is the true main purpose of the Star Wars system. This thought is particularly interesting in light of the fact that the Star Wars system was advocated and built by President Ronald Reagan at the same time he was working with the Russians to lessen the threat of a missile strike through detente and the now-famous summit meetings with soviet leader Mikhail Gorbachev.

Flying saucer recorded over western United States. (Photo courtesy Phil Imbrogno)

While all this was happening, some soviet military leaders actually praised and supported the Strategic Defense Initiative. Add to this Reagan's statements to the Geneva Summit about alien visitors, (See Chapter 3, Government At Work) then throw in the film footage taken from the space shuttle showing a UFO being fired at by what appears to be a burst of laser energy, and you have a whole new way to look at Star Wars. 15

What Is It: The Strategic Defense Initiative?
The Defense Support System (DSP), better known as Star Wars, is comprised of a series of satellites. Each satellite has varying capabilities for the detection of objects.

The Real Danger
On several occasions in the past the missile defense systems of both the Soviet Union and the United States went on full alert and a missile launch was almost triggered. The alerts had been caused by UFOs rapidly approaching earth from deep space and decelerating in the earth's atmosphere. The movement into the atmosphere alerted satellite sensors and computers that a missile launch had occurred. In particular, the Russians realized that they were at considerable risk of being mistakenly

attacked by a U.S. defense system that was being triggered by flying saucers.

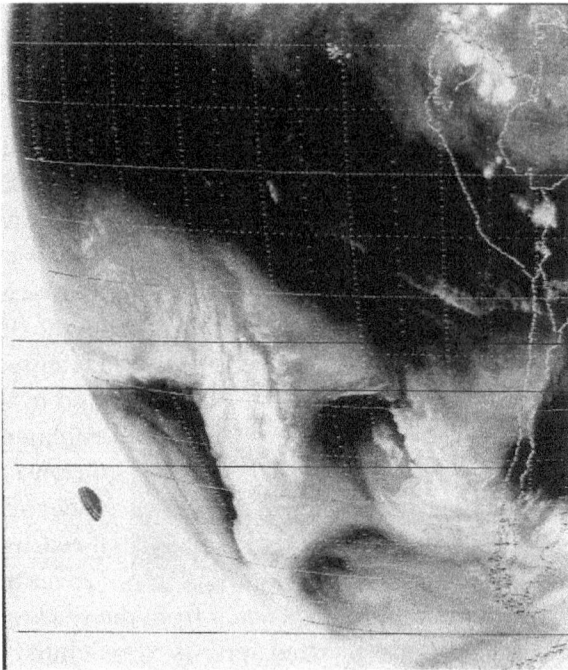

Another saucer breaks the atmosphere during a routine weather reconnaissance.
(Photo courtesy Phil Imbrogno)

UFOs and Security

In the June 1989 issue of the Soviet Military Review the leading article was titled "UFOs and Security." In it Aleksandr Kuzovkin states:

> We believe that lack of information on the characteristics and influence of UFOs increase the threat of incorrect identification. Then, mass transition of UFOs along trajectories close to those of combat missiles could be regarded by computers as an attack.

In the autumn of 1960 all bombers at Travis Air Force Base in the United States were put on red alert for an attack against the Soviet Union after the base radar detected "targets" flying via the North Pole to the U.S. territory. Suddenly the "targets" disappeared from the screen and were later explained as "radar reflections off the moon."

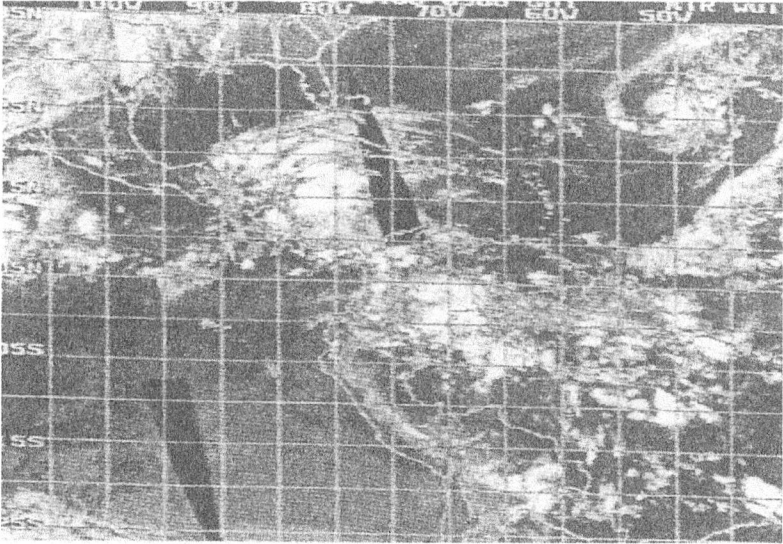

Huge triangle craft photographed in earth's upper atmosphere by weather satellites. (Photo courtesy Phil Imbrogno)

A Word About Meteors

Weather and spy satellites are also witness to some incredible meteor events inside the earth's atmosphere. About twenty times per month a large meteor descends through the atmosphere and disintegrates with a huge explosion. Some of the blasts are equal to 15,000 tons of high explosives, or the size of a small nuclear bomb. It is thought that such a meteor blast occurred just above the earth's surface in 1908 in Tunguska, Siberia. Known as the Tunguska blast, the detonation completely flattened hundreds of square miles of thick, heavy forest. 18

More About Tunguska

The blast in Tunguska is a well-known event. Tunguska is located in a remote area of Siberia in Russia near the Podkamennaya Tunguska River. It occurred on June 30, 1908 around 7:40 A.M. The event was an explosion so great that it was the equivalent of a thousand times the force of the atomic bomb dropped on Hiroshima in World War II. The blast completely flattened an entire forest of tress for hundreds of miles in all directions. The fireball was seen as far away as 500 miles!

Everybody has a different theory as to what exactly occurred. The explosion had all of the earmarks of a nuclear explosion. Scientists think that it was a meteor exploding within the earth's atmosphere, just above the planet's surface. Japanese scientists are convinced that the explosion was an **alien** spacecraft and have marked the site with a plaque commemorating it as an extraterrestrial event.

Confirmation of an Alien Event

A contact within the U.S. intelligence community told researcher and author Linda Moulton Howe, that the explosion was in fact caused by an alien spacecraft. The source said that aliens have told the U.S. government the explosion was the result of a nuclear power generator being accidentally ejected from an alien craft that was flying within the earth's atmosphere. [21]

Fastwalkers

Flying saucers picked up by spy satellites have been given the term *fastwalkers*, or FW for short. Sources who work inside the defense industry say satellites are detecting fastwalkers at a rate of three to four every month. One such person is Ronald Regehr, an aerospace engineer who has worked on the Defense Support Program for over 25 years. He wrote the performance/design specifications for each series of sensor systems, the operational software specifications, and edited the satellite performance reports. Regehr also prepared the SED (Sensor Evolutionary Design) Familiarization Manual, used to introduce the DSP to air force personnel new to the program.

Regehr was able to analyze pages from the Defense Support Program (DSP). The report is an evaluation written for the Air Force on the DSP's performance. The report indicates that the satellite defense systems are seeing objects coming in from deep space, in a curved trajectory, totally unlike that of a meteor. "I should know - I wrote that report for the first two years of DSP operation," says Regehr.

*A section of one of the coded DSP reports. Note some
of the lines reading: "UCF; UNUSUAL, Prob.FW"*
(Courtesy Ron Regehr)

Regehr points out that fastwalkers frequently slow down, curve, change
direction, and then leave the earth's atmosphere at less than escape
velocity. Meteors never exhibit such behavior. The behavior fits that of
an intelligently guided, powered craft.

> Fastwalker: In the jargon of scientific intelligence, a source of electro-
> magnetic radiation moving at high speed in the outer layers of the at-
> mosphere, which triggers the sensors of spy satellites.
>
> *Jaques Vallee*
> *Fastwalker, 1996*

Lost in Space

We have missing satellites and space probes. Some have malfunctioned,
some have crashed, some have exploded. Others have just disappeared,
both visually and electronically, never to be seen or heard from again.
The United States has lost two unmanned space probes heading for Mars
and three nuclear satellites. 11 In 1995 satellite NOAA 13 disappeared. 12
The Soviets have acknowledged losing six nuclear satellites and several

unmanned space probes. 14 Two Chinese satellites have also disappeared: Feyung I and Feyung II. 13

A Correlation to UFOs?

What do lost space probes and satellites have to do with flying saucers? No one really knows. However, there is a strong suspicion that in some cases there is a correlation; either that or the probes have been grabbed by **aliens**, for reasons I can only guess. Or, the government authorities have been up to their old tricks and are lying about what these satellites are really showing, a planet surrounded by flying saucers!

Missing Space Probes and Satellites

March 28, 1989
The Russian Probe, Phobos 2 was lost under mysterious and unexplained circumstances. Russian Colonel Marina Popovich has since stated that Soviet missions had determined that the probe's namesake, Phobos 2, one of the moons of Mars, is in fact artificial and hollow.

January 29, 1992
The Office of Strategic Defense Initiative (Star Wars) convinces NASA to send an unmanned probe to the moon. The probe, "Clementine I," is launched into a polar orbit around the moon. Because of it's high orbit it is able to map almost the entire surface of the moon.

Scientists are shocked to find that the surface variation in topography is up to twelve miles, not five miles as previously believed. They discover that some of the moon's mountains are a half-mile taller than Mount Everest, the highest mountain on earth. Clementine orbits around the moon for seventy-four days and then malfunctions. 4

September 1992
The Mars Observer is launched. The Observer is designed to provide an extremely detailed mapping of the entire surface of Mars using the latest technology, including short laser bursts bounced off the surface for pin-point accuracy. Originally, NASA has no plans to put a camera on board.

Why? Nonetheless, scientists fight NASA like cats and dogs. They win and an innovative new system of cameras is installed. 8

August 21, 1994
The Jet Propulsion Laboratory loses contact with Mars Observer just hours before it was scheduled to begin orbiting the Red Planet. This was the first failure of its kind in 17 years. Several different reasons are given for the loss of the Observer, but no really knows why. 8 The Mars Observer is never heard from again.

January 14, 1995
A NASA investigatory panel announces, "No one will probably ever know exactly what happened to the spacecraft." The panel's attempt to understand the Observer's silence was hindered because the spacecraft telemetry was turned off before the pressurization of its fuel tanks as it prepared to enter orbit around Mars. 9

January 1994
Turkish TURKSAT I and BULSAT I communications satellites are lost when a French Ariane launch vehicle's third-stage propulsion system fails. 1

July 1995
China loses its Apstar-2 satellite when launch vehicle explodes. Hughes Space and Communications Company and Great Wall Industrial Corporation disagree as to the cause of the explosion. 2

April 1995
United States satellite NOAA 13 vanishes from orbit.

November 17, 1995
Russia's Mars space probe is lost when a booster malfunctions and falls back to earth carrying 270 grams of live plutonium. 6 Two years later, health officials attribute a worldwide increase in lung cancer rates to highly active radioactive material being disbursed into the atmosphere from falling and disintegrating satellites.

November 22, 1995

Two Russian spy satellites are announced to have been lost by the
Russian Embassy. 7

December, 1995
Launch of Athena rocket from Vandenderg Air Force Base fails.

September 1996
The Cosmos 1275 satellite disintegrates. The crash is attributed to a
collision with space debris. 3

July 1997
Lewis satellite fails after being launched from Vandenberg on an Athena
rocket.

December 25, 1997
The final booster on a Russian-made Proton-K rocket fails. The "communications" satellite it was carrying falls into an orbit of only 125 miles
up instead of the 22,500 mile-high orbit it was planned for. The lower
orbit makes the satellite totally useless and subject to falling into the
atmosphere and burning up. 10

April 15, 1999
Delta rocket launched from Vandenberg AF base fails while carrying an
Orion satellite.

April 27, 1999
Athena rocket carrying an Ikonos 1 satellite lifted off at 11:22 A.M. from
Vandenberg Air Force base near Lompoc, California. Sometime before it
reached the intended 400 mile-high orbit, the Associated Press, NBC,
ABC, CNN and CBS news reported that the satellite simply disappeared.
No explosion, no crash, just gone. NBC news reported that this was the
third such satellite loss in less than 12 months at a total loss of over $3
Billion dollars!

April 28, 1999
Launch of a Cosmos-3M rocket carrying an ABRIXAS satellite fails, the
satellite is lost.

April 30, 1999

Titan 4 missile carrying a Milstar 2F-1 satellite is launced from Cape Canaveral. The launch fails and the satellite goes into the wrong orbit where it is useless and doomed to eventually fall and burn.

October 1, 1999

"Mars Probe Lost Due to Simple Math Error." On October 1, 1999, the front page of the *Los Angeles Times* as well as all major U.S. newspapers reported the following story:

> NASA lost its $125-million Mars Climate Orbiter because spacecraft engineers failed to convert from English to metric measurements when exchanging vital data before the craft was launched, space agency officials said Thursday. "That is so dumb," said John Logsdon, director of George Washington University's space policy institute ...The loss of the Mars probe was the latest in a series of major spaceflight failures this year that destroyed billions of dollars worth of research, military and communications satellites or left them spinning in useless orbits.

December 6, 1999

Mars Polar Lander enters Mars' atmosphere and fails to respond. NASA announces that it was crashed or lost in space. The craft is never heard from again.

August 11, 2011

The Pentagon's Hypersonic Plane Goes Missing. A test flight of the Falcon HTV-2, a hypersonic plane capable of reaching speeds roughly 20 times the speed of sound (15,000 miles per hour), ended unexpectedly early on Thursday when ground controllers lost contact with the arrowhead-shaped plane less than half an hour after it took to the skies. It simply disappeared on the edge of space and has never been recovered.

SCIENCE

- *The Universe*
- *Stars*
- *Time*
- *Gravity*
- *Life on other planets*

THE UNIVERSE

One of the problems in accepting the idea of space-traveling **aliens** is understanding what our traditional modern-day scientists already confirm as being true. The universe is so large and so strange that we are simply not able to incorporate it into our everyday experiences and thinking. Let's consider some things that may not be apparent.

Stars

We cannot see very many stars from where we stand. This makes it difficult to comprehend how many stars there really are. That is: How many suns actually exist? And remember, each sun has the potential of supporting many planets.

If you stand on the clearest and starriest of nights in a remote pasture in Wyoming (away from city lights) all the stars you can see with the naked eye will total less than three thousand. Is it any wonder we have difficulty comprehending the existence of billions and trillions of stars? And many of those stars are in fact entire galaxies each consisting of at least a billion stars. Many contain trillions of stars.

Get a Telescope

Modern telescopes confirm that there are well over 10 billion galaxies, each consisting of untold billions of stars. Galaxies are so big that each is considered to be an island universe unto itself. Even the largest tele-scopes can detect less than one tenth of 1 percent of our own galaxy's trillion stars.

A telescope doesn't just magnify items. It gathers light as well. This allows you to see more stars; for example, just looking at the same section of sky through a telescope will allow you to see ten times more stars than if you were just looking with the naked eye. Instead of three thousand, you could see and count thirty thousand!

Adding a camera and film lets the observer gather and store light. Using a camera and film allows you to record and store millions of stars. The retina in your eye can't do this, that's why you can't see all the stars that are really there with the naked eye.

Life on Other Planets

Our everyday assumption that we are the only intelligent life in the universe, until proven otherwise, stems partly from the small and limited number of stars we can actually see when we look up at night. Statistical-ly, if the universe consisted only of the stars we can see, there would be a chance we were the only folks in town. However, when we look at the staggering, true numbers of stars, it is logically and statistically impossible that there is no other life as intelligent as ours. If only one planetary system in a billion has intelligent life, then thousands of such worlds are hidden in any one galaxy alone.

A Single Grain of Sand

Take a trip to the beach, if you have one nearby. If not, just go stand in a sandbox at any playground. Take a magnifying glass with you. Reach down and pick up a handful of sand. Now, sift it in your hand until you have only a single grain in your fingers. Look at the grain of sand through the magnifying glass. Look at the facets in that grain of sand. It's a magnificent piece of nature, like a masterfully cut diamond.

Now make this assumption: This is the only grain of sand in the world that has a structure like this. All the other grains of sand in the world are plain, with no distinguishing characteristics. Does that make sense? It's a ridiculous assumption, isn't it?

Well, that's what modern scientists have done with our planet. They operate from the basic assumption that we are the only planet with life on it until proven otherwise; that all the other stars and planets in the universe are plain, no distinguishing characteristics, no life. This is even more ridiculous than the grain-of-sand assumption. I repeat: Does this make any sense?

The Numbers
While you're at the beach or in the sandbox, contemplate this: There are more stars in the universe than there are grains of sand on all the beaches on our entire planet! Scientists estimate that in our galaxy alone (the Milky Way) there are over 100 billion stars (suns).

Million vs. Billion
The words "million" and "billion" sound alike. People throw both words around and use them interchangeably as if they were close to each other or related to one another. They are not. There is a huge difference between a million and a billion. Here is one way to look at it:

> *If you have a million dollars, you can spend a thousand dollars a day for about three and a half years. But, if you have a billion dollars you can spend a thousand dollars a day for over two thousand years!*

A Different Way to Look at the Possibilities
If our solar system is average, and right now scientists believe that it is, then most solar systems have about ten planets.

That means our galaxy has a thousand billion planets. Just in our galaxy.

If only one planet out of thousand has life on it, then our galaxy alone has one billion planets with life on them!

If only one out every thousand of these life-bearing planets has intelligent life, such as our planet, then there are one million planets like ours with intelligent life, just in our galaxy alone.

If we make the assumption that humans represent an average rate of development, then half the planets (500,000) would be less developed than we are and half them (500,000) would be more advanced.

In 1943 during World War II the United States built ten thousand airplanes. Thirty years later we were in space. We accomplished both feats with technology that was less than a hundred years old.

This means 500,000 inhabited planets more advanced than we are, combined, could have built five billion spacecraft in a single year! 4

The Size of Stars
The size of a star can vary dramatically. There are very tiny stars the size of an asteroid, and there are huge stars. Some stars are so large that 25 billion Planet Earths could fit inside one of them. 2

Most of the Universe Is Invisible
Ninety percent of the mass in the universe is literally invisible to us. No light emanates from it and we cannot see it. Scientists know it is there because they are able to measure the gravitational pull these invisible masses exert on visible bodies. Not only that, but if you look at the entire spectrum of frequencies in the universe, man's five senses can only pick up a very small amount of them. Think of a dog whistle: Blow as hard as you can, you won't hear a sound. The whistle is out of your limited frequency range.

Distances
Distances are so great that it takes the light from most stars years to reach us. When we look up we can never see what is going on now, we can only see what has already happened.

To reverse this, suppose that there are people living on a planet circling a star in our galaxy. If they had a telescope pointed at the earth right now they would be seeing what you were doing in the sixties. They would look in and see people wearing bellbottoms! (For those readers who weren't born in the sixties, they wouldn't see you at all!)

Time

Much is made of the assumption that the stars are so far apart that no beings could travel to another star in a single lifetime. The key factor of course, is time. However, time is a very complex subject. Here are some things you can begin to think about when it comes to considering time. These facts are well known by our physicists and based to a large degree on Einstein's work.

Time is relative; it has nothing to do with distance. So stop making the assumption that it will take a certain amount of time to travel a certain distance. The two are completely unrelated. Many alien beings have clearly stated this. It is why they are able to travel vast distances across the universe almost instantaneously.

TRY THIS:

Put two dots on opposite ends of a sheet of paper. Traditional thinking tells you the shortest distance from one point to the other is to draw a straight line between the two. You then think you measure the time it takes to go between the two points.

WRONG!

The shortest distance is to fold the paper until the two points touch. This is how the aliens travel great distances without time being involved.

I know this sounds impossible, but time as we know it does not really exist. Time is only a reference point, just as a mile marker is a reference point. Look at it this way: If there is only one marker, what does that mean? Nothing! But if there are two or more they actually have meaning. They are references denoting something to you. This is well known and acknowledged by our physicists.

Different parts of our universe have different times. This is also a well-known and established fact. Here's an example: Let's say you have a twin sister. NASA gives her a ride to Jupiter where she sets up house and lives for the next 10 years. Jupiter has a different day than the earth (the amount of time it takes for the planet to make one revolution) and a longer year. So, at the end of the 10-year period, who's older, you or her? You have both lived in completely different time references.

Time is affected by gravity. The slight alteration in gravity caused by changing our distance from the earth's center (such as going to the top of the Empire State Building) is enough to produce a measurable change in the flow of time!

Time slows as you approach the speed of light. If you traveled in space at just below the speed of light for 10 years you would be and appear 10 years older. However, people on earth during the same time period will have experienced and aged 70 years!

Gravity

Since gravity plays a role in space travel as well as in the flow of time, here are a few words about one of our most misunderstood natural forces. When the space shuttle takes off it goes straight up vertically to get through the least amount of atmosphere as quickly as possible. When the shuttle attains the correct orbital height, they shut down the engines and the shuttle simply falls. The pull of the earth's gravity causes the shuttle to fall in an arc. The arc of the shuttle's fall matches the curve of the earth and the shuttle continues to fall endlessly.

Like Sky Surfing

The astronauts and the shuttle have not escaped gravity. When you see films of them cavorting around the cabin seemingly weightless, it is not because they are weightless, it is because they are falling! Just like a sky surfer before he opens his parachute. The astronauts are falling at a rate of 20,000 miles per hour!

Don't Jump

There is a lot of gravity up where the astronauts are. If you could build a skyscraper up to that orbital height (about 250 miles) and stand on the roof, you would still weigh about the same. You would not float off the roof of the building. In fact, if you jumped, you would go straight down.

Just Up the Coast

The astronauts in orbit are not that far away. They are about the same distance from earth as San Diego is from Santa Barbara, or about 250 miles.

> I have begun to feel that there is a tendency in 20th century science to forget that there will be a 21st century science, and indeed a 30th century science, from which vantage points our knowledge of the universe may appear quite different than it does to us. We suffer perhaps, from temporal provincialism, a form of arrogance that has irritated posterity.
>
> *Dr. J. Allen Hynek*

Albert Einstein

Once, while serving as a professor at Princeton University, the great physicist Albert Einstein was handing out that year's final exam. A student stood up and blurted out, "But Professor Einstein, this is exactly the same final exam you gave us last year!" Einstein turned and said, "Yes, you are right. It is the same exam. But, this year the answers are different!" Folks, this year all the answers are different for you too!

NIKOLA TESLA

Nikola Tesla was one of the greatest scientific minds who ever lived. His genius matched and in many cases exceeded that of Einstein. Whereas Einstein's work was primarily in theories and equations describing the universe, Tesla was an inventor. Tesla developed working models with most of his ideas. He actually demonstrated his theories and inventions, most of which were so astounding they could hardly be comprehended during his lifetime.

Tesla's Incredible Output

Nikola Tesla held over seven hundred patents. A short list of some of his inventions include the following:

- *Alternating current. (No, it was not Thomas Edison.)*
- *Radio (No, it was not Marconi.)*
- *Wireless communication. (Cell phones before there were ordinary phones.)*
- *Fluorescent lights.*

- *Induction motor.*
- *Radio-controlled vehicles.*
- *Rotating magnetic field principle.*
- *Tesla coil.*

The induction motor alone is responsible for virtually every electric motor you have ever encountered: vacuum cleaners, hair dryers, washers, refrigerators, fans, and on and on. You have probably never heard of the Tesla coil, but it is widely used in radio and television sets. 1

A Short Biography
Nikola Tesla was born in 1856 in what is now known as Croatia. He emigrated to the United States in 1884. He first worked for Thomas Edison. Edison gave Tesla a challenge and promised Tesla a handsome reward if he completed the seemingly impossible task. After working nonstop for two days Tesla produced what Edison had asked. Edison reneged on the deal, telling Tesla, "I was only kidding."

At that point Tesla left Edison and went on to establish his own laboratory. After inventing the system for alternating current, transformers, and electric motors, Tesla sold the patents to George Westinghouse. This was the beginning of the powerful Westinghouse Corporation. Some of the other things Tesla went on to accomplish were:

- *Developed shadowgraphs, which were later used by Roentgen in his discovery of X-rays.*
- *Tesla created man-made lighting in the 1800s.*
- *Tesla lit two hundred electric lamps 25 miles away without wires!*
- *Tesla installed the first power-generating machinery at Niagara Falls, bringing electric power to Buffalo, New York in 1896.*
- *Tesla discovered terrestrial stationary waves, proving the earth could be used as a conductor for electrical vibrations. 3*

The Current Significance of Tesla's Work
Much of Tesla's work is in the hands of the U.S. military, and only some of it is just now being understood in its entirety. Expert sources say his inventions and discoveries are being used successfully today in advanced weaponry, including particle-beam weapons, active space travel (far

beyond the capabilities of NASA's space shuttle) time travel, time-warping, antigravity devices, and through-the-earth communications.

The entire earth is permeated and surrounded by active electrical and magnetic energy of untold power. (Ever see a lightning storm?) Tesla's inventions can pull this energy from the atmosphere where it can be stored and used to drive a propulsion system at virtually no cost. Such a system is said to be used by the military to power aircraft and spacecraft at beyond supersonic speeds.

Tesla's Work Is Confiscated
When Tesla died on January 7, 1943 in New York City, the FBI made an immediate trip to his apartment to gather all his notes. These notes have never been released. Even today, the FBI maintains an extensive file on Tesla's discoveries. To this very day a request for information on Tesla's files through the Freedom of Information Act will result in receiving numerous pages with blacked-out passages.

A Word to Teachers and Students
The amazing thing is that most people have never heard of Nikola Tesla. If you are a teacher or a student, immediately check our list of Tesla material in the Bibliography. If you are teaching or studying science, knowledge about Tesla will revolutionize your life's work and your thinking.

Mini-note
In his day, Nikola Tesla was an international celebrity. Along with his other accomplishments, Tesla lit the Chicago World's Fair in 1893. He was considered so important that international press conferences were held each year on his birthday. The whole world wanted to know what he was going to do next. [7]

> Nature and nature's laws lay hid in night:
> God said, "Let Tesla be," and all was light.

> B. A. Behrend
> AIEE annual meeting, New York City, May 18, 1917

TEN SECRETS OF ALIEN SCIENCE

Another reason it's hard to integrate the idea of aliens, space travel, and seemingly supernatural events is because of our limited definition of the universe and how we think it works.

Historical Perspective

We, as humans, have done this before. In ancient times we discovered we were not alone. Humans in Western Europe discovered there were strange and marvelous cultures thriving on distant shores. The general population was shocked by this discovery. They were every bit as shocked as you are to discover that non-human, intelligent beings really exist in inner and outer space.

The cultures that Europeans discovered were neither better nor worse than theirs - just remarkably different. The same is true now. **Aliens** are not magicians or gods. They have simply had more time to develop their technology. A lot more time - but that is for another discussion. When sailors first encountered the compass they thought it was witchcraft. They thought no piece of metal could always point north all by itself.

In order to help you demystify technology, I want to share with you some concepts. A way of looking differently at our universe. Wherever possible I will tell you of work done by scientists that confirms what I am telling you. As such, I now share with you ten secrets of what you would call "**alien**" science.

This Is Not Your Father's Universe

Just considering what scientists have learned over the last 10 years changes the universe completely. It's doubtful your teachers or textbooks have caught up. It's a big shift, and at times it involves some complex concepts, so I am going to take things slowly, a step at a time, and perhaps give you a very different way of understanding how the universe really works.

Space

Space, as in "outer space," is not space the way you think of it. Start thinking of it like this: Imagine a yard of black velvet fabric, 3 feet square.

Now, ball it up and stick your hand in the middle of it. Notice how it moves, even wrapping itself around your hand. That's how space really is. It does those same things your fabric does. Our **alien** visitors know how to control its movement. They use this folding characteristic of space to travel quickly over and through great distances or ride along its edges.

Time

Excuse the pun, but time is not here today and gone tomorrow. Events that occurred in 1969 are still occurring right now. Just as you can travel through space you can also travel through time and through other dimensions. Think of time as a toy train track laid out in an oval. You can stop the train at any point and get off. Time is not just a series of occurrences; it is a series of destinations. Each occurrence is a point on the track that can always be traveled to, just like going to Chicago. And just like Chicago, it is always there! You can always go to any point at any time.

Subatomic Particles

You already know everything is made up of atoms. Atoms are made up of even smaller things known as subatomic particles. There are many different kinds, including quarks, protons, and gluons. The study of the behavior of these subatomic particles is known as quantum physics. Here's what you need to know: Whatever these subatomic particles can do, anything that exists can do.

Subatomic Behavior

Subatomic particles don't behave like anything you have ever seen, with one possible exception, which I will get to in a minute. Subatomic particles are literally packets of energy, not just tiny physical objects. They wink in and out of existence. In other words, sometimes they are in our dimension and sometimes they are in another dimension. This means that you and all that is around you is constantly winking in and out of existence. **Alien** beings have told human contactees that no more than 10 percent of any one of us is in existence in our reality at any one time. We are each like big, blinking neon signs. [5]

Particles or Waves

Subatomic particles can be either particles or waves or both at the same time! Think of a ping-pong ball flying in mid-air towards a mesh net on the ping-pong table. Just before it hits the net it changes form and like a light wave, just passes through the net. Then once on the other side, while still in mid-air, it becomes a ping-pong ball again! This is what subatomic particles can do. X-rays, light, and radio waves can all change from particles into waves and back into particles again.

What You See Is Often What You Get

There is much recent scientific evidence which suggests that merely observing a subatomic particle experiment will influence whether the energy packets will manifest themselves as a wave or a particle. If you are thinking waves and hoping for waves (instead of particles), that is what will occur, you will see and record waves. [6]

Like a Magician

If you knew how to control and utilize these naturally occurring subatomic capabilities, think of the things you could do. You could beam Scotty up, for real! It would seem like magic but it wouldn't be. It is simply physics and understanding how to work with the existing forces within our universe.

How To See Through Solid Objects

In 2010, I was sitting next to a man in the airport. We struck up a friendly conversation and discovered that we were both in the medical industry. I was in sales and he was in research and development for a very large and well-known company. After about 20 minutes, I happened to mention my interest in researching UFOS. (Oops!)

He got quiet, slowly turned and gave me 'The Look.' Then he whispered; "We know how to look inside of the human body." He then told me that his company had developed an instrument whereby they could look at a solid object and by adjusting the light frequencies that it received, you could look through a solid object. He then said " We looked at (body part) on the screen, made the adjustments and all of the skin and dermis structures melted away and we could completely see internal organs."

I wish I could describe the look on his face and the sound of his voice as he told me this story. I could tell he was still absolutely amazed as he re-lived the event.

That Exception

Now for that exception I mentioned earlier. The only large-scale items man has observed utilizing the properties of subatomic particles are: flying saucers!

Holograms

You will have to understand the basic concept of a hologram to gain a different perspective on our existence. This will help you understand not only how the universe functions, but how you function as well. There are two kinds of holograms: reflection and transmission.

Reflection Holograms

Reflection holograms are the kind you see on credit cards, and these are used to prevent forgeries since they are virtually impossible to duplicate. I am not going to talk about this kind of hologram here. However, just so you know, these reflection holograms are made up of several layers of images. It is usually just one image re-recorded a multiple number of times at different angles onto the film. Think of layers of a transparent onion, and you get the idea. When you look at a reflection hologram, your left eye sees a slightly different image than your right eye. Your brain combines the two images in a way that makes the image appear somewhat three-dimensional while still on a flat surface.

Transmission Hologram

A transmission hologram is a true hologram. It is a three-dimensional image projected into mid-air. In the movie *Star Wars* the robot R2-D2 projects a hologram (holographic image) of Princess Leia for Luke Skywalker to reveal a message she recorded. The holographic image appears in mid-air when a laser beam (energy source) of light passes through a plate (like a piece of film) that has a holographic image imbed-ded in it.

A Key Point

The universe really is a holographic projection! So are you! And once you get a handle on this hologram idea, you'll have a much better understanding of reality and how **alien** beings can do the things they do. Also, you'll learn remarkable things you can do! You will discover that many of the things we find so amazing as to deem them miracles, are in fact, simple examples of ordinary physics at work.

The Holographic Plate

The holographic plate, or piece of film, as we're going to call it, is a remarkable thing. Every part of the film has all the information on it. This is very important. One way to understand this is to compare it to a regular photograph. Let's say you have a picture taken with a regular camera of you and a friend standing together. When you get the photograph you rip it in half and end up with you on one piece and your friend on the other piece of the torn photo.

Now if you were to do exactly the same thing with a piece of holographic film that had both your pictures on it, each half would still have both your images on it! Although these images would be smaller than the original, if you beamed a laser through either piece of film you could still get a full-sized hologram! I know this is hard to understand, but just stay with me. You could keep cutting the holographic film into smaller and smaller pieces and both of you would still be on each tiny piece! Amazing, huh? Remember, each part of a holographic film contains all the original information. This is an important concept that we'll come back to shortly.

Unlimited Storage

One of the most remarkable things about holograms is their ability to store information. The amount of information that can be stored holographically is almost unlimited. Here's an example of how it works.

You could record the images of thousands of cars on the same piece of holographic film (plate). Every time you photographed a different car, you would simply hold the laser used in making the picture at a slightly different angle. Conversely, you could recreate the three-dimensional image of each car by changing the angle of the laser during the projection process.

One square inch of holographic film can store all the information contained in fifty volumes of an encyclopedia! 1

Your Brain Is a Holographic Computer

The human brain is like a piece of holographic film (plate). Each small part of your brain contains all the information you have. Your thought waves are the equivalent of a beam of laser light passing through a holographic plate. The resulting information is then projected into your consciousness and becomes reality to your perception. Not only that, but every cell in your body holographically contains the complete files of everything you have ever experienced, in full, living color and sound. And, they can be replayed.

Instant Replay

Everything you have ever seen or experienced is still available to you to re-experience. We must simply teach ourselves how to project our laser-thoughts at the correct angles to re-establish the hologram of infor-mation. This is not magic any more than windshield wipers on a car would be considered magic. With a car, you know where the windshield-wiper button is. With holographic information, you simply have not yet learned where the "play" button is. However, all humans have this capability.

Temple Grandin

Temple Grandin has a PhD and is a noted researcher, author and professor at Colorado State University. Grandin is a high-functioning autistic with near total recall. Grandin states that her memory is like watching full-length movies in her head that she can replay at will. She can mentally change the viewpoint of the images by altering the positions of lighting and shadows. 10

Near-death Experiences

The replay is what happens during near-death experiences (NDEs). There is a cascade of chemicals in the cells that triggers the complete holographic memory of your life to be released into your consciousness.

Our **alien** visitors also know how to access this holographic instant-replay of our lives.

You Have Unlimited Storage Capability

We also have virtually unlimited capacity in that little brain of ours. That's because the brain stores images, experiences, and memories holographically, not mechanically, as you have been led to believe. You've heard it said we only use 5 percent of our brains, right? That's because that's just our mechanical storage capabilities. The other 95 percent lies in what we can accomplish by utilizing the holographic capabilities that are built into our brains.

Scientific Confirmation

Humans store things in our consciousness in the form of complex holograms. Scientists have calculated that during our lifetimes we will each store approximately 2.8 X 10(20) or 280,000,000,000,000,000,000, bits of information. That's amazing, is it not? They have also correctly concluded that all the cells in your brain, combined, cannot store this vast amount of information. So, how do you do it? You store it holographically!

Instead of a laser beam, it is your thought processes, both conscious and unconscious, that become the energy source which passes through your holographic plates to store information holographically. When the process is reversed, the hologram that results is your reality!

What follows is information you may find helpful. People who have photographic memories are able to literally project the pages of a book they have memorized in front of themselves, holographically, and then simply read the pages. When people with photographic memories are recalling the things they can remember, you can observe their eyes following the words as if reading from a page. That is because they are. If you stop their eye movement, it ends the recall. [2]

Experiments by scientists have confirmed what I am telling you. During one such experiment, rats were laboriously taught the correct path through a maze. The scientists then removed various sections of the rat's brains. In some cases, they left no more than one-tenth of the brain. [3]

In each case, the rats still remembered exactly how to find their way through the maze. That is because all the information from the past experiences was still there, holographically stored on each and every tiny section of the brain.

Another scientist took out the brains of salamanders. He sliced them, diced them, and even scrambled them; then he put them back into the salamander. He even put them in upside down and backwards. He did this over seven hundred times. In every case the behavior of the salamanders returned to normal! 4 The results were so dramatic that even the television show *60 Minutes* devoted a segment to the experiments.

The same is true of you. Even some people who have had large sections of their brains removed due to illness or accidents still remember all. A university student in Sheffield, England had virtually no physical brain. His cerebral cortex was only one-forty-fifth the thickness of a normal human brain. Yet he was an honor student with an IQ of 130! This was because of his ability to access the holographic capabilities of his brain.

Mike, The Headless Chicken

On September 10, 1945 in Fruita, Colorado, farmer L.A. Olsen decided to slaughter one of his chickens (Mike). This was something he did routinely. His mother-in-law asked him to keep as much of the bird's neck on as possible, since it was her favorite part.

After decapitating the bird, it continued to flutter and flap for a few minutes as often happens when cutting off a chicken's head. About 10 minutes later, Olsen was stunned when Mike, the now headless chicken, regained his composure, began to fluff his feathers and started strutting around the barnyard like nothing had happened. Mike tried to peck for food and place his now missing head under his wing when he slept and do everything a normal chicken does.

Mike lived for four and a half years. Olsen fed Mike through an opening in his neck where the head had been. Before he died, Mike went on tour and was examined by scientists and medical experts from coast to coast. Mike was featured in *Time* magazine, *Life* magazine and the *Guiness Book of Records.*

Scientists concluded that Mike was able to function normally because part of his brain stem was left intact. This was apparently all that Mike needed to reconnect with his 'holographic' chicken faculties.

Mike eventually died from choking on a corn kernel. 'Mike, the Headless Chicken Day' is now celebrated annually in Colorado with picnics, fireworks, a 5K run, egg tosses, chicken jokes and lots of chicken salad.

What about amnesia? Or when I can't remember something? In both cases the information is still there, but stored holographically. You simply are unable to place your laser (thought waves) at the correct angle to recreate the hologram of information.

The Universe is a Hologram

The entire universe is a holographic projection. It is our thought energy that provides the (laser beam) energy to manifest the holographic image we call reality. We, each and every one of us, is a holographic plate (film). And just like a holographic plate, each of us contains all the information in the universe. Because of this we are literally connected to everything, and, everything is connected to everything.

This is not New Age philosophy. It is physics! When religious texts like the Bible and the Koran say you are connected and always return to the source, they mean it literally and physically, and not just in the spiritual sense.

A Giant Water Fountain

Another example would be a water fountain. Imagine a geyser-like fountain with a plume of water shooting up and then falling back down into the basin. The plume of water has a distinct shape, but it is still connected to all the rest of the water. If you turn the fountain off all the water returns to the basin and there is no way to pick out what drops of water were forming the plume. They are all one. Just as the water returns to the source and no longer has a certain form, so do you, eventually. And like the water, you are one with everyone and everything in the universe.

A Sea of Energy
The universe is composed of a sea of energy. The holographic plate you build in your brain merely interprets and sees this energy as a holographic projection you call reality. Reality is very much like the holodeck on the *Star Trek* series. You can change the program at any time and reality literally changes.

Prayers, Meditations, and Verbalizations
This is the reason prayers, meditations, and daily verbalizations work. They reconfigure the information on the holographic plate in your brain, thereby changing the projection you call reality. (For you tekkies: They etch a new interference pattern onto your holographic plate.)

So you can now begin to understand that the seemingly miraculous things that occur around flying saucers and **alien** beings are not miracles, and they are not magic. They are physics, plain and simple.

Instant Communication Over Unlimited Distances
Certain **alien** beings can communicate with each other instantly, regardless of the distance between the beings. The trader beings are known to be able to do this. What one knows, all of them know, instantly! This seems to violate Einstein's theory of relativity, which says nothing can travel faster than the speed of light. That is, until you understand the concept that these beings are not separate individuals. They are part of the same body of energy, just like the water in the fountain.

Scientific Confirmation
Scientists have confirmed this concept in studies with subatomic particles. The results of the studies seem to imply that subatomic particles, in this case, photons, can instantly communicate with one another. This would, again, seem to violate the light-speed law. 5

However, scientists are just now beginning to understand that the particles are not two separate objects. They are, in fact, one and the same! As are all the particles in the universe. Physicists call this property of nothing being separate as being "non-local."

Healing and Miracles

There is much discussion in the medical community about the nature of healing in the human body. Eastern medicine and Western medicine are being combined to gain a new perspective on how the body really heals itself from illness and disease.

Miracle healings are not necessarily miracles. Often times they are holographic reinterpretations. Once again, it is physics. By now you know experiments have shown that thoughts can dramatically affect the healing process. As a side note, it has also been discovered that thoughts can affect the working of machinery.

A New Hologram

People who experience miracle healings have been able to refocus their laser (thought patterns), which create a new hologram for themselves. Sometimes this happens consciously and by intent, other times it happens at a subconscious level. The new hologram of reality is created without the illness there. It changes the shape of the fountain and everything in reality joins to support this new reality, just as all the drops of water would support a new shape in a fountain.

Just consider these facts:

Emotionally disturbed and mentally challenged individuals have far lower rates of cancer deaths than the general population, about 4 percent as compared to the normal 25 percent. 6 It appears these individuals cannot as easily create a hologram (reality) of illness.

Placebos (bogus medication without any medicine in them) actually work 35 percent of the time! 7 The reason is because the patient's belief that the medicine is real changes the thought pattern and creates a new hologram (reality) of illness.

Big Pharma Gets Concerned

In 2002, the world's largest pharmaceutical companies put together a secret consortium to try and discover why they are seeing an increase in the effectiveness of placebos that is threatening future pharmaceutical sales. 11

A New Approach

We need to understand this: creating wellness is exactly the same process as creating illness. To put it another way, if you can create illness, you can create wellness. It is not magic - it is physics.

Hyper-Dimensional Physics

Our leading scientists have already discovered that you create reality from a sub-dimensional order of things. They call it hyper-dimensional physics. It is the same thing I have been discussing and referring to as the holographic reality.

Our ancient holy men and mystics have long known about this. They were able to tap into the holographic/hyper-dimensional reality of the universe. By understanding this, they could make things appear and disappear, like magic, but it's physics. It is simply having a greater control of your reality than most humans.

Flying Saucers Do the Same Thing

Alien spacecraft that disappear and reappear are doing the same thing. They are winking in and out of our dimension, our plane of holographic existence. It is not magic, it is physics!

What You See Is Not What You See

When you see something, you are not just *seeing* it. You are creating it holographically and forming it into reality. Many times there are parts of what you see that are actually being created holographically from the already-existing holographic plate in your brain. Your brain (holographic plate) provides information and fills in the parts of the scene you are not actually seeing.

Here is another way of understanding this process. In the middle of your eye's retina is a spot where the optic nerve attaches to the eye. At this spot there are no photo receptors. If you saw only what your eye actually "sees," there would be a hole in the middle of every scene you looked at. But there isn't. That's because the information already imbedded in your holographic plate fills in the missing pieces to complete the scene you see.

Scientific Confirmation

Through studies, scientists have determined that only 50 percent of what you see is actually seen by your eye and visual cortex. The other 50 percent is filled in holographically! This is why visualization techniques work so well for healing purposes and for learning things. Visualization utilizes a process that your brain is already doing all the time; filling the blanks and constantly re-creating reality.

How a Hologram Is Made

Let's say you want to take a holographic picture of a car so you can then project a three-dimensional image of the car, or a hologram. A laser beam of light is aimed at the car from several different directions at the same time. This is done through the use of mirrors and beam-splitters, which split the laser beam into two beams. The light bounces off the car and forms patterns on the film. Actually, it's a glass plate, but for simplicity's sake we're going to refer to it as a piece of film. These interference patterns contain the image of the car taken from all angles.

How a Hologram Is Projected

To produce the three-dimensional image we call a hologram the process is reversed. A beam of laser light is passed through the piece of film with the interference pattern on it. The result is that the light passing through the film recreates the exact patterns of light that were bouncing off the car when the hologram was made. The light patterns reform the exact, original shape of the car in three dimensions. Thus, the hologram.

Fourier Transforms

Fourier transforms are a set of equations that describe how the interference patterns translate the light patterns in the recording and projection of holograms. It has also been discovered that these exact same equations are used by the human brain to translate information during the thought process!

CATTLE MUTILATIONS

Cattle mutilations are instances where a domestic farm animal has been butchered with surgical precision. Although this is done mostly to cows it also happens to horses. In fact, the first case on record was a horse. The characteristics are such that they rule out a kill by wild predators such as coyotes and wolves.

The First Cattle Mutilation?

On April 21, 1897, Alexander Hamilton, the noted statesman, was awakened at night by loud humming noises coming from his cattle yard. He and two other men went outside and saw an "airship" slowly come down and hover over the yard. Here is how Hamilton described it:

> It consisted of a great cigar-shaped portion possibly 300 feet long, with a carriage underneath. The carriage was made of glass or some other transparent substance alternating with a narrow strip of some material. It was brilliantly lighted within and everything was plainly visible. It was occupied by six of the strangest beings I ever saw. They were jabbering together, but we could not understand a word they said. It seemed to pause and hover directly over a 2 -year old heifer, which was bawling and jumping, apparently fast in the fence. Going to her, we found a cable about a half-inch in thickness made of some red material, fastened in a slip knot around her neck, one end passing up to the vessel, and the heifer tangled in the wire fence. We tried to get it off but could not, so we cut the wire loose and stood in amaze-ment to see the ship, heifer and all, rise, slowly, disappearing in the northwest. Neighbor Thomas Link (4 miles away) found the hide, legs, and head in his field the next day and no tracks in the soft ground, which mystified him. 25

San Luis Valley

The first modern case on record occurred in 1967 in the San Luis Valley in southern Colorado. A horse owned by the King family named Lady was found dead in a pasture. Its flesh had been stripped completely from the skull, exposing the bare bones. The bones were so clean of flesh that the skull looked as if it had been sitting out exposed to the sun for weeks. However, the family had just seen the horse alive two days earlier. More confounding was the fact that there was absolutely no blood found near the body and no animal tracks of any kind nearby.

Several organs of the horse were missing and the cuts were made more precisely than the sharpest knife could have made. Remember, this was 1967, a good 20 years before surgical lasers were available.

Lady, Not Snippy

Since this case is the first, I want to keep the facts straight for you. The original reports stated the horse's name was Snippy. Those reports were incorrect. The horse's name was Lady. Snippy was Lady's mother and she was not harmed. Just to keep the record straight. 6

Other Witnesses

During the time when this mutilation occurred many people in the area saw UFOs and strange lights. Several other animals were found mutilated the same way. They were also found lying in the middle of a perfectly outlined circle cut or burned into the surrounding vegetation.

Cattle Mutilation. The tissue and jaw along with the tongue have been excised with surgical precision, exposing the bone and leaving no blood. (Photo courtesy Linda Moulton Howe.)

More Black Helicopters

Also seen in the area were black unmarked helicopters, which were extremely rare in 1967. Low-flying jets appeared in the area, which was also uncommon.

Native American Connection

The San Luis Valley is known to be a place of special significance to many Native American tribes. Among other things, it was the one place where many different tribes would gather each spring and there would be no conflict among them. It is said that this is the valley "where man was created."

Your Basic Mutilation

A standard mutilation exhibits one or more of the following characteristics:

- *Usually occurs with cattle, horses, or sheep.*
- *Jaw cut: A precision, surgical-like cut of surrounding flesh to completely expose the jaw bone and teeth. The tongue and surrounding glandular tissue has been removed.*
- *The sex organs, navel, and nipples have been surgically removed.*
- *The anus and surrounding glandular tissues have been surgically removed.*
- *No evidence of any blood, despite the severity of the procedures.*
- *No footprints of any kind leading to or from the animal.*
- *The animal is often found in the middle of a perfectly created circle.*
- *The cuts are made so precisely that a surgeon with a full operating room and a steady hand with the laser would have a difficult time matching these field cuts.*
- *The precision of the cuts and lack of blood rule out predator kills.*

Why Are Certain Organs Taken?

While there is no way to know for sure, a good bet is the fact that organ tissue retains things picked up in the environment like minerals, pesticides, etc. If you wanted to check the condition of the animal and what it is being exposed to, these organs would be the place to start.

What about Cults, Pranksters, and Coyotes?

Without a doubt, many so-called mutilations fall under these categories.

However, there have been far more of these mutilations than you probably realize. In the urban areas of the major cities in the country, cow news of any kind is no news. In the Midwest, though, it's a different story. Thousands of cattle have been lost over the years since 1967 in unexplained or strange circumstances. It just didn't make the big city papers.

Although many of these kills are explainable, about 40 to 50 percent are not, and this group fits the classic pattern of a cattle mutilation. For example, between 1975 and 1977 nearly two thousand cattle were mutilated in twenty-two states. If this had been accomplished by a group of people, individuals would have had to surgically attend to two cows a day for 2 years, over an area of twenty-two states. This is not likely. [1]

Predator kills are easily identified by experienced ranchers and veterinarians. Most of these kills could not have been done by a wild predator, especially since these kills involved the removal of only select organs.

No Flies, No Coyotes
Investigators report that when a "true" cattle mutilation has occurred, flies will not land on the carcass and coyotes won't touch it either. The carcass can lie out in the sun for weeks and never be touched by flies or coyotes. [4]

A Strange Harvest
The existence of cattle mutilations was brought to the attention of the public by Linda Moulton Howe. Howe researched and produced a documentary called *A Strange Harvest*. It was the first work that connected cattle mutilations to UFOs. The documentary won an Emmy Award in 1980. Her work concluded that animal mutilations appear to emanate from two places:

1. *UFOs*
2. *Unmarked helicopters and large vans seemingly owned by branches of the U.S. government.*

Linda Moulton Howe has continued her research and adds more documentation in her follow-up book *An Alien Harvest: Further Evidence Linking Animal Mutilations and Human Abductions to **Alien** Life Forms.*

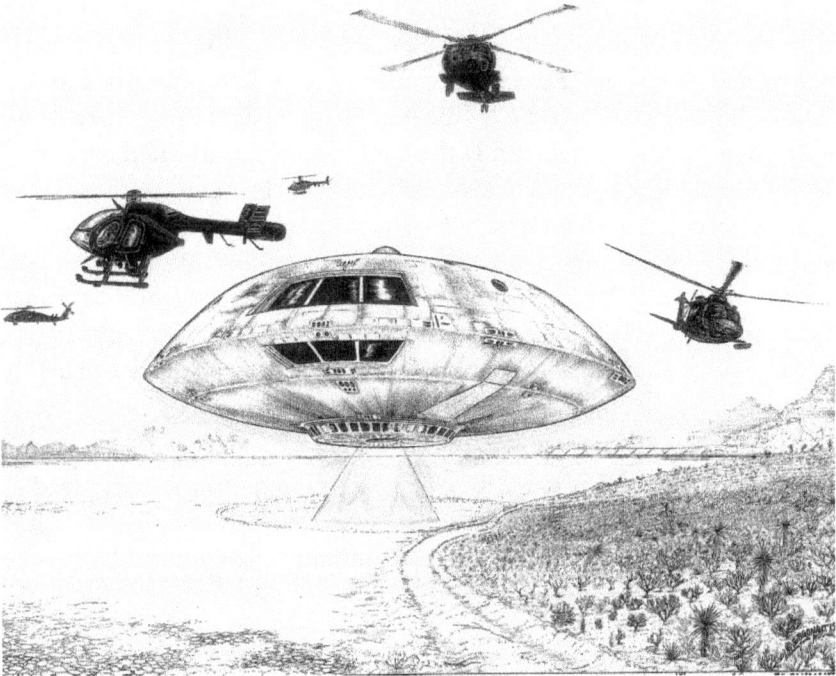

Black helicopters and large disk-shaped craft that are often seen in the areas where cattle mutilations have occurred. (© 1997 William L. McDonald)

In her most recent book, *Glimpses of Other Realities, Vol. II,* Howe tells of discussions she had with military intelligence operatives. They told her that the mutilations were in fact being done by the **aliens,** who were testing the animals for high levels of toxins that we humans have put into the atmosphere. They also told her that the black helicopters were a ruse to cover up the **alien** involvement in mutilations. 5. They didn't want the farmers to panic. It appears to be working, because most farmers when interviewed said they thought it was the government doing some kind of secret testing. 6

CROP CIRCLES

Crop Circles are elaborate designs formed in wheat and grain fields. The stalks of the grain have been laid flat, usually in a circular or flowing pattern.

Eighty-five percent of all crop circles appear in England in a concentrated area about 20 miles from Stonehenge. However, they appear annually all over the world, even near heavily populated cities. The first seasonal crop circles of 1996 were found in Laguna Beach, California. Many dramatic crop circles have appeared in Canada, Germany, Australia, Brazil, Japan, and the United States.

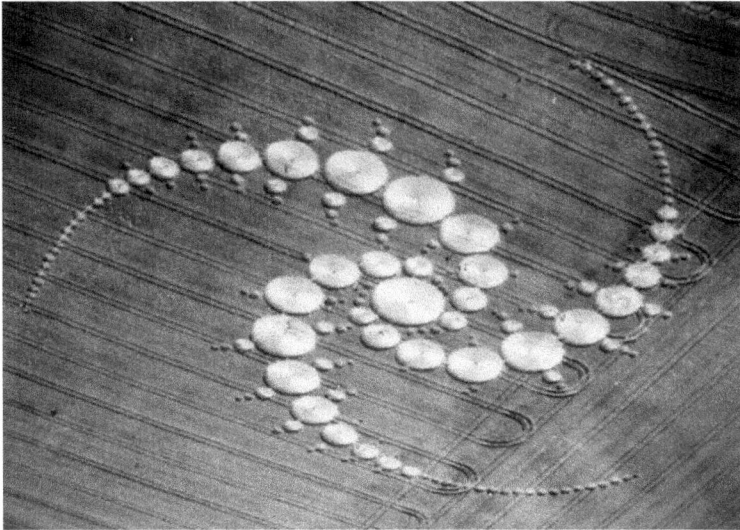

"Julia set" crop circle comprised of 96 perfectly formed circles.
(Photo courtesy Linda Moulton Howe.)

Some History
Crop circles first began appearing in grain fields in England in 1975. In 1990 the designs of these circles became increasingly more complex.

The Designs
Crop circle formations are absolutely stunning in their design, intricacy, and precise measurements. Many of them are huge, covering the space of ten football fields. When carefully measured, the geometrical designs are

accurate to within an eighth of an inch! This is true even if the formation is a thousand feet long! (That's the height of a hundred-story building.) For example, a hundred-foot circle will have an accurate and identical radius on all sides to within the thickness of a single stalk of grain.

Many crop circle formations are a thousand feet or more in length.
(Photo courtesy Linda Moulton Howe)

Pictograms and Insectograms

Some of the more complex designs are called pictograms. Insectograms are designs that resemble insects, although there is no apparent relationship of crop circles to insects. It's just a name.

Cellular Changes

The grasses involved in crop circles all exhibit cellular changes. Anyone, with little or no training and just using the naked eye can take a stalk of grain from a crop circle and compare it to another stalk from the same field that was not a part of the crop circle and clearly see the difference. Crop-circle grass has expanded nodes and stalks will be bent up to a 90-degree angle with no breakage.

You can see the expansion and change of every single cell of the crop circle grass with a basic elementary school microscope. Although many have tried, no one has discovered any process on earth that can duplicate these cellular changes.

Magnetic Fields and Radioactivity

Crop circles have a strong magnetic field in and around them, which is measurable. Many crop circles also exhibit strange patterns of radioactivity in which the level of radioactivity at a given spot will fluctuate up and down. According to our laws of physics, this is thought to be impossible because radioactivity is constant. That's why it is used for carbon-dating ancient artifacts.

Grass Direction

True crop circles often have several layers of grass in the design. Often the bottom layers of grass will flow in one direction, while another layer on top flows in the complete opposite direction. The grass has even been found delicately braided together. [2]

Metallic Disks

Often, thin metallic disks about the size of a quarter are found in crop circles. They have also been found near cattle mutilations. When these disks were analyzed by metallurgy labs at the University of Michigan and at MIT, they were found to be composed of a combination of titanium, silicone, and oxygen. Both labs concluded that no industrial match can be found on this planet.

Not only that, but when the disks were touched by any metal object such as tweezers or a pen, they immediately turned into a clear liquid. The labs theorized that the disks had somehow been electrically charged, with the charge maintaining the molecular structure of the disk. When touched with metal, the charge was grounded and dissipated, which allowed the "metal" to return to its true liquid form. [3]

Why do People Associate Crop Circles With UFOs?

First, because crop circles often appear in areas shortly after there have been UFO sightings. And second, because nobody on earth has been able to duplicate a true crop circle, certainly not at the cellular level, the assumption is made that it must therefore be extraterrestrial in origin.

Some Amazing Correlations

Most crop circles in England appear near the ancient structure known as Stonehenge. Many of the formations accurately reproduce the dimensions and configurations of Stonehenge to within a few centimeters.

Based on mathematical relationships and the theories of Euclidean geometry, the measurements of various crop circles appear to demonstrate many universal laws. Their measurements have been shown to correspond exactly to:

- *Notes of the musical scale.*
- *Electrical circuitry.*
- *DNA strands and genetic relationships.*
- *Sacred geometry/hyper-dimensional physics.*
- *Ancient symbols found only in such places as the pyramids of Egypt, Stonehenge, and Mayan and Aztec temples.*
- *Solar systems and asteroid trajectories.*
- *Mathematical equations.*
- *Advanced geometry.*
- *Molecular structure.*

Ironically, this list is an almost exact duplicate of the items the U.S. space program put onto the Voyager spacecraft in an effort to contact other life forms.

Three Dimensional Forms

Some crop circles appear to be footprints of an actual three dimensional form, much like a CAT scan. A CAT scan is a picture of a slice of a three dimensional object. For example, a CAT scan of your brain shows different regions from a slice of your brain, which is a three dimensional object.

Birds Fly Around Them

If we had the proper device, we might see that the crop circle is a slice of an invisible three dimensional form that surrounds it. In fact, when a flock of birds approaches a crop circle, it splits ranks to avoid flying above the formation (just as if a building or a solid object were there) and then reforms after passing the crop circle.

People who stand inside a crop circle often experience a dramatic rush of emotions and increased perceptual abilities.

What About Hoaxes?

Two farmers in England, both over the age of 65 when they announced themselves, claimed they were responsible for making crop circles by using wooden boards and string. Doug Bower and Dave Chorley claimed the crop circles were a hoax they perpetrated. These infamous jokers are now known simply as "Doug an' Dave."

As the crop circles began to get more publicity, they attracted thousands of sight-seers trampling across private crops and farm land. The claim by the farmers is well known to be an attempt by locals to stop this trespassing and loss in revenue from damaged crops.

Some Key Points

When asked to demonstrate how they made the circles, the farmers pushed down a few feet of grass with a board, but refused to create an entire formation.

Many crop circles have appeared on the same night, often hundreds of miles apart. Crop circles have also appeared in Canada on the same nights as these farmers claimed to have created circles in England.

The two farmers have been unable to recreate the cellular changes in the grain or the accompanying magnetic and radioactive fields. They also could not duplicate the 90-degree bends without breaking the grasses. And lastly, they could not get the grasses to flow all in the same direction.

Dave Chorley has since died and crop circles have continued to appear every year.

Eyewitnesses

A number of eyewitnesses claim to have seen crop circles created within a matter of seconds. The formations were so complex that it would have taken an army of people many hours just to attempt to create it by hand.

On July 8, 1996 three people all witnessed the formation of an elaborate crop circle. A groundskeeper and a security officer had walked by a wheat field at about 5:30 P.M. The field was completely normal. At the same time a pilot flew his plane over the field and stated that the field was normal. Less than an hour later the pilot flew back over the field and discovered a huge crop circle. He was so excited by his discovery he radioed it in to the Thruxton Airport. The security officer and groundskeeper were also shocked when they returned within the hour and found the crop circle.

The crop circle that the three witnesses found was the design of a very complicated mathematical equation which had been discovered by French mathematicians in the early 1900s, a calculation known as a Julia Set. The crop circle was comprised of 149 circles stretching over a square acre. 4

Videotape

Recently, a videotape surfaced which purported to show the actual creation of a crop circle. The video shows a ball of light descending from the sky. It rapidly circles a grain field, creating a crop circle and then shoots off into space at a high rate of speed. It all looks pretty impressive, except the guy who showed up with it is known to be a special effects whiz on the computer. So, odds are it's a fake.

Phone Home

Crop circles are a mind-boggling phenomenon. Their implications are dramatic, and they are studied very seriously by other countries in the world. Unfortunately, in the United States they are relegated to the front page of tabloids and to television shows like *Unsolved Mysteries*. The momentary claim of a hoax is all the American public is likely to hear about. These circles appear to be literal and congruent responses to the signals we sent out to the universe in the name of science.

Theories About Crop Circles

There are about as many theories about what crop circles are or what they mean as there are people on this planet. However, there is one theory that I feel stands head and shoulders above the rest, and here's why:

1. It is the only theory into which virtually every crop circle ever created seems to fit. In fact, according to this theory, every crop circle is needed, like pieces of a giant puzzle.

2. The person who discovered this applied a simple but logical approach and came up with an all-encompassing concept.

3. This theory seems to work and I have not seen a better, more thoroughly researched explanation.

Flying Saucer Theory
This is essentially what the theory says, that crop circles are really telling us how to construct our very own flying saucer. A former Air Force and commercial airline pilot for 24 years, Doug Ruby decided to take a simple approach in his investigation of crop circles: Why not treat them like schematics?

Blueprints
Ruby approached each crop circle as if it were a flat, two-dimensional schematic of a three-dimensional item, just like a blueprint is for a building. He started with the least complicated crop-circle designs first. Then, he simply built the item.

Energy Fields
After he built the first items, they didn't look like much. They looked like some partially constructed toy from a child's Tinker-toy set. Then Ruby had an intuitive thought: Why not spin the item, put it in motion? Voila! When the objects were spun they literally took on a whole other dimension. For example, it became apparent that one part that merely looked like a ball stuck on a pole was representing an energy field that could only be seen when it was spun. Without spinning the model these energy fields would have remained invisible.

A Logical Progression
Ruby also discovered that each crop circle builds on the other ones. Fortunately he started out with photos or diagrams of almost all the major crop circles that had ever been created, which gave him, essentially,

a full set of blueprints when he started, allowing him to actually see ahead as he constructed each model, just like an engineer or architect.

A Working Model

When scale models are built from these blueprints and they are all put together the crop circles tell us exactly how flying saucers are built, how they work, what powers them, and why they are shaped like saucers. The crop circles are an amazing presentation of a technical puzzle and Ruby's work ends up being sheer genius. Ruby has had confirmation of his theories and models from nuclear physicists and engineers. The crop circles even diagram the power source and tell how it works.

Adamski Beamships

When Ruby assembled models of the spacecraft from the crop circle schematics, the models look exactly like the type of flying saucer commonly referred to as the "Adamski beamships." Ruby's description of how the ships work confirms the statements of many people over the years about the rotating rings on the saucers as well as the interference with electrical devices.

Key Element

There is, however, one little problem - one that would prevent our scientists from building one of these craft to spec right now. The crop circles identify an atomic particle which has no charge as being the key particle in powering the ship. Our scientists say that's impossible. Of course, we now know that nothing is impossible!

Those Two Farmers

Remember those two old farmers I mentioned earlier? Well, they almost fouled up the whole works. After the farmers lied and said they were responsible for creating the crop circles, the next batch of circles appearing in 1991 and 1992 were pretty much ignored. People thought these two geezers were up to their old tricks, so these circles almost got lost forever. Fortunately some people took and kept some photos of them. Without these photos, Ruby might not have been able to complete the puzzle.

Equations

In addition to crop circles appearing in grain fields, large sets of numbers have appeared as well. In one instance, the following equation appeared in a Kansas grain field in 1991:

$$E \ 97 +$$

It appears to refer to Element 97 on the periodic chart of atomic elements. Element 97 is berkelium which has an atomic weight of 247. It is the element used to power flying saucers.

The Government

Shortly after this equation appeared it was eradicated by agents from the U.S. government, or people who said they were from the government. Anyway, it was a clear indication that someone doesn't want the crop circles deciphered.

Art or Engineering?

Whether you appreciate the crop circles as art or engineering, there is no doubt we are being communicated with by an amazing intelligence. It is clear this information is being given to all humanity out of love and caring. Do you think some people bent on evil intent would spend their time doing this? You're lucky to be here, right now.

If you have any interest in crop circles at all, whether as art or engineering, I highly recommend Doug Ruby's book. The title of Ruby's book *The Gift* tells exactly what the crop circles are: a gift!

DIFFERENT TYPES OF ALIEN BEINGS

- *The Traders*
- *The Travelers*
- *Other Beings*

The following information has been given to me by several individuals who have been in contact with **alien** beings for many years, but wish to remain anonymous at this time. As I have mentioned earlier, **alien** beings don't speak. They communicate through a combination of thought, feeling and images. This has been confirmed by world renown researcher Linda Moulton Howe, who has been told by U.S. Intelligence operatives that **alien** beings communicate with them in exactly this manner.

The Traders

There are beings known throughout the universe as *The Traders*. We humans tend to classify all **alien** beings as one. We sometimes refer to **alien** beings as the "little gray guys with big eyes." In many cases we are confusing these beings with the beings known as *Zetas*. I will tell you more about them later.

They are not guys. In some cases we would know them to be androgynous. There are many things about them we have difficulty understanding. Our science has not progressed enough to know some of these things. I will attempt tell you about them in terms you will understand.

For Billions of Years

Alien beings have been around for billions of our years, so long it is almost impossible for us to comprehend. We must understand that our years, our time, is not the same as it is for others throughout the universe. Part of this is due to our current inability to understand the true nature of what we call time, even within the realm of our own solar system.

Time as we know it does not truly exist in the way we think it does. It is simply a reference for our reality. Like a mile marker on a roadside, it only means something in relation to another marker.

An Intelligence Guides the Universe

These **alien** beings have been in existence long enough to observe the universe and know there is an order to all things. There is a creative intelligence that governs the universe. If you choose the word *God*, so be it. There is a connecting intelligence linking all things, big and small, in the universe. They have observed that a distant comet or even an exploding planet has a purpose.

The Real Birds and the Bees

The next thought is difficult for many of us humans to accept, but the fact is that without these beings we might not be here. They are not our creators anymore than the bee creates the flower. But without the bee carrying the pollen, the flower would not be. It is how all the universe works, and not just with flowers and insects, but with advanced sentient beings as well. So it may be with the relationship of alien beings to humans.

They Are All One

As a group, these **alien** beings are not a group of individuals. They are a group that has individuals. They are connected. There is no singularity. What one knows, all know. Have you ever watched a large school of fish in an aquarium? Have you ever wondered how hundreds of them can all turn instantly in the same direction at the same time? They are an example of being connected to a group consciousness. Each instantly knows what all the others know. These **alien** beings have a group consciousness.

The Man With No Name

Many **alien** beings don't have individual names the way we humans do. In their open interactions with humans they sometimes assign themselves individual earth-sounding names to make it easier for them to address us. Each individual has a frequency. It is a vibration others can feel. Humans also each have a distinct frequency. Like fingerprints, no two are the same. We have just not trained ourselves to sense one another's vibration. We generally rely on sight, or sound of the voice.

The Ultimate Explorers

Group consciousness has distinct advantages for exploration. If a group goes out and does not return, they know what happened. They do not need to send out a search party to find out what happened. They know instantly. Distance is not a factor. Their next step would be to simply not repeat what the first group did. This is very different from what we, as humans, would have to do. To know this will help us understand them.

They Lost Our Planet

A very long time ago these Trader beings discovered how to provide
enough energy to supply their entire planet from one source. They
utilized the energy of a thing our scientists refer to as a black hole. They
had the technology to "rope" a small black hole and pull it close to their
planet. They also learned that by feeding it they could increase its energy
output to give them even more energy. They began to feed it large
asteroids and small planets. However, a side effect of feeding it was that
it also grew in size and strength. As it grew it began to devour more and
more things, including things they never intended.

Out of Control

As it grew, it began to pull their planet into it. They could not stop it. It
grew out of control. They realized it would soon devour their planet.
Right up until the last minutes they did everything they could to try and
stop this from happening. In the last moments they abandoned our
planet. Their planet was consumed and lost. They had only enough time
to save themselves. All the other life forms – all the plants and animals
and all other living things - were lost forever.

Preserve All Life

They were devastated. A life form in the universe, once lost, cannot be
replaced. They set for themselves a mission. That mission is to preserve
all life forms in the universe. Not each individual, but a blueprint for each
species, subspecies, and any mutation. That is why they are known as the
Traders: They trade life; they preserve life. They also live by a rule: If they
take something they must leave something. That is the law of the universe. So, they don't just take life forms, they trade one for another.

Communication

Alien beings communicate with themselves and others by what we would
call mental telepathy. In fact it is more than that. It is a sharing of
thoughts, feelings, and other levels of understanding our scientists are
not yet aware of. It will surprise you to know that many alien beings have
no written language, they don't need one. They each know what every
one of them has ever known throughout time. These beings do have
certain symbols they use and sometimes project them mentally.

Their Intentions

We, as humans, are very concerned about what the intentions of alien beings are in visiting our planet. Many human Contactees have been told that we have nothing to fear. They have been told that alien beings have no weapons on their ships and they allow no one with weapons to travel outside of their own galaxy. They have no need for weapons. They could fly right through the center of our sun in their ships and feel no ill effect. They can travel through time, space, and distance almost instantly. Many other beings do have powerful energy tools, which like a hammer or screwdriver could be used as an item of self-defense.

Their purpose for being here has very little to do with us. They are here for their own purposes, most of which we are incapable of understanding. They have the same level of concern for us that we have for two-year-old children playing in a sandbox. We are unconcerned with what games they are playing. We will occasionally look to make sure they do not destroy the sandbox by playing with matches. Our nuclear toys are the matches. We may destroy many individuals, if we choose, but they will assure the continued existence of our species. They preserve life - all life.

What They Look Like

Humans, are very visual and we want to know what alien beings look like. Many are small compared to us - only 3 to 5 feet in height. Some are very slender; they have no need for additional body mass. It would simply get in the way. Their skin color ranges from gray to tan or beige. In relation to our bodies, their heads are larger than ours. Most of them have very little, if any, body hair. As I said earlier, they are sometimes androgynous, neither male or female. However, some of them can select to become either male or female at an appropriate time. Many reptiles and birds on our planet also have this capability.

The Eyes Have It

Their eyes are larger than ours, but by now you already know this. However, they are not as large as depicted on our television shows. Those shows depict the eyes of the Zeta beings, which are larger than the Traders. Their eyes also have the ability to polarize light.

Ears, Nose, and Mouth

The mouths of the Traders are more fully formed than the Zetas, but still much smaller than humans. They have very small teeth and eat a finely processed synthetic food. They have two small nostrils that function as a nose apparatus and small openings for ears.

Hands and Feet

Their hands have four fingers, with no thumb. They have no fingernails, but they do have little suction cups on the ends of their fingers. Two of their fingers can extend out in a manner similar to a cat's claw. They have thin legs and do not do much walking. They have the ability to float along by using an antigravity technology. Many humans have seen them do this.

How they Travel

The Traders' use spacecraft. They have the ability to travel between stars almost instantly. Contactees have been told that They are the only ones who have this technology. However, they do allow others to travel with them. They call these other species the *Travelers.* Most of them have the ability to travel between planets, but not between stars. Here is a simple way to understand it. These beings can focus on a given point in space. Then they basically pull space towards them and attach to it, like a rubber band. When they release they are instantly in that spot. Think of space as a piece of fabric, not empty space. Carl Sagan explains it quite well in his book and videotape *Cosmos.*

To make it even simpler, try this: take a piece of paper and put an ink dot on each end of the page. You were trained to think the shortest, fastest way to go from point A to point B was to draw a straight line between the points. In truth, the fastest way is to simply fold the paper and kiss the two points together. They fold space in just this manner and instantly jump from point to point. This is how **alien** beings navigate the universe.

Hey, How Did That Happen?

Some of our scientists accidentally triggered this instantaneous travel capability while trying figure out how one of the craft they recovered worked. While standing in one place, they suddenly found themselves in a completely different part of the room without ever having moved!

Imagine their surprise! Especially when they couldn't figure out how they did it or what actually happened!

Spacecraft

Aliens have many different kinds of spacecraft. What I have to tell you about them will take some getting used to. There are literally thousands of spacecraft in the immediate vicinity of our planet. Many are the Traders, many belong to others, who I will tell you about shortly. The Traders have the ability to cloak their ships just like in our *Star Trek* movies. They can also pop in and out of other dimensions at will and thus disappear from our sight instantly.

Size is Important

This will also be difficult for many of us to comprehend or believe at this time, but it has been communicated to some contactees that some craft are the size of our moon, stretching thousands of miles across. There are other craft ranging in size from 10 miles across to several hundred miles in diameter. These are what we call "small motherships." There are currently over seven thousand of these craft in our solar system right now!

There are larger "Super Motherships," which are over 6,000 miles in diameter are within one light year of our solar system. With their technology, any one of them could be here within minutes. There are over a thousand of the super motherships within this one-light-year distance from earth.

Flying Saucers

The craft we know as flying saucers are scout craft. They are generally carried into a planet's atmosphere by small motherships.

Cigar-shaped Craft

These are the small motherships, long and tapered at both ends. They generally contain eight to ten small flying saucers.

Moon Bases

Yes, there moon bases on the other side of our moon. Our space agency NASA is fully aware of their existence. Abductees and contactees have been told that **alien** beings have been actively observing our earth for over 200 million years.

Our Emotional Body
Each of us has within us something known as an emotional body. It is a source of untold potential. We are aware that certain countries in the Western world tend to view this capability as a weakness. The showing of emotions and feelings is but one small part of this ability. A hint: we, as humans, will never go to the stars until we value, develop, and under-stand the true abilities of the emotional body within us.

Race
The differences between the races on our planet is a source of great anxiety to us. The differences are also used by many to generate fear within us. Those differences between us are one of the greatest gifts in the universe. On other planets differences are revered; on ours they are feared. Do you know that ours is one of few planets that have different mixes of the same type of being? A great step in preparing us for interac-tion with alien beings will be for us as humans to learn to value our differences. They are treasures.

A source of great humor to many alien beings is this: We separate races almost exclusively by color of skin, when in fact the greatest differences between us as humans occurs between the sexes. To any outside observ-er, it would appear that men are a different race from women, not only in terms of physiology, but in terms of completely different societal interac-tions. A black male has far more in common with a white male than the white male has in common with any female.

Don't Call Us 'Alien'
Aliens do not like to be called "Alien." They prefer the term ET's or Extraterrestrials. They have emphatically told British contactee Steve Jones and others the following:

"We are anything but alien to you. We are you." 1.

Others Travel With Them

There are many beings in the universe, more than we can possibly imagine. It is very difficult for people who are living in a society like ours to accept this. We have believed for so long that there were no others, and now we are faced with a completely new reality. This will take some adjustment on our part. But whether we accept it or not, it is true.

The Traders are the only beings who can traverse between the stars. They do allow others to hitch a ride with them. These other beings attach their craft to their ships as the remora attaches itself to the shark in our oceans. These beings are also peaceful and carry no weapons. They would not allow others to travel with them if they attempted to carry devices of destruction. They are all here to observe our progress. We are not ready yet to join the others, but we are ahead of schedule, according to the Traders.

The Travelers

Those who travel with the Traders are known as the *Travelers*. They consist of many different kinds and races of beings. There are currently nineteen other races who have achieved Traveler status. Some of them will be discussed in this text. They are all here with intense and loving curiosity to observe your progress. It is an exciting event watching our transition. A world learning it is not alone is the equivalent to a new child being born. It is almost indescribable. Though these alien beings have witnessed this on millions of planets, it is still very exciting to them.

Several of the Traveler races are directly involved with monitoring and encouraging our growth. Again, we have nothing to fear. Any Traveler who brings harm to any sentient being will forfeit their right to travel with the Traders. Such a forfeiture is a serious loss and not taken lightly.

A One-light-year Limit

All races are allowed to develop space travel on their own, up to a limit of one light year. This corresponds to the distance of travel that can be achieved when a society discovers how to use Element 115. This limited distance is enough to explore space, but not enough to reach other stars and invade or conduct war on other societies located on distant planets. The Traders determine when a society is advanced enough to interact with others. At that time they allow them to attach their craft to theirs. Unfortunately, we have not yet reached this level, but we will.

Female alien.
(Drawing courtesy Christine "Kesara" Dennett.)

How They Live

As mentioned earlier, they eat small wafers made of processed vegetable matter which contains all the essential nutrients. They sleep very little because their metabolism is much slower and more efficient than that of humans. Their average life span is approximately 700 earth years.

The Traveler Races Speak

Zetas

They are known as Zetas because they come from the star system known to us as Zeta-Reticulum. This is a dual star system. That is, it has two suns instead of one, like Earth. The gravity on that world is nearly twice that of planet Earth.

Zeta being.
(Drawing courtesy Christine "Kesara" Dennett.)

Zetas are the ones we are most familiar with. It is their comrades whose bodies the U.S. government has recovered from some of their crashed scout ships. They ride along with the Traders to work with them. We recognize them because of their large almond-shaped eyes. They are larger than those of the Traders. Their mouths appear as mere slits to us. Like the Traders, they do not use them to communicate. They are the beings earth people see when they have what we call "abduction" experiences. That is not what really they are, but it is what we call them.

The Abduction Experiences

The experiences you call abduction experiences they refer to as *interactions*. We do not yet understand that these may be experiences we have agreed to. We may have graciously given our permission to participate in this process. The material taken from our bodies in most cases during these interactions amounts to less than the amount we would lose when getting a manicure for our fingernails.

This process appears to be a DNA-transfer technology. Apparently it is done to insure our DNA will flourish and thrive on other planets as well as our own. As I said, they are trading life and insuring its continued existence. They do this with great love for humans and with thoughts of protecting our genes. They thank us, and love us for our participation.

The Most Powerful Beings Ever Encountered

There is another reason for the "abduction" interactions. It seems that humans, are the most powerful beings some **aliens** have ever encountered. We have abilities beyond our greatest imaginings. Some **alien** races want to know how and why we have these abilities. They have encountered no other race of beings that have them. A source of some frustration to some of them is the fact that they cannot ask us about them, because we do not know we have them or how to access them.

A Connection to the Ultimate Power Source

There is an energy source that runs throughout the universe and flows through all dimensions. You may call it an energy grid, but it is so much more than that. It seems that humans, are directly plugged into this grid. Some alien races are not and they don't know how and why we are linked to it. It is said that we can literally create material out of thin air. That we are capable of moving the blocks of the Egyptian pyramids by sheer force of will, emotion, and intent.

Emotion and Intent

These two forces, emotion and intent, appear to be the things that link us to the ultimate universal power grid. They are under-appreciated by we humans. Particularly ignored is emotion. In our male-dominated societies, emotion is looked upon as a weakness and devalued as an attribute of the female gender of our species. These are the keys to the magic kingdom and we don't know what to do with them. We literally throw them away every day.

Fear

Our strongest emotion is fear. Even when we are happy, we manifest fear: fear that the happiness will disappear. By doing this, we literally guarantee that the happiness will disappear. This fear is so powerful that it is one reason aliens seldom pick up humans in groups. A group of us manifesting our fear all together would literally vaporize them on the spot! So, they pick us up individually and anesthetize us very quickly in order to protect themselves. The mantis beings often help other alien beings with this task.

Anything We Want

We humans, can literally have anything we want. We can manifest it by our emotions and intent. These two things link us to the universal grid and create it for us.

Humans Don't Need Spaceships

This may shock and surprise you. Alien beings have told many contactees that human beings do not need physical ships to travel in space. They find it rather humorous that we spend so much time trying to engineer and build 'hard' spaceships. If you want to delve a little more into the specifics of the science involved, I highly recommend David Wilcock's book; *The Source Field Investigations*. 3

Communication

Alien communication with humans is most interesting. Many humans who have encountered **aliens** say they "just know" what they are saying, even though no actual words are used. That is because they put forth a combination of feeling/thought/images most humans are not able to adequately describe. They have never experienced this before. When humans 'hear' aliens, they are making subjective interpretations of what they are feeling and think they are hearing from them. From the alien perspective it is like trying to talk to someone who has reduced levels of hearing. In effect, they have to shout their feelings/thoughts/images to us. It is very exhausting, but it works fairly well.

Fear and Secrecy

Because of this communication gap, humans will tend to hear/feel whatever is already in their consciousness. In the United States there is a lot of fear. People there tend to view their interactions with aliens as violations or abductions. It may surprise you to learn that other cultures on earth receive their experiences with aliens completely differently. In many countries people line up and wait to be interacted with by **aliens**.

The United States has fostered a high degree of secrecy and military activity surrounding the existence of **alien** beings. Other humans are threatened when certain segments of the government find out that people know of their existence. This is not so in other countries. This is not a criticism of the United States, just an observation and point of enlightenment.

Individual Interpretations

I cannot emphasize this enough: What people hear/feel from **aliens** is almost exclusively each individual's interpretation. This causes humans a lot of anxiety because we end up getting multiple versions of what they are all about. Probably none of them are all that accurate.

Love

It seems that humans have an infinite capacity for love. It is our greatest ability. At the current time it seems to be valued very little on our planet. However, that is changing and not just by our own desire but by forces in the universe we cannot yet begin to comprehend. Forget about propulsion systems - they will get us nowhere. Loving yourself and all that is around you will get you anywhere you wish to go.

A Gift

As a gift aliens have given us a little tip: Humans do not need spaceships to travel to the stars. Most other races do. However, as humans, have capabilities beyond our wildest dreams or imaginations. Some of these are referred to in our religious works. We simply don't understand the ancient language it was written in, or we have completely misinterpreted it. In some cases, we think if in fact these powers do exist they are reserved for the pious and what we call "holy" ones.

The reality is everyone has these abilities already built-in. You can learn to use them with about the same amount of effort it takes to learn to ride a bicycle.

The Mantis Beings

Should you encounter them, do not be alarmed by their appearance. There are many strange and wonderful forms in the universe. To us they appear as a six-foot tall being that resembles the insect we know as a praying mantis. Many people have seen them and have had difficulty convincing others they exist.

In our interactions with the Zetas, many of people can recall being "frozen" in place. This is one of the roles the Mantis beings play in the interaction. Often during interactions with beings from other places, humans begin to become frightened. To them it must appear that our response is to start to run around, making loud noises. The end result is to injure ourselves or others. In order to prevent this they briefly paralyze us.

Contactees and abductees have been 'told' that humans are the only beings in the universe that show their teeth when we are happy or angry. It is very confusing to some alien beings. Apparently, we are known for this trait.

You might say the Mantis beings are the anesthesiologists of the contact experience. They apparently have evolved over millions of years. They have an organ located in their midsection which can not only sense fear as a dog or wild animal would, but they can amplify the fear and radiate it back to the originator. This amplified energy is what disables our neurological system and freezes you. This is how they prevent us from hurting ourselves and them. They perform this duty with great love and care for us as humans. It's the equivalent of tranquilizing a tiger before giving it medical treatment.

The Reptilians

There are other beings visiting our planet which resemble 6-foot tall reptiles. Do not be surprised by their appearance. They are sentient and very advanced in their technology. They apparently are also contributors of certain sections of our DNA strands.

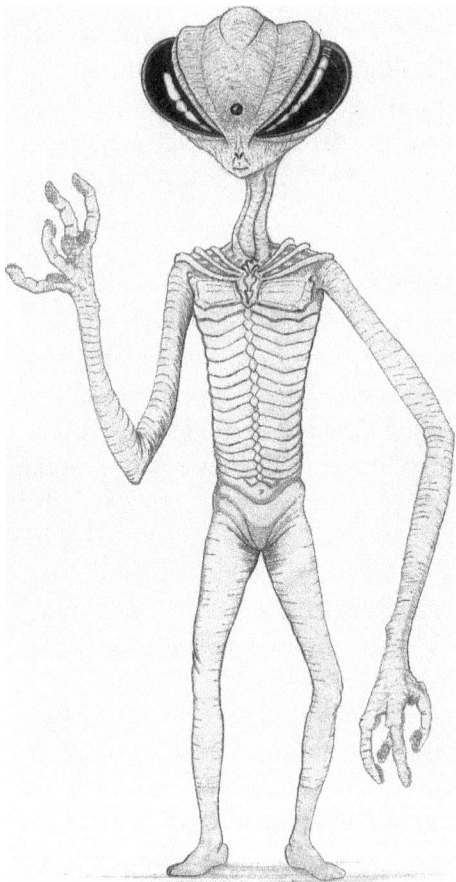

This is a drawing of the "Mantis" being. They are reported to be over 6 feet tall and are usually accompanied by the "Gray" alien beings. (©1997 William L. McDonald)

Their Purpose and Intention

These alien beings are here for many reasons, many of them beyond our comprehension. However, you may think of these beings as Lewis and Clark with scales. Among their greatest interest and curiosity is the marvelous variation in the land on our planet. The view here is truly magnificent. They have been to many worlds and there is none more beautiful and varied than ours.

It's Alive! Alive!

What you do not know yet is this: Almost every naturally occurring thing on our planet is alive. The earth itself is a living breathing being. This is not just a metaphor; it is a fact! Even the rock knows it is a rock! When you poison the environment you are poisoning a living being. Picture yourself giving a glass of arsenic to a child. It is what we do to our planet. Do we expect survival as a result of this behavior?

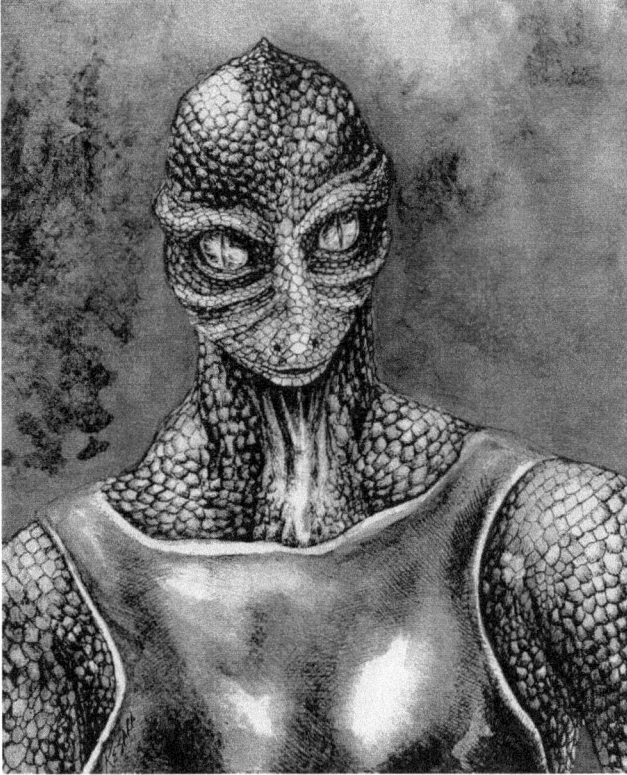

A Reptilian being. These beings have been reported by eyewitnesses worldwide. (Drawing courtesy Christine "Kesara" Dennett)

The Light

All living things emit light. This has been well-documented our television shows about nature and strange things. With Kirlian photography, leaves from a tree have been photographed, along with their light pattern. Many people call these light patterns auras. The light pattern for the entire leaf remains even after half of the leaf is cut away and removed.

Our Science Is Lagging Behind

All living things have this light emission, humans too. Our scientists are easily shown that a leaf has it, yet they scoff at the idea that a human has it as well. Our traditional science teachings do poorly at acknowledging things they can't attach a purpose to.

The Earth

The earth has light emanating from it. According to alien beings, mere decades ago, its light was bright and had the colors of a newborn baby. Now, its light is dim, with the colors of a human who is 90 years old or more.

It's Up to You

How can we improve things if we don't even acknowledge aliens are here? They are opposed to simply showing up and impacting our development. They have much they could teach us. There is much they could do to help the sentient being we call Earth.

They Must Be Invited

In order to assist our world, they must be invited, both by our actions and by our consciousness. There are many in official positions on our planet that know of their existence. They have chosen not to tell us about them for some reason.

The Nordics

There are beings that UFO researchers call the Nordic ones. They are as human-looking as you. Apparently, they have walked our streets and we have not noticed any difference. They are tall, six feet or more, and have blonde hair. Both males and females wear their hair long. As you can guess, they are gendered male and female the same as us.

Their Purpose and Intention

They are here to observe our interactions with one another and our societies at large. There are many things about humanity which are very intriguing. Some of the things they say, echo the words of the Traders.

Light Beings

Beings made of light also interact with humans and have appeared to people around the world. Some appear as balls of light and communicate telepathically. Others appear as 9-foot tall humans made of light. 2

Male and female "Nordic" beings that have interacted with many people world-wide. (©1997 William L. McDonald)

Our Differences

This is the most consistent, and they feel, important, aspect about our existence, the marvelous differences between each of us humans. Differences in body size, shape, and color. Differences in thought, consciousness, and behavior. We have no idea how rare that is. They have seen no other planet with such diversity in a single race. And we are a single race of beings, not a group of different races, as we often think we are.

They have told contactees that our planet is the only place where people with no morals, who would kill another, live side by side with those who are completely moral and would never kill another. This apparently does not occur in other societies, on other planets.

We Fear Our Treasures

Instead of valuing our diversity, we fear it. We fight it. We teach our children to fear and hate it. This is not a condemnation - just a remarkable observation.

Lost in Space

Have you noticed that almost all our recent space probes and satellites have disappeared or malfunctioned? There is a list of these very events in this book. If you have noticed, do you really think these are all inadvertent accidents? What are the odds of that happening?

Stay Put, For Now

We are being very politely, gently, and with loving care prevented from traveling in space any farther than we already have. Our governments are fully aware of the existence of extraterrestrial beings, yet they have gone to extraordinary and unbelievable lengths to keep the truth hidden from us.

The probes would have detected vast numbers of spacecraft circling our planet. Though all are here in peace and carry no weapons on their ships, the reaction of our governments would be to make every attempt to shoot some of these craft down. They have made every effort to do so in the past.

Like a Raindrop

We could launch every nuclear missile on our planet at one of their ships, all at once, timed to explode at the same time, and no one inside would even know anything had even happened. The effect would be no more significant than a single raindrop hitting one of our cars.

Right Through the Sun

Because of their inter-dimensional capabilities, they can travel right through the heart of stars with no effect. Our weapons are a complete waste of human potential. We can only kill each other.

Not Every Difference is a Threat

Back to the differences. There is such immense variety and diversity in the universe among living, sentient beings, so much so that our best science fiction writers could not envision it. If we as humans cannot tolerate each other for something as unnoticeable as a slight difference in skin shading, how can we possibly recognize and value sentient species on other worlds? We must learn to value each other. Until we can value ourselves the Traders will never jeopardize the existence of other species by allowing their exposure to humans.

Some Examples

There is a being on another planet who has more sentience and wisdom than all humankind put together. Yet, we humans, would look upon it and see only a tree. We would most likely cut this being into pieces and burn it for warmth.

There is another being with two heads, six legs, and a tail. It is green in color. It lives in small herds. It has an immense brain capability. The most complicated problems we would use a Cray or IBM mainframe computer to solve would be mere child's play for these beings. It can move physical objects by sheer force of mind. Based on alien observations, we humans would put a saddle on it or try to eat it.

If You're Real, Show Yourselves

This is a common refrain. And who can blame you? Our inner consciousness knows of the existence of alien beings. However, to express this inner knowledge you already have, is to expose yourself to ridicule and harassment by government officials.

Take the Step

We must take this risk. We must make this step. We have done so before on many occasions against much larger odds. The establishment of the United States as a country, the fight against Adolph Hitler, the ending of slavery, the right to vote for women and people of color. All these things took more effort than it would take to establish open contact with alien beings.

Things That Are Preventing Open Contact

Some of the things preventing open contact with alien beings are as follows:

Fear

Our fear of others, Our fear of the differences. Learn to love your fellow man and woman. Value her differences, cherish his skin color, see the value in all cultures. If we do these things, fear and hatred will disappear, and no one can ever force you to that place again. You would be shocked if you knew how little a change each individual would have to make to bring this about.

Personal Devaluation

We, as humans, devalue ourselves. We imagine that celebrities, athletes, people with wealth, and politicians are all better than we are. In our heart we know this is not true, yet our behavior says we believe they are better.

What will we do when we meet beings who can travel to the stars, cure all illness, create new life? These beings are no better than us. However, they are concerned by how we will respond. If we stammer and stutter over meeting an actor who can barely read his lines, we might revere as a god one who has extreme technology. It has happened before.
This is not fair to ourselves. We, as humans, are not yet ready to meet them openly. A shift in consciousness and learning to value ourselves will be their cue to appear.

They have given us a hint: Although we are not yet ready to join the other societies of the galaxies, we are ahead of schedule! That is why all the other beings are here observing us.

Permission

Everything that happens to us is done with our permission. Even the government secrecy surrounding the existence of aliens is done with our permission. Nothing can be withheld from us without our permission. We have given our permission for this. We have not yet given our permission to meet the aliens!

Powerlessness

We have taught our government and those around us that we believe we have no power. We believe we are powerless and the government has accepted our assessment. We love big events. The Super Bowl, the Olympics, the invasion of one country by another. It is quite amazing. During these events, we completely lose sight of ourselves and others. That is why the aliens do not hold a big landing event on the White House lawn.

ALIEN ABDUCTIONS

- *What happens during an abduction.*
- *Who gets abducted and why.*
- *The top investigators of the abduction phenomenon.*

Alien abductions! You have probably heard about alien abductions. They have been the subject of several movies and the popular television series *The X-Files*. It is a very complex phenomenon with many subtopics. The subject is emotionally charged, and not any one human on this planet has a complete understanding of all the aspects of the phenomenon. These abductions are a very important subject because they have become the source of much information about our alien visitors. This is a very complicated topic, so I'll take it one step at a time.

An Overview

These 'abductions' are real, and they are occurring worldwide. In short, alien visitors have been picking up and examining humans from all over the planet. All indications are that the number of people being picked up is in the millions worldwide. The patterns exhibited and the procedures performed are in many cases exactly like the ones we use to study wildlife and animals on our planet. Watch any nature show on television and you will see what I mean. We catch, tag, and take fluid samples from animals to study genetics, sociological interaction, and physical development. However, in this case, what complicates matters is the high level of our alien visitor's technology. Their technology is so far advanced that it causes problems when trying to document and understand exactly what is going on.

The Technology

We are dealing with alien beings with technology that goes beyond our imagination. Their technology defies our definition of physical laws. Some of the things you are about to read are seemingly impossible, and many of the things will simply be unbelievable or difficult comprehend. That's OK! I am not here to convince you of anything. I am simply sharing with you what has been reported by thousands of people around the world.

By many accounts several of the alien races are literally millions of years ahead of humans in technology. Think about this. Think of what we have developed just in the last hundred years. One hundred years ago there were no automobiles, airplanes, televisions, or telephones. Now imagine millions of years of such development. It's almost incomprehensible. Try this: write out a list of all the things we have now that we didn't have when your parents were your age. You'll be astonished!

Let's start with what a typical abduction experience looks like. Then I'll break it down and talk about some of the more intriguing aspects. At the end of the chapter I'll answer some frequently asked questions.

Defining Our Terms

Abductees

For the purposes of the discussion about what I call abductions, I am going to refer to the people being beamed up and examined in spaceships as abductees. The very terms abduction and abductee imply a violation or an act against your will, certainly something not in your best interest. In fact this may or may not be true.

A case can and has been made that abductees may be voluntary participants at a level of consciousness our scientists do not yet understand. The events could also be compared to a small child undergoing a surgical procedure in a modern hospital. If no one were available to explain things to her, she might easily conclude she is being punished, or at least that things are being done to her against her will. Just something to think about.

Experiencers

This is a term some people use instead of abductee. It is in recognition that these experiences may not truly be abductions. This term can also include contacts with alien beings that do not fit the abduction scenario.

Contactee

I consider this a whole different class of people. Contactees are people who claim to be in contact on an intellectual level with beings from other worlds or dimensions. There are many, many people around the world like this, and quite frankly, their stories sound every bit as credible as the abductees' stories. For the most part none of these people are attempting to make money or gain fame with their stories and there seems to be no motivation for them to make up such tales. The most well known contactees and their remarkable stories are profiled in the "Best Cases" section.

The Beginning of an Abduction Experience

Generally, abduction experiences happen in the home or while driving a car. Makes sense. If you want to abduct people you have to go where they are, especially late at night. And that's usually at home in bed or driving a car.

However - and this is important - abductions can and do occur any-where, from hotel rooms, hospitals, prisons, in the city, and out in the country. Forget that old stereotype that only Gomer in the backwoods gets beamed up. A Harvard-educated CEO of a major corporation is just as likely to be an abductee.

Abductees often feel that an abduction experience is about to occur. They may see strange lights in front of them or hear weird humming noises. They often feel apprehensive for no other apparent reason. They will often simply state, "I knew it was going to happen."

Usually at Night

Occurring most often late at night or in the early morning hours, the person will see figures or small beings at the foot of the bed. If they try to run, yell, or scream they find that they are paralyzed, except for their eyeballs, which for some reason, they can sometimes move. Even if they get a sound out, nobody else in the house can hear it. Everyone in the house will have been "switched off." Not asleep - their brains and central nervous systems will somehow have been disconnected. (More about this later.) A spouse lying in bed next to an abductee will appear more dead than alive.

How They Happen

The abductee is then literally floated out of bed and out of the house, right through solid walls, doors, and often through closed glass windows. If they're in a car, they'll be beamed right through the roof of the car. They will ride on a beam of pale blue light, usually accompanied by one or more small beings. Many abductees are floated into a small craft about thirty feet across. That craft then takes them to a larger mothership. Sometimes the abductee is beamed a tremendous distance from the house into the mothership.

When this happens, the abductee can see the ground, trees, and surrounding houses receding rapidly below. There is a lot of physical evidence confirming these beamings. Abductees have been returned to their beds with bits of leaves and branches in their hair that could only have come from the tops of tall trees that they brushed against while being beamed up.

Evidence

Speaking of evidence, there is plenty - lots of tangible things that clearly show that a person was physically displaced. These are not dreams or imagination. In addition to the aforementioned tree leaves there is:

- *Clothing that has been put on backwards.*
- *Band aids that have been removed and then put back in the wrong place.*
- *Stickers that an abductee put on his body in an effort to confirm his experiences. The sticker completely disappeared one night, only to show up in the same place on his body a week later. Yeah, yeah, I know - maybe it fell off in bed and stuck on him again later. No. He checked and changed the bed sheets after it first disappeared.* 13

- *Subdermal fluorescence left under the skin of abductees, which cannot be washed off. (Can be seen with a blacklight.)* 14
- *Full-color images of alien faces and hands left imbedded inside the glass of closed windows they have passed through.* 15

Who's on the Mothership?

When the abductee gets to the mothership, she may encounter an assortment of different beings there. I know, you thought they were all little gray guys with big eyes. Get ready. There are many, many different kinds of alien beings in our universe. If you don't get anything else from this book, understand that!

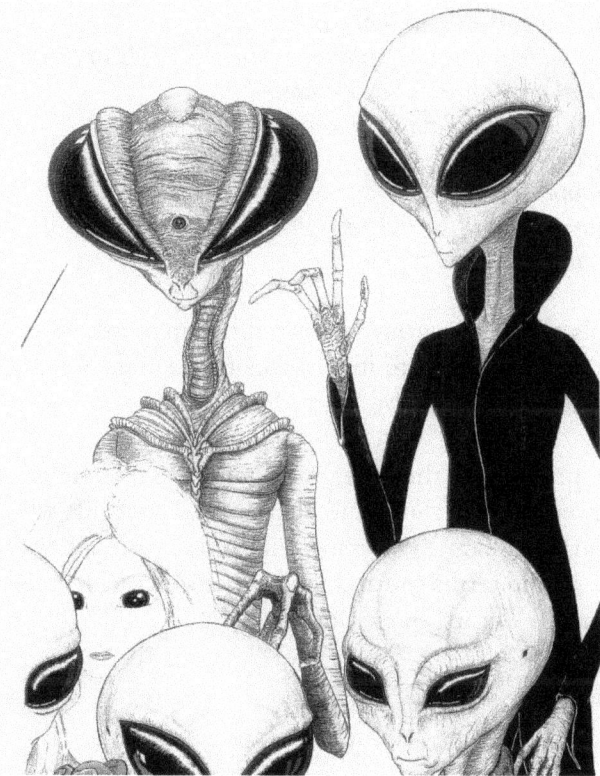

This drawing shows some of the different kinds of alien beings that have been reported by eyewitnesses worldwide (© 1997 William L. McDonald)

Sources from the intelligence community have told some researchers that covert U.S. intelligence operatives have interfaced with at least nine different kinds of alien beings that visit this planet. World-wide reports indicate that as many as fifty different races of alien beings have been here, such as the Mantis and Reptilian beings described before.

Medical Procedures

Once on board, the abductee is subjected to a whole host of medical and, for lack of a better term, psychological procedures. The procedures are very specific and consistent worldwide. No matter who is telling the story, no matter what country they are in, they describe exactly the same procedures. Here, briefly are some of the things that occur:

> * *Collect sperm or ovum.*
> * *Collect samples of skin, hair, or nails.*
> * *Place small devices or implants in various parts of the body.*
> * *Head and neck surgical procedures.*
> * *Check neurological functioning.*
> * *Extraction of fetus.*
> * *Brain/mind scan.*
> * *Creation of sexual scenarios.*
> * *Environmental mind tapes.*

For full details of the vast array and ramifications of the procedures, I recommend you read the definitive works in the area: *Secret Life* by David Jacobs and *Abduction* by John Mack.

During these procedures the little gray beings seem to function as worker bees. There are also gray aliens and alien/human hybrids who are a little taller and clearly in charge, very much like a doctor in an operating room. In fact these are the terms the abductees themselves use, referring to the beings present as doctors, nurses, and orderlies.

Weird Science

There are some odd things about these procedures:

1. They are mostly neurological and gynecological. Not once has an abductee reported having his heartbeat or blood pressure checked. So these are not medical examinations in the sense we

usually imagine.

2. The aliens still use very large needles! I have always wondered about this. They can float you through a solid wall, travel to the stars, and they're still using needles?! Abductees routinely report being stuck with large needles during these procedures.

Home Again

After these procedures they just float you on back home - until they come back in a couple of nights to get you again.

Who First Uncovered the Alien Abductions?

Great Ones, right here, right now! Have you ever wondered what it would be like to live during the same time as some of the great discoverers in history such as Columbus, Copernicus, or Leonardo da Vinci? These people were outside of the boundaries of current science and conventional thought. Though now known as geniuses, they were ignored and often ridiculed in their day. They were outside of the box.

Well, the people I'm going to tell you about now are outside of today's box. Here and now these pioneers are dislodging outmoded science and challenging us to examine undefined phenomena. One day their work will be as important to the world as that of Isaac Newton and Madam Curie. The good news is that these people are alive and you can watch and participate in their discoveries firsthand. Get a firm grip on your chair as you begin to explore the work of the world's foremost abduction researchers. Real life doesn't get any more exciting than this!

The Top Abduction Researchers

Here is a brief summary of five top researchers of the human/alien interactions we call abductions. The stories of their discoveries and the process that led to them is as important as their findings. The history provides a context, a framework. A man riding a horse through the middle of town is meaningless unless you know the event was surrounded by the American Revolution and the man's name was Paul Revere.

Therefore, how each person became involved with knowledge of the existence of an alien civilization is important. Each of these individuals has written at least one book about his or her experiences. The books are listed in the Bibliography. To understand the magnitude of their findings, you simply must read their books, cover to cover. Every one is fascinating, exciting, and true! I will say this, however: Be prepared to have your mind bent if you pick up these books.

Real People

One more thing about these people. They are real flesh and blood. They have names, faces, and e-mail addresses. You can talk to them, face to face. So much of the flying saucer/alien phenomenon is shrouded in secrecy, mystery, and just plain smoke; you rarely get a chance to attach a person to an event or research. This is the one instance you can actually get to know about the people involved. Their accessibility is almost as important as their discoveries. Wouldn't every physicist alive love to be able to pick up the telephone and call Albert Einstein? It's a rare privilege, and not one to be taken lightly. One day your grandchildren may ask you if you ever got a chance to see these people in person. Don't ignore the opportunity!

David M. Jacobs, Ph.D.

David Jacobs is a tenured professor of history at Temple University in Philadelphia. That's right, history! Sound like an unlikely discipline to end up researching alien abductions? Ironically, these abductions may end up being some of the most important historical events man has ever known. It's a sure bet David Jacobs' expertise at chronicling history will come in handy. It already has!

Jacobs got into this field of research almost by accident, as did many other UFO researchers. It was as if he were being pulled into it by some unknown force. Jacobs made an observation: UFOs had been reported for decades, if not centuries, and yet there was almost no information about them. You could go to any library and find volumes and volumes on leprechauns and the Easter Bunny, but nothing on something that has been witnessed by people all around the world for decades.

A spark was kindled and Jacobs did a dissertation on the subject. The dissertation was later expanded and published in 1975 as a book entitled

The UFO Controversy in America. The beginnings of his research career are well documented in his second book, published in 1992: *Secret Life: Firsthand Accounts of UFO Abductions*.

As we expand our contact with other beings in the universe we are going to need help from every area of study, including fields that have been ignored because they are not considered scientific, as well as those areas of study yet to be discovered. That means everyone has something to offer.

Who? Everybody!

Jacobs has discovered that people who are abducted come from all walks of life: doctors, secretaries, construction workers, housewives, and students. They are from every income level, from the very wealthy to people who are poor, and everyone in between; including all races, religions, and cultures. 2

Where? Everywhere!

David Jacobs has documented abductions from virtually any place you could find a human being: cities, rural roads, apartment buildings, hospitals, prisons, and major hotels. It can and does happen everywhere.

How Many People? A Lot!

Jacobs has spent over a decade conducting his research and investigations. He has worked with over three hundred abductees. Jacobs and his colleague Budd Hopkins together have received over fifteen thousand letters from people around the world detailing nearly identical abduction experiences. Based on their research, Jacobs and Hopkins estimate that approximately 7 percent of the world's population has been involved in abductions. In the United States alone that's 18 million people!

Time / CNN Poll

Not only that, but according to a Time/CNN poll, between 13 and 22 percent of the population acknowledges that they think abductions or at least contact is taking place on a regular basis. 14 That percentage equals 57 million people. By comparison, Jacobs' estimates seem to be well on the conservative side. Clearly, there is something taking place, and it's big!

How Often? All the Time!

If you're an abductee you could lose a lot of sleep. According to Jacobs, the lowest rate of abduction is at least ten times per year. That's almost once a month. The average rate is a hundred times per year! That's every three days! 3

Abductions Are Not Random

If you haven't been beamed up yet, you probably won't be. Jacobs has discovered that abductions are intergenerational.

1. Abductions are not random occurrences, like fishing.

2. They start when a person is a child. They are planned and repeated many times over a person's entire life.

3. They expand exponentially. Therefore, even if only one parent is an abductee, all the children from those parents will also become abductees. Even if you started with only a hundred abductees 50 years ago, think how many people you would have today.

4. Jacobs has been able to go back about 60 years and identify what appears to be some of the original abductees.

5. There is one exception: Adopted children do not get abducted even if their natural siblings do.

Flying Saucer Sightings Are Not Random

Flying saucers have a purpose. Flying saucers are vehicles transporting somebody to or from a location. They are not absently floating by like clouds. With this in mind, it could be that at least one of their main functions is transporting people for the purpose of abductions. People who are abductees see flying saucers all the time, often several times per week, whereas non-abductees can easily go a lifetime and never see a UFO. 4 The correlation strongly suggests that when people frequently see UFOs, it is in fact just before or immediately following an abduction event. A generalization can be made that it is rare to have one without the other. There are no adult onset abductions.

Abductions Appear to Be a Huge Project

By all accounts worldwide, the tables and devices involved in the medical procedures are all large and human-sized. The gray beings conducting the procedures are described to be between three and four feet tall, much smaller than humans. This means the equipment is intended for use on humans. Some of the spacecraft are huge with literally hundreds of examination tables in a single room. Think of the number of individuals and support systems it would take to build and maintain a ship this size with that amount of equipment. Enough capacity to routinely abduct people worldwide on a regular basis! This is a huge investment of resources and obviously very important to our alien visitors, not to mention the great lengths that have been gone through to keep this project secret. 5

More Proof: Physician, Heal Thyself!

As Jacobs continues to point out in his book, most of the alien procedures are gynecological and neurological. Our most compelling evidence is sitting in your doctor's filing cabinets! Physicians just didn't know what they were seeing, and when they did notice it, it was such an aberration it was simply dismissed.

For some doctors, it scared them, and they made agreements among themselves not to discuss it with anyone else. There have been several documented cases like this. Some additional things medical people regularly see in abductees:

- *Unexplained scars, scoop marks, and bruising.*
- *Deep bruising. So deep that X-rays clearly shown trauma all the way to the bone.*
- *Severe nosebleeds following an abduction.*
- *X-rays and CAT scans of implanted devices when the patient had no prior history of surgery.*
- *Three-pronged, deep-needle sticks that are spaced exactly the same on many abductees.*

UFO Healings

UFO Healings, by noted author Preston Dennett, follows and documents over one hundred cases of abductees who have been healed from grave illnesses by aliens using superior technology. Dennett acknowledges that all the cases may not be altruistic; it could be that some of these people were cured of illness so as not to lose a subject and disrupt the results of a monitored study. 8

John E. Mack, MD

John Mack is a physician and professor of psychiatry at Cambridge Hospital, Harvard Medical School, and the founding director of the Center for Psychology and Social Change. He is the author of nine books, winning a Pulitzer Prize in 1977 for *A Prince of Our Disorder*. *Abduction: Human Encounters With Aliens*, is Mack's latest book. He has investigated over a hundred cases of abductions. His book chronicles thirteen cases in depth. 6

Mack believes the investigation of human abductions is not just about aliens or UFOs. It is really about how we can expand our understanding of reality and awaken our human potential. 7 As we explore Mack's discoveries, let's see if we can step back and look at a bigger picture. Let's think of ourselves as a 3-year old child being taken through a hospital, seeing many things a child would not understand. As Mack says in the preface:

> When we explore phenomena that exist at the margins of accepted reality, old words become imprecise or must be given new meanings. Terms like "abduction," "alien," "happening," and even "reality" itself, need redefinition lest subtle distinctions be lost. In this context, thinking of memory too literally as "true" or "false" may restrict what we can learn about human consciousness from the abduction experiences. 9

A Psychiatrist is a Medical Doctor

After going to medical school to become a regular doctor, a psychiatrist then goes back to medical school and gets an additional degree in psychiatry. So how was a medical doctor pulled into alien-abduction research?

Mack heard about Budd Hopkins, an otherwise normal guy who had been working with people, spaceships, and aliens. Mack's reaction was typical: The guy must be nuts. Through a mutual acquaintance he ended up being introduced to Hopkins and his work. In spite of the insanity of it all, a few things triggered Mack's professional instincts:

1. Minute details of the experiences matched in almost every case.
2. The specifics about abductions had not been presented in mainstream media, so patients were not getting information from those sources, and at the time there had been no books published detailing the experiences.
3. There were physical marks, bruises, scars, and lesions supposedly caused by the experiences, which would not occur when someone imagines an experience.
4. In Mack's medically trained, professional judgment, none of the people seemed to be delusional or exhibit the signs of mental illness.

Mack then agreed to work with some patients and the rest is history.

Mack Identifies Three Kinds of Information

During John Mack's ongoing study of the abduction phenomenon, he was able to classify three distinct kinds of information available to us regarding these events. These three classes of information are extremely important and should be kept in mind at all times while studying any aspect of flying saucer/UFO/alien events. 10

1. Physical evidence left behind such as burned grass, scars, lesions, bruises, or implants. These things are easily recognizable by modern science.

2. Things we could understand with our science if we had more information or technology. Things which do not seem to violate

our understanding of how the universe works. An example might be an advanced propulsion system capable of interstellar travel.

3. Third - and this may be the most important category of all - things which do not fit within the framework of our universal laws. Things such as levels of consciousness we do not know how or have forgotten how to activate, along with unknown life forms who live only on those levels of consciousness.

Reading John Mack's book "Abduction" is an absolute necessity if you want to know more about alien abductions and the true capabilities of humans.

Budd Hopkins

We could call Hopkins the Godfather of alien abductions. I use *Godfather* as a term of respect and endearment. Hopkins was the first person to do continual, in-depth research into alien abductions. He has uncovered and tracked some of the most dramatic abduction cases in the world. His book *Missing Time* is a fascinating journal of discovery as he explores the unknown wonders of abductions and the life stories of the people being abducted. Much of the dialogue from the first hypnosis sessions is printed in full with appropriate notes.

I Just Wanted to Paint
Budd Hopkins was (and still is) an artist. He is a serious painter, it was what he did for a living. He knew nothing about UFOs and was not interested in them. Then in 1964 he saw an object which was more or less a UFO. Just a strange object. However, it was enough to pique his interest, so he read a few books on the subject.

In 1965 *Life* Magazine published an account of the now-famous Betty and Barney Hill case, the first abduction case on record. Hopkins believed the abduction was impossible, but he filed away the story in his memory.

A Push From A Friend
Ten years later in 1975 a man Hopkins had known well for 20 years just

happened to mention that he just had a strange experience. When Hopkins asked some questions, he discovered that his friend had seen an oval-shaped craft hovering in a nearby park while going home from work late one evening. Some small beings got out, collected soil samples, got back in the craft, and flew off. All this occurred at a distance of about 20 yards away from his friend. The next day Hopkins and his friend went back to the park and sure enough, there were fifteen small, 5-inch deep holes where the little beings had been. Unknowingly, Hopkins had been led into alien abduction research.

A Little Help From My Friends

Hopkins later enlisted the help of psychiatrist Dr. Robert Naiman to hypnotically regress some people who had similar strange experiences. Hopkins also got help from a neurosurgeon who was able to assist by confirming the neurological procedures that were being performed on abductees. The more he looked into the phenomena, the more people who had these experiences seemed to find Hopkins. By sheer word of mouth, more and more people were coming forward with the same kind of stories. Hopkins unexpectedly now had a new career, alien abduction investigations.

His Latest Work

Hopkins' latest book is *Witnessed: The True Story of the Brooklyn Bridge UFO Abductions*. It is a dramatic true-life thriller. It documents a multiple-witness abduction right in midtown Manhattan. The witnesses are extraordinary, including government agents and a world-renowned statesman! Known as the "Linda Cortile Case," the book sheds a whole different light on what some of these abductions might really be.

Linda Napolitano was beamed out of her apartment and into a hovering spacecraft in full sight of about a dozen people. The craft then dove into the East River and disappeared. In order to protect her identity, Hopkins referred to Napolitano as "Linda Cortile."

Betty and Barney

The first abduction on record, this case was discovered almost by accident. On September 19, 1961, Betty and Barney Hill were driving home on a road in rural New Hampshire. They were a racially mixed couple: Barney was black and Betty is white. The only reason I mention this is because in 1961 race relations were tense at best and a couple in such an environment would be less likely to want to draw any undue attention to themselves. However, because a physician initially thought it might be the underlying cause for emotional problems the couple later developed, their incredible story came to light.

As they drove down the highway, a disk-shaped object flew over the car. It stopped and hovered 200 yards away from them. They were avid birdwatchers, so they had binoculars with them in the car. Imagine Barney's shock when he got out of the car and saw through the binoculars that there were creatures in the portholes of the disk, looking back at him! Basically, he panicked!

He ran back to the car and the two sped off. Later they started feeling a little strange and noticed they could not remember the previous 30 miles they had just driven; also, their watches were no longer running, they had stopped cold.

Missing Time

Over the next several weeks Betty began to have weird dreams and the couple began to recall other odd things that had occurred on their road trip. Looking back, they realized their trip had taken 2 hours longer than normal and they couldn't figure out why. This later became the first recorded case of missing time. They also had no recollection of what they did during this 2-hour period of missing time.

Physical Evidence

The next day the Hills found twelve bright circles about the size of a half-dollar on their car. When they placed a compass over the circles the needle spun wildly.

Better See a Doctor

Barney began to exhibit a number of physical symptoms. A doctor attributed them to stress since there seemed to be no other cause. Barney was next referred to a psychiatrist, Dr. Benjamin Simon, in an effort to find the cause of the symptoms. As part of his treatment, Barney agreed to undergo hypnosis. After the first session, the psychiatrist decided that both Barney and Betty should be treated and hypnotized separately. The independent sessions were set up so that neither Betty nor Barney would have any conscious recollection of what they independently said. This was done so that neither could discuss with the other what they had told Dr. Simon. Each session was tape recorded.

What Really Happened!

Over a period of several months, Betty and Barney told Dr. Simon a story of what really happened that night. To say it was startling was an understatement, but both of them were telling the exact same story each from their own respective vantage point. That is, each story corroborated the other. They had been picked up by alien beings and taken aboard a space craft! They were both subjected to a number of medical procedures. Barney had sperm extracted and Betty recalled being told that the beings were performing a pregnancy test on her. Betty had a long needle inserted into her navel. This was decades before amniocentesis was developed by earth scientists.

The Star Map!

One of the most remarkable things about the Hill case, besides being the first abduction case on medical record, was a star map. The aliens had shown Betty a map consisting of stars and lines drawn between the stars. Betty was later able to draw the map while under hypnosis. They then asked her if she knew where her planet was on the map. When she was unable to tell them, they abruptly ended the conversation without telling her any more.

Movie of the Week

Though Barney died in 1969, NBC made a movie out of the Hill's case. Entitled *The UFO Incident*, it starred James Earl Jones and Estelle Parsons as Betty and Barney Hill.

The Little Gray Guys are Zetas

Marjorie Fish, an astronomer, took Betty's map and began to convert it into a three-dimensional model to see if she could find out where these beings were from. When a new catalog of stars, the Gliese Catalog, was released she was able to come up with a final version that seemed to make sense. The catalog allowed Fish to assign accurate distances between the stars. The map indicated that the beings were from a planet circling a twin (sun) star system, Zeta Reticuli, Which consists of two stars, Zeta 1 and Zeta 2. Zeta Reticuli is very close to us in terms of space distance. The planet is only 37 light years away (220 trillion miles). The two stars are also a billion years older than our sun. Fish's model was later confirmed by a computer. That is why the aliens we often call little gray guys are sometimes also known as Zetas.

Trade Routes

Some contactees were told in the 1960s that intelligent life is more often found in twin star systems, and that our solar system is unusual since we have life with only one sun. MIT astronomer Fred Rasio says, "You get the impression that most solar systems are not like ours." 15

On August 19, 1998, the front page of the *Los Angeles Times* featured an article about leading astronomer Andrea Ghez. Using the Keck telescope in Hawaii (the largest of its kind in the world) Ghez determined and declared that almost all new stars in the universe are, in fact, born as twins.

Betty Hill had been given additional information by her alien companions. They told her that the lines drawn between the stars were trade routes. The thick lines were busy trade routes, the thinner lines were routes used less often. Dotted lines represented occasional expeditions.

Some Things We Have Learned: A Remarkable Device

Here is a list of electronic devices we are all familiar with:

Digital Recorder
Television
Clock
Video camera
Radio transmitter
Electrical power generator
Cellular phone
Tape recorder
Multiband radio receiver
Computer
Computer operating system

Computer software programs
Power grid system
Fax machine
Scanner

Think of all the things each of these devices can do. Now imagine all these devices rolled into one small machine. Here's the point: You already own such a device. We all do. It's called our brain!

Alien abductions have taught us that we have innate abilities almost beyond comprehension. Some of our alien visitors know how to access any one or all these devices in our heads. They can literally play back a scene from your life at any point. They can play back the emotions you felt. Imagine if we could learn how to utilize the capabilities we already have built right in.

There is absolutely nothing to prevent us from starting to learn how to access these abilities now. In fact, we have a head start because we know they exist, thanks to alien abductions.

Some Alien Techno-marvels

Here is a short list of some of the things that have been observed and experienced by citizens from around the world. The alien beings can:

- Travel millions of light years in a matter of minutes. (Remember, time is not the same everywhere in our universe and a light year is a measurement of distance, not time.)
- Walk through solid doors, walls, and windows. (Remember, an atom is comprised mostly of space).
- Manipulate our perception of time and stop time as we know it.
- Bend and pull space.
- Lift objects using a beam of light.
- Move in and out of other dimensions.
- Control a human brain and nervous system with the mere touch of a finger.

The Military's Role in Abductions

This is an important area that is seldom discussed. There is plenty of evidence that many abductions are in fact generated and conducted by covert U.S. military forces. This is a hard fact to deal with but no discussion of abductions would be complete without it. CSETI (Center for the Study of Extraterrestrial Intelligence) founded by Dr. Steven Greer has uncovered over 150 eyewitnesses from defense contractors, NASA, the U.S. military, Central Intelligence Agency and other covert intelligence organizations that confirm the existence of extraterrestrial beings. Several of these witnesses confirm U.S. covert intelligence involvement with human abductions. Run, don't walk, to the CSETI website at www.cseti.org where you will find photos of some of these witnesses and their statements confirming knowledge of ETs.

Holographic Experiences

Greer's sources have stated that these covert agencies have the ability to create a "holographic" abduction so real that a person would easily pass a lie detector test. Abductee and eyewitness Pamela Hamilton has experienced such abductions and in a clear, unaltered state was taken by a group composed of both alien-looking beings accompanied by U.S. military personnel in uniform. Yeah, I know, this is hard to accept, but all indications are it's true. There are just too many witnesses to ignore, both as victims and people with knowledge of these activities from the inside. It's a big issue, folks, but you will have to deal with it sooner or later.

These covert organizations have the ability to impose a holographic experience on a person or group of people, even at a distance! This is real, not science fiction!

Melinda Leslie: Abduction Researcher

Melinda's special area of research has to do with the U.S. military. Many abductees have stated that they and others close to them have been abducted or re-abducted by members of the U.S. military. Melinda herself has experienced this. Melinda states:

> The hardest part of the abduction experience to deal with is the feeling that you must be going crazy. I cope with it because I insist on living a normal life.

Melinda works with others besides herself who are drugged, kidnapped, interrogated, and harassed by the U.S. military in an effort to find out what abductees know about the aliens. Members of the military also kidnap abductees in efforts to recover implants that aliens have placed in them.

An abduction by the military. Abductees are frequently re-abducted and examined by the military to gain information about alien visitors. (©1997 William L. McDonald)

Another abductee, Debbie Jordan-Kauble, also speaks of her traumatic experience in which she and companions have been drugged and kidnapped by members of the military. 16 Debbie's lifelong experiences with abductions is told in her book, *Abducted: The Story of The Intruders Continues*. Debbie is also the subject of Budd Hopkins' book, *Intruders*, and the television mini-series of the same name. Debbie has appeared on

Oprah Winfrey, *Sightings*, and *Maury Povich*. She can be reached at her website: http://www.ufocasebook.com/copelywoods.html

Melinda's body of evidence is large and impressive. It includes photos, medical lab tests, eyewitness accounts, and a growing number of people with the same testimony. Among them is Kim Carlsberg, whose story is recounted in *Beyond My Wildest Dreams*. If you have had similar experiences you can contact Melinda directly.

Website: http://www.alienexperiences.com/MelindaLeslie01.html.

E-mail: linnie@onebox.net

Yvonne R. Smith: Hypnotherapist

Yvonne Smith is a hypnotherapist, certified by the Hypnosis Motivation Institute, the first and only college of hypnosis in the United States to achieve national accreditation. She has been working with alien abductees since 1990.

A Place for Help

Yvonne also manages an investigative support group for abductees. She is the founder of CERO, which stands for Close Encounter Research Organization. CERO is an organization that provides a safe haven for those individuals who have undergone alien abduction experiences.

This is Serious Stuff

Investigating your own series of alien abductions is not to be taken lightly. As Yvonne says, "The decision to begin investigating troubling dreams or sketchy memories is one of the most important decisions you will ever make in your life. If you learn that you have, in fact, undergone abduction experiences, this knowledge will ultimately change your life, including your relationship with your family and friends."

More Medical Evidence

Some of the most compelling evidence of alien abductions comes from medical case histories. This evidence includes X-rays, photographs of unexplained marks, scars, and deep bruises. One of the best collections of photographs, X-rays, and case histories belongs to Yvonne Smith.

If you want help or more information, you can contact Yvonne or CERO in La Canada, California.
Website: www.ysmith.com
E-mail: Staff@ysmith.com
Phone: 818-383-6903

Frequently Asked Questions

How come people only remember this alien abduction stuff when they are under hypnosis?

Hypnosis is a critical subject when discussing alien abductions. Many abductees (but not all) only recall their experiences while under hypnosis. What prompts researchers to use hypnosis on these subjects is that they experience missing time and other strange things I will discuss below.

Hypnosis Controversy

First of all, to the general public hypnosis appears to be a strange thing. Many people don't believe it's real. Even the legal system and our courts of law cannot all agree on its validity. To many of us, our only experience with hypnosis is watching a hypnotist on TV or in a nightclub making your friend get up on stage and act like a chicken! We end up not knowing what really happened, or if anything really did happen. Besides, your friend is goofy and a show off anyway.

Second, hypnosis and its practitioners have come under fire recently for the use of hypnosis in investigating sexual-abuse cases. It has been charged that some therapists have imparted false memories of childhood abuse in patients during sessions of hypnotherapy. This is known as FMS, or False Memory Syndrome. As a result, the public questions even more the validity of using hypnosis to recount actual experiences. I will also mention here that there has never been a single alien abduction case that has turned out to be a masked history of sexual abuse or other traumatic cause. [12]

A Simple Way to View Hypnosis

If you have a computer or know something about them, then you know what hardware is. It is the computer itself, or the actual machine. You also know that software is the program or set of instructions that actually does the work. A computer has an operating system. Common operating systems you may have heard of are Windows 7, Linux, or any of the Apple Macintosh operating systems. The operating system is simply a set of electronic instructions that lie underneath the software instructions. You don't see them, but they allow the software to do its work. They are simply a series of commands to control electrical impulses.

Your brain is also a computer. It has a series of underlying electrical impulses, and you have your own built-in operating system. In both cases you can go into these underlying programs and get out data that is not normally visible. However, it is really there, and it is real data. Hypnosis simply accesses your own operating system. The information there is as real as you are. In fact, it is you. Please keep this in mind when discussing alien/human interaction.

Aliens Function at the Operating-system Level

Aliens, for the most part, only interact with humans on an operating system or subconscious level. It is at a different frequency we don't experience at normal consciousness. Think of it like attending a concert where all the instruments are dog whistles. You would need a special receiver or have to bring your pooch in order to appreciate the tunes. That receiver would have to convert the frequencies to ones you could hear. Well, your brain is a receiver and our alien visitors know how to access it and tune it - but you don't, - and the only way you can recall the music is to pull it up from your operating system through the use of hypnosis.

A Very Important Thing to Know

Abduction experiences recalled under hypnosis are consistently confirmed and validated by other people; specifically, by other people who have never met the original person who was hypnotized. Here is an example of what I mean:

Let's say Joe recalls under hypnosis that he was lifted into an alien spacecraft. He recalls being in a room and on his right is another person whom I will call Bill. When Bill is hypnotized separately he describes Joe exactly and the fact that Joe is to his left. When Joe is hypnotized he recalls that Bill is on his right. That is, their positions are respectively correct, and this is the case time and again when Bill and Joe have never met! Later when they do meet, they are shocked because they each remember the other even though they both agree that they have never met before except during their shared, remembered experience on the spacecraft.

This kind of experience occurs over and over again with alien abductions. This differs significantly from other hypnosis-recalled experiences such as many child-abuse cases where usually there is only one person with the remembered experience and no other people who can share or confirm it.

Hynopsis-recalled Events are More Accurate

In fact, events recalled under hypnosis are more accurate. They are not filtered by the subject's judgements or denial. If you take a group of people who witnessed a crime, any detective will tell you that each person will have a different version. Each filtered the incident through her own perception. If you hypnotize all the witnesses, their accounts will fall more in line with one another. Things recorded at the subconscious (operating system) level are more accurate, not less.

Screen-saver Memories

Many times when an abductee is hypnotically regressed the first couple of times he has vivid memories of seeing animals such as deer or owls with very large eyes. Abductees will also report just seeing eyes floating in midair in addition to other nonsensical memories. These are screen-saver memories, just like a screen saver on your computer. They are used by the alien beings to camouflage the true experience the abductee had. The true experience was recorded, but the hypnotist must be experienced enough to dig beneath the temporary screen saver.

Are Aliens Trying to Take Over the Planet?

No. Based on their technology, they clearly could if they wanted to. A case could be made that they are not trying to take over the planet, because they already own it! However, just discovering bits and pieces of these activities could cause a tremendous amount of fear and anxiety in people just now hearing about this for the first time, or for those realizing that all those vague reports that aliens actually exist are in fact, true.

From an observational standpoint, it appears the aliens are conducting a massive, long-term project involving many different aspects of humanity. These include but may not be limited to: our emotional, physical, and sociological conditions. The project involves genetics, as well as neurological and gynecological procedures. They have also imparted messages that we as a race of people need to be much more aware of the conditions we create on our planet because it affects not only our planet, but other portions of the universe as well.

Are You An Abductee?
(Compiled and reprinted with permission by Melinda Leslie.)

This is a list of fifty common indicators shared by most abductees. It is based on known research on the subject and Melinda's personal findings. It has been compiled to help you determine if you are an abductee. Of course, there may be other explanations for some of these occurrences, and this is in no way an absolute means of knowing if you are an abductee. If you or someone you know does fit any of these traits listed here, please seek the help of a qualified researcher or therapist. This list is not in any particular order.

- Have had missing or lost time of any length, especially an hour or more.
- Have unusual scars or marks with no possible explanation of how you received them, especially if you have an emotional reaction to them (i.e. small scoop indentation, straight-line scar, scars in roof of mouth, in nose, behind or in the ears, or genitals, etc.)
- Have seen balls of light or flashes of light in your home or other locations.
- Have a memory of flying through the air which could not be a dream.

- Have a "marker memory" that will not go away (i.e. alien face, examination needle, table, strange baby, etc.).
- Have seen beams of light outside your home or come into your room through a window.
- Have had vivid dreams of aliens or UFOs.
- Have had numerous UFO sightings in your life.

- For women only: Have had false pregnancy or missing fetus. (Pregnant and then not).
- Have awoken in another place than where you went to sleep, or don't remember ever going to sleep; for example, lying upside down in the bed or a car.
- Have had a dream of eyes such as animal eyes (like an owl or a deer), remember seeing an animal looking at you. Also applicable if you have a fear of eyes.
- Have awoken in the middle of the night startled.
- Have a strong reaction to pictures of aliens, either an aversion or being drawn to.
- Have unusual fears or phobias; for example: heights, snakes, spiders, large insects, certain sounds, bright lights, your personal security, or being alone.
- Have experienced self-esteem problems.
- Have awoken with marks, burns, or bruises with no explanation for how you could have received them.
- Have had someone who claims to have witnessed a ship or alien near you or has witnessed that you have been missing.
- Have had at any time blood or an unusual stain on sheet or pillow, with no explanation of how it got there.
- Have an interest in the subject of UFOs or aliens or an extreme aversion to the subject.
- Have been compelled to drive or walk to an out-of-the-way place or unknown area.
- Have the feeling of being watched all the time, especially at night.
- Have had dreams of passing through a closed window or solid wall.
- Have seen a strange fog or haze that should not be there.
- Have heard strange humming or pulsing sounds and you could not identify the source.
- Have had unusual nosebleeds or have awoken with a heavy nose bleed.
- Have awoken with soreness in your genitals which cannot be explained.

- Have had back or neck problems, T-3 vertebrae out often, or awoken with an unusual stiffness in any part of your body.
- Have sinusitis or nasal problems.
- Have had electronics around you go haywire or oddly malfunction with no explanation.
- Have seen a hooded figure in or near your home, especially next to your bed.
- Have had frequent or sporadic ringing in your ears, especially in one ear.
- Have a fear of doctors or tend to avoid medical treatment.
- Have insomnia or sleep disorders.
- Have had dreams of doctors or medical procedures.
- Have frequent or sporadic headaches, especially in the sinus, behind one eye, or in one ear.
- Have the feeling that you are going crazy for even thinking about these sorts of things.
- Have had paranormal or psychic experiences or have these abilities.
- Have been prone to compulsive or addictive behavior.
- Have channeled telepathic messages from extraterrestrials.
- Have been afraid of your closet now, or as a child.
- Have had sexual or relationship problems.
- Have to sleep against the wall or have your bed against the wall.
- Have a difficult time trusting other people, especially authority figures.
- Have a sensitivity towards certain lights or sounds.
- Have had dreams of destruction or catastrophe.
- Have the feeling that you are not supposed to talk about these things, or that you should not talk about "them."
- Have tried to resolve these types of problems with little or no success.
- You fit many of these traits but can't remember anything about an abduction.

ALIEN IMPLANTS

Many abductees have had small devices placed inside their bodies. Common locations are deep inside nasal cavities, behind the eye, in the back of the head and neck; or in the feet, toes, hands, or jaw. These implants are real. We have photographs, X-rays, and CAT scans of them in place. Several of them have been successfully removed by medical teams. Upon removal the implants sometimes disintegrate, but most often they don't. It is believed these implants are used to monitor activities or the physical condition of the people in whom they are placed.

Are They Really From Aliens?

Every indication seems to be that the implants are from alien beings. However, no one really knows for sure. Even those doctors who remove them and do research on abductions continue to use the term *alleged* alien implants. Wherever they come from there is little doubt something extraordinary is going on.

So I'll tell you some remarkable things about these implants, and then I'll tell you about a couple of doctors who remove them. They have made some astounding discoveries. By the way, if there are any physicians out there, pay attention!

The Implants

The implants are made of a metallic substance. Some are small and round, the size of a BB. Others are no larger than a pin-head. They come in many different shapes: round, triangular, spiral, and thin as a fine wire. They are clearly visible on X-rays, and hundreds of X-rays of these implants have been taken and documented by researchers. Most of the implants found so far have been placed on the left side of the individual's body.

An Organic Outer Covering

While in place, these implants are surrounded by an unusually strong covering of living tissue comprised of protein and keratin, the same stuff your hair and fingernails are made of. This covering is so strong and tough that surgeons cannot cut it with a hardened steel scalpel. This same scalpel can easily slice through bone. There is not anything on earth made by man that can match the strength of this simple outer covering.

Atomically Aligned

It is thought that this covering is so strong because all its atoms are atomically aligned. That is, all the atoms lie in one single direction, providing a level of strength not yet achievable by humans. The only creature on earth that can atomically align something is a spider; the tensile strength of a filament of spider's web is amazing, which is why it can stretch so far without breaking. By the way, the tight-fitting space suits found on the alien bodies recovered from crashed flying saucers were also atomically aligned.

After an implant has been removed from a person's body, it is then possible to cut through the tough outer covering, possibly because the aligned atoms and the surrounding tissue are no longer being charged or powered by the abductee's electrical energy field.

An Electromagnetic Field
Prior to being removed, the implants give off a very strong electromagnetic field. A Gauss meter (used to measure electromagnetic fields) registers off the scale when it is held next to the area of the body where the implant is located. However, once the implant is removed it no longer registers on the Gauss meter. The implication is that the person's own energy field is what powers the implant and allows it to generate the force field.

Nerve Bundles
While in place, there are large bundles of very sensitive nerves surrounding and growing into the implant; specifically, these are the same types of nerves that allow your hand to hold a glass with the right amount of pressure so as not to crush it, or to hold it so lightly as to drop it. These implants are often found in places where these kind of nerves don't normally grow, such as the back of the hand or in the jaw. Yet, an implant found in the jaw will be completely surrounded and penetrated by this kind of nerve tissue. 4

No History of Surgery
All the patients retained for study of the implants had no prior history or record of any surgeries. They had not had any accidents, and there were no other occurrences which would account for the implant being in place.

No Inflammatory Response
Not only that, but in all the cases studied there was absolutely no sign of inflammatory response, either chronic or acute. There was also no

wounding or scarring. There was no point of entry and no path of entry. Consider this: If we could insert metallic devices into the human body without any inflammatory response, then we would have the capability of doing complete organ transplants without any concern of rejection!

The Analysis

An electron microscope was used at a magnification of 100,000X and confirmed that tissue had grown right into the metallic surface of the implants. 1 The implants are comprised of eleven different elements.

Top Metallurgy Labs

These implanted devices have been examined by some of the world's leading metallurgy labs, including the lab at Los Alamos, New Mexico. Without knowing what the implants were or where they came from, the lab at Los Alamos concluded that the implants must be pieces of a meteorite, because no such metallic isotopes are found on earth. They put this in writing, in their lab report. 2

Operating under the same conditions, the metallurgy lab at the University of California at San Diego concluded that the metallic isotopes were "extraterrestrial." 5

Fluorescence

In a related but remarkable finding, researchers Derrel Sims and Dr. John Leir have discovered that people who have been abducted and physically touched by an alien being during the insertion of implants or during other medical procedures exhibit a fluorescence on their bodies. 3

The fluorescence is subdermal. That means it's not on the skin, but IN the skin of the abductee. It cannot be washed off. However, it does wear off in two to forty-eight hours. This fluorescence can be easily and dramatically seen when a blacklight is held next to the person's skin where an alien has touched him. It's really bright, as if the person had been painted with a bright neon yellow paint. Perhaps it is some form of antiseptic the alien beings use.

Just so you know that this is not as weird as it may seem, all organic substances emit a weak fluorescent light that is normally invisible to the naked eye. Researchers at Sandia National Lab in New Mexico are investigating ways to detect this fluorescence at crime scenes.

Meet Two Alien Implant Researchers

It's important to know that the men and women working to uncover the truth about flying saucers are not weirdos or crack-pots. You need to know that these people are real. They have families and jobs. They have no desire to stand out from the crowd and be ridiculed; however, they are willing to take the risk of being ridiculed on your behalf. They feel that your right to know the truth is worth the risk. Two such people are Derrel Sims and Dr. John Leir.

Derrel Sims

Derrel Sims works in the medical profession as a hypno-anesthesiologist, assisting in surgical procedures. Sims was abducted very early in his life, from the age of about 2 years old until he was about 17. He has complete conscious memory of his experiences. One of the things he remembers most vividly is that he noticed early on that his alien visitors did not have a belly button or a penis like he had.

Derrel Sims has spent most of his adult life trying to get to the bottom of exactly what is going on and why. He was one of the first people in the world to locate and identify alien implants. As he conducted his research, he began to accumulate X-rays of patients that clearly showed the location of these implants. Sims currently has the world's largest (and maybe only) private collection of alien implants, all of which were removed in a surgical procedure from living abductees.

Dr. Roger Leir

Like many researchers of the alien existence phenomenon, Dr. Roger Leir was initially exposed to the idea of flying saucers by his father. In 1947 his father showed him a newspaper headline, the now-famous first press release by Lt. Walter Haut of the Roswell saucer recovery. Years later Leir joined the MUFON (Mutual UFO Network) to find out if there really was anything to these UFO sightings. However, he was a member of the medical profession and as such was something of a skeptic. He did not believe extraterrestrials existed. Now, of course, he knows differently.

When Sims had a chance meeting with Dr. Leir, he asked Leir if he would be willing to attempt to remove some of the implants he had X-rays of. Leir agreed, and the rest is history, or at least will be history one day. Dr. Leir has removed most of the alleged alien implants himself. He removed the first implant in August, 1995. 6

Complete, unedited videotapes of the surgeries to remove the implants are available from Dr. Leir, who can be contacted on the web through MUFON, Ventura, California, at www.alienscalpel.com

Dr. Leir is board-certified by many boards, including The American Board of Foot Surgeons and the National College of Foot Surgeons. He has addressed many groups of physicians, including 250 surgeons and doctors at John Muir Hospital. He feels the most potent evidence of human/alien contact is to be found in the medical records of patients.

Skepticism

If you are skeptical that alien abductions are real, that's OK. Skepticism is healthy and normal. In fact, skepticism is essential for any truth to be born. Skepticism is as much a part of the learning process as labor pain is to childbirth. So let's step right up and acknowledge it once and for all.

Skeptics Box: An Opposing Hypothesis

For purposes of our discussion, let's assume alien abductions are not real. Assume they are figments of overactive imaginations or maybe some form of mass psychosis. Here's what you might want to contemplate as you read through this chapter:

People who claim to have been abducted all tell pretty much the same story. Their descriptions and experiences all fit within a very narrow range. The stories are pretty much identical, right down to the exact same descriptions of the instruments the aliens use. These abductions are reported from every corner of the globe. The descriptions are the same regardless of the person's language, country, race, age, culture, religion, sex, nationality, and geographical location. This alone is either an astounding fact or an astounding accomplishment.

Think of that old kid's game where you whisper a phrase into the next person's ear and pass it on. By the tenth person the phrase has mutated beyond recognition. No one can explain exactly how this false abduction story passed through all these barriers intact.

Explain the sheer numbers of people with the identical story. Even people who do not believe the stories acknowledge that 7 percent of the general population is making the claim. In the United States alone that equals 18 million people!

Does the Government Know About Abductions?

The answer appears to be yes. Clearly there are people within the government who know about this. Abductees often report being re-abducted by some sort of military personnel. They are frequently drugged and asked what they know about the aliens. These military types have also been known to attempt to remove some of the alien implants. See the profile of Melinda Leslie in the "Abductions" section for more information.

It's Only a Rumor

There is no doubt these abductions are occurring, and there is little doubt the government is aware of its magnitude. Since the public has gotten no information from officials whatsoever, rumors of their complicity are fair game. So here goes.

Inside sources say the government has made an agreement with a particular group of aliens which allows those aliens to use citizens in exchange for technology. However, the number of people who ended up being abducted far exceeded what the government expected, but now it's too late and they are (understandably) afraid the public will find out. The funny thing is that with their technological superiority, the aliens wouldn't need to make an agreement. That means they probably would have given the government the technology anyway.

Does this whole thing sound shocking and unlikely? Well, our government has a long history of allowing citizens to be used for experimental purposes. This behavior is not unlike previous government actions such as:

- *Marching U.S. soldiers into ground zero following a nuclear explosion to find out what the radiation would do to them.*
- *Field testing LSD on unsuspecting U.S. soldiers.*
- *Administering a useless placebo to African-American syphilis patients to see what would happen to them in the infamous Tuskegee Study.*

MORE ABDUCTION FAQs

- **What do you mean by missing time?**

When people have an abduction experience, often the only clue they have that something unusual has occurred is the fact that there seems to be a certain period of time they cannot account for. It is, simply, missing. A typical scenario would find a person driving in the car, looking at the car clock, looking at it again in what seems like a few seconds and voila! Three hours have gone by. Not only on the clock, but by other indicators such as a different slant of the sunlight or a different show playing on the car radio. We now know our alien visitors can simply switch a person on and off at will and the person will have no conscious recollection of what happened in between.

- **What Are Alien Implants?**

Many abductees have had small devices placed in their bodies. Common locations are deep inside nasal cavities, behind the eye, in the back of the head, and other places in the body. These implants are real. We now have photographs, X-rays, and CAT scans of them in place. Several of them have been successfully removed by medical teams. Upon removal the implants often disintegrate, but sometimes they don't.

By contacting UFO research organizations such as MUFON (Mutual UFO Network), you can easily put yourself in contact with individuals who can show you clear photos and X-rays of these tiny implants. With any effort at all, you could probably view one firsthand.

- **If there are so many abductions from common places how come nobody sees them?**

This is a very good question. Nobody really knows the answer. I do know this: Aliens have the ability to switch off the neural pathways of anyone nearby. They also have the ability to shift in and out of our dimension as well as control time. There have been reports that they have the ability to cloak their ships just like the Klingons on *Star Trek*. Airline pilots regularly report UFOs disappearing visually but remaining on the radar screen. One abductee recalled being abducted from a crowded swimming pool. As she was led away, she could see that all the people were freeze-framed, stopped in mid-action, including splashes of water coming from the pool!

Poll of Americans About Intelligent Life in the Universe

Percent who believe each of the following is true:

- *Intelligent beings from other planets have been in contact with humans: 22 percent.*
- *Intelligent beings from other planets have abducted human beings to observe or experiment on them: 17 percent.*
- *Intelligent beings from other planets have been in contact with members of the U.S. government: 13 percent.*

This data is from a telephone poll of 1,024 adult Americans taken for Time/CNN on June 4 and 5, 1996 by Yankelovich Partners, Inc. Sampling error is plus or minus 3 percent. [14]

THE ROLE OF SKEPTICS

* *Skeptics*
* *Debunkers*
* *Disinformation*
* *A Word About Carl Sagan*

People who are skeptical of new information are very important and very valuable. A person who is truly skeptical approaches new information with an open mind, but wants clear proof to change his mind about what he previously thought. The fact is we need these guys. Skepticism is a process of evaluation; a way to integrate new information.

A Process of Birth

Skeptics are absolutely necessary when moving to a new paradigm. They provide a frame of reference and a brake, so to speak, so society can move forward without gaining so much speed that we crash. The greatest transitions in human history all had opposing and skeptical forces. In fact, without opposition there can be no growth or change. The Chicago Bulls or the Green Bay Packers can't win a championship if they don't have other teams like the Knicks or the Cowboys to oppose them.

Copernicus discovered the earth was not the center of the universe. His views were met with tremendous opposition. The opposing forces withheld this information from the public for 200 years.

Once it was learned that the earth was round, it was still hundreds of years before all the world knew it.

When the microscope was invented and revealed the existence of micro-organisms, the discoverers were widely ridiculed by physicians who continued to practice surgery without washing their hands first.

Debunkers

A debunker is a person who is committed to proving that his way of looking at the world is the only way. Debunkers have a clear agenda and are opposed to anything that does not conform to their view. Unlike a true skeptic, a debunker does not have an open mind and is not seeking the truth, but rather just support for his position.

There are people who feel that their sole purpose is to "debunk" or offer disclaimers about the existence of flying saucers. It has long been suspected that some of these people are, in fact, paid by the U.S. government to do this. The most well-known of these debunkers is Philip Klass. Klass started his career as an aviation journalist. He's a pretty irascible old man. He can be very nasty in his attacks on people who know about UFOs.

Here is one thing that you should know about Phil. Investigator and former police officer Ted Oliphant picked up the phone and called Phil Klass. He asked Phil this question: "What do you think about the existence of UFOs?" After a long pause, Phil answered: "Oh, I suppose another civilization sends a probe here about every hundred years." So clearly, Klass knows the truth. 3

Disinformation

One of the ways the truth of the existence of flying saucers is kept from the public is with an active and aggressive campaign of disinformation. It works by providing misleading information to people who research the UFO phenomenon.

Here Is How They Do It

During the years I have been observing the UFO phenomenon, a clear pattern of deceit has emerged. Legitimate scientists and researchers are contacted by someone who has government credentials. He says he wants to share secretly acquired government information, documents, or photographs. Later, after the researcher bites the hook and incorporates this information into his own material, another government employee or other information source shows up with completely conflicting official documentation. This is then used to discredit the original researcher's entire body of work. This conflict also leads to other researchers in the field disavowing any connection to the person or any of his research.

In addition, different researchers are given different pieces of the puzzle, which leads to infighting and fragmentation among some investigators. Ironically, many of these bits of information are true, but all the pieces don't easily fit into any one picture. This is often clear to all parties involved, but like children they stay in the sandbox throwing sand at each other.

Carl Sagan

I have decided to include a few words about Mr. Sagan in this section. The decision to do this did not come easily and I wrestled with it for months while writing this book.

A Giant in the Cosmos

Carl Sagan's work was tremendous. The gift he gave the public was so great it cannot be measured. If there is one book every household should have (since we now know we are not alone in the universe) it should be Carl Sagan's book or videotape series *Cosmos*.

Almost single-handedly Sagan taught the world about science and the unlimited possibilities of the universe. In *Cosmos* Sagan describes with great hope and promise the items that were put aboard the two Voyager spacecraft. They were items intended to show people from other worlds who we are. Included in these items are information on our genetics, culture, mathematics, civilization, and the location of our solar system.

The Accusations

Many people who have studied the UFO phenomenon and can clearly see the truth of the existence of alien beings felt Carl Sagan was holding out, or even worse, playing the role of a debunker and lying to the public through failure to disclose what he knew. This is the reason I have chosen to put something about Carl Sagan in this section.

He Was Too Smart Not to Know

Many felt he was too smart and too well-connected not to know the truth. Not only that; it is just too easy to discover the truth. If anyone has even the slightest interest and simply asks around with the same level of intensity you would use to find a good dentist, you will easily confirm the existence of flying saucers. It just seems that someone of Sagan's reputation could have easily picked up the telephone, made a few well-placed calls and confirmed something he spent his whole life searching for.

Sagan was also chided in UFO circles about his off-handed comments inferring that UFOs were figments of people's imaginations.

Scientists Sometimes Do Dumb Things Too

Here is a statement made by Carl Sagan:

> I believe the search for extraterrestrial intelligence to be an exceedingly important one for both science and society... But I do not believe that the most efficient method of examining this topic is via the UFO prob-

lem. The best hope for such investigations is NASA's unmanned planetary program and attempts at interstellar radio communications. 2

It is interesting that Sagan saw UFOs as a problem instead of an opportunity. It sounds more like a military position. Even if there were only
one chance in ten million that UFOs were craft from other planets, you
would think a scientist would be ecstatic; people bet the lottery every day
and the odds of winning are only one in 25 million.

It never ceases to amaze me that the top brains in science use radio
waves to try to communicate with other beings in space. We don't even
use radio to communicate between countries. It's too primitive. Several
contactees have even been asked by aliens why we use radio for this
attempt to communicate, this is like using smoke signals to call your
friend.

My Conclusion

I have chosen to give Mr. Sagan the benefit of the doubt. I am going to
accuse him of doing the very best he possibly could for humanity. A
couple of points follow:

I did a brief, but by no means complete, look into Sagan's past writings. I
was unable to find any quotes or statements specifically denigrating
anyone's claims of the existence of flying saucers. It is quite possible he
really didn't know, as improbable as that seems. In reviewing some of his
work, it is clear Sagan was steeped in the traditional Western methods of
scientific thought. Even he recognized this. He may have simply been
held captive by his own view of the world.

"Extraordinary claims require extraordinary proof." This is a well-known
Sagan adage, and he is right. However, it does not take into account the
question of whether or not you will be able to recognize the proof when
you see it. In fact, the statement is self-limiting. Even though man
watched birds fly in the sky for thousands of years, up until 1912 scientists were still claiming heavier-than-air flight was impossible. Yet the
proof of the possibility was right in front of their faces all along.

Sagan fought to apply rigorous scientific methods to the investigation on UFOs. It's ironic because this was one of his greatest abilities, yet it cost him the most cherished information he could ever imagine, confirmation that we are not alone in the universe. That is, if he truly did not know, as his statements indicate.

Despite the tremendous opposition from many members of the scientific community, Sagan fought for and got a symposium held on UFOs at the annual meeting of the American Association for the Advancement of Science in 1969. Here are two statements Sagan made about this effort:

> The Associations should include in their programs doubtfully scientific areas of current public interest, such as astrology, extrasensory perception, and unidentified flying objects to show how these can be considered in a scientific way.

> We believe the scientific community is honor bound to keep the lines of communication open and to aid constructive discussion. We do not see how such a symposium can fail to serve science well. 1

The Last Word

Before he died, Carl Sagan said that if we find so much as a single microbe on a rock from Mars, it means the universe is teeming with life. He was absolutely correct.

REMOTE VIEWING

Remote viewing is the ability to leave your body and travel to other places and "see" what is there. It is also known as astral projection and soul travel. It is the same process described by people who have had near death experiences (NDEs). It's the part of the experience where they float above and can look down and see their body on the operating table, for instance.

While in this mode, one can not only see, but also feel what others are feeling and know what they are thinking. This has been a well-documented phenomenon through the ages. It is said that Napoleon

Bonaparte could do this, and that he nightly flew over his adversary's battle positions and gained a strategic advantage in combat.

How It Relates to Flying Saucers

A contactee who wishes to remain anonymous told us that aliens explained astral projection or remote reviewing to him like this:

> You humans, have the ability to project yourselves beyond your physical bodies. All humans have this ability. Most have simply not been taught how to use it. It is not a special talent any more than learning to ride a bicycle would be considered a special talent. Nor is it a spiritual gift. One who is truly despicable, such as a murderer, can also do this. However, not all beings in the universe can do this. Many of those you call alien beings cannot do this projection, even though they are technologically more advanced than humans. So from that standpoint this ability is quite special.

You Are Connected to All Things

When you do this projection you are able to recognize your connection to all things in the universe. It is this realization that permeates the entire culture of Native Americans.

Reserved For Priests and Spies

In many cultures throughout the ages the learning of this ability was reserved for priests. It was withheld from the general populace. When holy men do this projection they come back and tell you that they have been communing with God.

Secret government and quasi-government groups have trained people to do this projection for the purpose of spying. When spies do this, they come back and say they have been doing "remote viewing." The reason the government keeps information about this kind of projection secret is because if everyone learns how to do it there will be no secrets. In this projection mode, you can hear and feel what anyone else is thinking or feeling.

You can experience exactly what it feels like to be a grasshopper or even a rock. You can visit other planets and parallel universes. I do not mean this figuratively; I mean this literally. You will actually be there. You can even experience the complete consciousness of an entire planet. There are many on our planet who know this. They come to this knowledge from different avenues, some by simply learning to access it, some through meditation, others by breathing techniques, through physical exercise, or even through use of drugs.

They Visit Us

Our government spies have used remote viewing to visit spaceships to find out who the aliens are and what is going on. They want to know why there are so many spacecraft orbiting your planet. And, there are thousands of ships circling our planet right now and many more within one light-year's distance from us.

Do Your Own Remote Viewing

Our priests and spies have not yet realized that with this projection, humans carry with us our own expectations and interpretations. It is not possible to be completely objective because you are part of the whole. You are looking at the picture while at the same time being in the picture. Many of the things that you "see" are not really there. They are part of your mind's holographic projection. Some of it may be accurate, but much is not. Because your experience in the universe is so limited, it would be similar to a person in the 1700s seeing an automobile. How would he describe it? What would he call it? He has absolutely no point of reference and no experience whatsoever with such a machine.

Here Is a Secret

When you do this projection, the more you defend what you see the less likely you saw what you thought you saw. We humans, don't actually see very much. Our optical process sees only 50 percent of what is out there. Our mind fills in the blanks.

Our reality is much like a motion picture. It is really a series of still photos that are projected so rapidly in succession it appears real to you. When you learn to do this projection, you will notice that what you "see" has a much higher resolution than your regular eyesight. The images are absolutely crisp, sharp, and defined, unlike any you have seen before. That is because during this process you do not "see" with light reflection, you see pure energy patterns being reflected.

As you gain more experience with this projection process you will learn there are many different versions of reality, yet all of them exist. We should take what we learn from priests and spies who do remote viewing with a grain of salt. Better yet, you can learn to do this projection your-selves and "see" everything firsthand.

WORLDWIDE UFO RECOVERY EVENTS

This is a listing of all UFO Recovery events that are known. Nobody can guarantee the authenticity of any or all of them. The important thing is that you get exposed to the fact that flying saucers have been around for a long time and they are ubiquitous. There is no occurrence on our planet except the rising of the sun and the moon that occurs as consistently as the appearance of flying saucers.

Some of these events are actual crash retrievals; some of them are landing events. Others may be forms of the holographic projections some of the alien beings are capable of producing, and some may be outright lies or disinformation designed by the military or covert government forces to fake out interested private parties and UFO researchers.

Many of the events have collaboration from military insiders. Since the government has not been honest and forthcoming with the American people all these events are in play until proven otherwise. The list is long, but check it out.

A Long Time Ago

* *10,000 BC: Tibet*
* *2,000 BC: Grand Canyon, Arizona*
* *840 AD: Lyon, France*

1800s

* *1864 September: Cadotte Pass, Missouri*
* *1884 June: Holdredge, Nebraska*
* *1884 December 13: Sorissole, Italy*
* *1897 April 17: Aurora, Texas*

1900s

* *1908 June 30: Lower Tunguska River, Russia.*
* *1909 December 22: Chicago.*
* *1910: Puglia, Italy*
* *1925 September: Polson, Montana.*
* *1936: Black Forest, Germany*
* *1941: Cape Girardeau, Missouri*
* *1946 July 9: Lake Barken, Sweden*
* *1946 July 10: Bjorkon, Sweden*
* *1946 July 18: Lake Mjosa, Sweden*
* *1946 July 19: Lake Kolmjary, Sweden*
* *1946 August 12: Sweden*
* *1946 August 16: Malmo, Sweden*
* *1946 October: Sweden*
* *1947 May: Spitzenbergen, Norway*
* *1947 May 31: Socorro, New Mexico*
* *1947 July 2: Plains of San Augustine, New Mexico.*
* *1947 July 4: Roswell, New Mexico*
* *1947 July 31: Maury Island, Tacoma, Washington.*
* *1947 October: Paradise Valley, Arizona.*
* *1947 October 20: San Diego, California.*
* *1948 February 13: Aztec, New Mexico.*
* *1948 April: Aztec, New Mexico*
* *1948 July 7: Mexico (Just south of Laredo Texas)*
* *1948 July 8, Mexico City, Mexico.*
* *1948 August: Laredo Texas*
* *1949 July 5: Roswell, New Mexico.*
* *1949 August 19: Death Valley, California.*
* *1949 September 10: Albuquerque, New Mexico.*
* *1950 Mexico City, Mexico*
* *1950 Birmingham Alabama*
* *1950 May 10: Bahia Blanca Province, Argentina.*
* *1950 December 6: Guerrero, Mexico.*
* *1952 June: Spitzenberger, Norway*
* *1952 July: Washington DC.*
* *1952 August 14: Ely, Nevada.*
* *1953 April 18: Arizona.*
* *1953 May 20: Kingman, Arizona.*
* *1953 June 19: Laredo, Texas.*
* *1953 July 10: Johannesburg, South Africa.*
* *1953 October 13: Dutton, Montana.*
* *1953: Brady, Montana.*

* *1953: Fort Polk, Louisiana.*
* *1954: Mattydale, New York.*
* *1955 May 5: Brighton, England.*
* *1955 July: Vestra Norrland, Sweden.*
* *1957 July 18: Carlsbad, New Mexico.*
* *1957 September 14: Ubatuba, Brazil.*
* *1957 November 21: Reasty Hill, Scarborough, Yorks.*
* *1959 February 21: Gdynia, Poland.*
* *1959 September 17: Wormer near Amsterdam.*
* *1959: Italy, near Rome.*
* *1960: Spain.*
* *1960: Great Sand Dunes, Colorado.*
* *1960: March, New Platz, New York.*
* *1961: Timmensdorf, Germany.*
* *1961 April 28: Lake Onega, Russia.*
* *1962 April 18: Las Vegas.*
* *1962 June 12: Holloman Air Force base.*
* *1963: Atlantic Ocean.*
* *1963 July 16: Charlton, Wiltshire.*
* *1963 December 10: Fort Riley, Kansas.*
* *1963 December 10: RAF Cosford, England.*
* *1964 November 10: Fort Riley, Kansas.*
* *1965 January: San Miguel, Argentina.*
* *1965 December 9: Kecksburg, Pennsylvania.*
* *1966 October 27: Arizona.*
* *1967 January: Missouri.*
* *1967 August 17: Sudan.*
* *1967 October 6: Nova Scotia.*
* *1968 February 12: Orocue, Colombia.*
* *1968 March 25: Nepal.*
* *1970: Kankakee, Illinois.*
* *1971: Edwards Air Force Base.*
* *1972 April 7: New Zealand.*
* *1972 July 18: Morocco.*
* *1973 July 10: Arizona.*
* *1974: Detroit, Michigan.*
* *1974 Jan 23: Llandrillo, N. Wales.*
* *1974 May 17: Chili, New Mexico.*
* *1974 July 15: Spain.*
* *1974 August 25: Chihuahua, Mexico.*
* *1974 November 9: Carbondale, Pennsylvania.*
* *1974: Savonna, Italy.*
* *1975 April 5: Ohio.*
* *1976 May 12: Australia.*
* *1977: Western Australia.*

* 1977 January 10: Wakefield, England.
* 1977: Xenia, Ohio.
* 1977 June 22: Arizona.
* 1977 August 17: Mexico.
* 1977 May 26: Corinth, Georgia.
* 1977 November 16: Ellsworth AFB.
* 1978: Russia.
* 1978 May: Bolivia.
* 1978 January: McGuire AFB, New Jersey.
* 1978 May 6: Tarija, Bolivia.
* 1979 February 12: Pocono Mountains, Pennsylvania.
* 1979 February 24: Stackheads, Yorks.
* 1979 June 27: Oregon / Idaho border.
* 1979 August 21: La Paz, Bolivia.
* 1979 November 25: Grays Harbor, Washington.
* 1981 August 22: Argentina.
* 1983 January 12: Gallup, New Mexico.
* 1984 February 19: Coca Falls, Puerto Rico.
* 1986 December 29: Siberia.
* 1988 November: Afghanistan.
* 1988: Mt. Orab, Ohio.
* 1988 November 21: Gulf Islands, Florida.
* 1988 December 26: Dayton, Ohio.
* 1989: South Africa.
* 1989 July: Siberia.
* 1989 May 7: Botswana.
* 1989 September 28: Long Island, New York.
* 1989 November 4: W. Carleton.
* 1900 September 2: Greece.
* 1991 January: Gulf War Incident.
* 1991 August 18: Carleton.
* 1992 November 24, Long Island, New York.
* 1993 November: Yorks, England.
* 1993: Canada.
* 1994 January 12: Greeny Mt. Colorado.
* 1994 March 6: Mount Mutria, Guardairegia, Italy.
* 1994 December: Nullarbor Plain, Australia.
* 1995 August 17: Argentina.
* 1995 September 15: Lesotho.
* 1995 December 5: Somalia.
* 1996 January 14: New Orleans.
* 1996 January 20: Varginha, Brazil.
* 1996 February 15: Scotland.
* 1996 March 30: Hoosier National Park, Indiana.
* 1996 May: Boyle, Eire.

* *1996 October 3: California.*
* *1996 October 26: Scotland.*
* *1996 November 29: Franklin, Ohio.*
* *1996 December 25: China.*
* *1997 May 5: Puerto Rico.*
* *1997 July 1: Teresopolis, Brazil.*
* *1997 September 22: Scotland.*
* *1997 October 9: El Paso, Texas.*

UFO Events Without Specific Dates

* *Veneto, Italy.*
* *Shackleford Glacier, Antartica.*
* *Military base in Alabama.*
* *Australia.*
* *British Columbia, Canada.*

"Any sufficiently advanced technology is indistinguishable from magic."

Arthur C. Clarke

BEST CASES

- *Twenty-two of the best flying saucer cases.*
- *Celebrities and flying saucers.*
- *Famous encounters.*
- *Hynek classification system.*

I have included twenty-two cases for you to review. These cases are featured primarily for the large number of eyewitnesses involved or the magnitude of the event. Cases where alien beings were seen or interacted with also get a priority. I was more inclined to include cases in which a lot more additional information is available.

In each of the cases in this section specific individual details may vary from other versions you might have heard. Many of these cases are so well known that different versions develop as a result of the constant retelling of them by different people. In every case I have attempted to come up with the best factual account of each case. If I wasn't able to confirm something, it is noted.

The important thing is this: In each of the cases featured here there is absolutely no doubt, and it is irrefutable, that something extraordinary did occur. You will find many cases challenging your concept of reality.

The Ones I Like the Most

Some of the cases also appear in other sections of the book as well as this section. The twenty-two cases here are by no means all the well-documented sightings or encounters - just the ones I like the most or feel are important.

Contactee Cases

Contactee cases are cases where individuals have been contacted by alien beings. Contactee cases are just as real as plain sightings of craft. For most people there seems to be a two or three-step process. First, the person has to get used to the fact that flying saucers are real. When she (or he) accepts this, she then has difficulty envisioning the fact that there are "people" aboard these craft. She first tends to view the craft as clouds or just inert unguided objects.

Even some UFO researchers have a difficult time making the transition and accepting the idea of UFOs as occupied vehicles. So take your time. There is no need for you to hurry to integrate this concept. But rest assured: These craft contain beings, the beings are real, and they are contacting and interacting with humans all over this planet in great numbers.

Hynek Classification System

This is a system designed by Dr. J. Allen Hynek to classify sightings of UFOs. He developed it in the 1950s while he was doing research on UFOs for the U.S. military. Here it is:

Nocturnal Light
Any anomalous light(s) seen in the night sky whose description rules out the possibilities of aircraft lights, stars, meteors, and the like.

Daylight Disk UFOs
Seen in the distant daytime sky. The UFOs classed in this category can be other shapes as well, like cigars, eggs, and ovals.

Radar Visuals
Where UFOs are tracked on radar and can be seen at the place illustrated at the same time. A good example would be a disk-shaped object going 9,000 miles per hour and showing up on radar in 1950 when the world air-speed record was only 650 miles per hour.

Close Encounters of the First Kind
A UFO in close proximity (within approximately 500 feet) of the witness.

Close Encounters of the Second Kind
A UFO that leaves markings on the ground, causes burns or paralysis to

humans, frightens animals, or interferes with car engines or TV and radio reception.

Close Encounters of the Third Kind
A UFO which has visible occupants.

Two other classifications were later added to Hynek's original list. They are:

Close Encounters of the Fourth Kind
These include alien abduction cases.

Close Encounters of the Fifth Kind
Where communication occurs between a human and an alien being.

George Adamski, 1950: The First UFO Contactee

Anybody who studies flying saucers will invariably hear the name of George Adamski. Adamski was a controversial figure who popped up in the early 1950s. He was a kind of jack-of-all-trades, even doing a stint in the U.S. Cavalry in 1913. During Prohibition he came up with scheme to sell wine, he founded a monastery and started his very own order of monks! He called it the Royal Order of Tibet, despite the fact that it was located in southern California. Anyway, since it was a religious order he could sell all the wine he could make.

Mount Palomar
During World War II or shortly thereafter Adamski opened a hamburger stand near the Mount Palomar Observatory. Either the close proximity to Palomar or his burger's secret sauce got his juices going and he started referring to himself as Professor Adamski. Over the next few years Adamski claimed he had seen flying saucers near Mt. Palomar Observatory on at least two hundred different occasions.

A Trip to Venus
Adamski had many supporters, and in 1952 he claimed to have met human-looking aliens who said that they were from the planet Venus. He

also said he had been taken aboard spacecraft and taken to other planets in our solar system, which he described in vivid detail in several books.

The Controversy

The controversy surrounding George Adamski is thick. First, the conditions he describes on the various planets were thought to be impossible. There was also dispute about the photographs he said he took of the craft. Adding to this, the intelligence agencies of the U.S. and British governments befriended Adamski and sponsored a speaking tour around the world, and nobody knows right from left. To this very day there are those who will swear that everything he said was true and equally as many who say he was a con man. Since he died in 1965, none of these people have ever met him anyway.

Some Stuff Checks Out

Some of the things attributed to Adamski have proven to be accurate; specifically his descriptions and drawings of the spacecraft now commonly referred to as "Adamski" beamships. These saucers look like an inverted bell with the top of the dome squared off. The most prominent features are what look like three equally spaced balls attached to the bottom of the saucer. Since Adamski's claims were made in the 1950s, this type of craft has been seen by thousands of other people around the world. Adamski's drawings were dead on.

"He said Venus; We didn't!"

More recent contactees have been told by alien beings that the people they encountered in the 1950s frequently made the erroneous assumption they were from a planet in our solar system such as Venus. Rather than confuse the poor contactee, the aliens just said that they were from the "fourth or fifth planet."

As a note, aliens have stated that they do not consider earth to be the "third" planet in our solar system. They consider it to be the "seventh" planet. That's because they count planets as they travel into a solar system – not from the sun out, as we do.

Alien beings have also said that in all cases they were being accurate, but they did not specify which solar system or which dimension they were from. It is hard enough for people to understand it now, much less the early 1950s. In 1950 the movie monster Godzilla didn't even exist. George Would Have Loved It! He now has his own website and you can look it up at: www.adamskifoundation.com.

The Allagash Affair

The Allagash Waterway abduction. Four campers attract the attention of some unexpected visitors while fishing at night.
(Drawing courtesy Christine "Kesara" Dennett)

This case involves four credible witnesses. In 1976 four buddies: Chuck Rak, Charlie Foltz, and Jack and Jim Weiner decided to take a camping trip. All the men were students majoring in art. They left on August 20, a Friday evening, and drove out of Boston to a remote area, a lake on the Allagash Waterway.

When they arrived at the lake they set up camp on the lake's beach. They built a large bonfire which they knew from experience would last about between 4 and 5 hours. Then they hopped into the two canoes they had brought and headed out to do some night fishing. It was pitch black out on the lake and they planned on using the bonfire as a beacon to find their way back to the campsite.

Somebody's Watching

Shortly after moving to the center of the lake, Chuck got a strange feeling - as if someone were looking at him. Turning around, he saw a huge ball of light hovering about two hundred feet above a distant section of the lake. Chuck pointed at the object and said, "Hey, look!" The others turned to see a bright, perfectly round sphere of light pulsating and changing colors.

Charlie grabbed a flashlight and blinked it on and off at the object. The sphere, which had begun to slowly rise up, immediately stopped. Then it slowly headed towards Charlie and his buddies, growing in size as it approached.

Paddle!

The guys panicked and began rowing for their lives, not knowing what this strange glowing thing was. As they furiously paddled, a hollow cone of pale blue light shot out of the sphere and began advancing on the water towards their canoes. At that point they all blanked out.

The Fishermen Get Caught

The next thing they remembered was being back on the beach and getting out of their canoes. The object was still hovering overhead. Standing there, dazed, they looked at the object for 2 or 3 minutes before it shot off at super speed, straight up into the night sky, and disappeared.

All four men felt strange and disoriented. Despite the appearance and disappearance of a very strange object, none of them felt like talking about it. They did, however, notice that their bonfire had burned down completely, leaving only a few hot embers. To their knowledge, they had only been gone for about 30 minutes. The fire should have lasted at least four hours. This later turned out to be a classic case of "missing time."

Strangers in the Bedroom

Several years later Jim Weiner suffered a head injury. The injury caused a form of epilepsy known as tempero-limbic epilepsy. As part of his treatment he was asked if he was having any strange experiences. Jim then stated that he was having very strange and life-like dreams. He also frequently awoke to find strange creatures in his room at the foot of his bed. Jim's doctor referred him to Raymond Fowler, a serious UFO researcher.

Back in Time

Fowler had Jim hypnotically regressed, and the whole story about his camping trip to the Allagash Waterway came out. Jim and his three buddies had been picked up on the lake by the beam of light that had followed them. They were all taken aboard a spacecraft. They were examined and had samples of blood, semen, and urine taken. Skin, hair, and nail samples were taken as well.

Cross References and Drawings

All four witnesses to the Allagash incident confirmed the experience of the others. All their descriptions matched. All the men were artists and were able to provide detailed drawings of what they had seen. The drawings included the alien beings, the surroundings, and the instrumentation used for their examinations.

Double Your Pleasure; Double Your Fun

The aliens were particularly interested in Jim and his twin brother Jack. It turns out that these twins had been abducted almost since birth. Years later in May 1988, Jack was abducted again along with his wife, Mary. Jack recalls that they were literally "floated out of the house and across the lawn" to a waiting craft.

A Foreign Object

Shortly after Jack and his wife were abducted, Jack found a strange lump on his leg. It seemed to appear out of nowhere overnight. Jack's family physician was concerned that the lump might be cancerous and arranged to have a surgeon remove it. When the surgeon went in he found a small, strange-looking object. Since he didn't know what it was and had never seen anything like it, the surgeon sent it to the Center for Disease Control in Atlanta.

The Air Force Steps In

Later, in trying to find out what happened to the removed object, Jack discovered it was sent to a military pathologist in Washington, D.C. From there a United States Air Force colonel took control of it, and it was never seen again. When Jack went to ask the surgeon more about the object, the surgeon stonewalled him and refused to talk about it even though Jack had been his patient.

The full account and all the aftermath is vividly recounted in Raymond E. Fowler's book *The Allagash Abductions*.

Antonio Villas Boas

This is a famous close encounter that occurred October 16, 1957 in Brazil. It involves a young Brazilian farmer, Antonio Villas Boas, who was 23 years old at the time. The incident happened about 1:00 A.M. Antonio was tilling the fields on a tractor. This was something he did regularly. On the nights preceding this one he had seen a bright light in some of the distant fields.

A Big Red Star

As Antonio was riding the tractor he looked up to notice what he thought was an extremely bright red star. However, the "star" started dropping rapidly and was closing in on him! As it got closer, he could see it was actually a craft of some kind. The craft suddenly projected three legs out and landed. The lights from the craft were so bright they completely washed out the light coming from his tractor.

Scared to death, Antonio turned the tractor and stepped on the gas. But the tractor engine simply died. He got off and was trying to run when he was grabbed by a humanoid-like creature. As he fought the being, three more surrounded him. The beings somehow paralyzed him and dragged him by his feet into the craft.

Antonio Villas Boas, a young Brazilian farmer, meets a visitor from another world. (Drawing courtesy Christine "Kesara" Dennett)

No Clothes Needed

Antonio was taken to a small room. His clothes were taken from him and the beings coated his bare body with some kind of gel. The beings doing this were wearing tight-fitting space suits complete with helmets.

Through the clear face masks they wore Antonio could see finely featured faces with small blue eyes. The beings made strange sounds that sounded like little barks or yelps.

Antonio was then led into another room that had strange red letters written over the doorway. He was later able to write down what these letters looked like. In this room a blood sample was taken. There was an odd odor in the room that made Antonio feel nauseous.

Is That You, Barbarella?

Thirty or forty minutes later a young woman entered the room. She was about 5 feet tall, and according to Antonio, beautiful. The woman had an angular face with eyes that were catlike. She had long, white hair. She was nude and Antonio noticed that her pubic and arm hair was a strange, bright red. Antonio became aroused and the two had intercourse. That appeared to be the whole purpose behind his abduction. The woman also seemed to be relieved when the whole ordeal was over.

Child Support?

Before the woman left she pointed to her abdomen and to the ceiling. She made other gestures meant to convey to Antonio in no uncertain terms that he was about to become a space daddy! Antonio then began to feel a little angry. It was clear that "all they wanted was a good stallion to improve their stock." The beings then gave him a courtesy tour of the ship and dropped him off. Four hours had passed since he had been picked up.

Antonio Villa Boas later became a lawyer with four earth children of his own. To this day he can still remember every detail of his encounter without the use of hypnosis.

Belgian Triangles

This case or cases are often referred to as "The Belgian Wave of 1989." From November 29, 1989 until April 1990, huge numbers of craft sightings were seen in the skies over Belgium. It is estimated that nearly 90 percent of the entire population of Belgium saw spacecraft with lights on their perimeters, and there were over eight hundred close encounters in this 5-month period.

Triangles, Boomerangs, and Disks

The most common shape reported was a huge triangular-shaped craft. These craft flew so low and so slowly over townships that their outlines could clearly be seen from the ground, even at night. There were other shapes seen as well, including the well-documented boomerang-type craft; so-called because one side is longer than the other, just like a boomerang.

Military Confirmation

On many occasions F-16 military jet fighters were sent up to intercept the flying triangles. Radar in the jets locked onto hard targets, as well as radar on the ground. The records confirm, there is no doubt that large physical craft were there. Not only that, but F-16s are fast. They can fly twice as fast as a stealth airplane. In spite of this speed capability, the triangle ships just took off and left the F-16s in the proverbial dust.

So many credible people saw these craft that the Belgian government just couldn't ignore them, nor could they deem so many citizens to be deluded. Therefore, the Belgian Government became the first and only government in the world to officially recognize the existence of UFOs.

RAF Bentwaters

There are two air bases in England that are separated by a 1-mile-wide strip of forest known as Rendlesham Forest. That's why this case has two names: Rendlesham and Bentwaters.

NATO Air Bases

RAF Bentwaters is one of the two air bases, and the other is RAF Woodbridge. At the time they were both NATO air bases leased by Britain's Royal Air Force to the United States Air Force.

On December 26, 1980 at midnight, military guard units and civilians saw a craft land in the forested area between the two bases. Patrol units went out to investigate, and when they got there they found a diamond-shaped craft hovering about 6 feet off the ground. Some of the soldiers in the unit went up and touched it. They also noted strange symbols engraved on its side.

A Miraculous Display

The craft proceeded to do some amazing things. Smaller craft split off from it and accelerated instantly to amazing speeds, faster than any of our aircraft could go. Both air bases confirmed visual sightings and radar readings at the same time. In addition, videotapes were made, as well as audio tapes.

Sgt. Larry Warren says he witnessed a meeting between military brass and alien beings. The beings floated and were surrounded by a luminous protective bubble.

Dozens of Military Witnesses

There were dozens of military witnesses. If this event were not true, it would mean that all these men, many of them officers, would have conspired to make up a lie and risk being court-martialed.

The U.S. Military has withheld the videotapes from the public. However, British military brass has been more forthcoming. High-level officers have stated in taped interviews that something extraordinary definitely happened that night at Bentwaters.

Eyewitnesses such as Sgt. Larry Warren and Lt. Col. Charles Halt have been interviewed and openly state what actually occurred. Both men have been featured on television documentaries such as *Sightings* and *Unsolved Mysteries*. They have also been featured on many English broadcasts.

Key Points

One investigator, in an attempt to explain away the whole incident, says that all the men were looking at a lighthouse which is 5 miles away from the site. However, all the eyewitnesses were military men who had been stationed at Bentwaters for at least a year. They were used to seeing the lighthouse every night. They knew what it looked like. Not only that, but all the men said that they could see the lighthouse off in the distance while still looking at the craft sitting right in front of them.

This is one of the most heavily documented military cases of all time, in terms of eyewitnesses, visual confirmation, radar confirmation, even touching the craft - not to mention the video tape that was recorded and classified.

Brazilian Navy Case

While on training exercises on January 16, 1958 in the South Atlantic Ocean near Tinidade Island, forty-eight seamen and the ship's captain Carlos Alberto Bacellar all saw several flying saucers fly by them. The event was also witnessed by two civilians who were on board. Among the civilians was a technical photographer, Almiro Barauna, who had his cameras with him.

A Series of Photographs
Barauna was able to take an entire series of photographs. A series of photographs of a moving object is always impressive because they are hard to fake. Not only that, but these photographs were all taken in the presence of the military men on board the boat. The photographs were taken in broad daylight around noon and were developed immediately in a makeshift darkroom on the ship. Captain Bacellar personally watched the development process to insure the film was not tampered with.

The President Confirms It
On February 21 the president of Brazil, Juscelino Kubitschek, came forward and stated that the Navy had thoroughly analyzed the photographs and that he, the president, personally vouched for their authenticity.

Jupiter?
This case is so well documented it is not even funny, but it is also a good example of what typically happens. Years later a guy named Campbell said he had analyzed the photographs and the UFO was really the planet Jupiter. So fifty people all mistook Jupiter for something else? The

president of an entire nation jeopardized his reputation by stating that Jupiter was a UFO?

I don't know about you, but I have never seen Jupiter in broad daylight at twelve o'clock noon. And when you see the pictures, 'Jupiter' doesn't appear as a tiny spec - it's huge. Maybe it wasn't a space ship, but don't let people feed you ridiculous statements and tell you it was Jupiter!

The Brooklyn Bridge Abduction

"Linda Cortile" is a pseudonym Budd Hopkins used in his book Witnessed to protect the true identity of the subject of this abduction. Other names have been used for this case and later publications say the woman's real name is Linda Napolitano.

On November 30, 1989 about 3:00 A.M., a large flying saucer appeared over Manhattan in New York City. Two small beings floated Linda Cortile out of her twelfth-floor apartment on a beam of light. They passed her right through a closed glass window. (This is a common occurrence, although I don't know how they do it.)

A World Class Diplomat Sees It All
There were several eyewitnesses, and the event was seen by many people at different locations. Two of the witnesses were U.S. Secret Service agents. They were escorting the Secretary General of the United Nations, Perez de Cuellar. The two agents and Perez de Cuellar saw the whole thing from the Brooklyn Bridge, which they were crossing at the time. Like many other cases of a nearby hovering UFO, the magnetic field generated by the saucer knocked out all the electricity in the area, including the ignition system of the Secretary General's limo. They were a totally captive audience, along with other people on the bridge, who began to panic and start screaming.

Water Getaway
After picking up Linda Cortile, the saucer dove into the East River and disappeared. This too, is a common occurrence. There is plenty of

evidence to show that saucers use rivers, lakes, and oceans to travel. The U.S. Navy tracks as many saucers under water as above. Remember, two-thirds of the earth's surface is covered with water and humans have explored only about 5 percent of the area covered by our oceans. What better way to travel unseen and undetected?

The Return

Like many abductees, when Linda was returned to her room she found that her husband and son had been "switched off." This is a state of unconsciousness that all the other people in the house are put into when someone is abducted. The common statement made by abductees is that the other family members look more dead than alive. It's not a normal sleep state. Linda Cortile, recalling her return said, "I held a mirror under the nose of my husband and my son to see if they were breathing."

Canary Islands Case

The events of this case are well documented and have been witnessed by hundreds of people. The major newspapers said that "thousands of people had seen a spectacular luminous phenomenon." Included in the groups of eyewitnesses were civilians from all walks of life, including a physician, priests, and engineers. The event was also seen by the entire crew of the Spanish naval ship, Atrevida.

What They Saw

The Captain of the Atrevida filed his report as follows:

> At 21:27 hrs. on 22 June, 1976, we saw an intense yellowish-bluish light moving out from the shore towards our position. At first, we thought it was an aircraft with its landing lights on. Then, it became stationary. The original light went out and a luminous beam from it began to rotate. It remained like this for approximately two minutes. Then an intense halo of yellowish and bluish light developed and remained in the same position for 40 minutes.
>
> Two minutes after the great halo, the light split into two parts, the smaller part being beneath... the part from which the bluish nucleus

had come, vanished. The upper part began to climb in a spiral... its glow lighting up the land and the ocean. And, finally vanished.

This transparent luminous globe contained two extremely tall beings They were clearly seen by hundreds of citizens and military personnel in the surrounding area. The event was also witnessed by the entire crew of the Spanish naval vessel Atrevida. (Drawing courtesy Christine "Kesara" Dennett)

Transparent Globe

Later that evening in the nearby town of Las Rosas a physician, Dr. Francisco Padron, filed a formal deposition attesting to what he and other residents had seen. Dr. Padron had seen a large luminous sphere hovering over the road. Here's how he described what he saw:

It was made of a totally transparent and crystalline-like material, since it was possible to see through it the stars in the sky; it had an electric blue color but tenuous, without dazzling. It had a radius of about 30 meters, and in the lower third of the sphere you could see a platform of aluminum-like color as if made of metal, and three large consoles. At each side of the center, there were two huge figures of 2.5 to 3 meters tall, (10 feet!) dressed entirely in red and facing each other in such a way that I always saw their profile.

Then I observed that some kind of bluish smoke was coming out from a semi-transparent central tube in the sphere, covering the periphery of the sphere's interior without leaking outside at any moment. Then the sphere began to grow and grow until it became huge, like a twenty-story house, but the platform and the crew remained the same size. It rose slowly and majestically, moving slowly toward Tenerife. Suddenly, it reached enormous speed like none I ever saw in an airplane. Then, it disappeared in the direction of Tenerife.

The Taxi Driver
When Dr. Padron saw this event, he was riding in a taxi cab. The cab driver confirmed that he too saw the same thing. The driver stated:

A craft that looked as if it was made of transparent crystal, about 25 meters (85 ft.) high and 20 meters (65 ft.) wide, with two persons dressed in brilliant red inside.

A third witness observed the event as well:

The doctor's car and just above it the great blue ball. It was like a perfectly round globe, but very big, transparent, the stars could be seen through it. It had two man-like figures inside. I closed the doors and windows of my house and began to pray.

Other Confirmation
In 1994, the official Spanish Air Force files on this case were declassified and released to the public in an on-going effort to acclimate them to the existence of flying saucers. In the files were many more depositions confirming the events of June 22, 1976. There were also photographs of

the blue transparent globe as well as hard radar readings, as well as a report from the naval photo lab attesting to the authenticity of the photographs.

Celebrity Cases

Many noted celebrities have had their own encounters with flying saucers and aliens. Because of their fame they have frequently been brought into the inner circle and given information denied to the rest of us. For most of these cases there is no written documentation; however, others to whom they have confided have come forward and confirmed many of the details involved. In cases like this pay particular attention to the behavior of those involved. Ask yourself: What would cause a person to behave in the way he or she did? Is the behavior in line with the circumstances claimed? Well, here they are. Enjoy!

Jackie Gleason

The famous comedian was a close personal friend of then-President Richard Nixon. Gleason was very interested in UFOs. While playing golf in Florida with Nixon, Gleason asked Nixon what he knew about flying saucers and UFOs. The story goes that Nixon said he didn't want to talk about it, but indicated there was something to the rumors of their existence. Gleason hounded Nixon and insisted he tell him more. Nixon eventually relented and arranged for Gleason to be flown by Nixon's private presidential helicopter to nearby Homestead Air Force Base. There, under heavy security, Gleason was allowed to view the preserved bodies of several small alien beings.

Gleason was apparently very shaken by the whole experience. His wife at the time, Beverly McKittrick, recalls vividly how Gleason returned home visibly upset that night in 1973. A man by the name of Larry Warren was introduced to Gleason years later in 1986. Warren was there to speak about his own UFO experience and Gleason told him the story about Nixon letting him see the alien bodies. Gleason later built a home in the Catskill Mountains shaped like a flying saucer.

Dorothy Kilgallen

If you are under the age of 50 you have probably never heard of Dorothy Kilgallen. She was the Barbara Walters of her day. She was an extremely well known reporter and television personality.

Dorothy Kilgallen had learned through some of her sources that flying saucers were real. Apparently for this reason, the FBI and/or the CIA had bugged her phone. At one point in time, Kilgallen had made plans to go on national TV and tell the country the truth about the existence of flying saucers. I have no documents to back up any of this information. There was a CIA report dated August 3, 1962 and uncovered by reporter Milo Spiriglio that tends to confirm Kilgallen's knowledge about some UFO events.

Here is an excerpt from an article Kilgallen wrote that appeared in the *Fort Worth Star-Telegram*, May 23, 1955.

Flying Saucer Wreckage Assures Britons of Reality

I can report Sunday on a story which is positively spooky, not to mention chilling. British scientists and airmen, after examining the wreckage of one mysterious flying ship, are convinced that these strange aerial objects are not optical illusions, but are actually flying saucers which originate from another planet. The source of my information is a British official of cabinet rank who prefers to remain unidentified.

(Article then quotes the official.)

We believe, on the basis of our inquiries thus far, that the saucers were staffed by small men, probably under four feet tall. It's frightening but there is no denying the flying saucers come from another planet.

This official quoted scientists as saying a flying ship of this type could not possibly have been constructed on earth. The British government, I learned, is withholding an official report on the flying saucer examination at this time, possibly because it does not wish to frighten the public. In the United States, all kinds of explanations have been advanced. But no responsible official of the U.S. Air Force has yet intimated the mysterious flying ships actually vaulted from outer space.

About Milo Spiriglio's copy of the CIA memo: There is no way to know for sure if the document is authentic or not. After all, the CIA is not going to stand up and say, "Hey, that's ours!" But here are a couple of points:

Spiriglio is a court-certified document expert. 1 Other researchers are split fifty-fifty on its authenticity. Basically, nobody can prove it and nobody can disprove it.

Marilyn Monroe

The celebrity circles and reporters all knew Marilyn Monroe was having an affair with President John F. Kennedy, a fact that has now been openly revealed to the public. Marilyn Monroe made no secret of this. What you may not know is she also later slept with Kennedy's brother, Bobby.

Apparently intoxicated in a Reno Casino, Monroe stated verbally to others, that she was upset about being passed around by the Kennedy's and was going to tell some of their secrets. The secrets involved missile bases in Cuba, Kennedy's plans to assassinate Fidel Castro, and an air base that had "things from outer space" in it. Yes, I know it's a lot to handle, but let's take a couple of points one by one.

About Marilyn Monroe's death, there is no question this was no ordinary suicide. The circumstances were extremely suspicious. Several independent investigations have been conducted and many books written reviewing the death of Monroe. All evidence points to a homicide, not a suicide. Don't take my word for it, you can go to any bookstore and check it out for yourself. The books all contain reports, details, and the actual circumstances surrounding her death, including many things never told to the public at the time.

Author's Update

In early 2011, while having a conversation with a friend of mine named Greg, he told me the following:

Greg said that while he was in college, he worked part-time for a courier service. One of his regular stops was the Los Angeles County Coroners office. Over the years he built a casual friendship with coroner Thomas Noguchi. Noguchi is known as "The coroner to the stars." He conducted the autopsy on Marilyn Monroe. Noguchi told Greg that the level of barbituates in Monroe's blood was so high that it was impossible for that level to occur by taking them orally. The levels could only be that high if the drugs were injected. Yet, no syringe or needles were found in Monroe's house or vehicle.

The Final Conversation With Dorothy Kilgallen

Dorothy Kilgallen was a close friend of Marilyn Monroe, and she was one of the last people who spoke to Monroe merely hours before she supposedly committed suicide from a drug overdose.

The CIA memo obtained by Milo Spiriglio says that during their phone conversation, Monroe had told Kilgallen the very same things she had blurted out publicly in Reno, including the part about a military base with stuff from outer space.

John F. Kennedy

Author Jim Marrs conducted an interview with Bill Holden, who was a steward on Air Force One during Kennedy's presidency. As Holden tells it, in the summer of 1963 while on a trip to Germany he asked Kennedy, "What do you think about UFOs Mr. President?" Kennedy replied: "I'd like to tell the public about the alien situation, but my hands are tied."

The Mantell Case

FLIER DIES CHASING A FLYING SAUCER
New York Times, January 9, 1948.

This case involves the circumstances surrounding the death of Kentucky Air National Guard Captain Thomas F. Mantell, Jr. Mantell was flying in an F-51 fighter plane along with two other air national guard planes. All three pilots spotted a large UFO moving slowly overhead. It was also reported by the Kentucky state police and many citizens on the ground.

"I'm closing in for a better look." These were the words Mantell radioed in as he and the other three pilots climbed to intercept the UFO. None of the planes were equipped with oxygen, and the planes were running low on fuel. The other two pilots turned back after reaching 22,000 feet. At the time Air National Guard regulations stated you had to have oxygen on board to exceed 14,000. Mantell continued to climb until 30,000 feet.

Pilot Loses Consciousness

Mantell's plane then went into a spin. The plane crashed and Mantell was killed. Mantell was still strapped to his seat and his watch had stopped at 3:18 p.m., the time of impact. It was well known that weather balloons were often flying in the area. Initially, it appeared Mantell had simply chased a weather balloon too high, lost consciousness from a lack of oxygen, and crashed.

Now, as radio announcer Paul Harvey says, "Here's the rest of the story."

- The commander of Godman Air Base was personally watching the UFO through his binoculars for over an hour during Mantell's flight. This guy knew weather balloons and as the commanding officer for an entire air base, he didn't have time to stand around observing a weather balloon. What's important here is the behavior.

- Mantell's last radio transmission was: "My God, I see people in this thing!"

- According to Mantell's instrument panel, he had stayed up for over an hour after his plane had run out of fuel.

- A farmer who witnessed the crash said that as the plane fell and reached about forty feet, it was suddenly enveloped in a bright white light. Then the plane fell out of the light, flat, no longer spinning as before.

- Mantell died because his shoulder straps broke. He was thrown forward and the control stick punctured his chest. Had the straps not broken, judging from the remarkably undamaged condition of the plane, Mantell might have survived.

- There was no damage to surrounding bushes, trees, or ground. There were no scrapes on the bottom of the plane. Clearly there had been no forward or sideways motion. The plane had been rather gently dropped from a height of about forty feet. A plane spinning down from 30,000 feet would have been completely demolished along with Mantell and the almost-intact watch.

- Extraordinary sightings of similarly shaped UFOs were seen throughout the next several days over adjoining states. Some of the objects were seen traveling at incredible speeds.

- The events of this case are well documented in public and military records.

The Lonnie Zamora Case

This is another well-known, well-documented case. You may have seen it on television; it is featured regularly on *Unsolved Mysteries*. Here's what happened. Lonnie Zamora was a police officer in Soccoro, New Mexico. On April 24, 1964, after spotting a speeding car drive through the middle of town, Zamora raced after it to give the offending driver a speeding ticket. The driver kept going and headed out of town and into the desert. Zamora followed.

Up in the Sky!

After a few miles Zamora heard a loud roar and looked up in time to see a large flame descending from the sky, going down behind a nearby ridge. Zamora altered his course to check the flame out. He knew there was a dynamite shed nearby.

Leaving his car, Zamora walked around the small hill. There he saw a large oblong-shaped silver craft sitting on four legs. Standing next to it were two small beings in skin-tight jump suits. There was a red insignia on the door of the craft. The beings suddenly turned around and were completely surprised to see Zamora standing there. It was about 5:45 P.M. on a bright sunny day.

"Sam, Sam! Get Out Here, Now!"

Zamora was just as startled and ran back to his car where he radioed for Sergeant Sam Chavez to come out immediately and meet him. Zamora then heard the roar again. When he turned, the two beings were gone and the craft was lifting, up trailing a flame and kicking up dust. Zamora ducked behind his car, thinking the thing might explode. After reaching an altitude of several hundred feet, the flame stopped and the craft drifted silently over the mountains and disappeared.

Confirming Physical Evidence

Later when engineers were called to the site for inspection, they found a large burned area and four deep V-shaped holes were the four legs of the craft had been. The engineers determined that to have made holes that deep, the legs would each have had to support an entire ton for a total craft weight of 4 tons. This fact alone precludes a hoax being perpetrated by Zamora. The U.S. Air Force also agreed this event was real, stating: "Information obtained during the investigation revealed that the sighting was legitimate and there was no indication a hoax was being perpetrated."

The Gulf Breeze Wave

This case documents encounters with UFOs and aliens that Ed and Frances Walters had in Florida. Gulf Breeze is a small community just outside Pensacola, Florida.

Polaroid Photos

Beginning on November 11, 1987, Ed Walters and his family spotted a UFO hovering not far from his house. Walters grabbed his Polaroid camera and took a series of pictures. The fact that he used a Polaroid camera is important, and we'll talk about that in a minute.

As Walters was taking pictures, a beam of pale blue light hit him, lifting him off the ground. Walters fought physically and mentally and was dropped back down. Over the next several months, Walters, his wife, and his children saw more UFOs. Walters even saw an alien in his backyard and chased it away. Ed Walters took more photos, including one showing a blue beam of light hitting his wife.

A Past History

As Walters began to analyze what was going on, he realized that he had a long history of strange experiences. For the most part, he discovered what researchers already knew. People very seldom have a first alien experience as an adult. The experiences have been going on since child-hood, but the person doesn't think much about them and assumes that others have the same kind of *Twilight Zone* experiences from time to time.

The Walters' were not alone. Many other residents in Gulf Breeze were seeing UFOs at the same time - so many that Gulf Breeze got a reputa-tion as the place to go to see UFOs. People were out in lawn chairs every single night looking up at the sky. They were seldom disappointed. It seems that virtually every citizen in Gulf Breeze and many outsiders have seen UFOs there.

Charges and Counter-Charges

As is typical with many UFO sightings, there were charges and counter charges of a hoax being perpetrated by Walters and his family. However, this is a valid and important case. Here's why:

- *Ed Walters is no flake. He is a respected businessman with an excel-lent reputation. He is a contractor and developer in the construction business. It takes a lot to maintain a good reputation in that busi-ness. Not only that, but the charges of a hoax would mean his wife and children were active participants in a complete lie. That simply is not very likely.*

- *The photos. Part of the controversy stems from Ed Walters' photos of the UFOs. They are quite vivid and very clear. Some were also taken very close up at a distance of only about fifty yards. Some of these craft look a little hokey, like they are from a 1950s "B" movie. But, that's just how they look! These craft are said to be utility vehicles, like army tanks. Our modern-day tanks don't look much different now than they did in World War I.*

- *A side note about UFO photos. Photos taken of flying saucers are one of the greatest detriments to researching these craft. There have been many attempts at faking photos. Also, everyone has their own idea of what a real flying saucer should look like. If an actual photo doesn't resemble the viewer's concept, it's often labeled a fake.*

- *They're Polaroids! This is the most important part of the Ed Walters/Gulf Breeze case. Walters used a Polaroid camera. Polaroid film has a very sophisticated chemistry. Polaroid photos can't be faked! There is no negative to monkey around with, and any attempt to alter the image interrupts the development of the film and ruins the image. Also, the image begins to develop immediately upon exiting the camera. I know this because I worked for the Polaroid Corporation for 5 years.*

Experts Checked It Out

Experts from Polaroid were called in to check out Ed Walters' photos. They concluded that the pictures were real: that what was seen to be on the film was really there. In addition, they concurred that everything, such as the surrounding shadows, trees, and general distances, all these details were in proper proportion.

One more point. Many people feel it is significant that there is a nuclear submarine facility in Pensacola, near Gulf Breeze. The thinking is that the aliens are monitoring the nuclear arsenal.

An Iowa Family

I included this case because it represents many aspects of cases that occur. That is, there are a series of events which may involve not only family members but also friends and neighbors as witnesses. This is a case that was followed closely by experienced investigators from

MUFON (Mutual UFO Network). The main investigators were Beverly
Trout, Irene Barnes, Lawrence Lacey, and Robert Lyon. The entire case
history was originally published in the January 1998 issue of the MUFON
Journal.

The family is an affluent family residing in Iowa and wishes to remain
anonymous. For the purpose of relating the story I am going to assign
pseudonyms to each person to make it easier for you to follow along.

How It Started

On August 7, 1997, Bob, who was 21, was driving his 11 year-old
nephew to visit his grandmother (Bob's Mom). As they were driving
through Stone State Park, they could see an amber light through the trees
which appeared to be going in the same direction at the same speed they
were going. As they rounded a curve they could see that the object was
quite large, about 70 feet in length (the size of a seven-story building
laying on its side). The object was triangular in shape with three lights
defining its perimeter. It then banked to the right and came so close to
them they could clearly see the detail of its underside. Both Bob and his
nephew were a little freaked out and frightened by the whole experience.

I've Seen This Kind of Thing Before

The incident triggered the memory of two other incidents that had
happened to Bob. Two years before, Bob and another friend had seen a
blinding bright light suddenly appear in a bathroom. The light just
seemed to emanate from thin air, with no apparent source. Bob saw
several 4-foot-high beings. His friend also saw them. In another instance
Bob remembered translucent "angels" that appeared at the foot of his
bed.

Bob's sister had had some strange experiences of her own like this. She
said men "with bumpy skin and webbed hands" had been standing by her
closet.

Wild Kingdom

Back to August 7. As Bob and his nephew turned off the main road, just
after seeing the craft close up, something ran into their car, hitting hard
against the side. They looked out the window and saw a fur-covered

animal that was very muscular with a hump on its back. It was snarling, with huge teeth and blood-red eyes. Needless to say, they freaked and put the pedal to the metal to get to Grandma's.

Chupacabra?

Although this report sounds a little strange, it's not. There are many, many reports from around the world identical to this one. This creature also fits the description of the creature seen in Central and South America known as a *chupacabra*. There are all kinds of bizarre creatures which appear in heavily wooded areas when UFOs are around.

It's almost as if the aliens are letting the zoo loose for a little run and exercise. Hunters have also been chased by huge creatures they could hear and smell crashing through the brush, but could not see. The hunters swear they were being chased by something completely invisible!

The light in the house appearing from nowhere is very common, too. In fact, it is a standard precursor to an abduction experience, as well as beings hiding in the bedroom closet. Yeah, I know it sounds like a boogeyman thing, but grown, sane, and otherwise sophisticated adults have told me over and over again that alien beings will first appear in bedroom closets and then come through the door of the closet. And, I mean *through* the wood panel, without opening the door!

At Grandma's House

After they arrived at Grandma's, all three of members of the family saw an orange globe about a mile away. The globe pulsated and then split into two smaller globes. They continued to watch this display for 20 minutes.

Later that night Bob's young nephew had a strange nightmare in which he became paralyzed and felt a needle being stuck into him.

Strange Marks

Three days later on August 10 the grandmother noticed unusual puncture wounds on the boy's fingers and toes. Several weeks later, from August 20 to 24, the grandmother and some of her neighbors watched nightly as strange lights flew around the sky within a mile of her home. On several occasions, using binoculars, they could clearly see the triangular outline of flying craft. On two occasions the craft flew directly over her house. On August 27, the grandmother felt itching sensations on her thighs. To her dismay there had appeared overnight large red welts on her legs. In the middle of some of the welts were obvious puncture wounds. Later that same day Bob took his nephew home. It took three times longer than usual and Bob could not account for the lost time.

I Wish This Month Would End

Towards the end of the month Bob saw the ferocious looking hump-backed beast again. Bob's sister saw another strange animal that looked like a cross between a dog and a deer. She had never seen anything like it before. A month later on September 23 Bob and his sister saw a silver flying disk that came towards them. They panicked and drove off. On September 28, Bob had a large cigar-shaped craft fly over him. He could clearly see several rectangular windows on the ship. Bob felt as if he were getting communications from the beings in the craft. Bob and his family are now fairly certain they have been abducted.

An Incredible Journey

Philip H. Krapf had spent more than 25 years as an editor with the Los Angeles Times. Mr. Krapf had taken early retirement and was living in a suburban community just north of Los Angeles. At the age of 62, the last thing on his mind was flying saucers and extraterrestrial beings.

It Starts With "The Light"

Krapf's wife is a chiropractor and several times each month she leaves for a couple of days to see patients in some of the communities in California's large central valley. One night while his wife was out of town, Krapf was awakened by a bright light in his bedroom. Thinking it was coming from outside, he went to the window and looked out. Nothing was there. Not only that, but he noted that the shades were tightly drawn and there was no way for light to come in through the window anyway. Yet the light was still there, getting brighter and seeming to emanate out of thin air in the middle of the room.

The light then landed on Krapf and he found himself transported rapidly up into a spacecraft of some kind. He wasn't sure how he knew it was a spacecraft, but somehow, he just knew. He found himself surrounded by strange beings that weren't human. In his head, he knew he should be freaking out, yet he sensed that something within the light was keeping him calm.

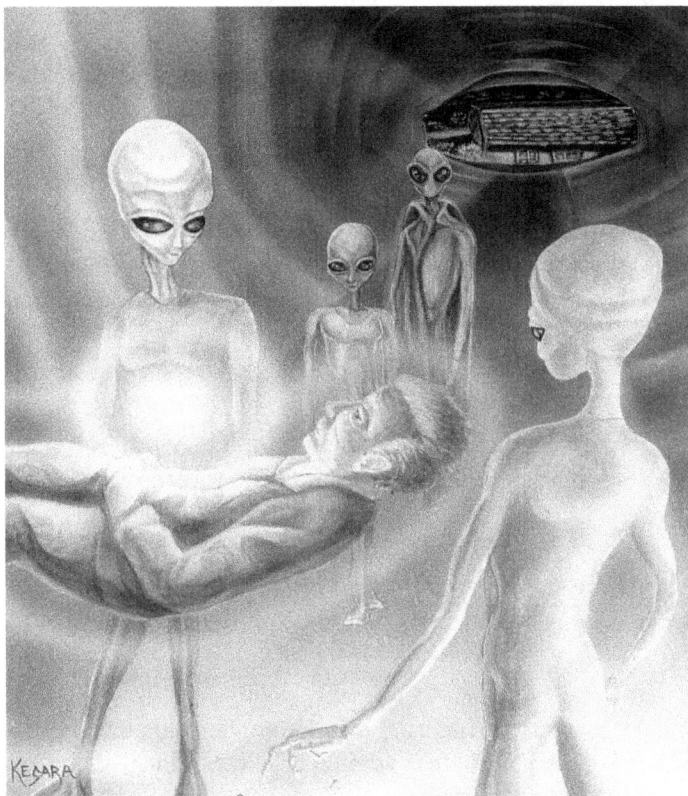

Phil Krapf is taken for the ride of his life. (Drawing courtesy Christine "Kesara"Dennett)

The light then landed on Krapf and he found himself transported rapidly up into a spacecraft of some kind. He wasn't sure how he knew it was a spacecraft, but somehow, he just knew. He found himself surrounded by strange beings that weren't human. In his head, he knew he should be freaking out, yet he sensed that something within the light was keeping him calm.

A Plan for Contact

His visit with the alien beings lasted several days. He was shown and told incredible things. The most amazing was that there was a world-wide plan going on right now to prepare the world for the inevitable contact the human race would have with these and other beings in the universe.

Krapf was told he was to play a key role in this process along with thousands of other hand-picked people around the globe. Some of the reasons he was picked were his complete lack of interest and knowledge about UFOs, as well as his skill as a wordsmith and editor.

The Most Important Part

Krapf was told that key people from all walks of life and professions were aware of our alien visitors and are going through an orientation to help the rest of us accept this fact when the time comes.

This explains why there is virtually no coverage of the huge numbers of flying saucer sightings daily around the world. Yet, we all know that unfounded rumors make the newspapers if the topic is considered "interesting" enough, and bogus stories like the completely false story about someone finding a deep-fried rat in a bucket of chicken make the headlines. Just the sheer number of people who think they see UFOs should ordinarily make the press. The reason they don't is what Krapf reveals:

> That key people in the media already know the truth about flying saucers. That's why absolutely nothing has been printed about this world-wide phenomenon!

Philip Krapf's first-hand account is truly remarkable and very, very enlightening. I can't encourage you enough to go out and get a copy of his book, The Contact Has Begun, which details his wonderful and true-life adventure.

A Powerful True Story

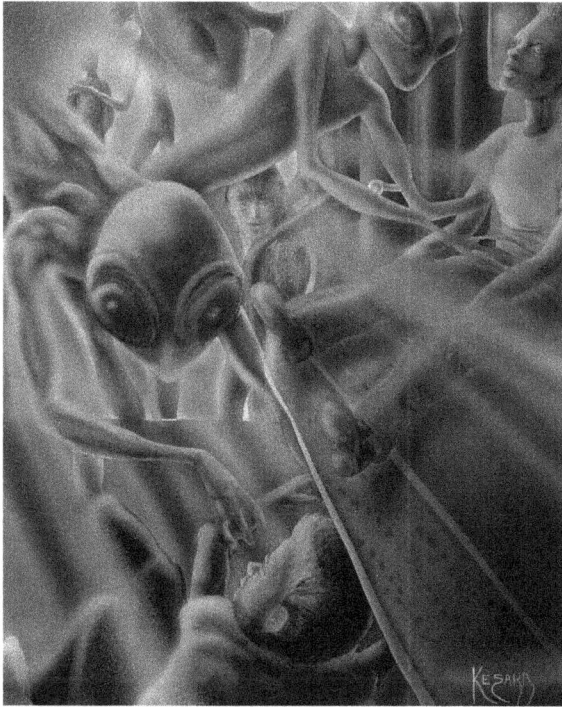

Alien beings abduct Monty and his family.
(Drawing courtesy Christine "Kesara" Dennett)

Of all the cases in this section, I actually think this is the most important one. It is stories like these that are occurring world-wide. Hundreds of people have told me they have had the same kind of experiences as the man who relates this story. If you, a friend, or a family member has had an alien encounter it is more likely to be like the case that follows than any of the others I have described in this section.

Here is how I found out about this particular case: I have a friend named George who is about 60 years old and retired. In October 1996 George attended his high school reunion. In the update year-book that is published after each reunion, George had written that many years ago he had a dramatic sighting of a UFO.

Shortly thereafter George received a lengthy typewritten letter from one of his former classmates, Monty. Monty related a 50-year history of his family's experiences with UFOs and extraterrestrial beings. The letter included drawings of the locations of some of the incidents.

George then called Monty and both of them discussed the whole case. The two men began a year-long series of telephone conversations about flying saucers and ETs. In February 1998 Monty sent George another letter, this time handwritten. George then related the story to me, as a personal friend. Both George and Monty have given us permission to share with you Monty's correspondence. What follows are three things:

- *Monty's original letter to George.*
- *Copies of Monty's original drawings.*
- *A discussion of Monty's February 1998 letter to George.*

Pasadena, California, 1951-52

"I believe it was early spring, just after dusk. I was on my bicycle, heading east on Garfias Street to North Roosevelt Street where I lived. I was 14 years old. There was a bright reflection on my left side. At first I thought it was a reflection on the power line. I realized this light was very high, very large, and the fastest thing I ever saw. It was directly above Mt. Wilson, about 1,000 feet and following the main ridge line, heading southeast over Monrovia Peak, Azusa, and Montclair, California. Then, south over Pomona. It was huge. Disk, oblong, white, orange and as big as two Pasadena Rose Bowls put together. It traveled that distance, approximately 50 to 60 miles in about 8 seconds, then shot straight up and out of sight.

"I was totally shook up and raced home a few more blocks and told my family. They listened, but were very skeptical. They knew I saw some-thing, due to my excitement. I know what I saw was real.

The next day, while reading the *Pasadena Star News*, there was a small article, 2 inches x 2 inches, explaining that several people at the Pomona Fairgrounds witnessed this unidentified object for a (few) seconds. An Air Force spokesman had no explanation for the event and that was it, end of discussion.

There is hardly a day goes by that I don't think of that incident of 45 years ago.

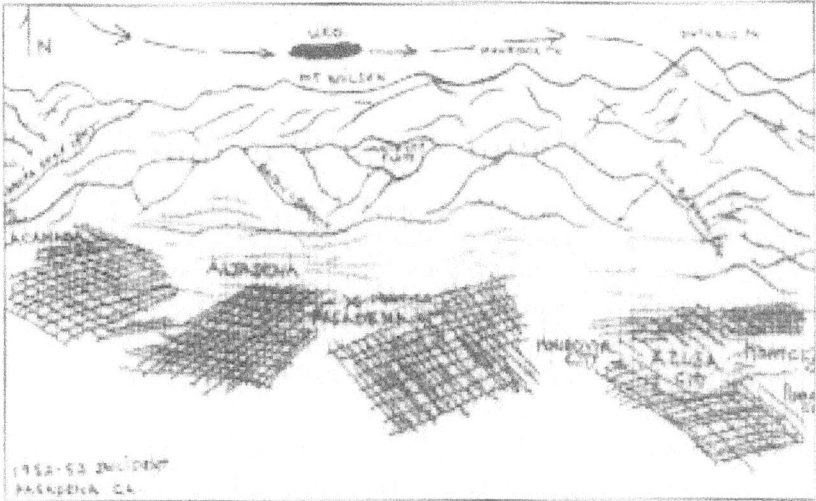

Drawing by Monty showing the location of stadium-sized craft he saw in 1952 near Pasadena, California.

San Bernardino, California, 1973-74

"My family: wife and four children (twins) Allen and Scott, 4 years old. David, 7 years old and Diana, 10 years old.

"We were on our way home from San Bernardino, California to our home in Twin Peaks, California, located in the San Bernardino mountains between Lake Arrowhead and Crestline. It was late, 10:30 to 11:00. I was driving a 1970 VW van. We were heading North on highway 18. I decided to turn off on Old Waterman Canyon Road, thinking I could save some time. This is a very narrow road, dark and curvy. This used to be the original road to Crestline and Lake Arrowhead. We were about halfway through, before this road intersects with the newer Highway 18.

"The next thing I remembered was waking up with the van parked on the side of this narrow road. In fact, we all woke up at the same time. I never pulled off the road to go to sleep. We were only 12 miles from home. I was dismayed, confused, and very relaxed. Our kids wanted to know why I pulled off and went to sleep, when in fact we were all asleep, or so we thought. We continued home. Betty and the kids went to sleep. When we arrived at home, it was 1:00 A.M. We had been asleep for one and a half hours in an area where I would never pull off, except for a flat tire.

"I was so baffled by this event that I found it difficult to carry out my duties for the U.S. Forest Service for a few days. My family never discussed this incident again, until December 1994, when my son, Allen, asked me if I remembered. 'Just vaguely,' I said, and that was the end of it.

December, 1995
"Allen asked me again about the incident. And in an instant, it all came back, what actually happened.

This is what I remembered on that night of 1974, 21 years after the fact.

"I exited Highway 18 onto Old Waterman Canyon Road and continued north where the road again intersects Highway 18. I was about halfway, approaching the switchbacks, when I saw lights in my rearview mirror. The lights were approximately 1 mile behind, very bright, and catching up with me. I thought the lights were two motorcycles racing, due to their high speed. I told my family to hang on, as I wanted to put distance between us and them. The lights were almost behind us, very quickly, when I realized the lights were above the road. I thought it must be a helicopter, but there was no noise. Our kids began to yell, "What is it Dad? Speed up."

"Now the lights were above us, bluish-white, and I thought there were two red lights. The car was losing power, not missing, just slowing down. Diana was now screaming, David was crying, and the twins were silent. My wife, Betty, began yelling, "It's the Lord. The angels are returning." The car stopped. It felt like the car was dragged to the side of the road. I couldn't move. I could see straight ahead but could not move my neck. It was like a blue fog. I heard the right sliding door open with a loud bang. No sounds from the kids. I heard the driver and passenger doors open. For an instant, I saw movement. I was out of the car. The next thing I remember is waking up, parked on the side of Old Waterman Canyon Road.

"My son Allen tells me what he saw and felt. When the lights were almost on top of us, his mother yelled, "They are angels." He somehow got under the middle seat. He could see between the floor and the cushion approximately 12 inches. The car pooped out, stopped. Lots of glowing blue light. So much that it illuminated through the 12-inch space he could see out of. He was curled up on the floor with his arm wrapped around the seat pipe bracket, and his hands were interlocked.

(Allen to his Dad) "I could see and think, but was paralyzed. The sliding door opens fast and a loud bang. The front doors open. I could see them through the open side door. They looked like giant bugs, long, spindly arms and huge bug eyes. Like a praying mantis. Dad, they take you and mom first. Mom was still screaming. Then Dave, Diana, and Scott. I'm last, but they couldn't release my grip from around the seat bracket bar. The bugs tell me to relax. I can't, nor would I voluntarily. My body becomes relaxed and they release my grip. I'm terrified and again, paralyzed. It was like I just floated out and up. Bright, bluish light. I'm inside a dark place and then I wake up, in the car, parked on the side of the road, wondering if I had a bad dream."

"Scott, Diana, Dave, and my then-wife Betty remember the event as I did. Betty refuses to discuss the event, becomes very emotional.

"This event remained hidden in our brains for twenty-one years, until December, 1995, when Allen said, "Do you remember?"

Twin Peaks, California, 1975

"Twin Peaks is on a ridge top that is located between Crestline, California and Lake Arrowhead. Our home was located on top of the ridge at approximately a 6,000-foot elevation. There was snow on the ground and I believe it was March or April when this next incident occurred.

"We lived in a two-story Victorian style home. It was very dark that night and all four children were on the second floor quietly playing, which in itself, was unusual. It was too quiet. My wife Betty and I were reading on the first floor. The kids began screaming their heads off, yelling and crying. An extremely bright, bluish light from outside completely enveloped our home, inside and outside. The kids ran downstairs and I ran outside. This very bright light had just moved to the north, below the ridge top. And light was radiating through the pine trees. This event lasted no more than 10 seconds.

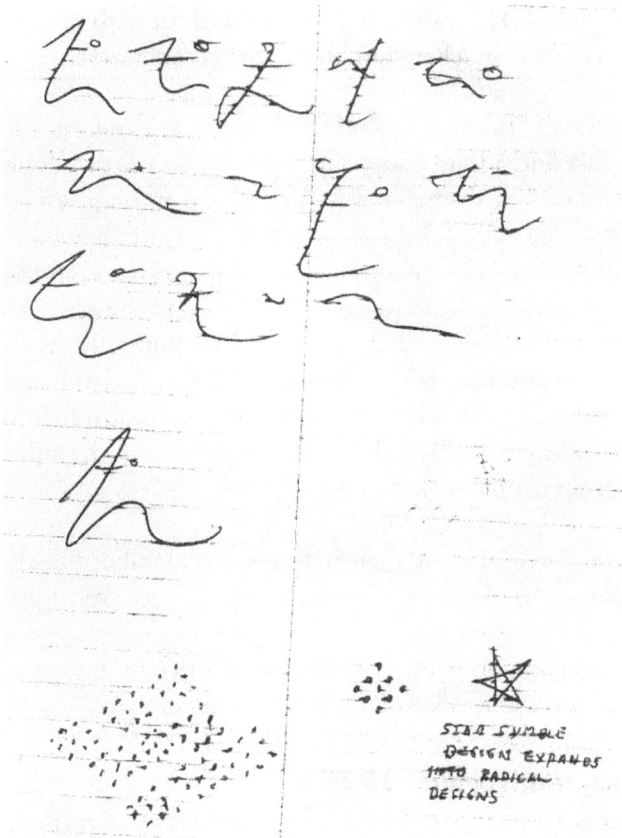

STAR SYMBOL
DESIGN EXPANDS
INTO RADICAL
DESIGNS

Symbol language being taught to contactees by alien beings.

"The kids were scared to death to go back upstairs. We were just baffled by what happened. There was no noise from the light. I asked local people if they saw this and none did. No reports were called in to the local sheriff substation. I just couldn't believe no one else witnessed this event. The *San Bernardino Sun* newspaper had nothing about unusual lights.

*Additional alien symbols from
Monty's hand-written letters.*

Hemet, California, 1993

"The last event took place from our home in West Hemet. It was an early fall night at approximately 10:00 P.M. I had just stepped outside and was looking towards the east. While looking towards the mountains, I noticed a very small, bright light that began to move extremely fast in one direction, then quickly shoot in another direction.

"No human could survive the G-forces of that type movement. I estimated this light would move 10 miles in one second, then instantly go in the reverse direction. This went on for about 30 seconds and the light shot out of sight. I believe this occurred east of the San Jacinto mountain range, near the Anza-Borrego desert. There was no mention of this event on radio or TV."

> My Thoughts (Monty): "I wish our government would quit spoon-feeding little tidbits of information. We all know something is going on and there is earthly involvement by humans. Until those who know the truth come forward, it will remain a mystery."

Monty
Hemet, California

Letter from Monty to George
February 24, 1998

"George,
Thank you for taking the time calling me on the *A&E* program. Good program covering all aspects of UFO abductions etc.

What bothers me, is all the records are gone on Roswell (destroyed) and probably on all sensitive UFO sightings and abductions that the Govt. kept secret. I don't think the Smithsonian museum in Washington D.C. has anything.

"What happened to me and my family has profoundly affected me. The ancient world engraved their events in stone. It worked for them, 8,000 years and it will work for me. I engraved a saucer and electrical force field with a hammer and cold chisel, summer of '97. I feel more people should put their important events in stone. It may take another thousand years to solve the secrets of government. It's nice to know that you are separating fact from fiction and keeping the awareness level up high.

Take Care, Monty

Oscar's Story

This case is a story told to me by a personal friend of mine named Oscar. Whenever I meet someone I make no secret of the fact that I have a great amount of interest in flying saucers. First, it keeps me true to who I am and what I am about. I am willing to listen to all kinds of guff from skeptics. As I said before, skepticism is an essential part of our growth process and the acceptance of the realization that we are not alone in the universe. Secondly, it frees people to tell me things they have experienced; things they have told no one else.

The "Look"

When someone comes forward to tell me about their flying saucer experiences, their demeanor changes. They start speaking in low tones. They invariably look around to see if anyone else is listening. It is not uncommon for them to unconsciously move 2 to 3 feet away from anybody else in the vicinity.

By the looks on their faces, you can tell the event affected them deeply and still does, no matter how many years have passed since their experience. These are the moments I live for. When I see "the look," I know I've struck gold and I'm about to hear a remarkable, true experience.

Such was the case with Oscar. Late one afternoon after a long day of meetings, I casually mentioned to Oscar that I was going back to my room to read some stuff about flying saucers. He got real quiet, but, he got "the look" on his face. He said, "OK. I'll see you in the morning." I like to arrive at meetings early to kind of stake out my space. Usually, I'm the first one there, but not this time. Oscar was waiting for me. With great trepidation, here is what he told me:

Phillipines: Young boys witness a school mate boarding an alien craft. (Drawing courtesy Christine "Kesara" Dennett)

A Man of God

The priest at Oscar's church had privately told him this story. The priest grew up in the Philippines. As a young boy, he remembered one year that a new kid showed up at school. It turned out that this kid was absolutely brilliant in his schoolwork. He was a phenomenal athlete. He was also very popular. The priest remembers that after several months the teacher began asking to meet the boy's parents. However, the boy always deferred or made up some kind of excuse. This was really odd because the town was so small that everyone knew everyone else and their families. Nobody knew this kid's family. And, no one really knew where he lived.

One day the priest and several of his friends decided to follow the new kid home. The kid headed out through some sugar cane fields, and eventually he came to a clearing. To the shock of the boys who were following, there was a small spacecraft of some kind sitting in the clearing. A door opened, and the kid walked in! The ship then lifted off and shot into the sky at a speed the boys had never seen before. To this day the priest maintains that every single word he told Oscar is true.

The Travis Walton Case

This is another well-known case, made even more famous since it was the subject of the motion picture *Fire in The Sky*. Here's the story.

On November 5, 1975, Travis Walton was a young man working for the National Forest Service, clearing brush in the Apache-Silgreaves National Forest outside of Snowflake, Arizona. He was on a work crew with six other men. While riding back from work in a single, large truck at about 6:00 P.M., the crew saw a red glow through the trees. Thinking it might be a budding forest fire, they decided to take a closer look.

The Light Beam

When they got to the location they found a large UFO hovering above a clearing in the forest. Walton got out and ran towards the craft. A beam of light shot down from the disk, striking him. It lifted him up from the ground, then knocked him back down, hard. The other men, in fear for their lives, jumped in the truck and took off, leaving Walton behind. A few minutes later they saw a light shoot straight up into the sky and disappear. They figured it was safe to go back and turned around to get Walton. When they got there Travis Walton was gone!

Or so the local sheriff thought. He immediately began an investigation into the murder of the missing Travis Walton. After all, the story his friends were telling sounded unbelievable. However, lie detector tests showed that the men were not lying and the sheriff was unable to break their stories.

Travis Walton sees the light.
(Drawing courtesy Christine "Kesara" Dennett)

The Return

Travis Walton showed up 6 days later and 12 miles from where he was last seen. Walton said that he had been taken aboard a spacecraft and kept there. At one point early in his adventure, Walton says he tried to run away down a corridor of the ship. During this time he encountered the classic small gray aliens with large heads and small mouths that never moved. He also saw some of the large Nordic aliens. These were men, over 6 feet tall, with muscular builds and long blond hair.

The Movie

The movie of Walton's experience is basically Hollywood hype. It's entertaining, but it also makes up a lot of things, in particular, the horrific scenes on board the ship where Walton is stored in some alien goo and later subjected to some kind of exam. These scenes were all made up by the movie producers. The case itself, however, is an excellent one and well-documented. Here's a few additional points about Walton's case:

- *The movie shows that there were only five men, when in fact there were seven, including Walton. Seven real witnesses to this event.*

- *In the 20 years since this incident took place, all the men have taken several lie detector tests each, administered by different examiners.*

- *They all passed every test given.*

Underwater UFOs

On January 3, 1979 Filiberto Cardenas was contacted by alien beings. While Cardenas and three of his neighbors were driving with him along a highway outside of Hialeah, Florida, their car suddenly stalled. The entire electrical system failed. It was about 6:00 P.M. and the headlights went out as well.

Buzzing and Lights

After getting out of the car Filiberto popped the hood. A very strange, loud buzzing sound began. Everyone in the car could hear it. Suddenly a bright, blue-violet light fell over Cardenas. He was instantly paralyzed, unable to move any part of his body. The light was coming from an odd-shaped craft above them. It was dark in color with poorly defined edges, almost like a blurry picture.

The light lifted Cardenas up, up, and above the treetops in full view of Fernando Marti, age 46; Marti's wife, Elizabeth, age 36, and their 13-year old daughter, Mirta. All three people witnessed the stunning event as the craft slowly flew off with Cardenas inside. Cardenas turned up about two hours later around 8 P.M. His story was dramatic.

Down, Beneath the Sea

The craft had taken Cardenas and lifted him into it. After traveling for some distance the craft dove rapidly into the ocean. Cardenas could see water rushing by through a nearby porthole. He felt and sensed that there was absolutely no resistance against the water. The ship cut through it like a hot knife through butter.

The beings who had spirited Cardenas away were small, but looked very human. They communicated with him through telepathy in perfect Spanish. They wore tight-fitting, one-piece jumpsuits.

Underwater Base

Cardenas was taken to and shown an underwater base that the aliens maintain. Several weeks later he was directed by the aliens through telepathy to go back to the same spot were the first encounter took place. Cardenas asked mentally if he could bring his wife, Iris. The beings said yes, because they considered Cardenas and his wife to be closely connected in a way that almost made them one.

During the next encounter the alien beings told Cardenas and his wife repeatedly how important universal love was for the health of the planet and the advancement of mankind. During the visit Iris asked if she could touch the beings in an effort to confirm that the event was really taking place. They allowed her to do so and she reported that the texture of their suits was smooth when you ran your hand along them in one direction, but rough, like fish scales or reptile skin if you ran your hand in the opposite direction.

Miami

On one occasion a contact took place at 10:00 A.M. At the very same time hundreds of people at Miami International Airport saw a large ship and two smaller disk-shaped craft. When interviewed later, all the eyewitnesses identified the same location as the place where the large craft was hovering. This location was the very same place where Cardenas and his wife were picked up and the ships were seen at exactly the same time as their encounter: 10:00 A.M. on February 21, 1979.

The Landing at Voronezh

Unidentified Flying Object Lands in Russia
New York Times, October 9, 1989

This is a very exciting case that, as usual, has had little publicity in the United States. However, it did reach our press as indicated by newspaper headline above.

Voronezh is a city located about 300 miles southeast of Moscow. It currently has about a million residents. On September 21, 1989, several children were playing on Mendeleyen Street. A strange craft landed nearby and two large beings got out, along with what can only be described as a robot ("a mechanical man"). The beings looked around for approximately 5 minutes, got back in the ship and took off.

Zavodsk Square

One week later several shiny disks landed all at once in different parts of the city. The most dramatic incident occurred downtown at a park in Zavodsk Square. A group of children were playing soccer in the park when the ships landed. A small being got out, accompanied by two "giants" over 10 feet tall. They, too, had a robot with them, and a floating globe.

When the citizens freaked out and started shouting at them, the beings and the craft suddenly disappeared only to reappear a few minutes later. One of the beings aimed a device at boy who apparently ran up for a closer look. The kid disappeared. Later after the ship took off, the kid reappeared; no harm done.

Soviet Newspaper Report

Tass, the official Russian News service, stated:

Scientists have confirmed that an unidentified flying object recently landed in the city of Voronezh. They have also located the landing site and found traces of aliens who made a short promenade about the park.

There were literally hundreds of eyewitnesses whose stories all concurred. There were deep holes left in the ground and scientists estimated from these holes that the craft weighed over eleven tons. In addition, there were increased levels of radiation and magnetization in the soil where the craft had been.

Alien landing at Voronezh, Russia
(Drawing courtesy Christine "Kesara" Dennett)

Such a furor was created in Europe over the landing that even famous French UFO researcher Jacques Vallee came to investigate. Mr. Vallee is the author of several books and many articles on the scientific investigation of flying saucers. The French-speaking character in the movie *Close Encounters of the Third Kind* who eventually arranged for Richard Dreyfuss' character to go aboard the spacecraft, was based on Jacques Vallee.

Voronezh, A Popular Place

Voronezh must be on the alien list of must-see places, because there seems to be a lot of activity around there. Two years later on August 20, 1991, an Aeroflot crew on flight 2523 heading for St. Petersburg spotted a large, bright saucer shortly after takeoff.

UFO Wave in Mexico City

July 11, 1991 was the date of a total eclipse of the sun, which could be end up being one the most important event in our century. The eclipse marked the beginning of a dramatic wave of sightings in Mexico City, the largest metropolis in the world. Since that date, virtually every day and every night somewhere in Mexico, UFOs, flying disks and large motherships are being seen and videotaped by thousands if not millions of citizens.

Former *60 Minutes* (Mexico) lead correspondent, Jaime Maussan has been the foremost investigator and chronicler of these extraordinary events. These strange craft are regularly seen around the smoldering volcano, Mt. Popocatepetl This volcano maintains the highest electro-magnetic fields ever recorded in the world.

Using his position as a well-known journalist and celebrity in Mexico, Jaime Maussan asked for the citizens of Mexico to send him any home videos they may have taken of these UFOs being sighted around the country. Within weeks, over 5,000 videos were sent to Maussan. He now has so many that they fill a warehouse. The videos show dramatic footage of moving formations, some involving more than 50 craft. There is also footage of huge metallic cylinders, craft spelling out formations and cigar shaped motherships.

As Maussan personally told me: "I have personally witnessed the sky filled with craft, while the traffic on all freeways and roads stopped as people got out of their cars and all pointed at the sky. And not one word about these events has ever appeared in a U.S. newspaper. I know, because I always check."

Maussan has a standing offer that he makes for all U.S. journalists: He guarantees that if anyone comes to Mexico City that they will see UFOs and flying disks for themselves. If they do not, he will pay for their round-trip airfare.

Jaime Maussan was born in Mexico City and earned a B.A. Degree in radio and television from Miami University in Ohio. Fluent in several languages, he has enjoyed a 25-year career in the media, during which he has received numerous awards. He is currently anchorman of the TV show *Tercer Milenio (3rd Milennium),* which is broadcast through Televisa Network, the largest Spanish language international network in the world.

Tercer Milenio is breaking every rating in Mexican television and is also leading the field in UFO investigative journalism in Latin America. Jaime also produces a radio program *Jaime Maussan, UFOs and other Mysteries,* and has produced 20 commercial videos for *Programas de Investigacion,* a leading independent production company in Mexico.

Carlos Diaz

Jaime Maussan has also been the lead investigator in the Carlos Diaz sightings. Diaz, a bright, educated, articulate businessman who lives in a remote part of Mexico, has captured dramatic still and video shots of hovering craft. Spectra-analysis of the film and videos show light frequencies, which have never been seen or recorded on earth before.

Maussan provided Diaz with an array of cameras and film, virtually guaranteeing that the footage could not be faked in all formats. In addition, Diaz has claimed to have met with human-like beings from these craft. Maussan has been closely following the Diaz case for over 8 years. Maussan has even spent months living at the Diaz house and has seen the craft himself.

NASA UFO FOOTAGE

Maussan has also been given some very dramatic footage of silver disks hovering around one of the NASA space shuttles. The footage taken from inside the shuttle is clear and unobstructed as it was shot through a porthole. The disks look exactly like those now commonly seen over Mexico City. I have seen the footage myself and it is spectacular!

Maussan states that he got the footage from a former NASA employee who got it into the hands of a scientist from another country. Jaime Maussan says: "Nobody in Mexico laughs about UFOs anymore, nobody!"

Watch The Skies

I was in a plane last week when I looked out the window and saw this bright light. It was zigzagging around. I went up to the pilot and said, "Have you ever seen anything like that?" He was shocked and said, "Nope." And, I said to him, "Let's follow it!" We followed it for several minutes. It was a bright white light. We followed it to Bakersfield, and all of a sudden to our utter amazement, it went straight up into the heavens. When I got off the plane I told Nancy about it.

Ronald Reagan
(while governor of California)
as told to Norman C. Miller, Washington Bureau Chief
The Wall Street Journal, 1972

I was the pilot of the plane when we saw the UFO. Also on board were Governor Reagan and a couple of his security people. We were flying a Cessna Citation. It was maybe 9 or 10 o'clock at night. We were near Bakersfield, California, when Governor Reagan and the others called my attention to a big light flying a bit behind my plane.

It appeared to be several hundred yards away. It was a fairly steady light until it began to elongate. Then, the light took off. It went up at a 45-degree angle, at a high rate of speed. The UFO went from a normal cruise speed to a fantastic speed instantly. If you give an airplane power, it will accelerate, but not like a hot-rod, and that's what this was like... the object definitely wasn't another airplane. But we didn't file a report on the object because for a long time they considered you a nut if you saw a UFO.

Bull Payntor, pilot (describing the same incident)

a. The phenomena reported is something real and not visionary or fictitious.

b. There are objects probably approximating the shape of a disc, of such appreciable size as to appear to be as large as a man-made aircraft.

General Nathan Twining
Chairman of the Joint Chiefs of Staff
(letter to the Commanding General of the Army Air Forces)
September 23, 1947

Flying saucers are being observed by citizens in every country of the world. (Courtesy Orange County Register)

Because of the developments of science, all the countries on earth will have to unite to survive and make a common front against attack by people from other planets. The politics of the future will be cosmic or interplanetary.

General Douglas MacArthur
New York Times, October 8, 1955.

We are not working with them, only contact.

Dr. Eric A. Walker
former executive secretary for the Defense Department
Research and Development Board.

ARGENTINA

The unidentified flying objects do exist. Their presence and intelligent displacement in the Argentine airspace has been proven. Their nature and origin is unknown and no judgement is made about them.

Between 1950 and 1965, personnel of Argentina's Navy alone made twenty-two sightings of unidentified flying objects that were not airplanes, satellites, weather balloons or any type of known vehicles. These twenty-two cases served as precedents for intensifying that investigation of the subject by the Navy. In the past two years, nine incidents have been recorded that are being studied by Captain Pagani and a team of military and civilian scientists and collaborators.

Captain Sanchez Moreno
Naval Air Station Comandante Espora
World Authority for Spatial Affairs
New York, 1979

BELGIUM

In any case, the Air Force has arrived to the conclusion that a certain number of anomalous phenomena has been produced within Belgian airspace. The numerous testimonies of ground observa-

tions compiled in this book (SOBEPS), reinforced by the reports of the night of March 30-31, 1990, have led us to face the hypothesis that a certain number of unauthorized aerial activities have taken place.

The day will come undoubtedly when the phenomenon will be observed with technological means of detection and collection that won't leave a single doubt about it's origin. This should lift a part of the veil that has covered the (UFO) mystery for a long time. A mystery that continues to the present. But it exists, it is real, and that in itself is an important conclusion.

Major General Wilfred De Brouwer
Deputy Chief, Royal Belgian Air Force
"UFO Wave over Belgium, An Extraordinary Dossier," Brussels, 1991

BRAZIL

The problem of flying discs has polarized the attention of the whole world, but it's serious and it deserves to be treated seriously. Almost all the governments of the great powers are interested in it, dealing with it in a serious and confidential manner, due to its military interest.

Brigadier General Joao Adil Oliveira
chief of the Air Force General Staff Information Service
(briefing to the Army War College), November 2, 1954

It is impossible to deny any more the existence of flying saucers at the present time. The flying saucer is not a ghost from another dimension or a mysterious dragon. It is a fact confirmed by material evidence. There are thousands of documents, photos, and sighting reports demonstrating its existence.

Brigadier General Joao Adil Oliveira
O Globo, Rio de Janeiro, February 28, 1958

CANADA

I made discrete enquiries through the Canadian Embassy staff in Washington, who were able to obtain for me the following information:

a. The matter is the most highly classified subject in the United States government, rating higher even than the H-bomb.

b. Flying Saucers exist.

c. Their modus operandi is unknown; concentrated effort is being made by a small group headed by Dr. Vannevar Bush.

d. The entire matter is considered by the United States authorities to be of tremendous significance.

Wilbert Brockhouse Smith
Department of Transportation memo
(stamped Top Secret), November 21, 1950.

ENGLAND

What does all this stuff about flying saucers amount to? What can it mean? What is the truth?

Sir Winston Churchill
memo to secretary of state for Air, Lord Cherwell, July 28, 1952

More than 10,000 sightings have been reported, the majority of which cannot be accounted for by any scientific explanation....I am convinced that these objects do exist and that they are not manufactured by any nation on earth. I can therefore see no alternative to accepting the theory that they come from some extraterrestrial source...

Air Chief Marshal Lord Dowding
commander-in-chief of RAF Fighter Command
Sunday Dispatch, London, July 11, 1954

UFOs defy worldly logic...The human mind cannot begin to comprehend UFO characteristics: their propulsion, their sudden ap-

pearance, their disappearance, their great speeds, their silence,
their maneuvers, their apparent antigravity, their changing shapes.

Earl of Kimberly
House of Lords, January 18, 1979

Many men have seen (UFOs) and not been mistaken. Who are we
to doubt their word? ... Only a few weeks ago a Palermo police-
man photographed one, and four Italian Navy officers saw a 300-
foot long fiery craft rising from the sea and disappearing into the
sky... why should these men of law enforcement and defense lie?

Lord Rankeillour
House of Lords, January 18, 1979

A very large number large number of sightings have been vouched
for by persons whose credentials seem to me unimpeachable. It is
striking that so many have been trained observers, such as police
officers and airline or military pilots. Their observations have in
many instances... been supported either by technical means such as
radar or, even more convincingly, by...interference with electrical
apparatus of one sort or another...

Lord Hill-Norton
chief of Defense Staff, Ministry of Defense
foreword to Above Top Secret, by Timothy Goode, 1987

FRANCE

I must say that if listeners could see for themselves the mass of re-
ports coming in from the airborne gendarmerie, from the mobile
gendarmerie, and from the gendarmerie charged with the job of
conducting investigations, all of which reports are forwarded by us
to the National Centre for Space Studies, then they would see that it
is all pretty disturbing.

M. Robert Galley, French Minister of Defense
radio interview, February 21, 1974

We can...say categorically that mysterious objects have indeed ap-
peared and continue to appear in the sky that surrounds us.

General Lionel M. Chassin
Commanding General of the French Air Forces
General Air Defense Coordinator, Allied Air Forces
Central Europe, NATO
foreword to Flying Saucers and the Straight Line Mystery, 1958

HUNGARY

*Around Szolnok many UFO reports have been received from the
Ministry of Defense, which obviously and logically means that they
(UFOs) know very well where they have to land and what they have
to do. It is remarkable indeed that the Hungarian newspapers, in
general newspapers everywhere reject the reports of the authorities.*

George Keleti
Minister of Defense, Nepszava, Budapest, August 18, 1994

INDONESIA

*UFOs sighted in Indonesia are identical with those sighted in other
countries. Sometimes they pose a problem for our air defence and
once we were obliged to open fire on them.*

Air Marshall Rosemin Nurjadin
Commander in Chief of the Indonesian Air Force
letter to Yusuke J. Matsumura, May 5, 1967 1

*I am convinced that we must study the UFO problem seriously for
reasons of sociology, technology and security.*

Air Commander J. Salutun
Secretary of the National Aerospace Council
letter published in *UFO News*, 1974

JAPAN

*Much evidence tells us UFOs have been tracked by radar; so,
UFOs are real and they may come from outer space... UFO photographs and various materials show scientifically that there are
more advanced people piloting the saucers and motherships.*

General Kanshi Ishikawa
Chief of Staff of Japan's Air Self-Defense Force
interview in *UFO News*, 1974

*I said that someone had to solve the UFO problem with far reach-
ing vision at the same time...From the point of "people" in outer
space, all human beings on earth are the same people, regardless
of whether they are American, Russian, Japanese or whoever.*

Toshiki Kaifu, Prime Minister
letter to Mayor Shiotani, Hakui City, June 24, 1990.

THE SOVIET UNION

*In spite of all the differences between us, we must all learn to pre-
serve our one big family of humanity. At our meeting in Geneva,
the U.S. president said that if the earth faced an invasion by extraterrestrials, the United States and the Soviet Union would join
forces to repel such an invasion.*

Mikhail Gorbachev
President of the Soviet Union
Soviet Life Supplement, May, 1987

*For skeptics and non-skeptics, this information can serve as offi-
cially documented proof of UFO validity. We hope that this open
acknowledgment of the phenomenon will put an end to ambiguous
speculations and will make the fact of its existence beyond doubt.*

*Now we have grounds to tell that UFOs are not optical or halluci-
nated phenomena, which were allegedly caused by global psycho-*

*sis. The objects have been spotted by technological means. Pictures
are available for specialists.*

General Igor Maltsev
Soviet Chief of Air Defense Forces
Soviet Military Review, June, 1989.

SPAIN

*Now, from a personal position, as Carlos Castro Cavero, I believe
that UFOs are spaceships or extraterrestrial craft...The nations of
the world are currently working together in the investigation of the
UFO phenomenon. Maybe when this group of nations acquire more
precise and definite information, it will be possible to release the
news to the world.*

General Carlos Castro Cavero
Spanish Air Force, commander of Spain's Third Aerial Region
interview with J. J. Benitez, 1976

ZIMBABWE

*This was no ordinary UFO. Scores of people saw it. It was no illu-
sion, no deception, no imagination.*

Air Marshal Azim Daudpota
The Times, London, August 3, 1985

*Although not speaking officially, as far as my Air Staff is con-
cerned, we believe implicitly that the unexplained UFOs are from
some civilization beyond our planet.*

Air Commodore David Thorne
director of general operations
letter to Timothy Goode, October 24, 1985. 2

A flying saucer flew over the control tower at Bulawayo Airport in
Zimbabwe on July 22, 1985. Dozens of people on the ground saw it as
well as control tower personnel. Two jet fighters were sent up to intercept it. It was described as the classic disk with a bubble on top.

ASTRONAUTS

We have contact with alien cultures.

Dr. Brian O'Leary
International Forum On New Science
Fort Collins, Colorado, September 18, 1994

I have no firsthand experience, but I have had the opportunity to meet with people from other countries who in the course of their official duties claim to have had personal firsthand encounter experiences... with extraterrestrials.

From what I now understand, and have experienced and seen the evidence for, I think the evidence is very strong and large portions of it are classified by governments.

Dr. Edgar Mitchell
NBC Dateline, 1996

I do believe that there is a lot more known about extraterrestrial investigation than is available to the public right now, has been for a long time... It's a long, long story. It goes back to World War II when all that happened and is highly classified stuff.

Dr. Edgar Mitchell
Oprah Winfrey Show, July 19, 1991

On the Apollo 14 mission to the moon, Dr. Edgar Mitchell became the sixth man to ever walk on the moon. In addition to having been an astronaut, Dr. Mitchell is also a scientist with a degree from MIT. He has also served as a Naval officer and a test pilot.

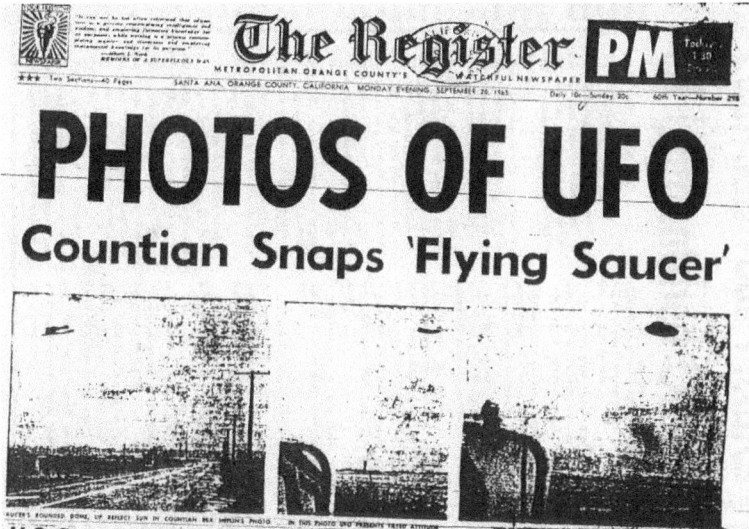

August 2, 1965. Citizens continue to sight and photograph flying saucers. (Courtesy Orange County Register)

I believe that these extra-terrestrial vehicles and their crews are visiting this planet from other planets, which obviously are a little more technically advanced than we are here on earth...We may first have to show that we have learned to resolve our problems by peaceful means, rather than warfare, before we are accepted as fully qualified universal team members.

Also, I did have occasion in 1951 to have two days of observation of many flights of them, of different sizes, flying in fighter formation, generally from east to west over Europe. They were a higher altitude than we could reach with our jet fighters of that time.

Col. Gordon Cooper
letter to Granada's Ambassador Griffith
United Nations, November 9, 1978.

I had a camera crew filming the installation (the installation of a precision landing system at Edwards Air Force Base in California) when they spotted a saucer. They filmed it as it flew overhead, then hovered, extended three legs as landing gear, and slowly came down to land on a dry lake bed!

*These guys were all pro cameramen, so the picture quality was
very good. The camera crew managed to get within 20 to 30 yards
of it, filming all the time. It was a classic saucer, shiny silver and
smooth, about 30 feet across. It was pretty clear it was an alien
craft. As they approached closer, it took off.*

*After a while, a high-ranking officer said that when the film was
developed I was to put it in a pouch and send it to Washington. He
didn't say anything about me not looking at the film. That's what I
did when it came back from the lab and it was all there just like the
camera crew reported.*

*I had a good friend at Roswell, a fellow officer. He had to be care-
ful about what he said. But, it sure wasn't a weather balloon like
the Air Force cover story. He made it clear to me what crashed was
a craft of alien origin, and members of the crew were recovered.*

Col. Gordon Cooper
National Enquirer, January, 1997.

*I'm one of those guys who has never seen a UFO. But, I've asked,
and I've said publicly I thought they were somebody else: some
other civilization.*

Eugene Cernan
Apollo 17 commander
"Cernan Says Other Earths Exist,"
Los Angeles Times, January 6, 1973

*I try to communicate with the life that's out there. I'm serious. It is
not that far out. When I'm circling around out there, I try in whatever ways I can to get them to come down here and get me.*

Story Musgrave
The Houston Post, December 1, 1993

Story Musgrave was a space shuttle astronaut who flew on the mission to
repair the Hubble space telescope.

RUSSIAN COSMONAUTS

*As regards UFOs, their presence cannot be denied: thousands of
people have seen them. It may be that their source is optical effects,*

but some of their properties, for instance, their ability to change course by 90 degrees at great speed, simply stagger the imagination.

Yevegni Khrunov
Soyuz-5 Spacecraft Pilot
"UFOs Through the Eyes of Cosmonauts," December, 1980

On May 5, 1981, we were in orbit (in the Salyut-6 Space Station). I saw an object that didn't resemble any cosmic objects I'm familiar with. It was a round object which resembled a melon, round and a little bit elongated. In front of this object was something that resembled a gyrating depressed cone, I can draw it, It's difficult to describe. The object resembles a barbell. I saw it becoming transparent and like with a body inside. At the other end I saw something like gas discharging, like a reactive object.

Then something happened that is very difficult for me to describe from the point of view of physics. Last year in the magazine Nature, *I read about a physicist... we tried together to explain this phenomenon and we decided it was a plasma form. I have to recognize that it did not have an artificial origin. I don't know of anything that can make this movement... tightening, then expanding, pulsating. Then as I was observing, something happened, two explosions. One explosion, and then 0.5 seconds later, the second part exploded. I called my colleague Viktor (Savinykh), but he didn't arrive in time to see anything.*

What are the particulars? First conclusion: The object moved in a suborbital path, otherwise I wouldn't have been able to see it. There were two clouds, like smoke, that formed a barbell. It came near me and I watched it. Then we entered into the shade for two or three minutes after this happened. When we came out of the shade we didn't see anything. But during a certain time, we and the craft were moving together.

Vladimir Kovalyonok
major general of aviation and cosmonaut
video-taped interview with Giorio Bongiovani
village of Kosnikov, Near Moscow, 1993
(videotape courtesy of Michael Hesemann and MUFON)

*Today it can be stated with a high degree of confidence that ob-
served manifestations of UFOs are no longer confined to the modern picture of the world, or the simple refutation of the orthodox
natural science paradigm. The historical evidence of the phenomenon, the singularity of its newly gained kinematic, energetic, and
psychophysical features allows us to hypothesize that ever since
mankind has been coexisting with this extraordinary substance, it
has manifested a high level of intelligence and technology. The
sightings have become the constant component of human activity.*

*It's necessary to carry out the popular ufological enlightenment,
since the probability for a meeting of a person with a UFO exists,
and this person should be ready for this event. Precautionary
measures are especially important. It's necessary to tell the truth,
which has been distorted previously by the politically engaged sciences and most recently by ufological dilettantes...The ufologists
should know all the UFOs landing places and contacts in their regions. They should know all the relations with the local authorities,
and in particular, with the police, the civil defense bodies, as well
as information, scientific and medical organizations.*

Pavel Popovich
major-general and cosmonaut
International UFO Symposium, MUFON, 1992

SCIENTISTS

*If we find so much as a single microbe on a rock from mars or the
moon, it means that the universe is teeming with life.*

Dr. Carl Sagan

*It now seems quite clear that the Earth is not the only inhabited
planet. There is evidence that the bulk of the stars in the sky have
planetary systems. Recent research concerning the origin of life on
Earth suggests that the physical and chemical processes leading to
the origin of life occur rapidly in the early history of the majority of
planets. The selective value of intelligence and technical civilization is obvious, and it seems likely that a large number of planets
within our Milky Way galaxy, perhaps as many as a million, are
inhabited by technical civilizations in advance of our own. Inter-*

stellar space flight is far beyond our present technical capabilities, but there seems to be no fundamental physical objections to preclude, from our own vantage point, the possibility of its development by other civilizations.

Dr. Carl Sagan
The Encyclopedia Americana
"Unidentified Flying Objects," 1963

The type of UFO reports that are most intriguing are close-range sightings of machinelike objects of unconventional nature and unconventional performance characteristics, seen at low altitudes, and sometimes even on the ground. The general public is unaware of the large number of such reports that are coming from credible witnesses...When one starts searching for such cases, their numbers are quite astonishing. Also, such sightings appear to be occurring all over the globe.

Dr. James E. McDonald
senior physicist, Institute of Atmospheric Physics University of Arizona;
testimony, U.S. House of Representatives, July 29, 1968

When the long-awaited solution to the UFO problem comes, I believe that it will prove to be not merely the next small step in the march of science but a mighty and totally unexpected quantum jump.

Dr. J. Allen Hynek
chairman of the Dept. of Astronomy, Northwestern University
scientific consultant to the Air Force for Project Bluebook.

I have begun to feel that there is a tendency in 20th Century science to forget that there will be a 21st Century science, and indeed, a 30th Century science, from which vantage points our knowledge of the universe may appear quite different than it does to us. We suffer, perhaps, from temporal provincialism, a form of arrogance that has irritated posterity.

Dr. J. Allen Hynek
letter to *Science Magazine*, August 1, 1966.

UFO sightings are now so common, the military doesn't have time to worry about them, so they screen them out. The major defense systems have UFO filters built into them, and when a UFO appears, they simply ignore it.

(Katchen specifically identified the radar network known as SAGE, semi-automatic ground environmental system, the North American tactical air defense system, that tracks all aircraft flights.)

The filters cut out all unconventional objects or targets and makes no record of UFOs. Unconventional targets are ignored, because, apparently we are only interested in Russian targets, possibly enemy targets. Something that hovers in the air, then shoots off at 5,000 miles per hour, doesn't interest us, because it can't be the enemy. UFOs are picked up by ground and air radar, and they have been filmed by gun camera all along. There are so many UFOs in the sky that the Air Force has had to employ special radar networks to screen them out.

Lee Katchen
NASA Physicist, June 7, 1968

Katchen made his statement based on seven thousand reports he personally examined.

CHINA

China UFO Research Organization (CURO) is a branch of the Chinese Academy of Social Sciences. This branch had over 20,000 members as early as 1985.

China is so vast, and UFOs are certainly being witnessed again and again all throughout China.

Wen-Qwang
The Journal of UFO Research
The People's Republic of China, 1981

More than six hundred UFO reports have been made in China during the past 5 years... UFOs are an unresolved mystery with profound influence in the world.

Professor Liang Renglin
Guangzhou Jinan University
China Daily, August 27, 1985 3

GERMANY

A Rocket expert considered to be one of the three founders of the space age, (The other two were Robert Goddard and Konstantin Tsiolkovsky) Hermann Oberth was invited by Dr. Werner Von Braun to come to the United States where he worked on rockets for the Army and NASA.

It's my thesis that flying saucers are real and that they are spaceships from another solar system. I think that they possibly are manned by intelligent observers who are members of a race that may have been investigating our earth for centuries. I think that they possibly have been sent out to conduct systematic, long-range investigations, first of men, animals, vegetation, and more recently of atomic centers, armaments and centers of armament production.

Professor Hermann Oberth
"Flying Saucers Come From a Distant World"
The American Weekly, October 24, 1954

They are flying by means of artificial fields of gravity... They produce high tension electric charges in order to push the air out of their paths, so it does not start glowing, and strong magnetic fields to influence the ionized air at higher altitudes. First, this would explain their luminosity...Secondly, it would explain the noiselessness of UFO flight...Finally, this assumption also explains the strong electrical and magnetic effects sometimes, though not always, observed in the vicinity of UFOs.

Dr. Hermann Oberth
Fate Magazine, May, 1962

It is my conclusion that UFOs do exist, are very real, and are spaceships from another or more than one solar system. They are possibly manned by intelligent observers who are members of a race carrying out long-range scientific investigations of our earth for centuries.

Dr. Hermann Oberth
UFO News, 1974.

These objects are conceived and directed by intelligent beings of a very high order. They probably do not originate in our solar system, perhaps not even in our galaxy.

Dr. Hermann Oberth
Mysterious Fires and Lights, David McKay, 1967

We cannot take the credit for our record advancement in certain scientific fields alone. We have been helped... (By) the people of other worlds.

Dr. Hermann Oberth
American Weekly, October 24, 1954

GREECE

Dr. Paul Santorini is a physicist and engineer who is credited with developing the fuse system for the atomic bomb at Hiroshima. This was the most complicated part of developing the bomb: how to detonate it. He also has several patents which cover the guidance systems for U.S. Nike missiles. While investigating UFOs seen over Greece in 1947 he said the following:

We soon established that they were not missiles. But, before we could do any more, the Army after conferring with foreign officials, ordered the investigation stopped. Foreign scientists flew to Greece for secret talks with me.

A world blanket of secrecy surrounded the UFO question because the authorities were unwilling to admit the existence of a force against which we had no possibility of defense.

Dr. Paul Santorini
UFOs: Interplanetary Visitors, R. Fowler, 1974

RUSSIA

Unidentified flying objects are a very serious subject which we must study fully. We appeal to all viewers to send us details of strange flying craft seen over the territories of the Soviet Union. This is a serious challenge to science and we need the help of all Soviet citizens. 4

Dr. Felix Y. Zigel
Soviet television broadcast, November 10, 1967

Observations show that UFOs behave sensibly. In a group-formation flight, they maintain a pattern. They are most often spotted over airfields, atomic stations, and other very new engineering installations. On encountering aircraft, they always maneuver so as to avoid direct contact. A considerable list of these seemingly intelligent actions gives the impression that UFOs are investigating, perhaps even reconnoitering... The important thing now is for us to discard any preconceived notions about UFOs and to organize on a global scale a calm, sensation-free and strictly scientific study of this strange phenomenon. The subject and aims of the investigation are so serious that they justify all efforts. It goes without saying that international cooperation is vital.

Dr. Felix Y. Zigel
Soviet Scientific Commission, Soviet Life, No. 2, February, 1968

Of special value are the archives set up by the commission. They contain over 13,000 reports connected with PEs (Paranormal Events) and with UFOs in particular.

(It's ironic, but this is almost exactly the same number of reports that were assembled for Project Bluebook, the U.S. Air Force's study of UFOs.)

UFOs have been seen to hover over ground objects, to chase or fly side by side with airplanes and cars, to follow geometrically regular trajectories, and to send out ordered flashes of light. In other words, such paranormals behave, from the viewpoint of human beings, quite often showing capabilities yet beyond the reach of the machines built on the Earth.

A. Petukhov and T. Faminskaya
All Union Council of Scientific and technical Societies Commission
Moscow Mir, 1989.

PSYCHIATRISTS AND OTHERS

A purely psychological explanation is ruled out...the discs show signs of intelligent guidance, by quasi-human pilots... the authorities in possession of important information should not hesitate to enlighten the public as soon as completely possible.

Dr. Carl Jung
Flying Saucer Review, Vol. 1, No. 2, 1955

It remains an established fact, supported by numerous observations, that UFOs have not only been seen visually but have also been picked up on the radar screen and have left traces on the photographic plate.

Dr. Carl Jung
"A Fresh Look at Flying Saucers"
Time Magazine, August 4, 1967

Incredible tales told by credible persons.

General John Samford

Military intelligence is a contradiction in terms.

Groucho Marx

"How does a weather balloon affect national security?"

Chris Wahl, 14 years old, Fontana, California

We already have the technology to move among the stars. What a shame it is that such breakthroughs are being hidden from humanity.

Ben Rich
former head of Lockheed Aircraft
(as told to Jan C. Harzan) MUFON California state section director.

Time is what keeps everything from happening all at once.

Yogi Berra
American Philosopher and Hall of Fame Catcher
` the New York Yankees

Concerns about national security intensify during war. During World War II, the government alerted citizens to the presence of enemy spies and saboteurs lurking just below the surface of American society. In a campaign that seemed to encourage mild paranoia, "careless talk" posters warned people that small snippets of information regarding troop movements or other logistical details could be useful to the enemy.

U.S. National Archives and Records Administration
Website, 1997

Words are ammunition. Each word an American utters either helps or hurts the war effort. He must stop rumors. He must challenge the cynic and appeaser. He must not speak recklessly. He must remember that the enemy is listening.

Civilians must have the war brought home to them. Every individual must be made to see the immediacy of danger to him... he must be made to understand that he is an integral part of the war front, and if he loses the war, he loses everything!

U.S. Office of War Information
Government Information Manual for the
Motion Picture Industry, 1943

We say glibly that in the United States of America, all men are created equal, but do we treat them as if they were...?

There is religious and racial prejudice everywhere in the land, and if there is a greater obstacle anywhere to the attainment of the teamwork we must have, no one knows what it is.

Arthur Upham Pope
Chairman of the Committee for National Morale, 1944

FAMOUS LAST WORDS

We are not bombing Cambodia.

President Lyndon Johnson

I didn't know anything about the Watergate affair.

President Richard Nixon

After that press conference, I excused myself... went into my office and I shut the door, and I sat there, blinds closed for half an hour, contemplating the impact that this could have on who we think we are.

Dan Goldin
NASA chief administrator, August 7, 1996

Our mission: To ensure ready access to essential evidence...that documents the rights of American citizens, the actions of federal officials, and the national experience.

National Archives and Records Administration
Online website
December, 1997

Flying Saucer Photographs From Around the World

- *Flying Saucers vs UFOs.*
- *Flying Saucers as vehicles*
- *Sizes and Shapes*
- *Photos*

> *For the most part the general public has not seen good, clear photographs of flying saucers. The resulting impression left with most people, therefore, is that there aren't any good, clear photographs. Nothing could be farther from the truth.*
>   Col. Wendelle Stevens, US Air Force (Ret.)

Col. Wendelle Stevens is a retired colonel who was in photo reconnaissance while in the military. In short, Col. Stevens is an expert in photography. Nobody has studied more flying saucer and UFO photographs than Col. Stevens.

The World's Largest Private Collection

Col. Stevens has the world's largest private collection of flying saucer photographs. Many of the images are just plain stunning. His collection contains over 15,000 photographs and negatives! They have been sent to him by people from all around the world.

Col. Wendelle Stevens, US Air Force (Ret.)

Col. Stevens has been kind enough to allow me to publish some of his photographs in our book. All published flying saucer photographs in this book are the courtesy of Col. Wendell Stevens and the UFO Archives. To quote

Col. Stevens directly: "Basically, my whole incentive has been to leave a legacy of information from our time to the young people of the future."

Each Photograph Is Thoroughly Researched

Col. Stevens researches and studies every photograph he receives. For the most part, the photos have all been taken by average people, in virtually every country on the globe. In some cases Col. Stevens has even been able to trace photos that had no information with them back to the person who took them. Here are just a few of the things Col. Stevens researches and records about each photograph:

- *Is there more than one photo? Is there a series?*

- *Who took it? When and how was it taken? (Date, time and place; weather conditions.)*

- *The type of film, the film emulsion, type of camera, F-stop and shutter-speed information.*

- *Was anyone else present? Did they see the craft? What did they say at the time?*

- *What was the photographer thinking? What prompted him to look up?*

- *Why did he have a camera with him? What was he doing before he saw the UFO?*

- *The appearance of shadows, distances, and the relationship of each item in the picture to the other items in the photo.*

- *Film speed and color balance.*

- *Camera make, model, serial number, date of manufacture.*

- *Lens type, focal length, focal plane.*

Do Any of the Photographs Ever Turn Out to be Fake?

Of course. There is always some Bozo trying to pull off a hoax. However, over 95 percent of the photos and negatives Col. Stevens receives from around the world, after being analyzed, appear to be genuine. People just don't seem to be that inclined to take the effort to fake a photo and then send it around the world for no money.

Photographs That Are Hard To Fake

Some of the most impressive photographs are those taken before 1985, well before sophisticated computers that could be used for faking a photo were readily available out of the studio. In addition, it's almost impossible to fake those that are part of a series of images taken with an amateur camera, one without a professional speed winder. They show the flying saucers hovering or moving slowly through the same background and terrain. This is something you could not accomplish by, say, throwing a pie pan.

Photos taken with a Polaroid camera are also very significant. Polaroids are virtually impossible to fake. I know, because I worked for Polaroid Corporation for 5 years. There is no negative to alter and the photo is developed instantly. Any tampering with the developing photo destroys the emulsion, which is comprised of seven distinct chemical layers.

Other types of photos virtually impossible to fake, are those showing flying saucers coming out of the water. The water can often be seen falling off of the ship. Try faking that.

As odd as it may sound, blurry photos are often good indicators of authenticity. Even sophisticated computers cannot duplicate blurry edges on a negative. A faked computer image always has sharp edges. The computer cannot merge portions of a fractal.

I also give special credence to photos taken by police officers, especially while they are on duty. An officer on duty is not likely to make up a story or try and fake a photograph. Many police officers carry Polaroid cameras to record traffic incidents and have used these cameras to record flying saucers.

Many clear photos have been taken of silvery flying saucers. Upon close inspection of the photo and negative, the surrounding scene and sunlight is accurately reflected on the skin of the craft. This is also virtually impossible to fake.

Tell-tale signs for the following specific types of forgeries and hoaxes are looked for:

- Double exposure.
- Reflected image.
- Photo paste-up.
- Montage.
- Use of a model: (curve illumination; lighter against dark objects; darker against lighter objects. Distance graying; focus; suspended model.)
- Crayon.
- Airbrush.
- Chemical Staining.
- Overlay.

Col. Stevens thoroughly reviews his investigation procedure in his book, *UFO Photographs Around The World, Vol. I.* Besides being an authenticating process, the narrative of what the people said and did and thought at the time the photo was taken is a fascinating record of some of humanity's first experience with craft built by people from other worlds and dimensions.

Objects Are Larger Than They Appear

Most UFO photographs have been taken by ordinary citizens using ordinary point and shoot cameras. Most of these cameras have 35mm or 28mm lenses. This means that the objects are being photographed with a wider than "normal vision" lens and the objects photographed will appear much smaller than they normally are. In reality, the objects will be almost two times bigger than how they appear in the photo. The average size of one of the small disk-shaped saucers is 30 feet across. That's the equivalent of a three-story building laying on its side. This has been confirmed not only by trained military observers, but also by radar.

Sometimes, a flying saucer will simply show up in the background. It is not unusual for the person taking the picture to say that the saucer wasn't there when they took the picture. They only saw it after the film came back from the developer. As strange as it may seem, many people are not only happy to give Col. Stevens their only copies of these images, but some of them also seem relieved. It's almost as if by giving away the photos, they are off the hook for dealing with the reality that flying saucers exist!

Historical UFO Photos

Mexico, 1883

The first UFO photographs were taken in 1883! They were taken in Mexico at the Zacatecas Observatory. 2 Professor A. Y. Bonilla was photographing the sun. In addition to the photos taken, Bonilla recorded that he observed 283 bright, luminous disks in the sky as well as 116 dark disks that moved across the face of the sun.

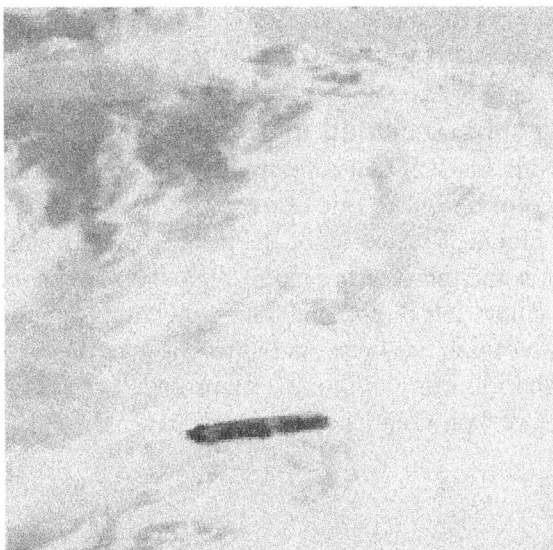

Photo of a cigar-shaped UFO taken in 1897.
(Courtesy Col. Wendelle C. Stevens (ret.), U.S.A.F.)

Chicago 1897

A large, cigar-shaped craft was photographed by Walter McCann while it was flying over Chicago on April 10, 1897. Later that same month, C. D. Lawrence, also of Chicago, photographed a cigar-shaped craft on April 26, 1897. This was 7 years before the first dirigible flew in the United States in 1904. These photos were taken 6 years before Orville & Wilbur Wright first flew a heavier-than-air craft at Kitty Hawk in 1903.

As an historical footnote: Just days before the Wright Brothers successfully flew an airplane for the first time, The New York Times ran an editorial stating that man would never be able to fly in a heavier-than-air craft. Even after the Wright Brothers had flown, *Scientific American* labeled the Wright Brother's flight a hoax. You have at least a thousand times more evidence of the existence of flying saucers right now in your hands than anybody had about the existence of airplanes, less than a hundred years ago!

1905, 1907, 1908, and 1914

Photographs of flying saucers were taken in these years as well. A photograph taken on July 27, 1907 shows a large cigar-shaped craft hovering above a group of tall-masted ships in Norway. Photographed by Obiettivo Sugli over the harbor, around noon, the shadow cast by the craft on the water is larger than any sailing ship in the harbor.

UFO Photographs Included in this Book

Though printed in black & white, the photos appearing in this book were all taken with color film, with one exception. This is a photo taken with black & white film in 1952. None of the photos have been treated in any way, except for some minor cropping of the edges. In the interest of authenticity, we have left the original flaws, including any marks, water spots and dirt. Nothing has been altered to improve the pictures you see in this book. The following photos are all provided courtesy of the UFO Photo Archives of Col. Wendelle C. Stevens (ret.), U.S.A.F.

UFO photographed over the harbor in Norway in 1907.
(Courtesy Col. Wendelle C. Stevens (Ret.), U.S.A.F.)

In Broad Daylight

This first photo was taken by a landscape photographer while photographing landmarks across the East River at 1:20 P.M. The photographer heard some nearby workmen shouting. They were pointing at something in the water. The water began to bubble furiously and suddenly this flying saucer shot out of the water. Five separate photographs of the saucer were taken with a professional camera. In several of the photos, water can be seen coming off the craft before it flew off at high speed. The photographer has requested to remain anonymous. Note: It is common worldwide for flying saucers to be seen emerging from bodies of water.

New York City, April 12, 1993.
(Courtesy Col. Wendelle C. Stevens (Ret.), U.S.A.F.)

The Meier Beamship

The following photo was taken on March 18, 1975 at 9:06 A.M. in Winkelriet, Switzerland. The photographer was Eduard "Billy" Meier. Meier was contacted by alien human-like beings who told him they were from the star system that we call Plieades. They told him they would allow him to take photographs of their ship as they flew in.

The alien beings referred to this craft as a "beamship." This is a 7-meter version, meaning that it is about 21 feet across. Like most flying saucers, this craft is bigger than it looks in the photograph.

As a reference, look at the size of the trees it is hovering over. Meier shot two rolls of 8MM movie film and five rolls of 35MM positive slide transparencies.

Nothing in this photograph has been altered. The photos and transparencies have been thoroughly analyzed by many photographic experts, including Col. Wendelle Stevens. The bottom line: It's real.

Winkelriet, Switzerland, 1975.
(Courtesy Col. Wendelle C. Stevens (Ret.), U.S.A.F.)

Just an additional note for you computer cynics. There was no computer or graphics software available to forge this photo when it was taken in 1975. Steven Jobs had not yet sold his first Apple Computer. It would not be until one year later when the first computer kit, the MITS Altair 8800 with a *total* memory of only 256 bytes, was available.

Two More Incredible Photos
The following two photos are representative of the quality and clarity of the photos in the collection amassed by Wendelle Stevens over the years.

Guanajuato, Mexico, July 1994.
(Courtesy Col. Wendelle C. Stevens (Ret.), U.S.A.F.)

Arturo Romero's son called him outside to take a photo of himself and his friend. The "friend" turned out to be a flying disk that had followed his son home from school.

July 6, 1990, 5:30 A.M. Palominos Island, Puerto Rico.
(Courtesy Col. Wendelle C. Stevens (Ret.), U.S.A.F.)

Taken by Guillermo Carde, while standing on another boat. The saucer emerged from the water and had water running off when the photo was taken.

June, 1978, Sunset, Barcelona, Spain
(Courtesy Antonio Ribera of Barcelona & Col. Wendelle C. Stevens (Ret.), U.S.A.F).

Taken by Sra. Montserrat Batilori of Barcelona, Spain. She took the picture while standing on her balcony watching a beautiful summer sunset. Just before taking the picture, three huge, luminous objects appeared in the sky flying in formation. Note how large these objects are when compared to the multi-story apartment buildings that appear in front of them.

Frequently Asked Questions

Q. How could aliens get from there to here if the distance between stars is so great?

We have to start looking at things a lot differently. The beings visiting our planet have been in existence 500 million years longer than human beings. We are not at the forefront of science. We will also have to update our knowledge of science, physics, and how the universe really works. Here are some things you need to know:

Time and Distance Are Not Related
I discuss this more in depth in the science section. But as Albert Einstein so eloquently pointed out, time and distance have nothing to do with one another.

Other Dimensions
Not all flying saucers come from outer space. Many come from "inner" space. It is well established that many of these craft come from other dimensions. Many contactees have been told this by alien beings. One such person is Hugo Batallanos from Latin America.

We know it's hard to comprehend these vast distances in space. However, in our local neighborhood there are over a thousand stars that are nearby. By "nearby," we mean within 54 light years of earth. In terms of space distances, any astronomer will tell you that particular distance is not just down the block, it's right next door!

Approximately half these stars are similar to our sun and probably have planets with life on them. Many contactees have been told by ETs that they are in fact from places much closer than we think, but our scientists are just not able to observe them at this time.

Distances From the Earth

THE MOON: 240,000 miles; 1.29 light seconds.
THE SUN: 93 million miles; 8 light minutes.
CLOSEST STAR: 400,000 trillion miles; 4.3 light years.
CLOSEST GALAXY: 1 million light years.

Traveling Speed
Traveling at 95 percent of the speed of light (186,000 Miles per second times .95) it would take eleven and a half years to get to the star system called Zeta Reticuli.

Making a slight increase to 99 percent the speed of light reduces the journey to Zeta Reticuli to take just 19 months. Remember, time slows as you approach the speed of light. And, by folding space, you get there almost instantly.

Our Technology is Way Ahead of You
Military insiders and aerospace engineers say we are at least 150 to 200 years ahead of where the public thinks we are in terms of spacecraft technology. Many believe the space shuttle is just a public relations display and research vehicle for launching science projects and sometimes deploying military satellites.
The true state of our technology is being hidden from the public, just as the existence of extraterrestrials is. Once you realize ETs are real, you can bet the farm that our technology could take us to other planets right now.

Ben Rich

"Anything you can imagine, we already know how to do."

Ben Rich
Former head of Lockheed Aircraft

Ben Rich was the former head of Lockheed Aircraft, the same company that developed the Stealth bomber and fighter planes. Several months before he died he made a stunning acknowledgment about the true state of our technology. It was made directly to a personal friend of mine, Jan Harzan, in front of fifteen other people. He basically said that physics as we learned it is all wrong and that the military already has star-travel capability. Here is a portion of the conversation they had:

> BEN RICH: "We already have the technology to go to the stars, but it would take an act of God for that information to be released to the public.
>
> JAN HARZAN: "How exactly does it work?"
>
> BEN RICH: "How does ESP work?"
>
> JAN HARZAN: "All points in space and time are connected."
>
> BEN RICH: "That's exactly how it works."

Thomas in Las Vegas

Several years ago I met a man I will call "Thomas" while attending a medical convention in Las Vegas. We got into a discussion about UFOs and technology. Here is what he told me: He said he had certain high level security clearances for a nearby military facility. He wouldn't say if the facility was Area 51 or not. He said he wasn't sure, because he was always brought to the facility in a van with the windows covered for the final leg of the journey. His tasks frequently had to do with aircraft.

To Europe and Back in Under Two Hours

Thomas said that on several occasions he had been placed on an aircraft and flown from Nevada to Europe and back in under 2 hours. That averages out to be 10,000 miles per hour! He couldn't identify the plane because he was boarded "blind" just like on the van. He, too, said our aircraft technology is so far ahead of where the public thinks it is they simply would not believe it even if someone told them the absolute truth of the real capabilities.

At the time Thomas told me this, there seemed to be no motivation for him to make it up. This happened years before I even thought about writing this book.

Check Your Ego at the Door

How can we possibly presume to know what a civilization can accomplish in as little as a hundred years, much less civilizations which are millions of years ahead of us in technology? Some quick facts:

- One hundred years ago we had no airplanes. One hundred years ago no human being had ever been in New York and Los Angeles in the same week, much less the same day!

- A simple $3 solar-powered calculator would completely astound and baffle Thomas Edison and Albert Einstein. Neither of them would be able to tell you the principles upon which it works.

- Fifteen years after the Wright brothers flew, many of the world's top scientists continued to publish articles saying that flight by man was impossible and could not be done.

- In the 1960s astronomers kept saying we couldn't go to the moon, but we did.

Astronomers vs. Engineers

A little side note about the last point. Astronomers are terrific scientists, unraveling wondrous riddles about the universe. Without them we wouldn't have a clue about the heavens. Listen carefully as they explain how things work. However, if you want to know how, and if, you can get someplace, call an engineer. When the media wants to know about possibilities of space travel, they always call the astronomers. They're calling the wrong people. The astronomers will tell you about the distances and forces in space, but the engineers will tell you how to get there. They will tell you space travel is very possible now with the technology we already have.

Q. How could they possibly keep something like this secret? They've never been able to keep secrets.

First things first: who is they? You will find this question and paragraph repeated several times in this book. That's because it's important. It will also help you keep things in perspective and not get caught in a place where you end up accusing everyone and everything.

The Military

They started out as the military. These were the people we asked to protect us during the world wars. They were our fathers, mother, cousins, and uncles. We asked them as a society to protect us from any and all things that may harm us in any way.

The Intelligence Agencies

These agencies grew out of the armed services. Their only purpose for existence is secrets! There are now agencies of this kind in both the military and civilian branches of the government. You know them as the FBI, CIA, NSA, and at least a dozen more you never heard of.

How They Got Started

As we said earlier and have documented in other chapters, the secrecy about UFOs started right after World War II. The military, after fighting two hellacious world wars back to back, was concerned with the continued safety of its citizens. Suddenly, less than two years after the end of World War II, the United States and other parts of the world were being flown over by what appeared to be ships coming from outer space and going over 10,000 miles per hour when the fastest planes we had were only going about 650 miles per hour.

The Saucers Were Not Dangerous

The first concern was: Were they dangerous? After a few years of flyovers and some saucer crashes, it became absolutely clear to the armed forces that they were not dangerous. This was obvious, because their technology was so vastly superior, they could clearly attack us if they so chose. It also became clear to the armed services that the beings in these ships had no harmful intentions. At that point the military was done. They handed over the responsibilities for flying saucers to the intelligence agencies.

Knowledge of the Saucers Was Dangerous

The world was just starting to get back on track after those two devastating wars. The intelligence agencies figured that knowledge about the existence of beings with vastly superior technology would throw the recovery into reverse and result in world-wide chaos and anarchy. A decision was made to keep this information secret, and you and your family were able to proceed with a normal life for the next 50 years.

The Black Arm

This is the only scary part of all this information, so I'll take it real slow. Somewhere in that 50-year time period between 1947-1997, another group of individuals grew out of the intelligence agencies and took over the control and management of the flying saucer/ET secret. I know this sounds like a conspiracy theory, but all the research I and many others have done point to this. Here are some specific examples of what I mean:

They is not the government as you think of it. There are no elected officials trying to keep this from you. In fact, the exact opposite is true. It is a fact that former U.S. Presidents Carter, Reagan, Ford, and Kennedy wanted and tried to get this information out to the public. In Carter's case, he asked to see the information on UFOs. He was told directly by people in the intelligence community that as president, he did not have a high enough clearance to even *see* the files.

Many congressmen and congresswomen have tried to get the information about the truth of the existence of UFOs out to the public.

They have been blocked in their efforts. This a secondhand story and unconfirmed, but it is said that then-Senator Bob Dole met with a UFO research group and told them Congress was trying to get the information to the public but was being blocked by some extremely powerful unknown group Congress referred to as "The Black Arm." It is said the Black Arm controls huge amounts of the American dollar. Remember, $80 Billion of your tax dollars each year goes into black operations and nobody knows what happens to it.

Clinton Gets Stonewalled.

Former Clinton confidante and Justice Department official Webb Hubbell recently wrote that finding out about UFOs was one of Clinton's two top priorities when he took office. The other was obtaining information on the Kennedy assassination. Here is what Clinton told Hubbell:

> *If I put you over at Justice, I want you to find the answers to two questions for me. One: Who killed JFK? And two: Are there UFOs?*

Hubbell goes on to say that Clinton was stonewalled and also denied access to UFO information. Somewhere in Washington that old "they" tail is still wagging the dog.

Secrets Can and Have Been Kept Successfully

Don't forget your role in this. It's easy to keep a secret if nobody asks about it. You've known about the possibility of UFOs for years, but you have never asked anyone about them. You haven't written your congressman. Your apathy and disinterest is any secret's best friend!

You are greatly underestimating what people can do if it is important enough to them. There have been many, many highly classified secrets kept from the public for decades.

The Ultra Secret

Early in World War II the U.S. and its allies had gotten their hands on a German encoding machine known as the Enigma Machine. This allowed the Allies to decode secret German radio messages. Thousands of men and women in the armed services of three countries (U.S., Britain, and France) knew this. Over 12,000 people in London alone, worked on this project. This was a key factor in winning the war. Nobody ever talked and the Germans never found out. It was known as the "Ultra" secret.

Even after the war the U.S. decided to keep it highly classified for another 20 years. They were afraid it would be used as an excuse by Germany for losing the war and thus revive Nazi activities. It wasn't generally known for 30 years until it was revealed in 1974. That's when *Time* magazine called it "the best-kept secret of all time." Of course now we know it's only the *second* best-kept secret of all time.

The point is: Thousands of people kept a huge secret for decades.

The Great Submarine Cover-up

In 1942 German submarines were actively sinking American shipping vessels just a few miles off the east coast of the United States. They sank literally hundreds of boats. This has been historically confirmed and certified. In an article appearing in the September 1999 issue of *UFO Magazine,* historical researcher Frank Rain describes what happened:

> The White House was desperately concerned for a number of reasons: The war had come to within binocular distance of America, but we were still almost a year away from having adequate numbers of ships and planes available to protect our eastern waters. Further, the Roosevelt Administration feared that if word of the number and severity of the u-boat incursions were to become widely known, there was risk of national panic...Thus lacking any course of corrective action, a policy of denial was enacted.

> First, an older admiral with no public profile, Adolphus Andrews, was put in charge of our eastern coastal defenses. Second, despite Andrew's repeated urgings for Washington to order coastal blackouts thereby making cargo ships more difficult to be seen against the shoreline, his requests were ignored so that the public's suspicions would not be raised. Third, certain trusted members of the eastern press were briefed about the situation and asked to refrain from reporting stories about it, which they agreed to do. Fourth, any report of German u-boat activity near the American coast was met with official skepticism or the reliability of the source questioned. Fifth, all evidence of torpedoed ships (wreckage and bodies) that washed up on shore was immediately impounded and disposed of by the military, while the local population was told that it was the result of a storm at sea and warned not to speak to anyone about it. And, sixth, those who were in the government information loop on this policy

were strongly informed that any breach of security would be considered treason, a crime punishable by execution.

Today few Americans have even the slightest notion that between December, 1941 and September, 1942, 292 vessels were torpedoed and hundreds of merchant seamen lost, most within sight of American beaches.

The entire story is told in detail in Homer Hickam's book: *Torpedoe Junction: U-Boat War Off America's East Coast, 1942*. Naval Institute Press, 1989 and Dell Books paperback, 1999.

FDR

 Franklin Delano Roosevelt served as President of the United States for thirteen years. He had been crippled by a bout with polio and was left a paraplegic. This information was successfully withheld from the public for his entire time in office and for decades afterwards. So hidden was this information that in 1996 when a memorial to Roosevelt was to be built in Washington DC, the U.S. Congress engaged in a heated debate as to whether he should be portrayed in a wheelchair. Opponents felt strongly that he should not, since the public that voted him into office and that he served, never knew of his condition.

Huge Gliders

Another World War II secret: Huge, silent gliders were built and quietly crossed German lines filled with American troops. The use of these gliders was kept secret and was unknown to the public for decades.

The Coup of 1934

In 1934 some of the biggest names in American business actually financed a coup in an attempt to overthrow President Roosevelt. The group was headed by the president of General Motors William S. Knudsen, Irenee du Pont, and members of the Morgan Bank. They put together $3 million dollars to do this, a huge sum of money in those days. The coup failed when a general in the Marine Corps refused to go along with it. This incident has been carefully deleted from your history books.

A Teaser Secret

When the Japanese bombed Pearl Harbor on December 7, 1941, there were no aircraft carriers in the harbor. Why? I'm not going tell you. You have to find out on your own.

Q. Why would the government continue to keep the existence of UFOs secret?

Why in the world would the government not tell us these things? Why would they cover it up? These are the two big questions. They are the questions asked most often and the most difficult to answer. The answers to these questions are probably never going to be known completely. After years of researching and investigating this topic, I find there are no concrete answers, but there are several things to consider. The best way to attempt to answer the cover-up question is to ask yourself a few questions. Here are some questions, suggestions, and exercises:

Ask yourself this: Did your mother or father ever sit down with you one-on-one and discuss sexual intercourse in complete detail?

Probably not! Based on this behavior, you could accuse your mom and dad of a huge cover-up. After all, weren't you eventually going to have a family and need this information? The reality is that your parents:

- *Were too embarrassed and uncomfortable with the topic.*
- *Didn't know that much themselves and were afraid to give you wrong information.*
- *Figured you would somehow learn on your own, the same as they did.*

This is exactly how the government/military felt when they discovered we were not alone in the universe. Except magnify the discomfort level by about a thousand-fold!

A Suggestion

Instead of using the terms *they* or *the government*, replace these words with *mom* and *dad*. That will take some of the edge off. It also lets each of us take some responsibility and recognize our own participation in this process. Think of it like this: Mom and dad graciously and generously gave us 50 years of not having to worry about something we had no control over anyway.

Define "the government." Who exactly is the government? Take a piece of paper and write it down. Be specific. Name names. Exactly which person or persons do you think kept this information from you?

To me, the government is my mailman. He's a good guy. I don t think he is withholding any information from me. Like 99 percent of all government employees, he is simply trying to do his job and pay his mortgage. The Government is *us*.

The Government Did What We Asked Them To

We the public have commissioned the government to protect us from people who speak a different language, have a different culture, look different, and eat different foods than we do. We have asked our military to go into armed combat in places as benign as Grenada and Panama. It would be a natural and expected response that they would seek to protect us from something as foreign as beings from another world. We have continued to accuse the government of doing exactly what we asked them to do - protect us!

It Started Out as an Extension of World War II

The people who were given the responsibility for protecting the American public didn't know what the intentions of our alien visitors were at first. Later it was determined there was no impending danger from them. The next concern was would the public hurt themselves due to panic? It was determined that the public would panic, so the secrecy lid was kept on.

Attendant Technologies

There are technologies which have been discovered and developed as a result of our interaction with flying saucers which would change everything immediately and drastically. For example, our scientists have been able to develop technologies and understandings which would render our dependence on fossil fuels and pharmaceuticals obsolete. Many industries and jobs worldwide would instantly disappear if they were put into place all at once. It is possible that the entire world economy could crash as a result of this.

Science, Society, and Religion

The people with access to this information were very concerned that our social and religious structures would not be able to integrate the information about the existence of alien beings, especially so soon after the end of the war. There was also concern that science would be turned on its head. The immediate result could have been a total disintegration of all social structures as we know them. The world was a very different place in 1947. The world probably could not have handled it then.

Now, It's a Combination of Things

Most of the people who first learned of this are dead. People who are now in official elected or appointed positions really don't have much info. In many cases the old records have mysteriously disappeared.

It also appears there is a group of people who do know and for some reason continue to try and keep it secret. Why? Nobody knows for sure.

Embarrassment

Don't discount this factor. If someone in an important position knows, who would be willing to come forward and admit they have been actively lying to the public for all these years? To single-handedly be the object of anger and scorn for an entire population?

The Government Knows Far Less Than You Think They Do

They are frightened and embarrassed at how little they do know after 50 years of investigating. The government knows that far more knowledge resides in the hands of individual citizens.

You will be surprised to learn the U.S. military regularly re-abducts abductees to find out from these people what they know about alien races because they have no other source of information.

If you lie long enough and big enough the lie becomes the truth. This lie has been told for over 50 years and now many people don't know what the truth is. It's not a cover-up if you choose not to know.

Do You Really Want to Know?

For whatever reason most people don't seem to want to know the truth about the existence of extraterrestrial beings. Most people have never asked for the information so the government simply never shared it. There have been clear indications that these things are real, at least for the last 50 years. Didn't this seem strange to anyone?

The government will tell you about extraterrestrials when you let them know in no uncertain terms that you are ready. When you indicate your readiness, cosmic forces will go into action and provide such overt, incontrovertible proof that no one will be able to deny it. But it won't happen until you make it happen.

Have You Ever Asked?

Have you or any members of your family ever written your congressman asking for any information that the government may have about UFOs or alien beings?

Eighty billion dollars of your taxpayers money goes annually into a black budget. The money is completely unaccounted for and unquestioned, even by congress. It is estimated that half of it, or $40 Billion dollars of it is used for UFO secrecy.

As citizens, we have taught the bureaucracy we call the government that we will accept without question anything they say or refuse to discuss. Think about it. You continue to pay thousands of dollars in taxes every year to the government and you have probably never read a single page of the tax code. You have no idea what it actually says. For all you know the last page could read:

"If you are reading this page you no longer have to pay any taxes."

In both cases, whether it involves taxes or extraterrestrials, the government has concluded you must not be very interested or concerned. So there is no need for them to discuss either of these topics with you.

These two questions: "Why wouldn't they tell us?" And "Why would they cover it up?" generate a lot of emotion, primarily fear and anger. Read this section two or three times. The more you do the more you will realize there is nothing to be angry about and even less to fear.

There have been a handful of people with a lot of authority and power who initially discovered the existence of alien beings. What started out as an effort to protect the citizens grew to a few people doing a disservice to all humanity. This can and will no longer continue. Events occurring now have guaranteed that. It is time to stop pointing the finger. Simply begin to ask for the information.

You Will be Greatly Surprised at the Following:

- *How willing old guard politicians are to share what they know. Several well-known politicians have made an honest effort to get this information to the public.*

- *How little information the government actually has beyond the fact that alien races exist. In 1997 Dr. Steven Greer, the founder of CSETI (Center for the Study of Extraterrestrial Intelligence) met with the director of the CIA, members of Congress, and senior military officers from the Pentagon. They wanted Greer to brief them, so they could learn more about the ET phenomenon.*

- *How much information the public, your friends, and neighbors have. They only need a safe forum to share the information with you without risk of being ridiculed. Some of the information they have to share is so dynamic you will need to hear it many times from many people before you can integrate it and begin to understand it.*

I leave you with these words: The *government* does not exist. *They* are you. There is nothing in this universe that can be hidden from you. You simply must take the steps to seek the information and ask for it in your own way.

Q. Why doesn't the media have this information?

There is no simple answer to this question either. There are, however, some things to consider.

The Topic Is Still Surrounded by Ridicule

The topic of UFOs and flying saucers is still surrounded by ridicule, just like the Wright Brothers and the idea of airplanes less than a hundred years ago. Besides naturally occurring cynicism, there has been a campaign - no, a war - waged against the American public to keep this knowledge secret.

And ridicule has been the biggest weapon. People are more afraid of being ridiculed than they are of death.

The Media is Like a Sports Franchise

If you're a sports nut, no doubt you have a favorite team. If it's a football team, then the ultimate goal of that team is to win the Super Bowl, right? Wrong. The ultimate goal of that team (the only goal) is to make money. Period. If you think otherwise you are being naive. The so-called media is no different. Their ultimate goal is not to bring you the news or any facts. It is simply to make money. And right now there is not enough information on this subject for them to make money, but there will be.

The Information Has Been Hidden

The important articles the media would need to present a story have been hidden. Dramatic videotapes and photos have been confiscated. People have been threatened with their lives. People who have worked for the military and for government contractors have all been sworn to secrecy. However, this is all starting to change. When that happens, and it will, the media will spread the word like crazy and make tons of money selling newspapers, magazines, and air time.

Q. Why don't scientists believe in UFOs?

In fact, many do. Some also have inside information. They are just afraid to come forward with it. Fear of ridicule (what else?) is the main reason. Also, a tremendous fear of losing their research funding. Another reason is that threats are routinely made against scientists who discover things that they are not supposed to find out.

Does not Fit Traditional Science

Many scientists are not sure, mainly because it does not fit within the framework of traditional Western science. Many scientists are about to learn some occurrences are not repeatable in the same way. Our entire scientific method is based upon being able to repeat something exactly in order for it to be true.

Hostages

Many scientists are being held hostage. They know some remarkable things. But they are being held captive through secrecy agreements and security clauses in their employment agreements.

The men and women at the space agency NASA are specific examples of scientific hostages. This list includes those people working at affiliated facilities such as the Jet Propulsion Laboratory in Pasadena, California. They know lots of things that should be told to the public. They are a civilian agency. It is a disservice to humanity to withhold this information. The scientists working there are being held incommunicado.

Q. Do UFOs really exist?

Yes. Not only now, but throughout the entire history of mankind there have been reports of UFOs. Even the Bible makes references to people and events that are most likely UFO-related. They have been recorded in ancient literature and artwork going back centuries.

Q. How big are UFOs?

UFOs come in many different sizes and shapes. Those most commonly seen are shaped like saucers, triangles, lop-sided boomerangs, cigars, balls, and spheres. These craft can also change shape or disappear at will. In terms of size they range from a few feet across (unmanned craft like robot drones) to manned craft that are several miles long. That' s for the craft that appear in our lower atmosphere. The craft that stay outside in space are sometimes over a 1,000 miles long.

Q. Where do they come from and why are they here?

There are many different kinds of aliens visiting our planet. It is said the U.S. government has identified at least fifty different kinds of beings visiting here. They are from all over the universe. Some of them also come from other dimensions our scientists are not yet able to identify.

Contactees and abductees have been told they are here for a wide variety of reasons, including but not limited to observation of our societies, research, preparing our planet to meet with alien races, and just plain sight-seeing.

2012 to 2015 Time Frame

More recently, human contacts have been told that our entire planet is about to find out that we are not alone. This is a BIG event in the universe. It is a rare event that all traveling alien beings want to witness. This is rare opportunity – some of them may not ever see this again in their lifetimes. And, this birth of ours affects the evolution of the entire universe, not just those who are witnessing it.

Q. What do they look like?

The variety is astonishing. You have no doubt seen images of the little gray guys with big eyes. There are also 6-foot tall reptilian beings that look like giant walking lizards, and beings that are over 6-feet tall and look just like a giant praying mantis. Contactees have been told that the variety of types of beings is so vast we would not be able to comprehend it at this time.

Q. Are cattle mutilations and crop circles related to UFOs?

No one is 100 percent sure but the answer is probably yes. In both cases UFOs are frequently seen in the area where these things have occurred.

Crop circles

Crop circles show patterns that relate exactly to complex mathematical equations including DNA, musical scales, and geometric relationships. They are done with extreme precision and no one on earth has been able to duplicate them in spite of the stories you may have heard about hoaxes. Real crop circles are accurate to within 1 millimeter and exhibit cellular changes and magnetic fields. No one on earth knows how to do this.

Cattle Mutilations

Cattle mutilations are done with extreme surgical precision with no residual blood left from the wounds. A full surgical team in a hospital would be hard pressed to duplicate this feat. Key glands of the animal are taken for some reason, most likely research. Complicating matters are the investigations of other animal kills that are not cattle mutilations but are lumped in with them. Some of these are attributable to wild predators such as wolves or coyotes; others are hoaxes.

Q. Why don't they just land on the White House Lawn?

They've done everything but that. Several times in the 1950s large numbers of flying saucers flew and hovered directly over the White House and Capitol building. It was well recorded in the major newspapers in Washington D.C. Different alien races have made it clear there is a *Star Trek*-type ban on interfering with the development of another species. They are fully aware that to land suddenly without properly preparing the public would cause mass confusion and fear. They are honor-bound to avoid this at all costs.

Q. What about abductees and contactees?

Abductees are people who are routinely picked up by alien beings. The purposes seem to be a large on-going research or monitoring project. They are also involved in genetic development projects. Abductees for the most part in the United States feel they are being kidnapped against their will. Citizens in many other countries, under the same conditions, feel they are contributing to the phenomenon and not being abducted.

Abductees as a group report a wide range of medical and psychological procedures being performed on them. When they return, abductees frequently have no conscious memory of what happened. However, many times they do. There are often physical marks on the body such as scars, beep bruises, and puncture wounds that were not there before the abduction took place.

The experience and descriptions of thousands of abductees around the world are identical, regardless of a person's culture, language, age, religion, geographical location, or prior belief system. Just the vast numbers of people world-wide reporting these events, alone, is one of the most amazing things in human history.

Contactees differ in that they don't feel they are being abducted. They usually have interactions and "conversations" with alien beings. We put conversations in quotes because any conversation is most often a mental projection. Often it is done with or without language. Sometimes it is a combination of language, feelings, or symbols. The communication is always telepathic and not spoken.

Who Gets Picked to be Abducted?

Abductions are not random. They run in families and they stay in families for generations. For instance, if one parent is an abductee then all that parent's children will also be. However, an adopted child will not be. This is why it is thought genetics are a key to understanding the whole phenomenon. People who are abductees are picked up very frequently. The average is a hundred times per year. That's every 3 to 4 days! And that's a low average. Many get picked up even more often.

How Can I Tell if I Have Been Abducted?

First of all, if you haven't been abducted yet, you won't be. Also, there are indications that the alien's project is winding down and being brought to a close. But to answer the question directly, there are some basic signs and symptoms. Not everyone exhibits any or all of them, but here are some clues. You may have been abducted if:

- *You have experienced periods of missing time lasting an hour or more. And we don't mean your last house party.*
- *You find strange scars, marks, or bruises you can't explain.*
- *You have really weird but very life-like dreams.*
- *You see UFOs, a lot!*
- *You have unusual physical problems or exhibit symptoms of post-traumatic stress.*

How Many People are Being Abducted?

A lot. Abductions are occurring in every country on our planet. The most experienced abduction researchers put the figure at 7 percent of the population. More conservative estimates put it at 2 percent. We feel the 7 percent figure is more accurate. Just counting the population of the United States (approximately 250 million) puts the number of people who have been abducted at nearly 18 million.

Q. Does our government have any of the advanced alien technology?

Yes. And some of it is already in your hands. As attested to by many scientists and military people like Col. Philip Corso, many of the things we commonly use today in fact come from recovered alien technology. Things such as fiber optics, solid state computer circuits, and night vision scopes and goggles.

Q. Is time travel related to UFOs?

In one sense, yes. Alien technology is so advanced that beings can travel great distances instantly and also travel inter-dimensionally. There are things about this kind of travel that allow them to travel in time as well. First, time literally slows as you approach the speed of light so time is not constant; it varies according to surrounding conditions. Gravity also affects the passage of time.

Time is Like a Train Track

Time is not linear. Picture a metro train like that goes from downtown, out to the suburbs, and loops back. Along the way it makes stops at different communities and you can get off at any one you choose. No matter what day you are on the train, the town is always there. It's the same with time and events. The events are always there. Time just connects them like the train tracks. The event doesn't just happen and it's over. You can travel to any event at any time and get off the train at that event.

Q. Are there really alien bases on our planet?

It appears the answer to this is yes. Many of them are jointly owned by aliens and human personnel said to be part of the U.S. armed forces. They are primarily underground, but the aliens themselves have many that are under water in oceans and deep lakes. Under water is a particularly good place to put a secret base. Man has still explored less than 5 percent of the world's ocean floors. Many, many photographs have been taken of UFOs emerging from water. In addition, many contactees have been taken under water to alien ocean bases.

Q. How many UFO reports are really UFOs? How many are hoaxes?

As a general rule, only about 10 percent of UFO reports are truly unexplainable. The remaining 90 percent turn out to be airplanes, helicopters, flares, missile launches, or astronomical events. Most reports are from honest people who saw something that appeared unusual to them. However, it's interesting to note that the now-famous Blue Book study conducted by the Air Force was unable to account for almost 40 percent of the thirteen thousand cases in their files!

Hoaxes?

There have been hoaxes. Some darn good ones too. What is remarkable is how few there have been. Estimates of the number of fake UFO reports are under 1 percent. Even the Air Force conceded that less than 1 percent of the reports are bogus attempts to deceive. People seem disinclined to spend a lot of time fabricating something that they probably couldn't make any money on.

A Fun Bogus Report

In 1997, in the Sea of Japan, a fast-moving object fell from the sky, hitting a Japanese fishing boat. The boat sank immediately and the fishermen were left swimming in the ocean. Fortunately none of them were injured. Upon being rescued, several of the men said that it must have been a UFO. One of the fishermen even said he thought he saw a creature just before the boat sank. The men were taken into custody and detained because of their claims. It was thought they were delusional. To make matters worse, one of the fisherman said that the space creature looked like a cow.

Holy Cow

The case gained some notoriety in Japan. Eventually the Russian consulate divulged the real facts: At an undisclosed location, some Russian military pilots decided to abduct a cow. They pulled the cow on board a transport plane. Later, while flying over the ocean, the cow kicked up such a ruckus that they decided to jettison it over the ocean. They figured no one would find out. Wrong. The poor cow ended up being the space creature that sunk the Japanese fishing boat.

Q. Could some flying saucer reports really be our own military?

Absolutely! As we pointed out in our section on modern technology, the military has some unbelievable aircraft. No doubt, some are so revolutionary they would appear to be alien if someone saw one fly by. We also know that the military has several recovered flying saucers and many private citizens have seen them going through their paces over Area 51 in Nevada.

Q. What about "cults" and flying saucers?

Since the bizarre suicide that occurred outside San Diego in 1997, many people want to know if aliens are tied to any strange cults. Our answer is no. There is really nothing to tie alien beings to something as weirdly human as a cult. Things are going to get a lot stranger as it becomes abundantly clear to the public at large that we are not alone in the universe and never have been. A lot of people are going to go slightly nuts, but there's no need for you to. We are a part of a vast universe/dimension and we are supposed to learn of their existence and participate in this transition.

Q. Why doesn't everyone know about flying saucers?

There are two very simple reasons. There are probably more, but here are the main ones. First, they don't want to know. This may sound trite, but it's not. There is plenty of evidence for the existence of something we call UFOs. Polls consistently show that 80 percent of the adult population feels something is going on and the government is hiding information.

This is a staggering fact. It has never before occurred in human history that 80 percent of the population recognizes that something is happening and less than one-tenth of one percent ever asks about it.

Fear of embarrassment and ridicule.

Don't take this lightly either. People are very afraid of these two things. Research shows that people are more afraid of embarrassment and ridicule than they are of illness or even death.

Q. What About religion? Is there a God?

The ramifications of these questions are enough to fill several books on this topic alone. But for right now, here are some simple guidelines for what the existence of flying saucers means for religion.

An Intelligence in the Universe

Research into flying saucers shows clearly that there is an intelligence at work in the universe far grander than our feeble intellect. Whether you call this intelligence God, Budda, Allah, or Mabel is up to you. This fact is easily discernible by the things you learn about when studying flying saucers, and even our alien visitors have told humans that there is an intelligence operating in our universe. By the way, our alien visitors refer to the universe as the Is-ness, as in "all that is." Our flying saucer research indicates that the intelligence we call God is a far more complex system of energy than we can possibly comprehend.

The Clergy

The big excuse always used as the reason the government won't tell the public about extraterrestrials is that the church couldn't handle it. If there is any one group that can be identified as being the most open to the possibility of extraterrestrials existing, it's the clergy. They are far more open-minded than the scientific community, which is sadly lagging years behind actual experience.

Every member of the clergy I have spoken to said that they would love to know about ETs. It would simply confirm what they have been saying all along; there is something grander than us.

The Vatican Already Knows

This may surprise you, but intelligence community sources tell us that the Vatican has long known about the existence of extraterrestrial beings. The Vatican has one of the world's top information gathering groups, reportedly second only to the world's acknowledged leader, Israel's Mossad. I use the term "information" instead of intelligence, because it sounds less militaristic.

Intelligence sources also say the Vatican has a direct downlink from the Hubble Space Telescope, something that even top scientists around the world don't have.

Vatican News

On April 5, 1998 it was announced that a Monsignor from the Vatican appeared on national television in Italy and stated that the current contact with extraterrestrial beings is very real. Monsignor Corrado Balducci is said to be an insider who is close to the Pope. He has made five appearances on national TV and discussed ETs. The prelate made two basic points:

1. *Balducci said the Vatican is receiving a lot of information about ex-traterrestrials and their contacts with citizens through their Nuncios (embassies) in numerous Latin American countries such as Mexico, Venezuela, and Chile. Balducci said that he, himself, is a member of a Vatican council whose responsibility is to figure out a way to handle the existence of extraterrestrial beings.*

2. *Balducci also said that the extraterrestrial encounters "are not demonic, they are not due to psychological impairment, they are not a case of entity attachment, but these encounters deserve to be studied carefully."*

Balducci's statements are particularly impressive in light of the fact that he is a Vatican expert on exorcism. (His official title translated is; 'Demonologist'.)

Rumors From the Intelligence Community

There are things which supposedly have filtered down from covert intelligence agencies such as the NSA, the CIA, and their military counterparts. These statements come up so often it is certain you will hear about it sooner or later, so I might as well stick your toes in the water for you.

Contacts within these agencies have stated that there are documents which say that alien beings have told our governments that they, the aliens, originated all religions on the planet Earth; that the alien beings are the architects of all religious doctrines. And, that is why there are remarkable similarities found in all the world's religions, despite originating from different cultures, and why many events depicted in the Bible are in fact descriptions of ET events and alien spacecraft.

Is it true, or is it just disinformation? Who knows. But if these documents do in fact exist and there is even a sliver of truth in these allegations, you can understand why any responsible government would be reluctant to share this information.

Twenty Things You Can Do

1. Face the fear.

Anyone who says that facing the prospect of the existence of beings from other worlds is not a little scary is lying. It is a challenge to the entire concept of your existence. Whether intentionally or unintentionally, deep down all your life you have been taught to believe otherwise. So this new information jeopardizes not just what you have been told about space beings, but what you have ever been told about anything. Now who can you trust? Who can you believe?

A Shock to the System
Because this information has been hidden from the public for so long, there will simply not be enough time to adequately prepare everyone. It would take another 50 years to do this gently and we don't have 50 years. These events are happening now!

Not only will individuals be shocked, but so will whole nations, governments, businesses, religions, and schools. After all, what are our science teachers going to say? The biggest thing in human history is occurring and they didn't have a clue?

There Is Nothing to Fear

There is nothing to fear. I have already established that the alien beings who are visiting this planet have vastly superior technology; otherwise they couldn't have gotten here. And, they have been here for a long, long time. Millions of years before mankind.

If they wanted to attack or take over New York, you and I wouldn't be here now. The military is already shooting at their ships. Your tax dollars are paying for this with ungodly amounts of money.

One B-2 bomber costs a billion dollars. That's enough to buy every school kid in America a new computer. And the cost of one of these bombers is cheap when compared to what is being spent every year on secret projects aimed at shooting down aliens!

Independence Day is only a movie. If you like the world we created, then keep doing the same old things. Like the idea of constant wars on the planet?

2. Hold Open Community Discussion Groups About Flying Saucers.

If you have ever talked about anything, you - and everyone else - needs to talk about this. This transition will be the biggest thing to ever hit this planet. It will affect everyone and everything.

You will also find that many of your neighbors already know a lot about this and have had some amazing experiences. Let them talk. If you listen, you'll learn things beyond your wildest imagination.

3. Reclaim Public Ownership of All NASA Photos

NASA has been withholding clear evidence of the existence of alien beings for decades. There is no nice way to put this: They have simply been lying to the public all these years while smiling in our faces and giving us an occasional pretty picture from the Hubble space telescope.

NASA is a public agency. As such, it is prevented by law from classifying information. I know they do some missions for the military, but all the space photos belong to us. Do you have any idea how much of your money they have already spent?

Righteous Indignation

A little righteous indignation is in order. We need some pressure put on them, and then release them from all responsibility. As scientists, they themselves are being held hostage. Allow them to come forward and tell what they know. Guarantee their safety and well-being. They just need to know you're not going to allow them to continue in their deceitful ways, no matter what. Their jobs and pensions will be dependent upon their honesty to the public. If we can't get that guarantee and be assured of it, then clean house. For their generous salaries, we can get some honest people.

4. Free Commercial Airline Pilots

Commercial airline pilots are also being held hostage by outdated, iron-clad bureaucratic laws. Our surveys show at least 25 percent of them have seen a UFO or experienced a UFO incident. Unbeknownst to you, the public, they are not allowed to talk about it. Don't believe me? Get a group of pilots in private and ask them, they will probably tell you the truth. If they report a UFO they will have to undergo psychological counseling or testing. If they persist in saying they saw what they saw they will be taken off of flight duty. And even worse things have happened to pilots who "talked."

The Instruments Go Haywire

Undoubtedly some arm of the government or some covert government group has a big influence in this. As I said earlier, somebody has gone to unbelievable lengths over the years to keep this information from the public. Another factor is the fact that flying saucers have a strong magnetic field of some kind around them, one which knocks out all electrical impulses. A good example is a scene in the movie *Close Encounters of the Third Kind*. Do you remember the scene near the beginning of the movie when Richard Dreyfuss' pickup truck conks out? That's what really happens. On an airplane, all the analog instruments go out. In a way, they are flying blind.

The Skies Ain't That Friendly Anymore

As you can well imagine, the airlines don't want the public to find out about this and have a panic over something the airline has absolutely no control over and no answer as to how to prevent.

The Attorneys Would Have a Field Day

If a plane goes down with no logical explanation, you can just see the legal boys going nuts. The airlines would have to admit they knew UFOs did this and then they would be liable for enough damages to put them out of business.

We Have to Take the First Step

Somehow, as matter of public policy, we have to openly recognize this fact. It may mean higher airfares to retrofit the planes with shielded instrumentation, but we can't bury our heads in the sand forever. No airline is going to propose it on their own, unless of course they are forced to by a sudden event which openly and irrevocably establishes the existence of flying saucers. And I assure you this will happen.

Here's an example of what I mean, an account of a very close call above New Jersey:

A HAM radio operator named John N. Gonzalez NZIXW, picked up the following conversation between the air traffic control tower at Newark airport in New Jersey and Flight 262 at 118.300 MHz. The date was Monday, November 17, 1997, sometime before midnight. The crew members of two other aircraft in the area witnessed the sighting and joined in the radio conversation. Here's the verbatim transcript:

JET #2: Watch out! The two (UFOs) are coming up to you.

FLIGHT 262: Well, Captain, the two up here are coming down to meet with you.

TOWER: Flight 262, what is your status?

FLIGHT 262: We have 236 souls onboard and 50,000 (pounds) of fuel. I think THESE DAMN THINGS ARE GOING TO HIT US. We are over Morristown just in case there is a collision with them. (Pause) They have taken off towards the northeast. And by the way, towards the northeast, it also looks like a meteor or space debris is coming down.

TOWER: Do you wish to report a UFO sighting?

FLIGHT 262: (pause) No, we have nothing to report.

JET #2: We heard you. I am making sure the passengers are all right. And, no, I have nothing to report, either.

JET #3: You guys have seen more than your share of UFOs. I know I have.

TOWER: Who are you? Please identify yourself. (There was no response.)

TOWER: Flight 262, go to the emergency frequency. We will meet the both of you there.

5. Learn this fact: You cannot solve any world-wide problems without first acknowledging the existence of flying saucers.

Sound a little far-fetched? If so, you are misunderstanding the magnitude of this occurrence. Among many other things, the existence of flying saucers means we understand far less about how the universe and our planet works than we ever imagined. There are huge pieces of the puzzle missing that will affect everything. To deny their existence is to deny a complete understanding of how our universe works and what you can do to make it, and our planet, better.

Not knowing this information is like not knowing there are microorganisms. Do you think any illness could have ever been cured without the knowledge that microorganisms existed? Well, the same thing applies here. The fact that alien beings exist and are real means the following things:

- There are other dimensions our scientists currently don't recognize. And these other dimensions affect the state of the very dimension we exist in. So nothing that is wrong in our dimension can be corrected without regard to the unseen dimensions.

- Our physics as we know them are completely wrong. This has even been stated in exactly these words by Ben Rich, the former head of Lockheed Aircraft.

- The greatest pollution on the planet is not environmental pollution - it is thought pollution. It is what prevents the curing of all the things wrong with our planet. Thought literally creates what exists. This has been told to us by alien beings and has been confirmed by the advanced understanding that physicists are reporting in the form of hyper-dimensional and quantum physics.

6. Try to get at least two U.S. military generals to go on record saying flying saucers don't exist!

Tell them you want to videotape it. Although most of these guys don't have firsthand knowledge, they have been exposed to enough to know aliens are real.

7. Look at this fact: Even insane and silly rumors get good coverage in traditional newspapers.

Look at the story about a rat being found in a bucket of fried chicken. It never happened, but you heard about it. Isn't it odd that you never hear anything about flying saucers in the traditional press? Even if flying saucers weren't real, you would think just the sheer number of people reporting them would be a huge story on mass psychosis or something -

yet there is nothing. If that doesn't tell you something is being suppressed, I've got some land to sell you.

8. Get a Night-vision Scope

With such a device, you can scan the skies regularly. Many flying saucers
that cannot be seen with the naked eye at night can be seen through a
night-vision scope. This has been reported many times. A person standing next to the viewer who does not have a night-vision scope cannot see
the craft, but the individual with the scope can. Don't just look high in
the sky. Scan the horizon and hills at tree-top level; they frequently travel
at these low altitudes and people just don't see them.

9. Get a Video Camera

Hot spots to tape UFOs are Mexico City and the Anza-Borrego desert in
southern California.

10. Check FEMA's Budget.

FEMA is the Federal Emergency Management Agency. It is an agency
that is supposed to help the public in emergencies like floods, earth-
quakes, and the like. So where is the money going? How come a big part
of the Federal budget is allocated to this agency and nobody ever sees the
money?

11. Learn to stop saying UFO.

The very word UFO says you have no idea what you saw. Idiots have
been making you and your friends believe you mistook the planet Venus
for an alien spacecraft for decades. Get a grip and get your power back.
If you see something you know is not a reflection and it's not an airplane,
tell people what you saw: a flying saucer!

It's a lot closer to the accurate truth than calling every sighting imagination or pizza nightmares or swamp gas. Flying saucers are real! If you see
a distant object out in the ocean, you don't say, "I saw an Unidentified

Floating Object." If you did, you would sound like an idiot. Now that you know flying saucers are real, just say so.

11. Take Your Own Personal Survey.

Ask friends or family members if they have ever seen a flying saucer. You will be shocked when you find out how many of them have seen one.

Not long after this book was originally published in print, I was contacted by an officer in military intelligence. We ended up talking for several hours. He told me that he specifically started taking a survey with each group of people he was assigned to train. He said that without fail, at least 3 out of every 10 people reluctantly admitted to having seen a UFO or having a very strange UFO experience. He stated, that now he could identify them before they even spoke. Upon asking the question, those people immediately became quiet and subdued and got "the look."

12. E-mail your congressional representatives.

Tell him or her to get with the program. Give them permission to act on your behalf. Even if you're not old enough to vote yet, e-mail them anyway. If enough of you do, they will soon get the message that they are behind the curve. Let them know that the simple knowledge that ETs exist should no longer be a matter of national security. You already know they exist, so what's up with the ruse?

13. Historians: Start documenting this transition.

This is the greatest transition in human history. Yet because of the secrecy and fear of ridicule for the past 50 years, the documentation of this event is being lost. The record of the initial contact with beings from other worlds is being destroyed or not even being recorded. Don't let this continue. Historians, get with the program!

14. Amnesty.

As citizens, guarantee unconditional amnesty to those in official or unofficial positions who have knowledge about flying saucers and who want to come forward and tell their stories.

15. Hold Family Discussions About This Topic.

The integration of this reality into our society is going to affect each and every person in a big way. Get ahead of the curve and start talking about it now. If you are in school, make sure your parents get a heads-up so they don't freak out on you.

16. Check out the relevant (and rapidly multiplying) websites.

Check out the websites of the best flying saucer organizations. A longer list can be found in the Appendix, but these few will certainly get you started.

Flying Saucers 101	www.flyingsaucers101
Aliens Information	www.aliens-everything-you-want-to-know.com
UFO Magazine	www.ufomag.com
MUFON International	www.mufon.com
MUFON Orange County, CA	www.mufonoc.org
The Disclosure Project	www.disclosureproject.org
CSETI	www.cseti.org
Enterprise Mission	www.enterprisemission.com
The Black Vault	www.theblackvault.com
Coast to Coast Radio	www.Coasttocoastam.com
Jeff Rense Radio	www.Sightings.com
David Wilcock	www.DivineCosmos.com/

17. Check you and your friends for fluorescence.

It has recently been discovered by researchers Dr. Roger Leir and Derrel Simms that alien abductees often have fluorescence on their bodies that remains after an abduction event. If you or a family member has had a recent abduction experience or recent contact with an alien being, simply take a small, hand-held black light and move it over the body. Dramatic bright fluorescence which will not come off when washed will be your own personal evidence of human/alien contact!

18. Contact or join your local flying saucer organization.

Most of these groups hold monthly lecture or discussion groups. Don't worry, there are no weird people there. (No weirder than any other typical slice of the population, that is.) Just ordinary citizens like you. You'll have a great time and learn a lot in a short period of time. Just attending one meeting will enlighten you greatly.

MUFON International Hotline: *1-800-UFO-2166*
MUFON Orange County, CA: *714-520-4UFO*

19. Remove the Ridicule Factor.

You are not nuts and neither are your friends or loved ones. Many of you have had extraordinary experiences. You must trust one another enough to begin to share them with each other. A lot of the fear surrounding this phenomenon is because people feel they have nowhere to turn if they have had an unexplained experience. In other countries friends trust what their friends tell them. Here in the U.S., the first thing we tend to do is to not believe a friend. Weird, huh? Well, it's time to change that. You are about to find out that reality is far stranger than any tale your friend could make up.

Thousands of people around the world have been contacted face to face by many different kinds of alien visitors. This is particularly true in countries which do not have a large element of ridicule running through their culture the way we do in the United States. There is also an active campaign of ridicule being waged against the citizens of the United States by those in positions of authority, who for some reason want to keep the existence of flying saucers and extraterrestrials secret.

Once you remove the ridicule factor, you will learn some astounding things. You don't need to believe everything you hear, especially the first time you hear it. However, let each person speak without attacking them. You can choose simply not to believe them, but let them speak. When you find out how many people have already had alien experiences, the volume will get so loud it will be impossible to ignore.

20. Relax and have fun.

Enjoy this. You are going to have the time of your life. This will be unlike anything you could ever imagine. You are one of the luckiest people in the entire universe. You are going to discover there are millions of alien beings out there, just waiting to find out what your reaction is going to be when you find out they exist. Columbus' voyage was peanuts compared to what you're about to do.

Oh, and let me be the first to tell you: If you are under the age of 20, *you* will have the opportunity to set your feet on the soil of another planet in your lifetime! I guarantee it!

What To Do Now

How to Report a UFO

Each year there are over a hundred thousand UFO sightings reported worldwide. Approximately one out of ten is truly an unidentified object; the rest are generally explainable once they have been investigated. Since the number of sightings has been increasing annually, there is a good chance you may see one. If you do it will certainly be an exciting event. Enjoy it and remember these tips:

1. Don't panic. Try to get your friends to come out so they can see it also. It always helps to have others corroborate what you saw.

2. Try to remember as much detail as possible. This could be one of the most exciting events in your life.

3. Attempt to estimate sizes, speeds, and distances. One way is to hold a quarter at arm's length and hold it up next to the object.

4. If you have a camera or video camera, get it and take photos, quick, before the object leaves. Don't stand around with your mouth hanging open.

5. Immediately write down everything you saw. Make drawings too; a picture is worth a thousand words.

6. If you encounter some kind of extraterrestrial being, simply consider yourself lucky, because your friends won't believe you anyway. Whatever you do, don't say "Take me to your leader." If you do, they'll probably collect you as an example of life with especially low intelligence.

7. Contact MUFON (Mutual UFO Network). This is the world's largest UFO organization. Here are five ways to reach them:

* *On the web:* www.mufon.com
* *By phone: 888-817-2220 or 513-871-8367*
* *By fax: 513-352-6345*
* *E-mail: hq@mufon.com*
* *U.S. mail: MUFON, 262 Wilmer Ave., Cincinnati, OH 45226*

Defining Your Purpose

- *Understanding exactly what it is you are trying to do.*
- *Learning you have a gift to give.*
- *How to give your gift.*
- *How to avoid wasting your gift.*

Give Someone A Gift

The sole purpose of sharing information about flying saucers should be to give that person a gift. It is an extraordinary gift. It is giving someone the opportunity to participate in life at a level they never knew before, allowing the recipient to do no less than help guide humanity to the next level of participating in the universe. It could end up being literally the greatest present ever given to a person during his or her lifetime. And, you get to give it!

Give Yourself A Gift

Do this first. You can't share something until you've acquired it yourself. Start by reading this book.

The Gift

The gift is the knowledge and confirming information that people on planet Earth are not alone, that we are part of a much larger community, and that we are actively involved with many other kinds of beings from other planets and other dimensions.

Who do you give your gift to? Someone you love, or someone who loves you. Choose your recipient carefully. This is a special gift from you. It takes love, caring, and energy to give this gift. You only have a limited supply of each. Make the best of your supply.

Your Children and Grandchildren

You love them, they love you. They've never seen an 8-track tape or a 45 record. They don't know Elvis and will never have heard a typewriter go "ding." They are also not stuck with foolish concepts like the earth is flat or the irrational idea that life developed only on this planet. If you listen carefully and pay attention, you'll probably discover they already know what you are trying to tell them.

Your Parents

You have already helped them with computers, cell phones and social networking – now you can help them with the real universe.

Your Best Friend

Enough said. This person has been with you through thick and thin. He or she won't bail out on you now. You owe them. So give the gift. Don't worry about the response - that's none of your business. Give it with love and let it go.

How To Avoid Wasting Your Gift

Don't try to convince anyone of anything. Don't give your gift to some-one you feel you need to convince. For instance, there are people like my sister in-law who say she wouldn't believe aliens existed even if they flew over her house and beamed her up. I told her, 'Trust me, I'm working on it.'

Convincing someone is not your purpose. If you give someone a toaster for a wedding present, you don't sit around trying to convince them it will toast bread. Hand over the instruction book, then get out of the way.

Either they'll figure it out or they won't. The same with this information. They may have to hear it several more times from several different people. So give the gift and move on.

No, Not That Guy!

Don't attempt to give your gift to people who can trigger you. You know who I mean: people like your neighbor who still thinks "the web" is what you find between a duck's toes. You would do anything to show this pompous person how stupid he really is. But, don't do it. Hold up. He is undeserving of your gift.

How To Give Your Gift

Be gentle, be loving, be kind. Tell your recipients you love them and you want to share something special with them. Then give them a copy of this book. Some basics to remember:

- *Flying-saucer information is a gift for you to give to someone else.*
- *What that person chooses to do with your gift is none of your business.*
- *Do not try and convince anyone of anything.*
- *Do not waste your gift on undeserving people.*

Share The UFO Witness Declaration

Let people know that you are no longer going to be intimidated, embarrassed or ridiculed for acknowledging the truth about the fact that we are not alone in the universe. Pass along the UFO Witness Declaration that follows.

THE UFO WITNESS DECLARATION

FACT: From 1982 to 1985, large triangular and boomerang-shaped UFOs were reported over the Hudson Valley by over 7,000 credible witnesses, including police and officials at the Indian Point Nuclear Power Plant.

FACT: In 1989 and 1990, large triangular and rectangular unidentified flying objects, one the size of an aircraft carrier, were reported over Belgium by over 2,000 witnesses, including police and military personnel.

FACT: In 1997, multiple sightings of mile long boomerang-shaped UFOs were reported over the state of Arizona by over 10,000 witnesses including police, military personnel and Republican Governor Fife Symington.

We make no claims as to the nature or origin of these UFOs. However, those who have taken the time and effort to conduct serious, in-depth investigations into these reports know that these sightings are of real, physical crafts and are indisputable FACTS.

Thousands of such sightings of physical crafts of unknown origin have been reported throughout the world for decades by credible witnesses, yet most who report such sightings are treated with ridicule, disbelief, scorn and even threats.

In light of the facts, we who have witnessed such unexplained crafts no longer accept this cynical mindset as realistic or credible.

Those who are witnesses to the UFO phenomenon know they exist for a fact. This is not an issue of speculation for such witnesses. However, we do not insist that non-witnesses must believe such objects exist, only that witnesses be treated with respect and that we deserve the same fairness and courtesy afforded to any individual or group who honestly expresses their point of view without fear of ridicule, punishment or persecution.

Recent polls clearly demonstrate that more than 50% of Americans believe that UFOs are a real phenomenon that deserves legitimate recognition and serious study by open-minded, qualified scientists, rather than being summarily dismissed as misperceptions, fantasies, hoaxes or hallucinations by cynical, unqualified debunkers. Over 36 million Americans have seen a UFO.

To put this statistic into political terms, these witnesses are also voters.

Therefore, we urge all who agree with the spirit of this declaration to send copies of this letter to their representatives, public officials, the media, the police, the military, airline officials, NASA, and all candidates running for any public office to assure them that our votes will go only to those who acknowledge the UFO phenomenon as real and deserving of

serious scientific investigation and who publicly endorse fairness and respect toward any witness who reports a UFO.
Developed and Reprinted by permission of Bashar.org

NOTES

INTRODUCTION

Putting Things in Context
1 ."Why Doctors Aren't Curing Ulcers," Brian O'Reilly, *Fortune*, June 9, 1997.

CHAPTER ONE: THE BASICS

Flying Saucers vs. UFOs
1. Bill McDonald, MUFON Journal, February, 1998
2. Jaime Maussan, MUFON Lecture, Los Angeles, CA, March 25, 1998

CHAPTER TWO: UFOs IN HISTORY

1. UFO: *The Continuing Enigma*, Readers Digest Association, Inc., 1993.
2. ibid
3. ibid
4. ibid
5. Annales Laurisseness, 900 A.D.
6. Jaques Vallee, *Passport To Magonia*, Contemporary Books, 1993.
7. John Carpenter, MUFON Lecture, Orange County, CA, March 25, 1998.
8. Mignes Greek, Dom J.B. McLaughlin
9. Jaques Vallee*, Passport To Magonia*, Contemporary Books, 1993.
10. Peter Brookesmith, *UFO: The Complete Sightings*, Barnes & Noble, 1995.
11. Time and Space: *Mysteries of the Unknown series*, Time-Life Books, 1992.
12. Eric Saunders, A Case History of UFOs in Turkey, UFO Magazine, England, May / June, 1996.
13. Peter Brookesmith, *UFO: The Complete Sightings*, Barnes & Noble, 1995.
14. Jaques Vallee, *Passport to Magonia*, Contemporary Books, 1993.
15. Conrad Lycosthenes, *A Chronicle of Prodigies and Portents*.
16. Peter Brookesmith, *UFO: The Complete Sightings*, Barnes & Noble, 1995.
17. ibid
18. Jaques Vallee, *Passport to Magonia*, Contemporary Books, 1993.
19. UFO: The Continuing Enigma, Readers Digest Association, 1993.
20. UFO Encounters, Golden Press, 1978.
21. *Ibid.*
22. Peter Brookesmith: *UFO: The Complete Sightings*, Barnes & Noble, 1995.
23. *Ibid.*
24. Jaques Vallee, *Passport to Magonia*, Contemporary Books, 1993.

25. Ibid.
26. *The Lost Books of the Bible and the Forgotten Books of Eden, Book of Protevangelion*, Chapter 13, Verses 1-10.
27. Ibid., Book of Infancy, Chapter 1, Verses 8-12.
28. John Carpenter, MUFON Lecture, Orange County, CA., March 25, 1998.
29. *Wonders of the Ancient World: National Geographic Atlas of Archaeology*, National Geographic Society, 1994.
30. Zita Rodriquez, *Reporte Ovni*, No. 37., Mexico City, 1994.
31. Peter Brookesmith, *UFO: The Complete Sightings*, Barnes & Noble, 1995.
32. John Carpenter, MUFON Lecture, Orange County, CA., March 25, 1998.
33. *The UFO Phenomenon, Mysteries of the Unknown*, Time-Life Books, 1992.
34. *Ibid.*
35. Kenneth C. McCulloch, *Mankind: Citizen of the Galaxy*, Rings of Saturn Publishing, Canada, 1985.
36. *Ibid.*
37. David Barritt, "Who Made the Giant Footprint?", Sunday Times Magazine, Vancouver, Canada, April 12, 1987.
38. John Carpenter, MUFON Lecture, Orange County, CA, March 25, 1998.
39. Cecil Jane, *The Voyages of Christopher Columbus*, Argonaut Press, 1930.

War of the Worlds
1. Hadley Cantrill, Princeton University Press, 1966.
2. *Ibid.*
3. American Institute of Public Opinion Poll, 1939.
4. CBS Poll, 1939.
5. *Fortune* Poll, 1939.
6. American Institute of Public Opinion Poll, 1939.

The World at War
1. *The Time-Life History of WWII*, Time-Life Books, 1989.
2. Gerhard L. Weinberg, *A World at Arms; A Global History of World War II*, Cambridge University Press, 1994
3. *World War II* CD-ROM, FlagTower, First Electronic Publishing, U.K., 1995.
4. *World War I*, CD-ROM, FlagTower, First Electronic Publishing, U.K., 1995.
5. U.S. National Archives & Records Administration Website, www.nara.gov/, 1997.
6. U.S. Office of War Information Government Information Manual for the Motion Picture Industry, 1943.

Los Angeles Air Raid
1. Peter Jenkins, *Los Angeles Evening Herald Examiner*, February 26, 1942.
2. Peter Brookesmith *UFO: The Complete Sightings*, Barnes & Noble, 1995.

Wartime UFOs
1. Jim Marrs, *Alien Agenda*, Harper Collins, 1997.

2. Peter Brookesmith, *UFO: The Government Files*, Barnes & Noble, 1996.
3. Peter Brookesmith, *UFO: The Complete Sightings*, Barnes & Noble, 1995.
4. Timothy Goode, Above Top Secret; The Worldwide UFO Cover-up, William Morrow and Company, 1988.

The Year: 1947
1. Jim Marrs, *Alien Agenda*, Harper Collins, 1997.
2. Memo to Commanding General, Army Air Force, from General Nathan Twining, Commander of the Air Material Command, September 23, 1947.
3. Timothy Goode, *Above Top Secret*, William Morrow and Company, 1988.
4. Richard Hall, Editor, The UFO Evidence, *The National Investigations Committee on Aerial Phenomena* (NICAP), Barnes & Noble, 1997.

Roswell
1. Don Berliner and Stanton Friedman, *Crash at Corona*, Marlowe and Company 1997, P.73.
2. *Ibid.* P.72.
3. *Ibid.*
4. *Ibid.*, p.73.
5. *Ibid.*, p.100.
6. *Ibid.*, Introduction.
7. Kevin Randle and Donald Schmitt, *The Truth About the UFO Crash at Roswell*, Avon Books, 1994.
8. *Ibid.*, p.198.
9. Don Berliner and Stanton Friedman, *Crash at Corona*, Marlowe and Company, 1997.
10. Jenny Randles, *UFO Retrievals; The Recovery of Alien Spacecraft*, Blandford Books, U.K., 1995.
11. Kevin Randle and Donald Schmitt, *The Truth About the UFO Crash at Roswell*, Avon Books, 1994.
12. *Ibid.*, Appendix B.
13. Don Berliner and Stanton Friedman, *Crash at Corona*, Marlowe and Company, 1997.
14. Interview with Kevin Randle, MUFON Journal, 1991.
15. Col. Philip J. Corso, *The Day After Roswell*, Pocket Books, 1997.
16. Don Berliner and Stanton Friedman, Crash at Corona, Marlowe and Company, 1997.
17. Jenny Randles, *UFO Retrievals*, Blandford Books, U.K., 1995.
18. Ted Loman, Lecture, Skywatch International Conference, Phoenix, AZ, November 15, 1997.
19. Kevin Randle and Donald Schmitt, *The Truth about the UFO Crash at Roswell*, Avon Books, 1994.
20. Don Berliner and Stanton Friedman, *Crash at Corona*, Marlowe and Company, 1997.
21. *Ibid.*
22. Kevin Randle and Donald Scmitt, *The Truth About the UFO Crash at Roswell*,

Avon Books, 1994.
23. *Ibid.*
24. *Ibid.*
25. *Ibid.*
26. Don Berliner and Stanton Friedman, *Crash at Corona*, Marlowe and Company, 1997.
27. *Ibid.*
28. *Ibid.*
29. Col. Philip J. Corso, *The Day After Roswell*, Pocket Books, 1997.
30. *Ibid.*
31. Derrel Sims and John Leir, MUFON Lecture, Orange County, CA., February 25, 1998.

Tuskegee Study
1. "Tuskegee Study of Syphilis in the Untreated Negro Male," 1932-1972.

Flying Saucers Over Washington DC
1. Peter Brookesmith, *UFO: The Complete Sightings*, Barnes & Noble, 1995.
2. Jerome Clark, *The UFO Files*, Signet Books, 1996.

Ten Year Review
1. Alan Griffin, Lecture, UFO Lectures of Orange County, Anaheim, CA July 27, 1996.
2. Memo from General Schulgen of the Air Intelligence requirements Division, Dated October 28, 1947.

CHAPTER THREE: THE GOVERNMENT AT WORK

Majestic 12
1. Stanton Friedman, MUFON Lecture, Orange County, CA., 1997.
2. Jaime Shandera, MUFON Lecture, Orange County, CA., July 23, 1997.

The Projects
1. J. Allen Hynek, *The Hynek UFO Report*, Barnes & Noble, 1997.

Area 51
1. *Secrets of Dreamland*, UFO Central Home Video, Venice, CA 1997.

The Men in Black
1. Peter Brookesmith, *UFO: The Complete Sightings*, Barnes & Noble, 1995.
2. Jim Marrs, *Alien Agenda*, Harper Collins, 1997.

The Disclosure Project
1. Steven M. Greer M.D., The Disclosure Project website, 2011

2. *Ibid.*

CHAPTER FOUR: NASA

1. Interview with Robert Oeschler, The Learning Channel - Videotape.

Modern Aircraft Technology
1. David Adair, Interview, *Sedona Journal*, February, 1998.
2. David Adair, Interview, Art Bell Radio Show, December, 1997.
3. Ben Rich, Personal Interview with Jan C. Harzan.

The Russian Experience
1. Sheila Ostrander and Lynn Schroeder, *Psychic Discoveries*, Marlowe and Company, 1997
2. *Soviet Military Review*, June, 1989.
3. Sheila Ostrander and Lynn Schroeder, *Psychic Discoveries*, Marlowe and Company, 1997.
4. *Ibid.*
5. *Ibid.*
6. Paul Dean, *Los Angeles Times*, November 20, 1991.
7. Abigail Lewis, Interview with Marina Popovich, *Whole Life Times*, July, 1991.

The Astronauts
1. Sheila Ostrander and Lynne Schroeder, *Psychic Discoveries*, Marlowe and Company, 1997, P.384.
2. Timothy Goode, *Above Top Secret*, William Morrow and Company, 1988, P. 384.
3. Carl Koppeschaar, *Moon Handbook*, Moon Publications, 1997.
4. MUFON Notes, Orange County MUFON, Spring, 1988, Vol. 4, Issue I.

The Moon
1. Sky and Telescope, *Harvard Astronomy Journal*, Lunar Conference, 1973.
2. Jim Marrs, *Alien Agenda*, Harper Collins, 1997.
3. *Ibid.*
4. *Ibid.*
5. George Leonard, *Somebody Else is on the Moon*, 1979.
6. Timothy Goode, *Above Top Secret*, William Morrow and Company, 1988, P. 386.
7. Jim Marrs, *Alien Agenda*, Harper Collins, 1997.
8. *Ibid.*
9. Sheila Ostrander and Lynne Schroeder, *Psychic Discoveries*, Marlowe and Company, 1997.

The Face on Mars
1. Richard C. Hoagland, MUFON Lecture, Orange County, CA. October 22, 1997.
2. Richard C. Hoagland, *The Monuments of Mars: A City on the Edge of Forever*, North Atlantic Books, 1994.
3. *ibid.*

4. Mark J. Carlotto, *The Martian Enigmas-A Closer Look: The Face, Pyramids and Other Unusual Objects on Mars*, North Atlantic Books, 1997.
5. Richard C. Hoagland, Mars I: NASA / Cydonia Briefings (Video Tape).
6. Richard C. Hoagland, Mars II: The U.N. Briefings - The Terrestrial Connection, (Videotape).
7. Bob Frissell, *Nothing in this Book is true, But It's Exactly How Things Are*, North Atlantic Books, 1994.

Star Wars and Weather Satellites
1. *Aviation Week and Space Technology*, January, 1994 Vol. 110, P. 27.
2. *Aviation Week and Space Technology*, July 31, 1994, Vol. 116, P. 21.
3. *Ad Astra*, Sept.-Oct., 1996, Vol. 6 P. 10.
4. *Discover*, January, 1995, Vol. 15, P. 92.
5. *Ibid.*
6. *Time*, December 2, 1995, Vol. 119, P. 72.
7. *Ibid.*
8. *Science,* September 3, 1993, Vol. 251, P. 1254.
9. *Science*, January 11, 1994, Vol. 256, P. 197.
10. *Science,* September 3, 1993, Vol. 251, P. 1254
11. *The Nation*, December 15, 1995, P. 5.
12. Philip J. Imbrogno, *UFO Universe*, Vol. 1, 1997 P. 41.
13. *Ibid.*
14. *The Nation*, December 15, 1995, P. 5.
15. *Larry King Live*, January, 1997.
16. A. Dmiryuk, *Pravda*, November 16, 1979.
17. William J. Broad, New York Times, January 25, 1994.
18. *Ibid.*
19. *Los Angeles Times*, Front Page, December 26, 1997.
20. Ronald Regehr, Personal Interview, 1997.

CHAPTER FIVE: SCIENCE

1. Bob Berman, *Secrets of the Night Sky*, William Morrow, 1995.
2. Carl Sagan*, Cosmos*, Ballantine Books, 1980.
3. Ronald W. Clark, *Einstein: The Life and Times*, Avon Books, 1972.
3. Richard P. Feynman, *QED, The Strange theory of Light and Matter*, Princeton University Press, 1985.
4. Col. Wendelle Stevens (Ret.), *UFO Photographs, Vol. I,* UFO Photo Archives, 1985.

Nikola Tesla
1. George Trinkhaus, *Tesla: The Lost Inventions*, High Voltage Press.
2. George Trinkaus, *Radio Tesla*, High Voltage Press.
4. Inez Hunt and Wanetta Draper*, Lightning in his Hand: The Life Story of Nikola Tesla.*

4. R.A. Ford, *Tesla Coil Secrets.*
5. *Nikola Tesla 1856-1943: Lectures, Articles, Patents*, Tesla Book Company.
6. Margaret Chaney, *Nikola Tesla...Man out of Time.*
7. John O'Neill, *Prodigal Genius*, Omni Publications, Hawthorne, CA.

Ten Secrets of Alien Science
1. Richard Restack, *Brain,* Warner Books, 1979.
3. David A. Pollen and Michael C. Tractenberg, Alpha Rhythm and Eye Movements in Eidetic Imagery, *Nature,* May 12, 1972.
4. Karl Lashley, *Physiological Mechanisms in Animal Behavior*, Academic Press, 1950.
5. Paul Pietsch, Shufflebrain, *Harpers Magazine*, May, 1972.
6. David Bohm, *Quantum Implications*, edited by Basil J. Hiley and F. David Peat, Routledge & Kegan Paul, U.K., 1987.
7. Jeanne Achterberg, *Imagery in Healing*, New Science Library, 1985.
8. Thomas J. Hurley III, " *Placebo Effects: Unmapped Territory of the Mind / Body Interactions,* " *Investigations*, No. 2. 1985.
9. Personal Interview with Anonymous Contactee, February 28, 1998.
10. Temple Grandin, . "How does visual thinking work in the mind of a person with autism? A personal account". *Philos Trans R Soc Lond B Biol Sci* **364** (1522): 1437

Cattle Mutilations
1. Jim Marrs, *Alien Agenda*, Harper Collins, 1997.
2. Linda Moulton Howe, *A Strange Harvest*, Documentary.
3. Linda Moulton Howe*, An Alien Harvest: Further Evidence Linking Animal Mutilations and Human Abductions to Alien Life Forms*, Paper Chase Press, 1998.
5. Linda Moulton Howe, *Glimpses of Other Realities - Vol. II: High Strangeness*, Paper Chase Press, 1998.
6. *Ibid.*
7. Ted Oliphant, MUFON, Orange County Lecture and Videotape, April 25, 1998.

Crop Circles
1. Doug Ruby, *The Gift: The Crop Circles Deciphered*, Blue Note Books, 1997.
2. Ted Oliphant, MUFON Lecture, Orange County, CA, April22, 1998
3. *Ibid.*
5. Linda Moulton Howe, Glimpses of Other Realities-Vol. II: High Strangeness Paper Chase Press, 1998.

Different Types of Alien Beings
1. Steven Jones, MUFON Lecture, Orange County, CA, May 18, 2011.
2. *ibid.*
3. David Wilcock, *The Source Field Investigations*, Dutton, Penguin Group 2011.

Alien Abductions

1. David M. Jacobs Ph.D., *Secret Life*, Simon & Schuster, 1992.
5. *Ibid.*
6. David M. Jacobs, Lecture, MUFON, Orange County, CA., June 25, 1997.
7. *Ibid.*
8. *Ibid.*
9. John E. Mack M.D., *Abduction*, Charles Scribner's Sons, 1994.
10. *Ibid.*
11. Preston Dennett, *UFO Healings*, Wild Flower Press, 1996.
12. John E. Mack M.D., Abduction, Preface, Charles Scribner's Sons, 1994.
13. *Ibid.*
14. *Sedona Journal*, June, 1995.
15. John E. Mack M.D., *Abduction*, Charles Scribner's Sons, P.18.
16. David M. Jacobs Ph.D., MUFON Lecture, Orange County, CA., June 25, 1997.
17. *Time Magazine*, June 23, 1997, P. 66.
18. Fred Rascio, Discover Magazine, September, 1997, P. 82.
19. Debbi-Jordan Kauble, UFO Lectures of Orange County, Anaheim, CA., March 1, 1997.
20. Derrel Sims and John Leir, MUFON Lecture, Orange County, CA. February 25, 1998.
21. *Ibid.*

Are You An Abductee?

1. Melinda Leslie, Corona Del Mar, CA., 1997.

1. Dr. Roger Leir, MUFON Lecture, Orange County, CA., February 25, 1998.
2. Dr. Roger Leir, Metallurgy Analysis, Los Alamos Labs, 1997.
3. Derrel Sims, MUFON Lecture, Orange County, CA. February 25, 1998.
4. *Ibid.*
6. Dr. Roger Leir, Metallurgy Analysis, University of California at San Diego, CA, 1997.
7. Dr. Roger Leir, MUFON Lecture, Orange County, CA., February 25, 1998.
8. Ronald Regehr, MUFON Notes, MUFON, Orange County, CA., 1998.

The Role of Skeptics

1. Carl Sagan and Thornton Page, Editors, *UFO's A Scientific Debate*, Barnes & Noble, Cornell University Press, 1972.
2. Ted Oliphant, MUFON Lecture, Orange County, CA, April 22, 1998.

Remote Viewing

1. Jack Hauck, Lecture, Anaheim, CA., 1997.
2. Jim Schnabel, *Remote Viewers, The Secret History of America's Secret Spies*, Dell Publishing, 1997.
3. Sheila Ostrander and Lynn Schroeder, *Psychic Discoveries*, Marlowe and

Company, 1997.

World-Wide Recovery Events

1. CSETI, Project Starlight Briefing Document, April, 1997.
2. CSETI, Website, www.cseti.org.
4. Kevin D. Randle & Donald R. Schmitt, *The Truth About the UFO Crash at Roswell,* Avon Books, 1994.
5. Jenny Randles, *UFO Retrievals, The Recovery of Alien Spacecraft*, Blandford Books, U.K., 1996.
6. Don Berliner and Stanton T. Friedman, *Crash at Corona*, Marlowe and Company, 1997.

BIBLIOGRAPHY

"A Mind/Brain/Matter Model Consistent with Quantum Physics and the UFO Phenomena," Thomas Bearden, MUFON Symposium Proceedings, 1979.

"A Reference Guide to Foreign UFO Documents," J. Antonio Huneeus, MUFON Symposium Proceedings, 1996.

"A Review of Selected Aerial Phenomenon Sightings From Aircraft 1942 to 1952," Richard F. Haines, MUFON Symposium Proceedings, 1983.

"A Review of Selected Sightings from Aircraft-1973 to 1978", Richard F. Haines, Ph.D., MUFON Symposium Proceedings, 1979.

"A UFO Propulsion Model," Frederick E. Alzonfon, Ph.D., MUFON Symposium Proceedings, 1982.

A World Beyond, Ruth Montgomery, Fawcett Crest, 1971.

Abducted. The Story of the Intruders Continues, Debbie Jordan & Kathy Mitchell, Carroll & Graf, 1994.

Abduction-Human Encounters with Aliens, John E. Mack, M.D., Charles Scribner's Sons, 1994.

"Abductions in Africa - Worldwide Similarities," Cynthia Hind, MUFON Symposium Proceedings, 1993.

"Above Top Secret," Timothy Goode, MUFON Symposium Proceedings, 1989.
Above Top Secret: The Worldwide UFO Coverup, Timothy Goode, William Morrow, 1988.

"African Encounters: Case Investigations," Cynthia Hind, MUFON Symposium Proceedings,1981.

Agency: The Rise and Fall of the CIA, John Ranelagh, Weidenfeld & Nicholson, Pocket Books, 1996.

"Albert Einstein," Boris, Podolsky, and Nathan Rosen*, Physical Review* 47, 1935.

Alien Agenda, Dr. Clifford Wilson, Signet Books, 1988.

Alien Agenda, Jim Marrs, Harper Collins, 1997.

Alien Contacts and Abductions, Jenny Randles, Sterling Publishing Co., Inc., 1994.

Alien Encounters, Mysteries of the Unknown Series, Time-Life Books, 1992.

Alien Identities, Richard Thompsen, Govardhan Hill, Inc., 1993.

"Alien Roots: Six UFO Entity Types and Some Possible Earthly Ancestors," Alvin Lawson, Ph.D. MUFON Symposium Proceedings, 1979.

Aliens Among Us, Ruth Montgomery, Ballantine books, 1985.

Aliens From Space, Major Donald E. Keyhoe, Panther, 1975.

An Alien Harvest, Linda Moulton Howe, Paper Chase press, 1989.
"An Alien Harvest," Linda Moulton Howe, MUFON Symposium Proceedings, 1989.
"Analysis of Humanoid Reports" David F. Webb, MUFON Symposium Proceed
ings, 1976.
"Angina Pectoris and the Placebo Effect," Herbert Benson and David P. McCallie
Jr., *New England Journal of Medicine* 300, No. 25, 1979.
An Invitation To The Dance, Steven Jones, Little Star Publishing, 2010.
"Apollo Over the Moon: A View From Orbit," Harold Masursky, C.W. Colton,
Farouk, El-Baz, *Today* 12, #9, February, 1979.
Are The Invaders Coming?, Steven Tyler, Tower Books, 1968.
Australian Ufology: A Review, Journal of UFO Studies, Vol. 2, Keith V.
Basterfield, V. Godic, M. Rodeghier, 1990.
Behind the Flying Saucers, Frank Scully, Henry Holt & Company, 1950.
Behind The Flying Saucer Mystery, George Adamski, Paperback Library Inc.,
1961 and 1967.
Beyond Earth: Man's Contact with UFOs, Ralph and Judy Blum, Corgi Books, 1974.
Beyond My Wildest Dreams, Diary of a UFO Abductee. Kim Carlsberg, Illustrations
by Darryl Anka, Bear & Company, 1994.
Beyond Supernature, Lyall Watson, Bantam Books, 1988.
Beyond the Brain, Stanislav Grof, State University of New York Press, 1985.
Bible and Flying Saucers, Barry Downing, Avon Books, 1970.
Bible Code, Michael Drosnin, Simon & Schuster, 1997.
Black Holes and Warped Space-Time, William J. Kaufmann, W.H. Freeman, 1979.
Black Holes: The Edge of Space, The End of Time, Walter Sullivan, Doubleday,
1979.
Born to Heal, Ruth Montgomery, Fawcett Crest, 1973.
"Brazil: Censorship of UFO Reports," *Flying Saucer Review, Vol. 19, no. 6*, 1973.
*Can Quantum-Mechanical Description of Physical Reality Be Considered Com-
plete?* Technology Publishing, 1995.
"Case For The Extraterrestrial Origin of Flying Saucers," Stanton T. Friedman,
MUFON Symposium Proceedings, 1979.
"Case History of UFOs in Turkey," Eric Saunders, *UFO Magazine*, U.K. Quest
Publications International Ltd., May/June, 1996.
"Case of the Extraterrestrial Origin of Flying Saucers," Stanton T. Friedman,
MUFON Symposium Proceedings, 1979.
Casebook of a UFO Investigator, Raymond E. Fowler, Prentice-Hall, 1981.
Catchers of Heaven, Michael Wolf, Dorrance Publishing Co., 1997.
"Cattle Mutilations That Defy Conventional Explanations," Walter H. Andrus, Jr.
MUFON Symposium Proceedings, 1983.
Centuries of Contact, John S. Carpenter, Videotape, 1997.
Cracking The Bible Code, Jeffrey Satinover M.D., William Morrow, 1997.
Demon-Haunted World, Carl Sagan, Random House, 1995.
Dialogues With The Angels, Tricia McCannon, Horizons Unlimited, 1996.
Divine Encounters, Zechariah Sitchin, 1996.
Chronicle of Prodigies and Portents, Conrad Lycosthenes, Adventures Unlimited
Press, 1991.

CIA and the Cult of Intelligence, Victor Marchetti and John D. Marks, Coronet May, 1987.

Clear Intent, Lawrence Fawcett and Barry J. Greenwood, Prentice-Hall, 1984.

Communication with Extraterrestrial Intelligence, Carl Sagan, M.I.T. Press, 1973.

Communion, Whitley Streiber, Beech Tree Books, 1987.

Comprehensive Briefing Document: CSETI Project Starlight, The Center for the Study of Extraterrestrial Intelligence, Steven M. Greer M.D., Version 1.1, April, 1997.

Contact Has Begun, Philip H. Krapf, Hay House, 1998.

Conversations with God Book 2, Neale Donald Walsch, Hampton Roads Publishing, 1997.

Conversations with God, Book 1, Neale Donald Walsch, G.P. Putnam's Sons, 1995.

Cosmic Blueprint, Paul Davies, Simon & Schuster, 1988.

Cosmos, Carl Sagan, Ballantine Books, 1980.

Craft of Intelligence, Allen Dulles, Harper & Row, 1963.

Crash at Corona, The Definitive Study of the Roswell Incident, Don Berliner and Stanton T. Friedman, Marlowe & Company, 1992

Crashed UFOs: Evidence in the Search for Proof, William L. Moore, Direct, 4219 Olive St., Suite #247, Burbank, CA 91505, 1985.

"Crop Circles: Brief History and Overview," Dennis Stacy, MUFON Symposium Proceedings, 1991.

"Crop Circles: is There a UFO Connection?," George Wingfield, MUFON Symposium Proceedings, 1994.

"Current Brazilian UFO Wave," A.J. Gevard, MUFON Symposium Proceedings, 1996.

"Cydonia Hypothesis," John E. Brandenburg, Ph.D. MUFON Symposium Proceedings,1989.

Dark White: Aliens, Abductions, and the UFO Obsession, Jim Schnabel, Hamish Hamilton, 1994.

Day After Roswell, Col. Philip J. Corso with William J. Birnes, Pocket Books, 1997.

Dead Sea Scrolls, Dr. Jonathan G. Campbell, Ulysses Press, 1998.

Death of Ignorance: New Age Science, Dr. Fred Bell, Pyradyne Inc, 1980.

Decoding the Bible Code, John Weldon, Clifford Wilson, Barbara Wilson, Harvest House Publishers, 1998.

Development of David Bohm's Ideas From The Plasma to The Implicate Order, Edited by Basil J. Hiley and F. David Peat, London: Routledge & Kegan Paul, 1987.

"Differences Between Perceptions of Ufology in America and Europe" by John L. Spencer, MUFON Symposium Proceedings, 1990.

Dimensions: A Casebook of Alien Contact, Jaques Vallee, Contemporary Books, 1988.

Dirty Work: The CIA in Western Europe, Edited by Philip Agee and Louis Wolf, Zed Press, 1978.

Disclosure, Steven M. Greer M.D., Crossing Point, Inc., 2001.

Discoverers, Daniel J. Boorstin, Vintage Books, 1985.

Don't Think Like a Human, Kryon Book II, Kryon Writings, 1994.

Doomsday Conspiracy, Sidney Sheldon, Warner Books, 1991.

Earth: Pleiadian Keys to the Living Library, Barbara Marciniak, Bear & Company Publishing, 1995.

Eckankar-The Key to Secret Worlds, Paul Twitchell, Illuminated Way Publishing, 1987.

Egyptian Language: Easy Lessons in Egyptian Hieroglyphics, Wallis Budge, Dover Publications, 1976.

Einstein: The Life and Times, Ronald W. Clark, Avon Books, 1971.

Encounters: A Psychologist Reveals Case Studies of Abductions by Extraterrestrials, Edith Fiore, PH.D. Ballantine Books, 1989.

"ET Contact: The Religious Dimension," Dr. Barry H. Downing, MUFON Symposium Proceedings, 1990.

"Evidence for Life Beyond the Mars Face", Vincent DiPietro, MUFON Symposium Proceedings, 1996.

Experiments in Distance Influence, Leonid Vasiliev, E.P. Dutton, 1976.

Exploring Inner and Outer Space, Brian O'Leary, Ph.D., North Atlantic Books, 1989.

Extraordinary Popular Delusions and the Madness of Crowds, Charles Mackey, London, 1841.

Extraterrestrial Civilizations, Isaac Asimov, Fawcett, 1979.

Eye and Brain: The Psychology of Seeing, Richard L. Gregory, Princeton University Press, 1983.

Eyewitness to History, Edited by John Carey, Avon Books, 1997.

Field Guide to Extraterrestrials, Patick Huyghe, Avon Books, 1996.

"Fifty-Six Pilot Sightings Involving Electromagnetic Effects", Richard F. Haines, Ph.D.,MUFON Symposium Proceedings, 1992

Fingerprints of the Gods, Graham Hancock, Crown Publishers Inc., 1995.

Fire In The Sky: The Travis Walton Experience, Travis Walton, Berkeley, 1993

"First Scientific Results from Voyager 2," *Science*, Vol. 206, no. 4421, November 23, 1979.

First Three Minutes: A Modern View of the Origin of the Universe, Steven Weinberg, Basic Books, 1986.

Flying Saucer Conspiracy, Major Donald E. Keyhoe, Hutchinson, 1957.

"Flying Saucer Technology," Stanton T. Friedman, M.S., MUFON Symposium

Flying Saucer Story, Brinsley Le Poer Trench, Ace Books, 1966.

Flying Saucers, Dr. C. G. Jung, Mentor Books, 1959.

Flying Saucers Are Hostile, Brad Steiger, Joan Whritenour, 1967.

Flying Saucers Are Real, Stanton T. Friedman, And/Or Press, 1977.

Flying Saucers from Outer Space, Major Donald. E. Keyhoe, Henry Holt & Co., 1953.

Flying Saucers: Top Secret, Major Donald E. Keyhoe, G.P. Putnams Son's, 1960.

Flying Saucers: Twenty Years, 1947-1967, Editors of United Press International and Cowles Communications, Inc.,Look Magazine Book Division, 1967.

Flying Saucers-Serious Business, Frank Edwards, Lyle Stuart, 1966.

Forbidden Archeology, Michael A. Cremo, Richard L. Thompson, Bhaktivedanta Book Publishing, 1996.

"Forbidden Science: The UFO Phenomenon and the Research Community," Jaques Vallee, Ph.D., MUFON Symposium Proceedings, 1992

Forgotten Future, Boros Attila, Android Lap-Es Konyvkiado, Budapest, Hungary, 1995.

From Out of the Blue, Jenny Randles, Berkeley, 1993.

"Further Evidence Linking Animal Mutilations and Human Abductions to Alien Life Forms," Linda Moulton Howe, M.A., MUFON Symposium Proceedings, 991.

"Future Physics and Anti-gravity," William F. Hassel, Ph.D., MUFON Symposium Proceedings, 1977.

Galaxies, Timothy Ferris, Sierra Club Books, 1980.

Gift, The Crop Circles, Deciphered, Doug Ruby, Blue Note Books, 1997.

Gifts of Unknown Things, Lyall Watson, Simon & Schuster, 1976.

Glimpses of Other Realities - Volume 1: Facts & Eyewitnesses, Linda Moulton Howe, Paper Chase Press, 1994.

Glimpses of Other Realities - Volume II: High Strangeness, Linda Moulton Howe, Paper Chase Press, 1998.

"Global UFOLOGY - Worldwide Cases, Official Policies and Ufological Attitudes," J. Antonio Huneeus MUFON Symposium, 1992.

Gods of Eden, William Bramley, Avon Books, 1989.

"Great Moments in Medical Research," Daniel Seligman, *Fortune 117*, No. 5 February 29, 1988.

Gulf Breeze Sightings, Ed Walters and Francis Walters, Avon Books, 1991.

Healer Within, Steven Locke and Douglas Colligan, New American Library, 1986.

Healing and the Mind, Bill Moyers, Doubleday Books, 1993.

"Healing Remission and Miracle Cures," Brendan O'Regan, Institute of Noetic Sciences Special Report

Hidden History of the Human Race, Michael Cremo, Richard L. Thompson, Bhaktivedanta Book Publishing, 1999.

Hidden Mysteries: ET's, Ancient Mystery Schools and Ascension, Dr. Joshua David Stone, Light Technology Publishing, 1995.

Higher Techniques to Inner Perfection, Bryce Bond, Inner Light Publications, 1991.

Hoagland's Mars: The NASA-Cydonia Briefings - Videotape.

Hoagland's Mars: The U.N. Briefings-The Terrestrial Connection, Videotape.

Hollywood vs. the Aliens, Bruce Rux, Frog Ltd. Books, 1997.

"Holographic Memory: Karl Pribram Interviewed by Daniel Goleman," Daniel Goleman, *Psychology*

Holographic Paradigm, Renee Weber, New Science Library, 1982.

Holographic Universe, Michael Talbot, HarperCollins, 1991.

HotDogs, Heroes & Hooligans, Michael L. LaBlanc, Visible Ink Press, 1994.

How I Learned Soul Travel, Terrill Will Illuminated Way Publishing, 1987.

Hynek UFO Report, Dr. J. Allen Hynek, Barnes & Noble, 1997.

"Hyperspace (Virtual State) Engineering," Thomas E. Bearden, M.S., MUFON Symposium Proceedings, 1980.

Imagery In Healing, Jeanne Achterberg, New Science Library, 1985.

Implicate Brain, Karl H. Pribram, Quantum Implications, edited by Basil J. Hiley and F. David Peat, Routledge & Kegan Paul, 1987.

In Armour Bright, Frank Scully, Chilton, 1963.

In Search of Ancient Astronomies, E.C. Krupp, Doubleday, 1978.

Incident At Exeter, John G. Fuller, MJF Books, 1966.

"Information Retrievals: A Case for UFO Cover-Up," William Spaulding, MUFON Symposium, 1979.

"Inside Revelations on the UFO Cover-up," Richard Boylan, *NEXUS*, 5:3, April-May, 1998, p.45-50.

Inside The Spaceships, George Adamski, Arco/Spearman, 1956.

"Instrumented Sensing, Recording and Documentation of Transient Phenomena in UFO Events," Ray Stanford, MUFON Symposium Proceedings, 1980

Intangible Evidence, Bernard Gittleson, Simon & Schuster, 1987.

Intelligence War, Colonel William Kennedy, Salamander Books, 1983.

Intelligent Life in the Universe, I.S. Shklovskii and Carl Sagan, Dell, 1976.

Interrupted Journey, John G. Fuller, MJF Books,1966.

Intruders, Budd Hopkins, Ballantine Books, 1987.

Invasion From Mars, Hadley Cantril, Princeton University Press, 1940.

Investigation and Analysis of Sound Pulses Recorded During a Period of UFO Activity in Bragg Creek, Alberta, Canada" by Dennis R. Regan, Ph.D. And William K. Allan, MUFON Symposium Proceedings, 1979.

"Invisibility And The UFO Abduction Phenomenon," Budd Hopkins, MUFON Symposium Proceedings, 1993.

June 24, 1947: How It All Began. The Story of the Arnold Sighting, Bruce S. Maccabee,

Kryon: Don't Think Like a Human!, Book II, Lee Carroll, Kryon Writings, 1994.

Kryon: The End Times, Book I, Lee Carroll, The Kryon Writings, 1992.

"Legion of the Bewildered Silent and Related Topics," J. Allen Hynek, Ph.D.,MUFON Symposium Proceedings, 1979.

Let's Face The Facts About Flying Saucers, Gabriel Green, Warren Smith, Popular Library, 1967.

Letters to the Air Force on UFOs, Edited by Bill Adler, Dell Publishing, 1967.

Lost Books of the Bible and the Forgotten Books of Eden, World Bible Publishers, 1926.

Love, Medicine and Miracles, Bernie S. Siegel, Harper & Rowe, 1986.

Magellan's Voyage, Antonio Pigafetta, Dover Publications, 1994.

Magellan's Voyage, Vol II, Facsimile of the Original Manuscript in French, Antonio Pigafetta, Yale University Press, 1969.

Majestic, Whitley Strieber, G.P. Putnam's Sons, 1989.

Mankind: Citizen of the Galaxy, Kenneth C. McCulloch, Rings of Saturn Publishing Manitoba, Canada, 1985.

Mars and It's Canals, Percival Lowell, Macmillan, 1906.

Mars as an Abode of Life, Percival Lowell, Mcmillan, 1908.

Mars, Percival Lowell, Houghton Mifflin, 1896.

Martian Enigmas, Mark J. Carlotto, North Atlantic Books, 1997.

Martian Landscape, Viking Lander Imaging team, NASA SP-425, U.S. Government Printing Office, 1978.

Meaning of Relativity, Albert Einstein, Princeton University Press, Fifth Edition.

"Medical and Surgical Aspects of the UFO Abduction Phenomenon," Dr. Roger K. Leir, MUFON Symposium Proceedings, 1996.

Message From the Pleiades, Vol. 1: The Contact Notes of Eduard Billy Meier, Edited by Wendelle C. Stevens, UFO Archives, 1990.

Message from the Pleiades, Vol. 2., The Contact Notes of Eduard Billy Meier, Edited by Wendelle C. Stevens, UFO Archives, 1990.

Mind Reach, Russell Targ and Harold Putoff, Delacorte Press, 1977.

"Mind as Healer," Signe Hammer, *Science Digest, 92*, No. 4, April, 1984.

Miracle in the Void, Free Energy, UFOs and Other Scientific Revelations, Dr. Brian O'Leary, Kamapua'a Press, 1996.

Missing Time, Budd Hopkins, Ballantine Books, 1981

"Missing Time: A Psychologist Examines the UFO Experience," Aphrodite Clamar, Ph.D. MUFON Symposium Proceedings, 1981.

Monuments of Mars: A City on the Edge of Forever, Richard C. Hoagland, North Atlantic Books, 1987.

Moon Handbook, Carl Koppeschaar, Moon Publications, 1995.

Most Significant UFO Sightings in Germany, Dipl.-Phys. Illobrand Von Ludwig

"Must We Stand Idly By? Social Reaction to UFO Reports," Ron Westrum, Ph.D., MUFON Symposium Proceedings, 1976.

Mysteries of the Past, L. Casson, R. Claiborne, B. Fagan, W. Karp, American Heritage Publishing Co. Inc., 1977.

Mystic Places, Mysteries of the Unknown Series, Time-Life Books, 1992.

"Neurophysiology of Remembering," Karl Pribram, *Scientific American 220*, January, 1969

New Cell. New Bodies, New Life!, Edited by Virginia Essene, S.E.E. Publishing, 1991.

"Newspapers and UFOs" by Walter Greenawald, MUFON Symposium Proceedings, 1979.

Night Siege-The Hudson Valley UFO Sightings, Dr. J. Allen Hynek and Philip J. Imbrogno with Bob Pratt, Ballantine Books, 1987.

Nothing in This Book is True, But It's Exactly How Things Are, Bob Frissell, Frog, Ltd. Books, 1994.

Omega Project, Dr. Kenneth Ring, William Morrow, 1992.

Our Ancestors Came From Outer Space, Maurice Chatelain, Pan Books, 1980.

Out There: The Government's Secret Search For Extraterrestrials, Howard Blum, Simon & Schuster, 1995.

Over The Rainbow: Quantum Physics Discovers The Holographic Universe, F. Joe Lewells, Ph.D.

Passport to Magonia, Jaques Vallee, Contemporary Books Inc., 1969.

Peak Performance: Mental Training Techniques of the World's Greatest Athletes, Charles Garfield, Ballantine Books, 1989.

Philadelphia Experiment-UFO Conspiracies, Brad Steiger, Inner Light Publications, 1990.

"Placebo Effects: Unmapped Territory of Mind/Body Interactions," Thomas J. Hurley III, *Investigations,* No. 1. 1985.

"Placebos Are Getting More Effective. Drugmakers Are Desperate To Know Why.", Steve Silberman, Wired Magazine, August, 2009.

"Post Abduction Syndrome," David M. Jacobs, Ph.D. MUFON Symposium Proceedings, 1988.

"Preliminary Analysis of Medical Injuries as a Result of UFO Close Encounters," Richard C. Niemtzow, M.D. & Ph.D., MUFON Symposium Proceedings, 1980.

Preparing for Contact, Lyssa Royal & Keith Priest, Royal Priest Research Press, 1994.

Psychic Discoveries, Sheila Ostrander and Lynn Schroeder, Marlowe & Company, 1997.

Psychic Exploration: A Challenge to Science, Edited by Edgar Mitchell and John White, G.P. Putnam's Sons, 1974.

"Public Reaction to Alien Contact: A Study," Raymond W. Boeche, MUFON Symposium Proceedings, 1988.

Puzzle Palace, James Bamford, Sidgewick & Jackson, 1983.

Pyramid Power, Max Toth and Greg Nielsen, Destiny Books, 1985.

Pyramid Truth Gateway Universe: The Purpose, Intent and Overview of Extraterrestrial Visitations, Reg T. Miller, Pyra Publishing, 1997.

QED-The Strange Theory of light and Matter, Richard P. Feynman, Princeton University Press, 1985.

Ray Stanford, MUFON Symposium Proceedings, 1980.

Real X-Files (One-hour Documentary) Channel Four, Great Britain, Jim Schnabel and Bill Eagles.

Realms of the Human Unconsciousness, Stanislaus Grof, E.P. Dutton, 1976.

"Recent Field Investigations into Claims of UFO Related Injuries in Brazil," Jaques Vallee, Ph.D., MUFON Symposium Proceedings, 1989.

Red Limit: The Search by Astronomers for the Edge of the Universe, Timothy Ferris, William Morrow, 1977.

"Red Skies: The Great 1989 UFO Wave In The U.S.S.R.," J. Antonio Huneeus, MUFON Symposium Proceedings, 1990.

"Religious Dimension to the UFO Phenomenon," Ted Peters, Ph.D., MUFON Symposium Proceedings, 1979.

Remote Viewers: The Secret History of America's Secret Spies, Jim Schnabel, Dell Publishing, 1997.

Report on Unidentified Flying Objects, Edward J. Ruppelt, Ace Books, 1956.

Reporte Ovni, Zita Rodriquez, Vol. 37, Mexico City, 1994.

"Retrievals Of The Third Kind," Leonard H. Stringfield, MUFON Symposium Proceedings, 1978.

Revelations: Alien Contact and Human Deception, Jaques Vallee, Ballantine Books, 1991.

"Roswell Incident: Beginning of the Cosmic Watergate," Stanton T. Friedman and William L. Moore, MUFON Symposium Proceedings, 1982.

Roswell Report: Fact VS Fiction in the New Mexico Desert, Headquarters United States Air Force, 1995.

Ruth Montgomery: Herald of the New Age, Ruth Montgomery with Joanne Garland, Fawcett Crest, 1986.

"Scientific Method of Investigating UFOs," John L. Warren, Ph.D., MUFON Symposium Proceedings, 1977.

Scientific Study of Unidentified Flying Objects, Dr. Edward U. Condon, Bantam Books, 1969.

Scientists Confront Velikovsky, Edited by Donald Glodsmith, Cornell Unversity Press, 1977.

Secret Life-Firsthand Accounts of UFO Abductions, David M. Jacobs, Ph.D., Simon & Schuster, 1992.

Secret Science Behind Miracles, Max Freedom Long, Robert Collier Publications, 1995.

Secrets of the Night Sky, Bob Berman, HarperCollins, 1995.

Self-Aware Universe, Amit Goswami, Ph.D., Penguin Putnam, Inc., 1995.

Shufflebrain: The Quest for the Holographic Mind, Paul Pietsch, Houghton Mifflin, 1981.

"Sightings from An African Casebook," Cynthia R. Hind, MUFON Symposium Proceedings, 1997.

"Significance of Multiple Participant Abductions," John S. Carpenter, MUFON Symposium Proceedings, 1996.

Silent Invasion: The Shocking Discoveries of a UFO Researcher, Ellen Crystall, Marlowe & Company, 1991.

"Sixth Witness in the Linda Cortile Abduction Case," Budd Hopkins, MUFON Symposium, 1995.

Skylab Explores The Earth, NASA, SP-380, U.S. Government Printing Office, 1977.

Soul Traveler, Albert Taylor, Verity Press, 1996.

Source Field Investigations The, David Wilcock, Dutton, Penguin Group, 2011.

Source The, Art Bell, Brad Steiger, Paper Chase Press, 1999.

Soviet Psychotronics: A State of Mind, Richard Groller, Military Intelligence, October, 1986.

Space, Time and Medicine, Larry Dossey, New Science Library, 1982.

Space-Gods Revealed: A Close Look at the Theories of Erich Von Daniken, Ron Story, Harper and Row, 1976.

"Spanish Air Force UFO File: the Secret's End," Vincente-Juan Balleser Olmos, MUFON Symposium Proceedings, 1993.

Stars: A New Way to see Them, H.A. Rey, Houghton Mifflin, 1970.

Starseed Transmissions, Ken Carey, Harper, San Francisco, 1995.

Story of Rock and Roll, Paul Du Noyer, Carlton Books, 1995.

Stranger at the Pentagon, Dr. Frank E. Stranges, Inner Light Publications, 1967.

Strangers Among Us, Ruth Montgomery, Fawcett Crest, 1979.

Superforce, Paul Davies, Simon & Schuster, 1948.

Supermind: The Ultimate Energy, Barbara Brown, Harper & Row, 1980.

Sychronicity: The Bridge Between Mind and Matter, F. David Peat, Bantam Books, 1987.

Tantric Mysticism of Tibet, John Blofeld, E.P. Dutton, 970.

The Adventure of Self-Discovery, Stanislav Grof, State University of New York
   Press, 1988.
This Island Earth, NASA SP-250, Nick W. Orans, U.S. Government Printing Office,
   1986.
Time and Space, Mysteries of the Unknown Series, Time-Life Books, 1992.
Time-Life History of World War II, Time-Life Books, 1989.
Timetables Of Technology, Bryan Brunch and Alexander Hellemans, Touchstone,
   1994.
Tissue Changes in Unexplained Animal Mutilations, John H. Altshuler, M.D.,
   MUFON Symposium Proceedings, 1991.
Torpedoe Junction: U-Boat War Off America's East Coast, 1942, Naval Institute
   Press, 1989, Dell Books, 1999.
Treasure of El Dorado, Joseph Whitfield, Treasure Publications, 1991.
"Tribal Reactions to UFOs in Africa," Cynthia Hind, MUFON Symposium Proceed-
   ings, 1984
Truth About the UFO Crash at Roswell, Kevin D. Randle & Donald R. Schmitt,
   Avon Books, 1994.
"Udate on Majestic-12," Stanton T. Friedman, MUFON Symposium Proceedings,
   1989.
"UFO Abduction Phenomenon: What Might it Mean for the Human Future?," John
   E. Mack, M.D. MUFON Symposium Proceedings, 1995.
UFO Abductions: A Dangerous Game, Philip Klass, Prometheus, 1989.
UFO Contact From Undersea, Lt. Col. Wendelle Stevens (Ret.), Stevens, 1982.
"UFO Contactees: Captive Collaborators or Cosmic Citizens," R. Leo Sprinkle,
   Ph.D., MUFON Symposium Proceedings, 1980.
UFO Controversy in America, David M. Jacobs, Ph.D., Indiana University
   Press, 1975.
UFO Crash/Retrievals: Amassing the Evidence, Leonard H. Stringfield, Direct: 4412
   Grove Avenue, Cincinnati, Ohio 45227.
UFO Encounters, Golden Press, 1978.
UFO Encyclopedia, Jerome Clark, Omnigraphics, 1993.
UFO Evidence-The National Investigations Committee On Aerial Phenomena
   (NICAP) Edited by Richard T. Hall, Barnes & Noble, 1997.
UFO Experience: A Scientific Enquiry, J. Allen Hynek, Ballantine Books, 1972.
UFO Files, Jerome Clark, Publications International, Ltd., 1996.
UFO Healings-True Accounts of People Healed by Extraterrestrials, Preston
   Dennet, Illustrations by Christine 'Kesara' Dennett, Wildflower Press, 1996.
"UFO Interference And Self-Starting Engines," James M. McCampbell, MUFON
   Symposium Proceedings, 1983.
"UFO Light Beams: Space-Time Projections," Alan C. Holt, MUFON Symposium
   Proceedings, 1984.
UFO Phenomenon, Mysteries of the Unknown Series, Time-Life Books, 1992.
UFO Photographs Vol. I, Wendelle Stevens, UFO Photo Archives, 1986.
UFO Photographs Vol. II, Wendelle Stevens, UFO Photo Archives, 1986.
UFO Report, Irving A. Greenfield, Lancer Books, 1967.
"UFO Research: An International Perspective," David Haisell, MUFON

Symposium Proceedings, 1982.

UFO Retrievals, Jenny Randles,, Blandford, 1996.

UFO The Complete Sightings, Peter Brookesmith, Barnes & Noble, 1995.

UFO The Continuing Enigma, Readers Digest Association, Inc., 1991.

UFO The Government Files, Peter Brookesmith, Barnes & Noble, 1996.

UFOs A Manual for the Millenium, Phil Cousineau, HarperCollins West, 1995.

UFOs And Extraterrestrials in History, Yves Naud, Ferni Publishers, Geneva Switzerland, 1978, Vol.1-4.

UFO's A Scientific Debate, edited by Carl Sagan and Thornton Page.

UFOs and How to See Them, Jenny Randles, Barnes & Noble, 1997.

"UFOs and World History: Proof of an Old Interrelationship Between the Human Race and Advanced ET Intelligence," Robert O. Dean, MUFON Symposium Proceedings, 1994.

"UFOs as a Space-Time Singularity," J. Allen Hynek, Ph.D., MUFON Symposium Proceedings, 1978.

UFOs Explained, Philip J. Klass, Random House, 1974.

"UFOs, Extraterrestrial and the New Science," Brian T. O'Leary, Ph.D. MUFON Symposium Proceedings, 1990.

"UFOs: Four Questions for Theological Seminaries, "Rev. Barry H. Downing MUFON Symposium Proceedings, 1988.

UFOs Over America, Jim and Coral Lorenzen, Signet, 1968.

UFOs: The Public Deceived, Philip J. Klass Prometheus Books, 1983.

UFOs: The Whole Story, Jim and Coral Lorenzen, Signet, 1969.

"Unified Field Theory And The UFO," Henry C. Montieth, Ph.D., MUFON Symposium Proceedings, 1980.

Universe And Dr. Einstein, Lincoln Barnett, Sloane, 1956.

"Viking 2 Mission Results", *Science, Vol. 194*, no. 4271, December, 1976.

"Viking Mission 1 Results*," Science, Vol. 194*, no. 4260, October, 1976.

Vimana Aircraft of Ancient India and Atlantis, David Hatcher Childress, Adventures Unlimited Press, 1991.

Visitors from Within, Lyssa Royal & Keith Priest, Royal Priest Research, 1996.

Voyages of Christopher Columbus, Cecil Jane, Argonaut Press, 1930.

Walking Between The Worlds, Gregg Braden, Radio Bookstore Press, 1997.

Watchers, Ray Fowler, Bantam Books, 1990.

We Are Not Alone, Walter Sullivan, Bantam Books, 1964.

"What the Government Would Know About UFOs if They Read Their Own Documents," Peter A. Gersten, J.D., MUFON Symposium Proceedings, 1981.

"What The Russians Know About UFOs", George Knapp, MUFON Symposium Proceedings, 1994.

"Who Made The Giant Footprint?," David Barritt, *Sunday Times Magazine*, Vancouver British Columbia, Canada, April 12, 1987, p. 48-49.

"Who Speaks for the Witness? Medical and Ethical Issues in Abduction Research David A. Gotlib, B.Sc., M.D. MUFON Symposium Proceedings, 1990.

Wholeness and the Implicate Order, David Bohm, London: Routledge & Kegan Paul, 1980.

Wonders of the Ancient World: National Geographic Atlas of Archaeology

National Geographic Society, 1994.

"Why the Cover-Up?" Richard Gottlieb, MUFON Symposium Proceedings, 1977.

Why The Ets Visit In Peace, Reg T. Miller, Pyra Publishing, 1999.

Witnessed-The True Story of the Brooklyn Bridge UFO Abductions, Budd Hopkins. Pocket Books, 1996.

World At Arms: A Global History of World War II, Gerhard L. Weinberg, Cambridge University Press, 1994.

World Before, Ruth Montgomery, Fawcett Crest, 1976.

World History From 1500, J. Michael Allen & James B. Allen, HarperCollins, 1993.

World's Best "True" UFO Stories, Jenny Randles & Peter A. Hough, Sterling, 1994.

You Are Becoming A Galactic Human, Virginia Essene and Sheldon Nidle, S.E.E. Publishing, 1994.

UFO Organizations

MUFON - International Headquarters:

MUFON (Mutual UFO Network)
MUTUAL UFO NETWORK, INC.
262 Wilmer Ave.
Cincinnati, Ohio 45226
UFO Hotline: 888-817-2220
Phone: 513-871-8367
Fax: 513-352-6345
E-Mail: hq@mufon.com
Web: www.mufon.com

The world's oldest and largest UFO research organization. Started in 1969 by Walter H. Andrus, MUFON International has over 5,000 active members worldwide. Membership is $35 annually and includes a subscription to MUFON's monthly journal.

MUFON Chapters

MUFON Orange County, California
5267 Warner Ave. #275
Huntington Beach, CA 92649
Phone: 714-520-4UFO or 714-520-4836
E-mail: mufonoc@cox.net
Website: www.mufonoc.org

MUFON Los Angeles, California
P.O. Box 94
El Segundo, CA 90245-0094
Phone: 818-483-0864
E-Mail: contact@mufonla.com
Website: www.mufonla.com/

MUFON San Diego, California
P.O. Box 771
Solana Beach, CA 92075
Phone: 760-753-2456
E-Mail: contact@MUFONSanDiego.com

Website: www.mufonsandiego.com
Twitter: www.twitter.com/MUFONSanDiego

MUFON Sacramento
E-Mail: info@mufonsacramento.info
Website: www.mufonsacramento.info

MUFON WEBSITES / E-MAIL CONTACTS:

MUFON Headquarters	www.MUFON.com
Arizona	www.phoenixmufon.com
Arkansas	www.ArkansasMUFON.org
California - San Diego	www.MUFONSanDiego.com
California - Los Angeles	www.mufonla.com
California - Orange County	www.mufonoc.org
California – Sacramento	www.mufonsacramento.info
Colorado	www.comufon.org
Connecticut	www.newenglandmufon.com
Delaware	jventre1@comcast.net
Florida	FLMUFONSD@AOL.COM
Georgia	www.mufonga.org
Hawaii	lornah@mufonsd.org
Illinois	www.mymufon.com
Iowa	jimkingr@gmail.com
Kentucky	www.kymufon.org
Louisiana	vwalker605@aol.com
Maine	www.newenglandmufon.com
Massachusetts	www.newenglandmufon.com
Maryland	dcborton@comcast.net
Michigan	www.mimufon.org
Minnesota	www.mnmufon.org
Mississippi	ndwvitality@gmail.com
Missouri	www.missourimufon.org
Nebraska	www.mufon-ne.org
Nevada	mcmalzahn@gmail.com
New Hampshire	www.newenglandmufon.com
New Jersey	majorstar@verizon.net
New Mexico	burleson@dfn.com
New York	sarfalvo@roadrunner.com

North Carolina   mcmalzahn@gmail.com
Ohio   www.mufonohio.com
Oklahoma   lanekend@aol.com
Oregon   www.oregonmufon.com
Pennsylvania   www.mufonpa.com/wordpress/
Rhode Island   www.newenglandmufon.com
South Carolina   cherylgilmore1@yahoo.com
Tennessee   www.tnmufon.com
Texas - Austin   www.austinmufon.org/blog/

Texas – Dallas/Fort Worth   www.mufondfw.org
Texas – Houston   www.houstonmufontx.org
Texas – San Antonio   www.mufonsanantonio.com
Utah   www.mufonut.webs.com
Vermont   www.newenglandmufon.com
Virginia   susan.swiatek@gmail.com
Washington DC   dcborton@comcast.net
Washington State   lmchilds@comcast.net
Wisconsin   LEWISC@post.uwstout.edu

MUFON INTERNATIONAL CHAPTERS

Argentina   claudiodelrosario06@gmail.com
Australia   gem60@optusnet.com.au
Austria   helmut.lammer@oeaw.ac.at
Belgium   Pieter.hendrick@pandora.be
Canada   andremorin45@sympatico.ca
Finland   B.borg@kolumbus.fi
Germany   i.v.ludwiger@t-online.de
Israel   shjuval@bezeqint.net
Portugal   marcoagpinto@mail.telepac.pt
South Africa   mufon-sa@icon.co.za
Switzerland   swissufo@swissufo.ch
Turkey   agozisik@gmail.com
United Kingdom   ducan.campbell123@nt1world.com

BUFORA (British UFO Research Association)
Clarendon House, 117 George Lane,
South Woodford, London, E18 1AN
Telephone: 08445 674 694
E-Mail: enquiries@bufora.org.uk
Website: www.bufora.org.uk

International UFO Congress
3116 S. Mill Ave., #153
Tempe, AZ 85282
Phone: 480-302-2147
Phone: 1-877-UFO-0110
Fax: 480-302-2140
E-Mail: contact@ufocongress.com,

Website: www.ufocongress.com,

The Disclosure Project
Dr. Steven Greer M.D.
PO Box 265
Crozet, VA 22932, USA
Website: www.disclosureproject.org

CSETI (Center for the Study of Extraterrestrial Intelligence)
Dr. Steven Greer M.D.
PO Box 4556
Largo, MD 20775, USA
Phone: 1-301-249-0727
Fax: 1-877-92-CSETI (1-877-922-7384) [USA Only]
or 1-301-576-8041
E-Mail: **coordinator@cseti.org**
Website: www.cseti.org

Alien-Human Hybrid Research
Advanced Professional Counseling Services
Cristianne Quiros,
Riverside, CA
Phone: (909)633-0900
Fax: (951)784-9784

Close Encounters Research Organization (CERO)
Director: Yvonne Smith
La Canada, CA, United States
Telephone: +1. 818.383.6903
E-mail: staff@ysmith.com buy latin music Rodrigo Y Gabriela
Website: www.ysmith.com

J. Allen Hyneck Center for UFO Studies (CUFOS)
Box 31335
Chicago, IL 60631
Phone: (773) 271-3611
E-Mail: Infocenter@cufos.org .
Website: www.cufos.org

The Fund for UFO Research, Inc.(FUFOR)
P.O. Box 7501
Alexandria, VA 22307
E-Mail: fufor@ufoscience.org
Website: www.ufoscience.org

Intruders Foundation
UFO Abduction Research Organization
P.O. Box 30233
New York, NY 10011
Phone: 212-645-5278
Fax: 212-352-1778
Budd Hopkins – Executive Director
E-Mail: IFcentral@aol.com
www.intrudersfoundation.org

National UFO Reporting Center
P. O. Box 700
Davenport, WA 99122
E-Mail: director@ufocenter.com
Director: Peter Davenport
UFO Reporting Center Hotline:(206) 722-3000.
www.ufocenter.com

National Investigations Committee on Aerial Phenomena (NICAP)
www.nicap.org

International Center For Abduction Research (ICAR)
7715 Crittenden Street #129
Philadelphia, PA 19118-4421
Director: David M. Jacobs PhD
E-Mail: djacobs@ufoabduction.com
Website: www.ufoabduction.com

National UFO Center
Ret. Major George Filer
E-Mail: majorstar@verizon.net
Website: www.nationalufocenter.com

UFO Publications

UFO Magazine
PO Box 245
Lambertville, NJ 08530
To Subscribe: 1-888-UFO-MAGA
E-Mail: webmaster@ufomag.com
Website: www.ufomag.com

MUFON UFO Journal
2619 11th Street Road, Ste 21
Greeley, Colorado 80634
UFO Hotline: 888-817-2220
Phone: 970-817-2166
Fax: 970-352-5365
E-Mail: hq@mufon.com
Web: www.mufon.com

Filer's Files
Ret. Major George Filer
E-Mail: majorstar@verizon.net
Website: www.nationalufocenter.com
Website: www.ufofiler.com

Flying Saucer Review
FSR Publications Ltd, PO Box 585,
Rickmansworth WD3 1YJ, England.
E-Mail: lunula9@aol.com
Website: www.fsr.org.uk

Sedona Journal of Emergence
Light Technology Publishing
PO Box 3870
Flagstaff, AZ 86003
Phone: 928-526-1345
Phone: 800-450-0985
Fax: 928-714-1132
E-Mail: subscriptions@lighttechnology.net
Website: www.sedonajournal.com

UFO AFRINEWS
Reports of UFO events in Africa, 1988-2000
Harare, Zimbabwe
www.ufoafrinews.com

Fate Magazine
PO Box 460
Lakeville, MN 55044
Website: www.fatemag.com

UFO Newsclipping Service
#2 Caney Valley Drive
Plumerville
AR 72127-8725 USA
E-mail: ufons@webtv.net
Web: www.ufoinfo.com/newsclip.shtml
($6.00 per month)

British UFO Newsclipping Service
(British papers only)
CETI Publications
247 High Street
Beckenham, Kent, BR3 1AB
England

General Publications

Huffington Post – United Kingdom
www.huffingtonpost.co.uk

Huffington Post – United States
www.huffingtonpost.com

UFO Websites

There are hundreds of UFO websites on the internet. Go to these three websites first and you will be linked to all the best websites about Flying Saucers, Aliens and UFOs, including MUFON chapters world-wide.

Flying Saucers 101: www.flyingsaucers101.com
Aliens: www.aliens-everything-you-want-to-know.com
UFO Magazine: www.ufomag.com

Index

About the Author

HAROLD BURT

I live in Southern California, halfway between San Diego and Los Angeles. I run my own publishing company and a separate corporate marketing firm. For the last 30 years I have worked in sales and marketing management, primarily in the medical/pharmaceutical fields. I have spent most of my career with Fortune 500 companies, the names of which any physician or nurse would instantly recognize.

I stay actively involved with the Orange County Chapter of MUFON (Mutual UFO Network), where I have served on the Board of Directors. I love sales and marketing, but I have come to know that my real purpose in being on Earth is to help people adjust to and accept the fact that, as Jodi Foster says in the movie, *Contact:* "We are not alone!"

I am also the co-author of *Unsolved UFO Mysteries*, published by Time Warner Books. I am currently working on several other books and educational projects.

Contact Info:

E-Mail
Harold@FlyingSaucers101.com

Websites
Website: www.Flyingsaucers101.com
Website: www.Aliens-Everything-You-Want-To-Know.com

Blogs
www.Flyingsaucers101.com

Social Media
www.FaceBook.com/FlyingSaucers101
http://Twitter.com/FlyingSaucers10

Book Club Discussion Questions and Topics

What did you find surprising about **the facts** introduced in this book?

How has reading this book changed **your opinion** of a certain person or topic?

Does the author present **information** in a way that is interesting and insightful, and if so, how does he or she achieve this?

How has the book increased **your interest** in the subject matter?

What is the **central idea** discussed in the book? What issues or ideas does the author explore? Are they personal, sociological, global, political, economic, spiritual, medical or scientific?

Do the issues **affect your life**? How so – directly on a daily basis, or more generally? Now or sometime in the future?

What **evidence** does the author use to support the book's ideas? Is the evidence convincing...definitive or ...speculative? Does the author depend upon personal opinion, observation, and assessment? Or is the evidence factual – based on science, statistics, historical documents, or quotations from (credible) experts.

What kind of **language** does the author use? Is it objective and dispassionate? Or passionate and earnest? Is it polemical, inflammatory, sarcastic? Does the language help or undercut the author's premise?

What are the **implications** for the future? Are there long or short-term consequences to the issues raised in the book. Are they positive or negative...affirming or frightening?

What **solutions** does the author propose? Who would implement those solutions? How probable is success?

How **controversial** are the issues raised in the book? Who is aligned on which sides of the issues? Where do you fall in that line-up?

Talk about **specific passages** that struck you as significant – or interesting, profound, amusing, illuminating, disturbing, sad? What was memorable?

What have you learned after reading this book? Has it broadened your perspective about a difficult issue - personal or societal?

Questions provided courtesy of LitLovers, 2012